In Sickness and in Power

In Sickness and in Power

Illness in Heads of Government during the Last 100 Years

David Owen

Westport, Connecticut
London

Library of Congress Cataloging-in-Publication Data

Owen, David, 1938–
   In sickness and in power : illnesses in heads of government during the last 100 years / David Owen.
     p. ; cm.
   Includes bibliographical references and index.
   ISBN 978-0-313-36005-3 (alk. paper)
   1. Heads of states—Mental illness.   2. Heads of states—Mental illness—History—20th century.   3. Heads of states—Health and hygiene.   4. Heads of states—Health and hygiene—History—21st century.   5. Federal government—History—20th century.   6. Federal government—History—21st century.   I. Title.   II. Title: Illnesses in heads of government during the last 100 years.
[DNLM: 1. Famous Persons.   2. Mental Disorders.   3. Federal Government—history.
 4. History, 20th Century.   5. History, 21st Century.   6. Political Systems—history.
WZ 313 O97s 2008]
RC451.4.S64.O94 2008
616.89—dc22   2008013655

English language edition, except the United States and Canada,
published by Methuen.

First published in Great Britain 2008 by
Methuen Publishing Ltd
8 Artillery Row
London
SW1P 1RZ

Library of Congress Catalog Card Number: 2008013655

ISBN: 978-0-313-36005-3

Published in the United States and Canada by
Praeger Publishers, 88 Post Road West, Westport, CT 06881
An imprint of Greenwood Publishing Group, Inc.
www.praeger.com

10 9 8 7 6 5 4 3 2 1

To Maggie Smart

Who has worked with me for over thirty years
and for whom no words of thanks can be enough.

Contents

Acknowledgements

Many people have helped in the discussion and writing of this book and to all of them I offer my personal thanks.

John Wakefield, whom I have known since the late 1970s and with whom I have campaigned politically on the euro, deserves very special mention. He has, with surgical precision, cut out one fifth of my manuscript but in doing so has enhanced the argument and greatly improved the book.

Doctors of medicine, including my son Gareth, at the Institute of Psychiatry, King's College London, have been an immense help, as has Argyrios Stringaris, also at the Institute of Psychiatry. I have been lucky to have had the advice of Paul Flynn, a metabolic physician at the University of Cambridge; Dr Kevin Cahill, professor in tropical medicine and director of the Center for International Health and Cooperation in New York; Professor Gabriel Kune, emeritus professor of surgery, University of Melbourne; Dr David Ward, consultant cardiologist, St George's Hospital, London; and Professor Anne Curtis, Yale University. I have also been fortunate to have been able to interview Dr Claude Gubler, President François Mitterrand's personal doctor, and Dr Georges Flandrin and Dr Abbas Safavian, who treated Shah Mohammad Reza Pahlavi.

A number of writers and journalists have helped: Dr Lawence Altman, medical editor of the *New York Times*; the late R. W. Apple, also from the *New York Times*; Daniel Finkelstein of the London *Times*; Kevin Maguire of the *Daily Mirror*; and Norbert Both, who also helped with my previous book *Balkan Odyssey*. I have been given valuable advice by Richard Reeves, presidential biographer of Kennedy, Johnson and Reagan; his assistant, Peter Keating; R. D. Thorpe, biographer of Anthony Eden; and Peter Merseburger, biographer of Willy Brandt. Thanks are also due to Lord Desai, Jean Rosenthal and Simon O'Li from Paris.

I am grateful to the following libraries whose staff have gone out of their way to help. First and foremost the House of Lords library; then the University of Birmingham, whose library houses Anthony Eden's 'Avon papers', The British Library, The John F. Kennedy Presidential Library, the Massachusetts Historical Society in Boston and the library of the University of Liverpool, which holds all my personal archives.

Very special thanks go to my wife and literary agent, Debs. Also to Alan Gordon Walker and Jonathan Wadman at Methuen.

References to English-language sources pose some difficulty since this book is being published in the UK and the USA. I have referenced mainly from my own library, even if the editions it contains were not the first published. I have also quoted from either the hardback or the paperback editions depending on which were in my possession. Similarly the editions I borrowed from libraries have determined which edition is referenced. In a rough and ready way I hope this reflects the editions that are most easily accessible. On spelling I have followed common usage, whether in the quoted passages or when discussing a particular country: for instance, the US Department of Defense but the UK Ministry of Defence.

The chapter notes are extensive. They are designed to provide background information on illnesses for non-medical readers and detail about international and domestic politics for readers who have a non-political background. Medical terms have been drawn from *Black's Medical Dictionary*, 41st edition, edited by Harvey Marcovitch (London: A. & C. Black, 2005) and *Oxford Concise Colour Medical Dictionary*, 3rd edition (Oxford: Oxford University Press, 2004).

Any errors of fact or mistaken interpretations are solely my responsibility.

Introduction

> From inability to let well alone, from too much zeal for the new and
> contempt for what is old, from putting knowledge before wisdom, science
> before art and cleverness before common sense, from treating patients as
> cases and for making the cure of the disease more grievous than the
> endurance of the same, good Lord deliver us.
>
> Sir Robert Hutchison (1871–1960), 'The Physician's Prayer'

I have always felt that this physician's prayer, with 'voters' replacing 'patients',
could be a politician's prayer as well. For politicians too hold the lives of
people in their hands. This is most obviously the case when they govern at a
time of war, but it is not only then. Politicians, and especially heads of
government, take many decisions which have far-reaching effects on the lives
of the people they govern and may even, in the most extreme cases, affect
whether they live or die. Hutchison's prayer is that physicians should
remember that their first duty is not to make things worse, important when
iatrogenic disease is so prevalent. It is the politician's duty to intervene only
when intervention is likely to improve the status quo and to resist the
clamour for action for its own sake. Bismarck's famous remark that politics is
the art of the possible expresses the same insight that there needs to be
modesty in ambition. For both politicians and physicians, competence, and
the ability to make realistic judgements about what can and cannot be
achieved, are essential attributes. Anything that impairs that judgement can
do considerable harm.

The inter-relationship between politicians and doctors, politics and
medicine has fascinated me for all of my adult life. No doubt my own
background as both a doctor and politician has fuelled my interest and
influenced my viewpoint. In particular I have been interested in the effect on
the course of history of illness in heads of government. Such illness raises many
important issues: the impact on decision-making; the dangers inherent in the
illness being kept secret; the difficulty of removing ill leaders, in democracies

as well as in dictatorships; and, not least, the responsibility that illness in heads of government places on their doctors. Should their loyalty be exclusively to their patient, as would normally be the case, or do they have an obligation to take into account the political health of their country?

Over the generations, many members of my family have been doctors of medicine or worked in professions related to medicine. Many also practised politics, predominantly at local level, and some managed to be involved in both medicine and politics.[1] Perhaps that is why I have found it quite normal that medicine and politics should play the role of natural partners in my life. Although at times medicine has been crowded out by politics, my love for it has never weakened. Even when I was Foreign Secretary I was still somewhat pedantically calling myself a medical practitioner in official documents, as if somehow I never saw my political career as anything other than temporary. I certainly never thought of politics as a profession. I lived from one general election to another, never certain that I would be re-elected to represent my highly marginal constituency seat in Plymouth. In the end, though, I became the city's longest-serving MP, stepping down in 1992 after twenty-six years in the House of Commons.

My life combining medicine and politics started when I was first adopted as a parliamentary candidate in 1962 while a mere junior doctor at St Thomas' Hospital, which stands on the banks of the river Thames directly opposite the Palace of Westminster in London. In some ways medicine had brought me into politics. In 1959, as a medical student, I had joined the Labour Party because of the poverty and poor housing I saw in the area of south London that St Thomas' serves. We treated the patients' illness but they went back to the same damp, crowded flats and pretty soon they were in hospital again. Just after qualifying as a doctor in 1962, I was asked to put my name forward to be the Labour candidate for a large rural constituency, not a seat Labour could win. The reason I took this step puzzles me to this day, but I believe it was to stop myself becoming what I used to call a 'medical vegetable', someone obsessed only by medicine. I had seen my close contemporaries, on first qualifying as doctors, become absorbed in medical matters to the detriment of many other aspects of life – they stopped reading newspapers and found no time to listen to the radio or watch TV.

When the time came to fight the 1964 general election I took three weeks' unpaid leave. I managed to win just enough votes not to forfeit a financial deposit. On my return to hospital, politics took a back seat and I concentrated on medicine. I specialised at St Thomas' in neurology, which also involved undertaking some psychiatry. It was a stimulating environment and soon I was engaged in pure research into the chemistry of the brain.[*] Then, quite unexpectedly in the summer of 1965, I was asked by a Labour alderman in Plymouth if he could put my name forward for what was virtually my home constituency, Plymouth Sutton. It was widely believed that there would have to be another general election in 1966 and this was a marginal seat. In retrospect, I should have known that when I was chosen as the candidate, my selection might change my life; but though it's difficult to believe, I still did not realise that I was likely to become an MP. Nevertheless I was making a choice of sorts – I wanted at least to have the chance of painting on a broader canvas. I may not have made a final decision to choose politics, but I was open to the possibility that the electors might choose politics for me. Even so I was still surprised when on the day after polling day, in 1966, I suddenly found myself a member of the House of Commons.

For the following two years I criss-crossed Westminster Bridge continuing to work on the chemistry of the brain in my laboratory in St Thomas's while also attending Parliament on the other side of the river. All this abruptly came to an end when I was appointed minister for the navy in 1968, for it is a long tradition that ministers of the Crown are not allowed to undertake any other job. In 1970, after the Labour government lost the general election, I remained an MP and went into business part time. This involved the computer modelling of the decision-making process in major companies, some in the pharmaceutical industry. Since 1995, I have served on the board of Abbott Laboratories, a large US health care company.

---

[*] My fellow research worker in St Thomas' Medical Unit was a brilliant neuroscientist, C. D. Marsden, who later became professor of neurology at the National Hospital for Neurology and Neurosurgery in central London. We wrote up our research on the effect of adrenaline on physiological tremor in the *Journal of Physiology*, on peripheral beta-adrenergic receptors concerned with tremor in *Clinical Science* and on Mechanisms underlying emotional variation in *Parkinsonian Tremor in Neurology*. The effect of B adrenergic blockade on finger tremor and Achilles reflex time in anxious and thyrotoxic patients was described in *Acta Endocrinologica*.

Adrenaline, called epinephrine in the United States, is a vitally important hormone secreted by the medulla of the adrenal gland, which is located on top of the kidneys. It prepares the body for 'fright, flight or fight'. It also has widespread effects on the circulation, muscles and sugar metabolism. The action of the heart is increased, the rate and the depth of breathing are increased and the basal metabolic rate can rise. Adrenaline can be given by injection for anaphylactic shock due to an allergic response, commonly a bee or wasp sting. It can also be given for cardiac arrest.

Labour won the two general elections in 1974, and once again medicine and politics ran in tandem, although in a rather different way, as I served as minister of health for two and a half years.[2] No job I have ever done since, whether being Foreign Secretary from 1977 until 1979, leader of the Social Democratic Party (SDP) from 1983 to 1987 and 1988 to 1990 or co-chairman of the International Conference on the Former Yugoslavia from 1992 to 1995, has given me as much personal satisfaction.

Overall, I practised medicine for six years and I learned much from the fascinating experience. All of it informs this book, but one aspect has particular relevance. The consultants, neurologists and psychiatrists for whom I worked at St Thomas' Hospital tended to treat a number of prominent politicians and I had seen the strains and stresses of political life within the confidential context of the doctor–patient relationship. I helped treat a senior politician who had become addicted to alcohol and another who was severely depressed. I saw the pressures under which they lived and began to wonder how much of a factor stress played in their illnesses. I treated other patients suffering from drug addiction, whether heroin, amphetamines or tranquillisers. Patients were referred for a second opinion from all parts of the country, often suffering from rare conditions and providing a unique insight. I had, by then, become highly specialised and used to joke that I was a doctor from the 'head up', being focused entirely on the brain. Even my compulsory six months' surgery was spent as an ophthalmic eye surgeon, an experience which would not now meet the statutory requirement for general surgical experience. Had I stayed in medicine I suspect I would have tried to become a professor in neuropsychiatry.

It was during those medical years that my lifelong interest began in how government decisions are taken, particularly at the highest level. I watched spellbound in 1962 as the Cuban Missile Crisis developed and, three years later, as the Vietnam War unfolded. In 1972, after working in the Ministry of Defence, I wrote a book on defence decision-making, its deficiencies, complexities and dangers.[3]

Many know Lord Acton's famous dictum, 'Power tends to corrupt, and absolute power corrupts absolutely.'[4] But Acton preceded that with a plea to judge those who hold power by a higher standard than those who do not: 'I cannot accept your canon that we are to judge Pope and King unlike other men, with a favourable presumption that they did no wrong. If there is any presumption it is the other way against the holders of power.' The Pulitzer Prize-winning historian Barbara Tuchman wrote that we are less aware that power breeds folly; that the power to command frequently causes failure to think; that the responsibility of power often fades as its exercise augments. The overall responsibility of power is to govern as reasonably as possible in the interest of the state and its citizens. A duty in that process is to keep well-informed, to heed information, to keep mind and judgement open and to resist the insidious spell of wooden-headedness. If the mind is open enough to perceive that a given policy is harming rather than serving self-interest, and self-confident enough to acknowledge it, and wise enough to reverse it, that is a summit in the art of government.[5]

The extent to which illness can affect the processes of government and the decision-making of heads of government, engendering folly, in the sense of foolishness, stupidity or rashness, was an issue I faced quite directly on a number of occasions once I became Foreign Secretary and it has interested me ever since. I was also fascinated by those leaders who were not ill and whose cognitive faculties functioned well but who developed what I have come to describe as hubris syndrome. Acts of hubris are much more common in heads of government, whether democratic or not, than is often realised and hubris is a major contributor to Tuchman's definition of folly: 'a perverse persistence in a policy demonstrably unworkable or counter-productive'. She continued: 'Wooden-headedness, the source of self-deception is a factor that plays a remarkably large role in government. It consists in assessing a situation in terms of preconceived fixed notions while ignoring or rejecting any contrary signs. . . . Also the refusal to benefit from experience.'[6] A characteristic of hubris is the inability to change direction because this involves admitting that one has made a mistake.

Bertrand Russell once wrote: 'The concept of "truth" as something dependent upon facts largely outside human control has been one of the ways in which philosophy hitherto has inculcated the necessary element of humility. When this check upon pride is removed, a further step is taken on the road towards a certain kind of madness – the intoxication of power'[7] (see also Chapter 7). Leaders intoxicated with pride and power are often described by laymen as having become 'unhinged', 'barmy', even 'mad', though these are not terms the medical profession would use about them. Democratic societies, especially those which have evolved out of absolute monarchies, have developed systems of checks and balances to try to protect themselves from such leaders. But these mechanisms – Cabinet, Parliament and the media – are not always effective. Under despotic leaders, where there are no democratic controls and few internal mechanisms, short of a coup, to remove them, there is often little that can be done. External condemnation and international sanctions have so far proved of only limited value while external military force has had questionable success.

I was lucky to serve in the governments of two British Prime Ministers, Harold Wilson and James Callaghan, neither of whom became intoxicated with power and both of whom were largely fit. I was with them, kicked out of power by the voters in 1970 and 1979 respectively. It did not feel at the time to be a good thing, but it was a very salutary experience, underlining that in a democracy a politician is the servant of the people, and that power is loaned and can be withdrawn.

During his first premiership, from 1964 to 1970, Wilson was in excellent health, although in opposition in the early 1970s he developed some cardiovascular trouble which made him reluctant to stay on too long. When he found himself, somewhat to his surprise, back in No. 10 in 1974 he was troubled that his photographic memory was beginning to deteriorate. Additionally the same old political and economic problems kept recurring and he no longer had his previous energy and elan. Wilson surprised everyone by voluntarily stepping down in 1976 and in retirement a few years later developed overt Alzheimer's disease with a serious progressive deterioration in the functioning of his brain (see Chapter 2).

James Callaghan succeeded Wilson despite being several years older. Callaghan had had a prostatectomy in 1972 when in opposition but recovered well and in 1974 became Foreign Secretary. He remained in good health as Prime Minister and he tackled the necessity of dealing with the International Monetary Fund with vigour and political skill. He lost the general election in 1979 to Margaret Thatcher but left office with dignity and grace. He went on to be the longest-lived former British Prime Minister ever and in a long conversation with him in the summer of 2004 I found his recall of names and events remarkable. Callaghan died just short of his ninety-third birthday in 2005.

I was also able to watch at fairly close quarters four other British Prime Ministers, Edward Heath, Margaret Thatcher, John Major and Tony Blair. It is against this unusual background of more than forty years' involvement in medicine and politics that I have tried to examine past incidents of ill health in heads of government worldwide and to set their illnesses alongside political events at the time so that readers can judge for themselves the inter-relationships.

Public discussion of illness in political leaders is reasonably straightforward when the illness is described as physical but is less so when it is described as mental. This is because, regarding mental illness, the general public and professional practitioners do not speak such a shared language as they do when talking about ordinary physical illness. There is also a mismatch between what the press and public talk about as mental illness and what the medical profession are ready to diagnose as mental illness. When the press and public use terms such as 'madness', 'lunacy', 'psychopath', 'megalomania' or 'hubris' – some or all of which have been used about despots as diverse as Adolf Hitler, Idi Amin, Mao Zedong, Slobodan Milošević, Robert Mugabe and Saddam Hussein on one hand and democratic leaders as different as Theodore Roosevelt, Lyndon Johnson, Richard Nixon, Thatcher, Blair and George W. Bush on the other – they are using words which the medical profession has either long abandoned, redefined or severely restricted. Madness and lunacy for doctors are terms which have been totally replaced by whether a defined mental disorder is present. Psychopathic behaviour has been narrowed into specific personality disorders and megalomania to delusions of grandeur. Usually heads of government who are popularly dubbed as in some sense mad are not considered to have any mental illness by the medical profession.

Depression and mental illness is commonly found and cannot be regarded as an automatic disqualification for public office. Abraham Lincoln is a most interesting case of how a leader's qualities can be forged through their depression. Few heads of government have borne that affliction for a longer period than Lincoln and yet he refused to be bowed down by it. As a young man he had profound mood swings, more down than up, and even wrote an essay on suicide. 'I may seem to enjoy life rapturously when I am in company. But when I am alone I am so often overcome by mental depression that I dare not carry a penknife.' On 25 August 1838 the *Sangamo Journal* carried an unsigned poem, 'The Suicide's Soliloquy', which points strongly to having been written by Lincoln. Lincoln was by common consent one of the greatest US Presidents and through all the stress of the Civil War 'he retained an unflagging faith in his country's cause'.[8] It is probable that overcoming or learning to live with his depression contributed to Lincoln's character as President. He had two major breakdowns and his depression in his twenties became more persistent in his thirties but the author of a book on the subject has found no evidence of mania, though he thinks it is possible that Lincoln had hypomania, characterised by heightened energy.[9] Hypomania is discussed on p. 7 in relation to Theodore Roosevelt, and it was a diagnosis also made about Nikita Khrushchev; see Chapter 4, p. 171.

Where professionals do diagnose political leaders, retrospectively, as having suffered from a mental illness, the public is often less willing to accept the diagnosis, especially when the leaders in question happen to have become national heroes. Diagnosis of bipolar disorder* is a case in point. To be diagnosed as suffering from bipolar disorder, someone has to have a history of at least one clear-cut manic episode and at least one episode of an affective disorder, usually presenting as depression but which can also present as anxiety. In the past the manic episode often had to be very florid for the diagnosis to be made and the reluctance to diagnose was, in part, because there was no treatment. Once lithium† was found to be a successful treatment for bipolar disorder, doctors were readier to make the diagnosis.

In diagnosing the manic phase of bipolar disorder doctors look for a number of signs and symptoms which cumulatively can make the diagnosis. To the psychiatrist the early phase of mania is called hypomania; some liken it to

---

* Bipolar disorder used to be called manic depression. Mania affects approximately 1 per cent of the population, while the less-than-manic forms dominated by depression affect 4-5 per cent. (P. Thomas, 'The Many Forms of Bipolar Disorder: A Modern Look at an Old Illness', Journal of Affective Disorders (2004), vol. 79, supplement 1, pp. 3–8.) Symptoms overlap with schizophrenia, attention deficit disorder and personality disorders. Bipolar disorder is one of the mental illnesses which has responded well to drug therapy, initially lithium but now more frequently sodium valporate, a drug also used for treating epilepsy. Sir Aubrey Lewis, one of the great British psychiatrists, noted many years ago a general tendency to under-diagnose recurrent depression and manic depression in favour of schizophrenia in the United States. Gradually that gap has closed over some seventy years to the extent where American practitioners are now perhaps more ready to diagnose bipolar disorder than their British counterparts. Schizophrenia is an overall title for a group of psychiatric disorders that have at their core disturbances in thinking, behaviour and emotional responses. It is not the 'split personality' that it is commonly thought to represent.

† Lithium is an alkaline metal discovered by a Swedish chemistry student, Johan Arfvedson. He named it from the Greek for 'stone', lithos, where the metal was found. In early Greek and Roman times mineral water, now known to contain lithium, was prescribed and Soranus, a physician from Ephesus, prescribed it for manic insanity and melancholia. US Presidents Grover Cleveland and William McKinley were treated at a spa called Lithia Springs in Georgia and its bottled water is still sold. The Australian psychiatrist John F. Cade used lithium carbonate on ten manic patients in 1949 with dramatic results and this was confirmed in the first double-blind trial by the Dane Mogens Schou. It took until the early 1970s for lithium to become accepted as the treatment of choice for manic depression. (Ronald R. Fieve, 'The Lithium Breakthrough', in Moodswing: Dr Fieve on Depression, rev. ed. (New York: William Morrow, 1989).)

falling in love, an exhilaration when one becomes enthused, full of energy and bounding self-confidence. Hypomania leads into bipolar-II disorder, milder than the depression and mania of bipolar-I, both of which used to be lumped together as manic depression. Estimates vary but more than fourteen million people in the United States suffer from mood disorders, depression or anxiety and of these more than two million are likely to suffer from bipolar disorder, to distinguish it from the unipolar disorder of depression alone. There have been many genetic and biochemical studies of bipolar disorder but the biological underpinning remains uncertain.

In diagnosing the manic phase of bipolar disorder doctors look for a number of signs and symptoms which cumulatively can make the diagnosis:

1. Increased energy, activity and restlessness
2. Excessively 'high', euphoric mood
3. Extreme irritability
4. Racing thoughts and talking very fast, jumping from one idea to another
5. Distractibility, inability to concentrate well
6. Little sleep needed
7. Unrealistic beliefs in one's abilities and powers
8. Poor judgement
9. A lasting period of behaviour that is different from usual
10. Increased sexual drive
11. Abuse of drugs, particularly cocaine, alcohol and sleeping medications
12. Provocative, intrusive or aggressive behaviour
13. Denial that anything is wrong
14. Spending sprees.[10]

A recent paper by three American psychiatrists claimed that Theodore Roosevelt and Lyndon Johnson had had bipolar disorder while President.[11] That they had both had depressive illnesses is beyond dispute. But some have questioned the diagnosis without more evidence of specific episodes of mania. What is interesting about the retrospective diagnosis of bipolar disorder in other political leaders as well is that the public seem ready to accept that their heroes suffered from bouts of depression but are less willing to acknowledge manic behaviour as symptomatic of mental illness. It has been suggested, for example, that Winston Churchill suffered from bipolar disorder. No one denies that he was frequently cast into deep sloughs of depression, which he himself called his 'Black Dog' moods. But there is considerable resistance to the diagnosis of mania – either because of a feeling that he never had obvious clinical episodes or because, even if they might have occurred, there was little pathological about them, and people prefer to see Churchill as a unique figure. Theodore Roosevelt arouses a somewhat similar reaction amongst some Americans (see Chapter 1).

It may be that people expect, even want, their leaders to be different from the norm, to display more energy, work longer hours, appear exhilarated by what they are doing and full of self-confidence – in short, to behave in ways that, taken beyond a certain point, a professional would mark down as manic. So long as those leaders are attempting to achieve what the public wishes them to achieve, it does not want to be told that they are mentally ill. But when those leaders lose the support of their public, it becomes a very different matter. Then the public is ready to use words long discarded by the profession to describe mental illness, as a means of expressing its objection to the way its leaders are behaving.

It is here, perhaps, that things become most interesting, at least as regards the health of the body politic even if not of the leaders themselves. This is when a political leader behaves in ways not just that the public disapprove of but instinctively interpret as being the result of a change in mental state: of the leader having 'lost it', having become 'unbalanced', 'unhinged', 'out of control'. Even though there may not be manifest in that behaviour sufficient symptoms to warrant any professional diagnosis of mental illness, the public are convinced that the leader is not just simply making mistakes but showing some sort of mental incapacity to take rational decisions. Here, medical language is, as yet, of little use. We are forced, instead, to speak in more traditional terms at least until we acquire, if we ever do, medical understanding of what may be the cause of such loss of capacity.

One such traditional term, no longer part of the professional lexicon but, it seems to me, a wholly legitimate word for the public to use, is 'megalomania'. I was myself charged with 'a display of megalomania' by a journalist friend in the summer of 1987. By using the term he was saying not simply that he thought what I was doing was wrong (in resisting a merger of the Social Democratic Party with the Labour Party) but that it was the consequence of a mental state I had got myself into at a time, after I had resigned as leader, when the SDP was breaking up.[12] The medical profession may not use the term 'megalomania', but that does not mean that no one else should. Megalomania can be an occupational hazard for politicians, and its manifestation in a developed form, hubris, is a legitimate topic of study for the medical profession.

'Hubris' is not yet a medical term. The most basic meaning developed in ancient Greece, simply as a description of an act: a hubristic act was one in which a powerful figure, puffed up with overweening pride and self-confidence, treated others with insolence and contempt. He seemed to get kicks from using his power to treat others in this way, but such dishonouring behaviour was strongly condemned in ancient Greece. In a famous passage from Plato's *Phaedrus*, a predisposition to hubris is defined: 'But when desire irrationally drags us toward pleasures and rules within us, its rule is called excess [*hubris*].'[13] Plato saw this 'rule of desire' as something irrational that drags men into doing the wrong thing through acts of hubris. In his *Rhetoric*, Aristotle picks up the element of desire Plato identifies in hubris and argues that the pleasure someone seeks from an act of hubris lies in showing himself as superior. 'That is why the young and the wealthy are given to insults [*hubristai*, i.e. being hubristic]; for they think that, in committing them [acts of hubris], they are showing superiority.'[14]

But it was in drama rather than philosophy that the notion was developed further to explore the patterns of hubristic behaviour, its causes and consequences. A hubristic career proceeded along something like the following course. The hero wins glory and acclamation by achieving unwonted success against the odds. The experience then goes to his head: he begins to treat others, mere ordinary mortals, with contempt and disdain and he develops such confidence in his own ability that he begins to think himself capable of anything. This excessive self-confidence leads him into misinterpreting the reality around him and into making mistakes. Eventually he gets his comeuppance and meets his nemesis, which destroys him. Nemesis is the name of the goddess of retribution, and often in Greek drama the gods arrange nemesis because a hubristic act is seen as one in which the perpetrator tries to defy the reality ordained by them. The hero committing the hubristic act seeks to transgress the human condition, imagining himself to be superior and to have powers more like those of the gods. But the gods will have none of that: so it is they who destroy him. The moral is that we should beware of allowing power and success to go to our heads, making us too big for our boots.

The theme of hubris has fascinated playwrights, no doubt because it provides the opportunity to explore human character within highly dramatic action. Shakespeare's *Coriolanus* is a study in it. But the pattern of the hubristic career is one that will immediately strike a chord in anyone who has studied the history of political leaders. The hubristic posture has been described by the philosopher David E. Cooper as 'excessive self-confidence, an "up yours!"

attitude to authority, pre-emptive dismissal of warnings and advice, taking oneself as a model.'[15] Another philosopher, Hannah Arendt, who admired ancient Athens, has written about the shortcomings of its ruler Pericles, who was possessed by 'the hubris of power', and has compared him unfavourably with Solon, the lawmaker of Athens.[16] The historian Ian Kershaw aptly titled the two volumes of his biography of Hitler 'Hubris' and 'Nemesis'.[17]

What interests me, watching political leaders, is hubris as a description of a kind of loss of capacity. This pattern is very familiar in the careers of political leaders whose success makes them feel excessively self-confident and contemptuous of advice that runs counter to what they believe, or sometimes of any advice at all, and who start to act in ways that seem to defy reality itself. Nemesis usually, though not always, follows.

I want to find out whether hubristic behaviour of this sort amongst political leaders can be linked to certain personality types that predispose someone to act hubristically; and whether, indeed, such personality types create a propensity in those who have them to enter careers such as politics. Even more interesting is whether some political leaders who do not have such personality types may, nonetheless, start to behave hubristically simply as a consequence of being in power. In other words, can the experience of being in power itself bring about changes in mental states which then manifest themselves in hubristic behaviour? I believe it would be meaningful to speak of this as a hubris syndrome that can affect those in power. A syndrome happens to someone, it is nature at work, a collection of features, be they signs or symptoms which have a greater chance of appearing together than independently.

The behavioural symptoms which might trigger the diagnosis of hubris syndrome typically grow in strength the longer a head of government remains in office. He or she needs to present, I suggest, more than three or four symptoms from the following tentative list, before any such diagnosis should be contemplated:

- a narcissistic propensity to see the world primarily as an arena in which they can exercise power and seek glory rather than as a place with problems that need approaching in a pragmatic and non–self-referential manner;
- a predisposition to take actions which seem likely to cast them in a good light – i.e. in order to enhance their image;
- a disproportionate concern with image and presentation;
- a messianic manner of talking about what they are doing and a tendency to exaltation;

- an identification of themselves with the state to the extent that they regard the outlook and interests of the two as identical;
- a tendency to talk of themselves in the third person or using the royal 'we';
- excessive confidence in their own judgement and contempt for the advice or criticism of others;
- exaggerated self-belief, bordering on a sense of omnipotence, in what they personally can achieve;
- a belief that rather than being accountable to the mundane court of colleagues or public opinion, the real court to which they answer is much greater: History or God;
- an unshakeable belief that in that court they will be vindicated;
- restlessness, recklessness and impulsiveness;
- loss of contact with reality; often associated with progressive isolation;
- a tendency to allow their 'broad vision', especially their conviction about the moral rectitude of a proposed course of action, to obviate the need to consider other aspects of it, such as its practicality, cost and the possibility of unwanted outcomes: a wooden-headed refusal to change course;
- a consequent type of incompetence in carrying out a policy, which could be called hubristic incompetence. This is where things go wrong precisely because too much self-confidence has led the leader not to bother worrying about the nuts and bolts of a policy. There may be an inattention to detail which can be allied to an incurious nature. It is to be distinguished from ordinary incompetence, where the necessary detailed work on the complex issues involved is engaged in but mistakes in decision-making are made nonetheless.

Most syndromes of personality tend to manifest themselves in people by the age of eighteen and stay with them for the rest of their lives. The hubris syndrome is different in that it should not be seen as a personality syndrome but as something which manifests itself in any leader but only when in power – and usually only after they have been wielding it for some time – and which then may well abate once power is lost. In that sense it is an illness of the office as much as of the person. And the circumstances in which the office is held clearly affect the likelihood that a leader will succumb to it. The key external factors would seem to be these: overwhelming success in achieving and holding power; a political context in which there is minimal constraint on the leader exercising their personal authority; and the length of time they stay in power.

The medical profession is not yet ready to pathologise the sort of damaging, hubristic behaviour which the public instinctively, if imprecisely, talks of in terms of lunacy, insanity and madness. But just because the profession, rightly, wishes to be very controlled in its use of language does not mean that these questions are not very much in need of asking by philosophers and lawyers as well as the medical profession. In this book I do not pretend to answer these questions definitively. In Chapter 7 I draw on my book *The Hubris Syndrome*,[18] a paperback published in the UK in 2007, while omitting some of its detailed supporting argument relating to Iraq.

In looking at illnesses in heads of government in the twentieth century, between 1901 and 2007, to be precise, Chapters 1 and 2 consider many cases of illness in heads of government over that whole period. There are then five chapters covering specific case histories: Chapter 3 examines the illness of the British Prime Minister, Sir Anthony Eden, during the Suez Crisis of 1956; Chapter 4 compares the behaviour of President John F. Kennedy in 1961, during the Bay of Pigs fiasco and while meeting Nikita Khrushchev, with that displayed the following year in the Cuban Missile Crisis, and relates them to his health and the changes in treatment that took place in between these events; Chapter 5 concerns the illness of the Shah of Iran during his last five years in power; and Chapter 6 looks at the case of President François Mitterrand of France, who suffered from prostate cancer for almost his entire fourteen-year period in office, eleven of them without the public knowing. In Chapter 7 hubristic behaviour is discussed in relation to President George W. Bush and Prime Minister Tony Blair over Iraq. Finally, in Chapter 8, I consider some of the safeguards that society needs to address as a consequence of illness in heads of government.

Part I

Illness in heads of government during the last 100 years

1

1901–1953

> The peacemakers, however, had to deal with reality, not what might have been. They grappled with huge and difficult questions. How can the irrational passions of nationalism or religion be contained before they do more damage? How can we outlaw war? We are still asking these questions.
>
> Margaret MacMillan[1]

This chapter examines illness amongst political leaders who held real power or influence in the years from 1901 to 1953, while the next chapter covers 1953–2007. This period of just over a hundred years saw great changes in international politics and medical science. By 1918 the United States of America had emerged as a world power; by 1945 it was the world's strongest. In Chapter 2 we will see that by 1989, despite defeat in Vietnam, America had become the world's single superpower as the Soviet empire crumbled. Yet by 2006 American power had been checked in Iraq and Afghanistan, and China was becoming a new world force.

The prosperity of Britain during the first part of the twentieth century was bled by two devastating wars that started in Europe. After the Second World War Britain gradually lost its empire piece by piece, most dramatically with independence for India, granted in 1947. Economic weakness forced withdrawal from east of Suez, a process that was virtually complete by 1967 (see Chapter 2). In 1973 the United Kingdom joined the founding six members of the European Economic Community, to make a community of nine, with Denmark and Ireland. Today the European Union comprises twenty-seven countries, a unique venture with its destiny uncertain.

The twentieth century was a period when huge advances were made in medical treatments. Ronald Ross and Alphonse Laveran, two of the scientists who helped prove that mosquitoes transmitted malaria, the world's most serious endemic disease, were awarded the Nobel Prize for Medicine in 1902 and 1907 respectively. Penicillin had only just begun to be manufactured when it was given to Winston Churchill for his severe pneumonia in 1943. Medical diagnosis improved progressively throughout the century, transformed by microbiological techniques, blood chemistry, X-rays, electro-cardiograms (ECGs) and ultrasonics. More recent breakthroughs have come from the knowledge stemming from molecular biology and the discovery of DNA, and from magnetic resonance imaging (MRI) and positron emission tomography (PET) scans. The extraordinary range of treatments and drugs available has altered the nature of the health problems of political leaders and thereby the impact of illness on policy-making. People live longer and their working life has grown longer.

All of this is not to suggest that the issues concerning illness and its effects on heads of government, with which this book deals, sprang from nowhere simply in 1901. One of the most bizarre episodes of illness involving a head of government was the oral cancer of US President Grover Cleveland. On 1 July 1893 Cleveland was operated on for cancer of the jaw in great secrecy aboard a yacht in New York harbour. He was strapped upright in a chair against the mast of the *Oneida* and given nitrous oxide followed by ether. A large part of the jaw was then removed. The press were merely told that he was suffering from toothache. An account of what happened appeared in a Philadelphia newspaper but was denied. Cleveland is the only President so far to serve one term, then lose an election and yet be re-elected for a second term. He died in 1908 aged seventy one, of causes unrelated to his oral cancer.[2]

The truth began to become known only in 1917. In 1928 a member of the medical team revealed details of the operation and the nature of the tumour was eventually revealed in March 1980.[3] Cleveland's story, particularly the secrecy involved, would have fitted very well with the examples given in this book. But nineteenth-century medicine was very different from that practised in the twentieth century and the lessons from history are therefore somewhat less, hence the focus on the last hundred years or so.

The following case histories over this period of heads of government who were ill or thought to have been ill have no continuous medical strands to bind them together, and I have not sought to artificially group them, being content to let them be assessed chronologically within the context of their times. Some of the leaders are democratic, others are dictators or despots. The histories are in some respects brief medical records of individual patients. But medical knowledge is built up on such case histories and in Chapter 8 I attempt to bring together the lessons from them all and make recom-mendations for the future.

Theodore Roosevelt

Theodore Roosevelt was a man of phenomenal energy. He was Vice President to William McKinley, who was assassinated on 14 September 1901. Roosevelt was forty-three years old when he took office as President. He was re-elected in 1904 and stepped down, aged 51, in 1909. To many Americans his presidency can be measured against the great administrations of Lincoln and Washington. Edmund Morris, Pulitzer Prize-winning biographer of Roosevelt, explains his febrile character by citing the short but perceptive essay of a French writer, Léon Bazalgette, writing 'that these floods of apparent aggression, half fierce, half humorous, were more indicative of energy than of serious thought. They were part of the excess that was part of Roosevelt's nature. The weir had constantly to spill, to keep the deep water behind clear and calm.'[4] To the layman words such as megalomania and hubris do not go amiss when attached to Roosevelt. A man of phenomenal energy, who suffered from periodic depressions, his rise up the political ladder was extraordinary.

Roosevelt, after some lobbying on his behalf, was appointed assistant secretary of the navy on 19 April 1887. He quickly made his mark, virtually putting the navy on a war footing. Exactly a year later Congress voted for Cuban independence. President McKinley signed the resolution next day with its promise, once liberation had been achieved, to leave government and control to the people of Cuba. On 23 April the President called for 125,000 volunteers as the regular army numbered only 28,000 men. Within days Roosevelt's Rough Riders of frontiersmen were born and 'Teethadore', as Roosevelt was called in the *New York Press*, because of prominent front teeth, was embarked on his course of becoming the most famous man in America. It was as Colonel Teddy Roosevelt that he led his men in a cavalry charge to victory at the battle of San Juan Hill on 1 July 1888, in the Spanish–American War. He went on to storm his way to the governorship of New York and then to be nominated as the Republican candidate for Vice President.

To some people's surprise three leading American psychiatrists wrote a paper in 2006 claiming that it was highly likely that Roosevelt, while President, had suffered from bipolar-I disorder.[5] Nevertheless they concluded that his symptoms had not interfered with his effectiveness or performance in office. Some have claimed Roosevelt was the happiest man to have lived in the White House, others that he became deluded and insane. On 31 January 1908 Roosevelt wrote a special message to Congress, audacious and controversial and aligning himself with the progressive left. The *New York Times* wrote of his tendency towards 'delusion', especially with regard to conspiracies against himself. The *New York Sun* called it a 'pretentious diatribe' better referred to psychologists.

From childhood Roosevelt suffered from asthma and periodic diarrhoea, which was called in the family *cholera morbus*. At Harvard a doctor warned him that his heart had been affected by his asthma and body-building exercises.[6] Advised to slow down, otherwise his life would be short, he refused to comply. In July 1883 as New York State legislator he had a bad attack of asthma and diarrhoea, which he later described as a nightmare. On 14 February 1884 his mother died of typhoid fever; eleven hours later his wife, Alice Lee, died from kidney failure, called Bright's disease, after giving birth to their first child. Roosevelt was devastated. His diary entry had 'a large black and a single anguished entry. "The light has gone out of my life."' He was twenty-five.[7] Roosevelt took refuge in physical exercise as a way of overcoming the grief which he called 'Black Care' and which, he explained, 'rarely sits behind a rider whose pace is fast enough'.[8] After spending time on the ranch riding and exercising, he had another attack of asthma for a fortnight in late March/early April. Yet while ranching he gained in strength and William Roscoe Thayer, a biographer who knew him at Harvard, prophesied that this magnificent specimen of manhood 'with the neck of a Titan and with broad shoulders and stalwart chest' would have to spend the rest of his life struggling to reconcile the conflicting demands of a powerful mind and an equally powerful body.[9] Yet he had another attack of asthma in September 1887 when his new wife, Edith, was close to having a baby. There is little doubt, therefore, that anxiety was an aspect in bringing on these asthmatic and diarrhoea attacks. Anxiety is an affective disorder which can be as diagnostic as depression in bipolar disorder.

Theodore Roosevelt's brother, Elliott, was a serious alcoholic and eventually died following an epileptic fit. In late 1891 Elliott had legally challenged an insanity claim in a newspaper and published a denial of any madness. Theodore took to his bed for eight days thereafter, perhaps as a result of the stress of dealing with his brother. As governor of New York in 1899 Theodore confessed to being 'a wee bit depressed' that spring, which Edmund Morris writes was 'a Rooseveltian euphemism for submersion in the Slough of Despond'.[10] There is therefore clear evidence of clinical anxiety and depression affecting the health of a man who at the age of forty-two was in other respects seen as in vigorous, robust health and was the Vice President of the United States.

Roosevelt was climbing the highest peak in the Adirondacks in New York State when he was told by a ranger that McKinley had been shot. He was President for more than seven years and his anxiety and asthma during this period seemed to recede into the background and are not felt to have affected his decision-making as President. 'In youth, the aggressive impulse had predominated but in maturity he had strengthened himself to a state of containment, like a volcano sheathed in hardened lava. For three years there had been no serious fissures'[11] prior to assuming the Presidency. In the White House Roosevelt, perhaps to get rid of his aggression, used to box regularly for exercise. During a sparring match he was blinded permanently in his left eye, but the public were never told.[12]

There is no clear-cut case of an incontrovertibly manic episode in Roosevelt's life. But there is some evidence of manic tendency. Roosevelt 'slept erratically, but after his 18-hour work day the little sleep he had was sound and refreshing – a sine qua non of the hypomanic state'.[13] Yet the distinction between lay people describing Roosevelt as showing signs of megalomania and doctors diagnosing him with hypomania is a fine one. After the 1904 election victory, in a mood of elation, Roosevelt announced that he would follow the example of George Washington and not run for re-election in 1908. It is claimed that he was in a manic rage when he attacked the *New York World* and the *Indianapolis News* for criminal libel in 1908, and in a fiery message to Congress on 15 December, he replied to the assertions that there was some corrupt action by or on behalf of the United States government in connection with acquiring the title to the Panama Canal from the French Compagnie Universelle du Canal Interocéanique, saying, 'The stories were scurrilous and libelous in character and false in every essential particular.' He went on to attack Joseph Pulitzer, the proprietor of the *New York World*, who wrote to the *New York Times* saying he objected strongly to Roosevelt's policy of

> imperialism, militarism, and jingoism; his general lawless and autocratic temper, his contempt of Congress, and his abuse of the courts. I am really sorry that he should be so angry, but the *World* will continue to criticize him without a shadow of fear, even if he should succeed in compelling me to edit the paper from jail.[14]

Temper tantrums apart, in office Roosevelt had a formidable record of achievement. Aware of the strategic need for a shortcut between the Atlantic and Pacific, he ensured the construction of the Panama Canal. His interpretation of the Monroe Doctrine prevented the establishment of foreign bases in the

Caribbean and assumed the sole right of intervention in Latin America to the United States. Cuba was liberated and the armed forces in the US were strengthened. He secured peace in 1905 between Japan and Russia, for which he received the Nobel Prize. At home his clean-up of politics was accompanied by a fall in the lynch rate. His trust-busting established rules for a market economy. Over the handling of black soldiers in the Brownsville incident in August 1906 Roosevelt made and acknowledged serious mistakes. Roosevelt left office as the first great political environmentalist, having created five national parks and eighteen national monuments. He achieved this by cajoling authority out of Congress or by making executive orders. He had a fierce temper, was domineering, impatient and at times bellicose, but he was also much loved.

A respected figure but with powerful enemies, Roosevelt stepped down incapable of settling for a life of inaction. He soon regretted having chosen President Howard Taft as his successor. Taft was ineffective and suffered from apnoea, a breathing-related sleep disorder,* which, along with his obesity, made him lethargic and not up to the job. Roosevelt then, most unwisely, decided to fight both Taft and Woodrow Wilson, the Democrat nominee, as a third-party candidate. He was shot at during the campaign, but was saved by a steel spectacles case he kept in his breast pocket. He went on speaking despite a blood-stained shirt, with a bullet lodged in his chest, proclaiming, 'It takes more than that to kill a Bull Moose!' In November 1912, against a split Republican Party, Wilson won the election. Thayer wrote of this ill-fated electoral challenge: 'If he could not rule he would ruin. The old allegation that he must be crazy was of course revived.'[15] After Roosevelt fought and lost – though he beat the incumbent, President Taft – he 'suffered from what his family delicately referred to as a 'bruised spirit'; so concerned were they about his state of mind that they discreetly asked his doctor, Alexander Lambert, to come for a visit. Roosevelt, who had become a political pariah, confessed to Lambert, 'I have been unspeakably lonely. You don't know how lonely it is for a man to be rejected by his own kind.'[16]

---

* Obstructive sleep apnoea syndrome was not diagnosed until the second half of the twentieth century. Apnoea is a temporary cessation of breathing when sleeping with a reduction of nasal inflow to less than 30 per cent of normal for more than ten seconds. The syndrome is defined as when there are more than five periods of apnoea in any one hour, leading to daytime sleepiness. It is treated by giving oxygen at night through continuous positive airways pressure devices and, where there is an abnormality of the pharynx, by applying mandibular or jaw advancement splints. Snoring is a feature and complications can involve heart failure and high blood pressure.

Once again Roosevelt sought to overcome his depression with adventure and physical exertion and headed off on an expedition on 4 October 1913 to chart the River of Doubt in Brazil. That river, which now bears his name, is a tributary of the Amazon, winding its way for nearly 1,000 miles through the Brazilian rainforest. There Roosevelt was reborn and revitalised, despite nearly dying at one stage on the expedition. With his life in peril he told his son Kermit to take the expedition on and leave his ailing father behind with the vial of morphine he took on his travels for just such an eventuality. Kermit refused and with an infection in his leg and high fever Roosevelt was very lucky to survive. He returned a hero to New York harbour on 19 May 1914. A few years later, a shadow of his former self, Roosevelt was refused permission by President Wilson to go to France to fight in the First World War, where later he lost his son Quentin.

On 6 January 1919 Theodore Roosevelt died aged sixty. His friend and fellow naturalist, John Burroughs, said of this quite remarkable man, who had periodic depression and anxiety and may have wrestled throughout his life with bipolar disorder: 'The world is bleaker and colder for his absence from it. We shall not look upon his like again.'[17]

Henry Campbell-Bannerman

When Henry Campbell-Bannerman assumed office in Britain in 1905 on the resignation of A. J. Balfour, he was the first person officially to be given the title Prime Minister, his predecessors being First Lord or First Minister of the Treasury. His government included three future Prime Ministers: Herbert Asquith, David Lloyd George and Winston Churchill. A Liberal landslide followed when Campbell-Bannerman called the election of 1906. He had become leader of the Liberal Party in 1899 and led them in Parliament against the Boer War, a controversial stance which triggered abusive letters, including one from, of all people, a clergyman, who wrote, 'You are a cad, a coward and a murderer, and I hope you will meet a traitor's or a murderer's doom.' He didn't quite do that, but as his period in Downing Street progressed, Campbell-Bannerman became progressively sicker. In June 1907, he had a second heart attack and disruption of the conduct of government was avoided only by allowing Asquith, the Chancellor of the Exchequer, to take over more and more of his duties and in effect act as his chief of staff. A year earlier he had been broken by the death of his wife, to whom he had been devoted. His ill health continued along with repeated heart attacks. He 'never resigned of his own free will, fighting on his death bed to hang on to the Premiership'.[18] It was only when his doctors took matters into their own hands that he was virtually forced to resign. He remained in No. 10 until he died almost three weeks later on 22 April 1908.

Campbell-Bannerman's main legacy was South African reconciliation. He paved the way for the great Liberal Party reforms and supported votes for women at the height of the suffragette movement in 1906.[19] To that extent, despite his illness, he was a surprisingly successful Prime Minister.

So, right at the beginning of this chronicle, many of the themes of this book are already present: a head of government, a British Prime Minister, sick in office with heart disease; the subsequent need for others to take charge in order to keep disruption to a minimum while keeping the outside world from knowing the true extent of the problem; another head of government, a US President, governing actively and successfully despite having a history of mental illness. The interesting feature is that in the case of Campbell-Bannerman the doctors, unusually, showed their muscle and demanded resignation, whereas in almost every other case described in this book, the medical advisers to heads of government never exerted anything approaching such authority.

Campbell-Bannerman is unique in that he is the only Prime Minister so far to die in 10 Downing Street, a place he once described as a 'rotten old barrack of a house'. Yet his is not the worst case of incapacity in this 106-year period. That distinction belongs to the US President Woodrow Wilson, who, though not dying in the White House, had the most incapacitating illness of any serving President.

Woodrow Wilson

Woodrow Wilson had had hypertension, or raised blood pressure, for many years before he became President in 1913 and had many neurological incidents from 1889 onwards, which were probably vascular in origin. A normal person's blood pressure is around 120 millimetres of mercury systolic and 80 millimetres diastolic, expressed as 120/80.* In hypertension, the systolic blood pressure in the arteries is high and the diastolic usually also rises, reflecting the pumping of

---

*Systole is the period of the cardiac cycle when the heart contracts. It usually refers to the ventricular systole, which lasts about 0.3 seconds. Diastolic pressure is lower because the ventricle is relaxing and refilling.

the heart and the force exerted on the arteries. Hypertension over time produces changes in the artery walls and predisposes them to clot formation or thrombosis. In Wilson's case, retinal artery changes had been recorded as early as 1906. In 1919, while attending the Paris Peace Conference, Wilson's judgement was not only impaired but 'he was prone to do things which were "unnatural" for him'. Others said that he had developed a one-track mind.[20] By May of that year he was unable to shift his political positions reflectively and had become prejudiced and intransigent.[21] Clearly his capacity to negotiate effectively had a pathological basis in the brain and he was showing signs of dementia,[*] the result of numerous small strokes. He was described as being, 'increasingly egocentric, suspicious and secretive and less discreet in references to people'.[22]

The European reaction to Wilson was an early sign of the clash of cultures which George W. Bush triggered, resulting in an Americophobia in Europe on a far greater scale. It was whispered that Wilson talked to the conference like Jesus Christ, and the French Prime Minister, Georges Clemenceau, called him mentally afflicted, a sufferer from 'religious neurosis'.[23]

Through the last week of September 1919, Wilson suffered a progressive thrombosis of a major artery in the right hemisphere of his brain, in other words a stroke.[24] His consciousness became impaired on 2 October, by which time he had developed massive damage to the brain with a complete paralysis of the left side of his body and the loss of the left side of his whole visual field. His speech was weak and slurred. Wilson also developed what is called 'neglect syndrome', ignoring one whole side of his body.[†] The President's state of denial was medical in origin, but no such excuse can be called in aid to explain the denial by his wife and by his personal physician, Admiral Cary Grayson. They quite simply lied about his condition. Grayson had been appointed Wilson's physician when he was a mere junior officer in 1913 because, by chance, he had sewn up a cut on the President's sister. They became friends and Grayson lost all objectivity in his care of the patient.

---

[*] Dementia is a deterioration in mental function occurring in around 10 per cent of people over the age of sixty-five and 20 per cent over the age of seventy-five. It is caused by progressive brain disease, which can be vascular, degenerative or due to a tumour, usually malignant. The frontal lobe of the brain contains the motor cortex and those parts of the brain which are concerned with behaviour, personality and learning.

[†] In Wilson's case, he ignored the left side of his body and he explained away the existence of his left-sided paralysis by referring to himself as being 'lame'. This inattention and disregard of paralysis is well recognised in major strokes of the right cerebral hemisphere of the brain and can lead to a complete unawareness of illness or anosognosia. Very bizarre forms of denial or rationalisations can result.

On 6 October, at the first Cabinet meeting without Wilson, the Secretary of State, Robert Lansing, asked Grayson to inform the Cabinet about the President's illness. Grayson told them that Wilson was suffering only from a 'nervous breakdown, indigestion and a depleted nervous system'. When Lansing mentioned that part of the constitution which provided for the Vice President to assume the office of President during any period of incapacity, Grayson made it clear he would not sign any certificate of disability and repeated thereafter that the President's intellect was unimpaired. In fact, Wilson could neither read nor dictate and lay in a darkened room dealing with no government business for weeks. He was unable to hold a Cabinet meeting until 13 April 1920, nearly seven months after the stroke. He was clearly incapable of making important decisions during this period and although he once discussed resigning with Grayson, neither of them took the matter any further.

Many times since then and in different countries, a head of government's medical adviser has lied or misled the public about his or her patient's health, putting the patient's interest before that of the state. In Wilson's case lying was made easier because Grayson was a serving naval officer treating his patient as his Commander in Chief and following the wishes of a superior officer.

There is little doubt that Wilson should have stepped down in 1919, at least for a period, until it was clear whether or not he was going to recover. There were real policy consequences of his failure to do so. For instance, had Wilson stepped down and been succeeded by the Vice President, Thomas Marshall, he might have persuaded Congress to ratify the treaty establishing the League of Nations. What was needed was for two key people in the debate on the league, Senator Henry Cabot Lodge opposing and Senator Gilbert M. Hitchcock supporting, to be helped to reach a compromise. If that had been done, the league, with the United States the leading nation within it, would have been a far more effective organisation and might have helped prevent the Second World War.

As part of his denial of his medical condition, and to demonstrate who was in control, Wilson petulantly dismissed Lansing because Cabinet meetings had been held in his absence and without his permission. In the meantime, Wilson's wife, Edith, started dealing with his workload. For some months, his wife and his doctor between them gave the false image of a working President. Later, Edith Wilson began to be spoken of as America's first woman President. Woodrow Wilson, meanwhile, was not contemplating resignation at all. Indeed in that summer of 1920 he was thinking of standing for a third term. Misleading information and photographs were put out to Democratic Party delegates in San Francisco, hoping to sway the vote. Fortunately, they gave merely sentimental backing rather than political support to their President and voted for Governor James M. Cox of Ohio as presidential candidate, with Franklin D. Roosevelt the vice presidential candidate. This Democratic ticket was surprisingly heavily defeated by the Republican candidate, Warren Harding. Wilson held his last Cabinet in March 1921 and died on 3 February 1924.

David Lloyd George

On 6 December 1916, the Welshman David Lloyd George became British Prime Minister. In a complicated manoeuvre he and a significant number of Conservative members of the wartime coalition had pressurised Herbert Asquith to accept a revised form of War Cabinet, which he did on 3 December but then rejected on the 4th, creating a schism within the Liberal Party whose residues can still be detected today.

Asquith's health when in office was pretty good, and it was actually helped by a near collapse on 2 April 1911, when he complained of having felt giddy for three weeks and appeared exhausted, having been dealing over many long hours with the first national coal strike. His doctor diagnosed hypertension and warned him to substantially reduce his alcohol intake, which was mainly in the form of wine and brandy at dinner. It is claimed that henceforward 'he seems to have taken a firm hold on his alcohol consumption. But reputation once tainted is rarely regained.'[25] Certainly his health improved for the remainder of his period in office.

Comparisons between Lloyd George and Asquith are notoriously difficult. Roy Jenkins, speaking about Asquith in 1987 and reflecting on the biography he had written in 1964, tried hard to be fair:

> He had knowledge, judgement, insight and tolerance. . . . Nevertheless, I think he was in office too long and his style was unsuited to the demands of wartime leadership. It was not so much that Lloyd George when he replaced him, was a better war leader. His errors of strategic judgement and his ineffectiveness in controlling a High Command backed by the King were just as great as were those of Asquith. But Lloyd George had the zest and the brio to behave as though he were a better war leader, and that was half the battle.[26]

This account, however, underestimates Lloyd George's two significant interventions: to force the Admiralty to accept the convoy system in 1916; and in 1918 to insist on meeting the Ludendorff offensive with an attack by fresh troops from Britain, and to persuade the Americans to commit troops.[27]

It was a grim time in the war and Lloyd George's elevation to head of government came as a tonic for public opinion. The German submarine threat was starting to imperil the Merchant Navy and the nation's crucial supply lines. Victory seemed far off, defeat possible. Fatefully, none of Asquith's supporters were ready to serve under Lloyd George and many Conservatives had qualms, to say the least, about the steadiness of the mercurial new Prime Minister. Unlike Winston Churchill's coalition in 1940, where Churchill, by then a member of the Conservative Party, had the majority of MPs, the Lloyd George coalition was dependent on Conservative MPs' support and he could not rely on half of his own Liberal MPs nor on the Irish National Party. Lloyd George, however, proceeded to make a virtue of this weakness: he introduced what the Conservatives wanted, a small War Cabinet of five members. Lloyd George was the only Liberal. Andrew Bonar Law, the Conservative leader, became Chancellor of the Exchequer and Leader of the House; Arthur Henderson, the leader of the Labour Party, continued in office; two Conservative peers, Earl Curzon and Viscount Milner, proconsuls and proven administrators of the Empire, were brought in as ministers without portfolio. The Prime Minister, in effect, by this arrangement, contained himself. It worked because every day after breakfast Lloyd George would walk along the connecting passage from 10 to 11 Downing Street and spend around an hour with Bonar Law reviewing the day's business and submitting his own imaginative ideas to Bonar Law's practical, critical mind.[28] In this way potentially the most hubristic British Prime Minister in the last century constrained his charismatic and creative personality. It was a Cabinet structure which contributed massively to his success over the next two years. Lloyd George's biographer, John Grigg, wrote that his power over the War Cabinet 'was due to force of talent and personality rather than to the inherent strength of position' and that while he was bold, positive and decisive he was not autocratic and 'set much store by conciliation and liked, if possible, to carry people with him'.

Lloyd George retained good health throughout his period in No. 10; there was no history of depression and he only had periodic throat infections which appeared to be related to times of tension. In September 1918 he had a bad attack of influenza for nine days and a shaky convalescence. When at eleven o'clock on the eleventh day of the eleventh month in 1918 the war ended, with the announcement of the armistice terms, it was appropriate that Lloyd George was acclaimed as 'The Man Who Won the War'.

On 14 November 1918 a general election was announced to take place in a month's time with votes to be counted after Christmas on 28 December. The coalition planned to continue in office and fought on a joint Lloyd George–Bonar Law manifesto. For the first time women could vote and in the 'khaki election' the coalition won 473 of the 707 seats in the House of Commons.

Max Aitken, later better known as the newspaper proprietor Lord Beaverbrook, was a Unionist MP for Ashton-under-Lyne from 1910 until 1916. He served with the Canadian forces in France and joined Lloyd George's government as Chancellor of the Duchy of Lancaster in 1918. He generously wrote of Lloyd George's period as wartime Prime Minister in his book, published in 1963, about Lloyd George's decline and fall:

> Here was a man who had done battle with the most dreadful foe his country had ever faced. Great fleets and grand armies had moved at his command. The utmost perils had left him undaunted. He was ever fertile in inspiration and resource. He subdued not only the enemy without, but also the enemy within. He had to contend with recalcitrant colleagues, stubborn Admirals, treacherous Generals, who were quite ready to conspire behind his back, and even to involve the King himself in their intrigues. He looked on tempests and he was not shaken.[29]

As the year 1921 opened few dissented from Bonar Law's opinion: 'Lloyd George can be Prime Minister for life if he likes.' But according to Beaverbrook, '1921 ushered in two cruel years which were to rip away all the gold brocade and the tinsel too.' While Beaverbrook was not the most dispassionate of men, he knew much about the wielding of power and by the time he put pen to paper analysing Lloyd George, he had also served under Churchill as Minister for Air Production, Minister of Supply and Lord Privy Seal. In contrast to his praise for the wartime period he was a bitter critic of Lloyd George's prime ministership after the war, when he felt that hubris was at the root of his problems:

> The Greeks told us of a man in high position, self-confident, so successful as to be overpowering to all others. Then his virtues turned to failings. He committed the crime of arrogance. His structure of self-confidence and success came

tumbling down. He struggled against fate, but he was doomed. So it was with Lloyd George in the year 1921 and into 1922. Then all was over. His plans good and bad came to nothing. He fell and never rose again.

The brilliant schemes and stratagems which he resorted to in war, outwitting Generals and Politicians, Peers, Prelates and the King, and all to save Britain, he now applied with daring and skill to save himself from defeat by the Members of the House of Commons. He was confident that what he had done once, he could do again. To keep the seat of power, the place of patronage, he was prepared to stand out as the leader of Empire-minded men – or appear as the Liberal Apostle of Free Trade: as the Man of Peace in Europe – or the Man of War against Turkey and France: as the hammer of the Russian Bolsheviks – or their noble conciliator: as the Tribune of the British working classes – or the Champion of the Tory Landlords against Labour: stern enemy of the Irish – or their tender friend spreading his covering wings about another Celtic race ground under the heel of the oppressor. He took up each position in turn during those tragic years of 1921 and 1922. . . . Sometimes and simultaneously he took up contradictory standings. His daring was wonderful to look upon. But to those who never forgot his greatness in his great days, the spectacle wore thin and ere long became pathetic.[30]

A more balanced view of this postwar period, chronicling some of its undoubted achievements, comes from the historian Kenneth O. Morgan: 'For all its failures, the Lloyd George Coalition of 1918–22, alone of peacetime British governments this century, tried to harness political consensus for positive ends.'[31] Morgan, in contrast to Beaverbrook, gives credit to Lloyd George for social reforms that far surpassed those of 1909–13, with the implementation of universal state unemployment insurance, the new expenditure on pensions and social security, the creation of the Ministry of Health, a measure of justice for agricultural workers and education reforms. These measures stalled on Treasury demand for retrenchment. But already the seeds of destruction were traceable in Lloyd George's style, 'the dangers of Caesarism . . . intuitive, erratic diplomacy and confused, ill-prepared encounters'.[32] Morgan goes on to describe how by June 1921 Lloyd George seemed 'a desperate man' and that this underlaid his 'temporary physical breakdown'. 'With the stamp of personal authority so emphatic on the government's programme on all fronts, the press naturally used the Prime Minister as its essential target'[33] and this was symbolised by him summoning the Cabinet to Inverness, near where he was convalescing, highlighting the image of a 'one-man band, goaded into unnatural harmony by a frenetic conductor of aberrant genius'.

While he was selling honours, manipulating friends and enemies and bestriding the world stage, nemesis struck Lloyd George at a famous meeting of Conservative MPs at the Carlton Club, and he was forced to resign that same day, 19 October 1922. It could all have been so different if he had acknowledged political reality. In late June 1920, supported by Churchill and Charles McCurdy, Lloyd George presented his Liberal colleagues serving in the government with a plan for merging the coalition Liberal and Conservative parties. At the peak of his powers, Lloyd George's plan was somewhat surprisingly defeated. Thereafter he was a Prime Minister without a party. He should have resigned then as Prime Minister and either accepted to serve under a Conservative leader or taken to the back benches. While Lloyd George bitterly regretted his Liberal colleagues' refusal to merge, in an interesting contrast his wife, who never liked the Tories, was very pleased.

Even if Lloyd George out of office had not been able to heal the division within the Liberal Party before the next election, he would have been better placed to eventually do so and return as Prime Minister sometime after Asquith died in 1928, leading at least the largest single party in the House of Commons. Instead he fought on as Prime Minister, gripped by the need to stay in power and not ready to release himself from the total hold that power now had over him. In doing so he carried the political enmity of Stanley Baldwin and Ramsay MacDonald, who were ready to combine at almost any price to keep Lloyd George from returning to power.

Tracing Lloyd George's downfall one can see that the mistakes and errors he made were born out of hubristic actions. Firstly, he was mesmerised by the world stage. After he signed the treaty of Versailles on 28 June 1919, having negotiated it for months in Paris, he continued to spend an inordinate amount of time hammering out difficult issues in special conferences. He attended no fewer than thirty-three between 1919 and 1922.[34] The conference habit was summed up in a *Punch* cartoon of that name. Secondly, he came to believe he was indispensable. By 1920 Churchill was complaining as War Secretary that the Prime Minister had virtually taken over the running of the Foreign Office and historians have written about these years as the start of a form of presidential government.[35] The two friends did work together over the Anglo-Irish treaty but gradually they drifted further apart than at any other time in their long association. Lloyd George even came close to being contemptuous of Churchill's judgement:

The trouble with Winston is that he's always taking action. *He will insist on getting out his maps.* In 1914 he got out his map of the Dardanelles, and think where that landed us. And after the War I had to think what to do with him. I wanted him in my Cabinet, of course, but what's the safest place *after a war* for a man who will get out his maps? The *War Office*, of course, I thought. He'll be safe there. But was he? Before I could look round, he's got out his maps of Russia and we were making fools of ourselves in the Civil War.[36]

Churchill also believed that Britain did not have enough troops on the ground in the Middle East and elsewhere. To Lloyd George, Churchill had 'Bolshevism on the brain'.

Differences with a Liberal colleague, like Churchill, within the coalition, were compounded by Lloyd George's differences with Conservative MPs and peers. Lord Curzon, the Foreign Secretary, wrote to his wife on 21 April 1921: 'He wants his Forn. Sec. [*sic*] to be a valet, almost a drudge, and has no regards for the civilities of life.' In March 1922 Lloyd George sacked his Secretary of State for India, Edwin Montagu; speaking at the Cambridge Liberal Club, Montagu said: 'The head of our government is a Prime Minister of great but eccentric genius. He has demanded the price which it is within the power of every genius to demand – the complete disappearance of the doctrine of Cabinet responsibility. He is a great genius – but a dictator.'[37] Lloyd George was now an autocrat, not a democrat.

Meanwhile, British military involvement in Palestine, Turkey and Mesopotamia (what we now call Iraq) were leading to heavy casualties and many MPs began to sense a restlessness amongst the electorate. The failure of President Wilson to prevent the defeat in the US Congress of Article 10 of the Versailles treaty, which stated that a signatory promised to 'respect and preserve against external aggression the territorial integrity and existing political independence of all Members of the League', led to America not participating in the League of Nations. All this affected Lloyd George's prestige at home as the successful peacemaker.

These factors were material when it came to the Carlton Club meeting and Baldwin's warning that Lloyd George's 'dynamic force' had broken up the Liberal Party and could well break up the Conservative Party. Lloyd George's charm and contrary personality are well reflected in a letter he wrote (out of power) in September 1923 to Bonar Law, with whom he had worked so well for five years. Bonar Law was very ill and his earlier resignation in March 1921 had removed the last check on Lloyd George's presidential style. They remained friends perhaps because while Lloyd George was deeply ambitious, Bonar Law hardly knew what ambition was:

My dear Bonar,

I was amused when Max [Aitken] told me last night that on your return to the House of Commons you meant to spend the rest of your years supporting the Government of the day in all its difficulties. I told him that I had exactly the same design for my own future but that when I imparted it to you my patriotic professions were invariably received with incredulity. You were right. I find it most difficult to be a tolerant judge of the defects of my successors! Impartiality is a virtue that wears badly. Mine is already in tatters. I have just written a preface to a book in which I slang everybody with perfect impartiality. I was delighted to see you once more & to see you looking ever so much better than I did when I passed through a similar experience.

We must have another meal at Max's. He was in a condition of ribald high spirits last night.

Ever sincerely

D.Ll.G.[38]

Lloyd George, 'the Welsh Wizard', or 'the Big Beast of the Forest' or 'the Goat', as he was called by some, was the most multi-skilled politician of the twentieth century. He had an eloquence unmatched and a rare negotiating genius. He was the most radical Chancellor of the Exchequer and for his first three years, the best Prime Minister. Yet he was also the first British Prime Minister to be toppled after developing hubris syndrome. Unconstrained from 1920 onwards, his admiration for presidential governments, first for Theodore Roosevelt and then for Franklin, developed apace. Later he even admired Hitler too much for his own good. His hubristic temperament was always there but ran in democratic harness until 1921. Thereafter he paid everyone less and less regard and even lost his respect for Parliament. He died on 26 March 1945. Churchill said, in a most remarkable eulogy in the House of Commons two days later: 'As a man of action, resource and creative energy, he stood, when at his zenith, without a rival.'

Paul Deschanel

Extraordinarily, at the same time as President Woodrow Wilson was ill, something very similar was happening in France. President Paul Deschanel's wife was signing official acts for her husband because he was acting very bizarrely. Deschanel was one of the most brilliant literary and political figures of his time and as a young man had been elected to the Académie Française. He was elected President of France on 17 January 1920 with an overwhelming majority of 734 votes out of 888 voting members of Parliament. Soon after his election, though, rumours of extravagant behaviour started circulating. He surprised crowds, for instance, by enthusiastically kissing the mouth of a First World War solider who had a severely mutilated face. Then, on 23 May, Deschanel disappeared from his presidential train while travelling from Paris during the night. He had either fallen from an open window, which would explain the fact that he was slightly hurt in his leg, or just walked off the train while it was making a technical stop. He ended up in his night clothes and with blood on his face in a gatekeeper's house at a railway crossing. His assertions that he was the President of the Republic and had fallen off the train were met with hilarious incredulity until a doctor, who was called in, recognised him. Deschanel apparently said, 'I have a complete gap in memory between the moment I opened the door of my compartment and the moment I awoke here.' It has been claimed that Deschanel suffered from Elpenor's syndrome, characterised by a 'state of half-consciousness with disorientation in space and half-automatic movements occurring, on waking, in people who, shortly before, went to sleep in an unusual place after having drunk too much or having taken hypnotic drugs. This state may lead to a fall or to misdemeanours.'[39] It is claimed Deschanel had taken 50 centigrams of a hypnotic drug, Trional.

It is also claimed, perhaps somewhat improbably, that on another occasion Deschanel received the British ambassador, the Earl of Derby, stark naked except for his decorations. The British Foreign Office, from whom I enquired, have no record of this alleged incident. There was also an occasion when the President was found walking fully clothed in a shallow lake at Rambouillet. On 15 September 1920, under the headline 'President's health broken', newspapers reported that after consulting the Prime Minister he had decided to resign. Deschanel voluntarily did so on 21 September after only seven months in office.

It is now thought that in addition to Elpenor's syndrome Deschanel developed frontotemporal dementia.[40] This is a degenerative brain disease that often starts with uninhibited behaviour. He died aged sixty-seven on 22 April 1922, with no mention of any brain disease or post mortem examination.

Warren Harding

Woodrow Wilson's successor, Warren Harding, was a handsome, healthy-looking man, only fifty-five when he came to office. But in fact he had had heart trouble for some years beforehand with shortness of breath, and he died before the invalid Wilson. Harding was not a towering figure. He had fought an inactive 'front porch' campaign and had few distinctive qualities. Memorably, Senator William McAdoo described Harding's speeches as resembling 'an army of phrases moving over the landscape in search of an idea. Sometimes these meandering words would actually capture a straggling thought and bear it triumphantly, a prisoner in their midst, until it died of servitude and overwork.' Harding's looks deceived about his health as well as his abilities. He suffered from depression and had had heart symptoms for many years, at one stage in 1918 being unable to complete a lecture because of them. As President, he began to complain of chest pains in 1922, his blood pressure rose and he appeared exhausted. On 2 August 1923 Harding died. His wife refused a post mortem, but there is little doubt, despite differing accounts of his last few moments, that his death was cardiovascular in origin, leading to a stroke.

Calvin Coolidge

On the day after Harding's death, the Vice President, Calvin Coolidge, was sworn in as President by his father, a notary public, by the light of a kerosene lamp late at night in the family farmhouse at Plymouth Notch, Vermont. He was re-elected in 1924, trouncing the Democratic presidential candidate, John Davis, by 382 ballots to 136 in the electoral college vote, with Robert La Follette, standing for the Progressives, winning 13 ballots. On 27 August 1927, Coolidge stunned everyone by announcing, 'I do not choose to run for President in 1928.' It may be that he was influenced by the health of his wife, Grace. She had 'little energy and was losing weight';[41] like him she was grieving for the death of her younger son from a septic toe and worried about her mother's illness. Grace was diagnosed as having a tumour on the kidney in the summer of 1928. In fact she outlived him. It was his own bereavement depression, following his son's death, which caused him voluntarily to leave the White House, although he may have had a heart attack in the White House in 1925;[42] if true this may have contributed to his decision.

In 2006 Coolidge was authoritatively diagnosed as having had a major depressive disorder while in office.[43] Whereas many people still see depression presenting in terms of despair, anxiety can be just as important a presenting feature of depression and so it was with Coolidge. As a boy he had been shy and sensitive, with allergies that led to asthma and a congestion in his nasal passages that left him with a distinctive 'quacking quality to his voice'. He used a throat spray but kept this quiet. He was very sensitive to his nose and throat difficulties throughout his life and to his chronic indigestion. Described as a dull lawyer, 'an odd stick around town', he had amazed everyone by marrying a vivacious, humorous, outgoing attractive schoolteacher who liked his dry wit, bore his temper tantrums and put up with his secretive nature and enjoyment of isolation. He slept for up to eleven hours a day. A journalist wrote, 'His ideal day is one in which nothing whatever happens.'

The surprising thing is that a man with depressive anxiety who relished eventless days should ever have got anywhere near being President. Indeed, a leading writer on US Presidents has labelled Coolidge the 'Great Enigma.'[44] In his home was an embroidered quote prominently displayed:

> A wise old owl sat on an oak.
> The more he saw, the less he spoke;
> The less he spoke, the more he heard;
> Why can't we be like that old bird?

He started in politics running for the school committee. In 1906 he was elected to the Massachusetts legislature, the General Council, retiring as was the local practice after two one-year terms. He became mayor of Northampton, serving two terms, and thereafter was in public office for twenty years as state senator, governor and then Vice President. All this time, he was an honest, competent but plodding elected official. Yet his ever-present anxiety left him with little relish for the job of President and in 1924 he had written to his father: 'I hope this is the last time I shall ever have to be a candidate for office.'

There is little evidence that his mental state damaged his presidency. His remark that 'the business of America is business' summed up his attitudes, economy in government and the reduction of debt. His depressive anxiety may have been particular to him but, as his biographer wrote, he, 'like Hoover, Roosevelt, Truman and even Eisenhower after him, suffered from the rarest form of Potomac fever – that which afflicts only Presidents. That form decreed that he could view no prospective successor with equanimity.'[45] His melancholy came out even more in retirement and in his letters. Coolidge died on 5 January 1933, of a coronary thrombosis.

British Prime Ministers Bonar Law, Baldwin, MacDonald and Chamberlain

After the toppling of the robust figure of David Lloyd George, successive British Prime Ministers were hit by health problems, which probably contributed to a build-up to the politics of appeasement. In October 1922 Andrew Bonar Law took over from Lloyd George as Prime Minister, when he already knew that he had laryngeal cancer. By April 1923 he could no longer speak in the House of Commons. He resigned in May and died in October. It is not known whether or not his doctor, Sir Thomas (later Lord) Horder, advised him against becoming Prime Minister in the first place,[46] or, if he did, why Bonar Law ignored the advice and hid his true condition from his colleagues. Stanley Baldwin became Prime Minister on Bonar Law's resignation, and it is an oddity of his career that he twice rose to that job as a result of the incumbent having to stand down because of ill health. The second time, the ill Prime Minister was James Ramsay MacDonald.

MacDonald, with no previous ministerial experience, became Britain's first Labour Prime Minister when his party won the largest number of seats, though not a majority, in the inconclusive election of January 1924. He held the office for only nine months before a second election brought Baldwin back to power. MacDonald became Prime Minister again in 1929, holding the post until 1931. When the national economic crisis hit, he fatefully rejected John Maynard Keynes's advice and refused to devalue sterling. His Cabinet could not swallow the tough economic measures that were needed as a result. Under pressure from George V to continue in office, MacDonald decided it was his duty to head a coalition National Government. The Conservative contribution was so huge that MacDonald inevitably became their political prisoner.

Initially MacDonald had the advantages of incumbency and of his considerable political presence and bearing. But with only three former Labour Cabinet ministers to support him and thirteen Labour MPs,[47] he began to feel the isolation of being separated from almost all of his old Labour colleagues. That might have been easier to take if he had been a younger man and his wife had still been alive. Slowly ill health began to diminish his standing. MacDonald suffered from glaucoma and had a number of eye operations and by 1933, more alarmingly, his mental functioning was deteriorating and he was probably suffering from mild dementia. By 1934, when he was sixty-eight, his impact on British policy-making had become limited and he was little more than a figurehead. Baldwin was the key figure in the National Government, making the important decisions.

On 4 March 1935, in a defence White Paper which bore MacDonald's initials, the argument was made that serious deficiencies in the country's defences could only be put right with additional expenditure. How far MacDonald really believed this is unclear. He had opposed both the Boer War and the First World War because he felt England was not itself in danger. He had thereafter done everything to champion disarmament so it was very difficult for him now to accept that rearmament was essential. It is possible that had he been younger and fitter he might have come to the conclusion that rearmament was necessary when Hitler took power in 1933. But Macdonald was an idealist over disarmament and only a reluctant realist.

On 7 June 1935 MacDonald stepped down as Prime Minister and Baldwin took over for the third time. To add to his troubles, he lost his seat in the general election of November 1935 but managed to return to the Commons the following February by using the anomalous position of a Scottish University seat and remained in the Cabinet as Lord President of the Council. He left government when Baldwin retired in May 1937 and he died of heart failure on 7 November that year. He was by then in all respects a shadow of his former self.

Baldwin for many years did not suffer from any serious illness and is sometimes depicted as the only Prime Minister to have resigned completely voluntarily. I do not think this is true. He had grown increasingly deaf and this was judged by some close to him as a major factor in his desire to step down and hand over to Neville Chamberlain. In 1936, as Chancellor of the Exchequer, Chamberlain's

> principal source of concern related to Baldwin's own health and constitution. Depressed, obviously deafer, unable to sleep and in a 'strained nervous condition', over the summer Baldwin suffered such a complete breakdown that his physician declared that three months complete rest was the minimum necessary for him to recover his strength.[48]

When Chamberlain took over, on 28 May 1937, Britain responded with some enthusiasm to someone who was initially a vigorous and active Prime Minister, even though already sixty-eight years old. He had for a long time been doing the work of Prime Minister. Now he seized the opportunity to play on the world stage. His personal diplomacy during two weeks in September 1938 was disastrous and Munich will reverberate as the first summit conference, on 29–30 September, and a warning to all future summiteers of the dangers of believing that personal relations can overcome all problems. 'More dangerous still was the idealism (and hubris) of a politician who believed he could bring peace to Europe.'[49] It is often forgotten that there was huge public support for Chamberlain's search for peace. That policy was dubbed 'appeasement' by its opponents. Winston Churchill, the advocate of rearmament, had been consigned to be a prophet in the wilderness and written off by many commentators, one of whom had described him as a 'beached whale'. But despite their differences, Churchill did not initially turn his fire on Chamberlain.[*] Only in the House of Commons on 5 October did Churchill unleash his full invective, calling the Munich settlement 'a total and unmitigated defeat'.

It is interesting to analyse Chamberlain's state of mind at Munich. He was exhausted and the day after his heady return to Heston airport and his unprecedented appearance with the King on the balcony of Buckingham Palace he admitted to his sister that he had come nearer to a nervous breakdown 'than I have ever been in my life'.[50] His mood was exultant and he appeared to have been successful in ending the prospect of war. He had acted throughout with a small inner Cabinet and had marginalised his antis. Today apologists for Chamberlain claim he gained time for UK rearmament. That was not his objective. He deluded himself about Hitler's trustworthiness and his sinister ambitions.

There is no record of Chamberlain's visiting Lord Horder, his doctor as well as Bonar Law's, or any hint of his having any serious illness during the period leading up to his Munich visit to Hitler in 1938. Nor in the months after he had declared war on Germany in September 1939 did Chamberlain appear ill. When he stepped down as Prime Minister on 10 May 1940, illness was not, on the face of it, a factor in his resignation. But very soon afterwards, on 24 July, Chamberlain was diagnosed as suffering from advanced cancer when an X-ray revealed a partial stricture of the bowel. At Churchill's

---

[*] When Anthony Eden courageously resigned as Foreign Secretary on 20 February 1938, even though the policy of seeking peace by appeasement was seen to have failed, Churchill was quick to sign a round robin in the House of Commons in support of Chamberlain's policy. He told the Chief Whip, David Margesson, on 17 March that the Prime Minister's point of view and his were not divergent. (David Dutton, *Neville Chamberlain* (London: Arnold, 2001), p. 112.) Eden's resignation never became the rallying point to remove Chamberlain.

insistence he remained a member of the War Cabinet. But he became very ill and an exploratory operation showed inoperable and incurable cancer. He resigned on 3 October 1940 and died on 9 November.

There is no concrete evidence that Chamberlain's undiagnosed cancer had any serious effect on his decisions as Prime Minister. But by 1939 it would be surprising if it had not had some effect. While we know all too little about the early effects of cancer,* there is evidence, in part anecdotal, that cancer brings on the process of ageing, that it is more likely to be accompanied by depression and that it is often accompanied by a general slowing down of brain and body. Exhaustion and stress were taking their toll on Chamberlain by 1938. By March 1939 R. A. Butler, usually known as 'Rab', then a minister in the Foreign Office, described how, on learning that the Italians had invaded Albania, he went over to No. 10 to tell the Prime Minister what had happened. Chamberlain was at the open window of his study feeding seed to the birds, and was rather annoyed at Butler's arrival. He expressed amazement at Butler's distress at the news, saying, 'I feel sure Mussolini has decided not to go against us.' When Butler talked about the threat to the Balkans, Chamberlain dismissed it, saying, 'Don't be silly. Go home and go to bed,' and continued to feed the birds.[51] The capacity for self-delusion is the most worrying aspect of this story, and the fact that it was recorded by Butler, a politician who supported Munich and appeasement, makes the testimony all the more convincing. It is possible that Chamberlain was a victim early on in his premiership of hubris syndrome.

After Munich, with pending cancer and existing gout,† Chamberlain was acting well below his potential. A limerick circulating in the Foreign Office summed up the mood in Whitehall in 1939 about him:

---

* Cancer means a malignant tumour, irrespective of which tissue the cells grow from and where it is in the body. Cancer cells can lie dormant for years. For instance, it has been calculated that a small bowel cancer of around 2–3 centimetres across will have been present on average for five years before being diagnosed. There is a body of epidemiological evidence which shows a statistically significant positive association between major ongoing work stresses and the subsequent diagnosis of cancer. There is some evidence, although it is not conclusive, on how life stress might operate as a cancer trigger, namely that stress lowers the immune state, thus allowing dormant cells to multiply rapidly. (R. Kune and G. Kune, 'Proof of Cancer Causation and Expert Evidence: Bringing Science to the Law and the Law to Science', *Journal of Law and Medicine* (2003), vol. 2, no. 1, pp. 113, 120–1.)

† Gout occurs when there is a raised concentration of uric acid in the blood plasma and in parts of the body. It is deposited in tissue as sodium monourate and this leads to a swelling and pain in the joints. The cause is not known but there is a hereditary element. Rare before the age of

> An elderly statesman with gout,
> When asked what this war is about,
> In a written reply
> Said, 'My colleagues and I
> Are doing our best to find out.'

A better defence of Chamberlain is that certainly by 1939 he had become more realistic about Hitler and was buying time as the rearmament programme built up, knowing that Britain had to fight. Nonetheless, a new and fitter Prime Minister in No. 10, throughout 1939, could have made a difference in those critical months and might have helped check Hitler's territorial advances. But at that stage the leader chosen to replace Chamberlain would not have been Churchill. It would almost certainly have been Lord Halifax. Though highly intelligent and a patriot, and nicknamed the 'Holy Fox', he did not fully recognise that Britain had to fight through the peril in 1940 following Dunkirk and the fall of France to defeat Hitler.

Adolf Hitler

The popular assumption of Adolf Hitler's madness rests in part on the enormity of his crimes but also, perhaps, on his style, or at least on his rhetorical style as captured in newsreel footage of his speeches at the vast Nuremberg rallies. He appears to be ranting like a madman. In fact this footage is misleading: his rhetorical range was huge and he could speak quietly, even emolliently. Hitler could be courteous and display good manners. He hid his rages. Many of the people who saw the very realistic German-made film *Downfall*, released in Britain in 2005, showing Hitler's last days in the bunker in Berlin, were surprised not to see a monster.

Hitler certainly did at times rage like a madman but from a medical point of view, mental illness can be diagnosed only when a mental condition renders a patient incapable in some way and in Hitler's case it would be impossible to argue that whatever his mental make-up may have been, it left him incapable. Quite the contrary. He rose to power and then consolidated

forty, it can be accompanied by urinary calculi (stones), which are composed of urates. When associated with kidney disease long-term prophylactic treatment is with allopurinol, which lowers blood urate levels. Pain responds to non-steroidal anti-inflammatory drugs. Precipitating factors are alcohol and rich animal-derived food.

absolute power in himself by the most brilliant and careful calculation and self–discipline.

The world depression which had begun in 1929 in the United States, with the sudden collapse of the New York stock market, hit Germany very hard, particularly in 1931. In the harsh economic climate of the time, Hitler saw the political opportunities that reparation payments, foolishly still insisted upon by the Allies, gave him. He moved with consummate skill to exploit them. Alan Bullock, in a biography of Hitler, wrote: 'In 1930 the mood of a large section of the German nation was one of resentment. Hitler, with an almost inexhaustible fund of resentment in his own character to draw from, offered them a series of objects on which to lavish all the blame for their misfortunes.'[52] The list was a long one, mainly focused on the Allies (especially the French), reparations, the Weimar Republic, financial speculators, big business, communists and above all Jews. Hatred of the treaty of Versailles was widespread in Germany and under its terms three million Germans still lived in Poland, Czechoslovakia and Austria while Austria could not unite with Germany.

Hitler calculated that his best route to power lay in keeping the country's ageing and infirm president, Paul von Hindenburg, in office. Field Marshal Hindenburg had emerged somewhat undeservedly from the First World War as a military hero and had become President of Germany in 1925, even though he was already showing his age and was dubious about the whole idea of a democratic republic. Hitler saw he could exploit the constitution, which gave Hindenburg considerable power, to use the armed forces to clamp down on opposition and to suspend the constitution itself. Hitler's strategy was to make use of Hindenburg's power over the German army to keep it onside during a legal handover of power from the physically failing President to himself.

By late 1932 Hindenburg was coming under pressure from industrialists and bankers to let Hitler become Chancellor. Hindenburg's son, Oskar, met Hitler and was won round. Then on 4 January 1933, Franz von Papen, the former Chancellor, and Hitler met and did a deal which Papen convinced Hindenburg he should support. Hitler was to be Chancellor, Papen Vice Chancellor and General Werner von Blomberg Minister of Defence. On Monday 30 January 1933 Hitler was asked to form a government by Hindenburg. Again, with calculating shrewdness, Hitler put only three Nazi Party members into the government. Then the Reichstag was dissolved and elections were called. Now the Nazi stormtroopers came out on the streets with a vengeance. The Communists split the Social Democratic vote and the Nazi Party won the election with 43.9 per cent of the votes, giving them a bare majority in the Reichstag. The subsequent proscription of the Communist deputies allowed an enabling law which gave Hitler unbridled power to be passed by the necessary two thirds majority.

Before the vote on 21 March the Nazis and the army were reconciled at a dramatic formal ceremony in the Potsdam Garrison Church to mark the opening of the Reichstag session. The visibly ageing President Hindenburg and the young Chancellor walked down the aisle together. Hitler in his speech lauded the Field Marshal President, then walked over and, bending low, grasped the old man's hand. In this gesture Hitler dramatised the reality: he had secured the army, was legally the head of government and on course to hold absolute power.

From April 1933 Jews were dismissed from their jobs in the public services, in the legal profession and in the universities. On 21 June 1934 a crisis developed and Hitler went to see Hindenburg, now virtually senile and very sick. He was told by Blomberg that the President was about to declare martial law and hand power to the army unless something was done to curb the power of the two million-strong SA, the Nazis' stormtroopers. On 29 June, perhaps significantly the day that Dr Ferdinand Sauerbruch, an eminent German doctor, was called to see the President, Hitler and Hermann Goering, fearing that even on his sick bed Hindenburg might declare martial law, moved quickly. That night they arrested and killed Ernst Röhm, the leader of the SA, and many others. Hindenburg, in as much as he knew what was happening, and above all his supporters in the military, were delighted.

Hindenburg died on 2 August and it was announced immediately that the offices of President and Chancellor would be merged and that Hitler would become head of state as well as Supreme Commander of the Armed Forces of the Reich. The law announcing the change was signed amongst others by Papen and Blomberg. That same day the officers and men of the German army took the oath of allegiance, not to the state or the constitution but to the Führer of the German Reich and People, Adolf Hitler. In a plebiscite on 19 August, the German people endorsed the change to Führer and Reich Chancellor by an overwhelming majority – 89.93 per cent of the 95.7 per cent of the electoral roll who voted, or 86.06 per cent of the entire electorate. This was helped by publication of President Hindenburg's Political Testament, endorsing Hitler but without his personal reference where he stated his wish for the restoration of the monarchy. Hitler waited a long time – until 4 February 1938. Then at the last Cabinet meeting of the Third Reich, he assumed Blomberg's title and office as Commander in Chief of the Armed

Forces in addition to his own title of Supreme Commander and got rid of the post of War Minister. The once all-powerful German army was now totally subjugated to the will of Hitler in form as well as substance. No man suffering incapacity as a result of mental illness could have acted with such skill.

Slowly, relentlessly, once Hindenburg had died, Hitler began to dismantle Cabinet government and it ceased to exist after the successful occupation of the Sudetenland in October 1938. Domestic policy was for Hitler a minor diversion of his time; his thinking and calculations were focused on foreign policy and in systemically rearming in defiance of the Versailles Treaty and in planning for and expanding the frontiers of Germany, which had begun in March 1936 with the occupation of the demilitarised zone of the Rhineland leading up to the French border. Since the start of the Spanish Civil War in July 1936 Hitler's long-standing opposition to Bolshevism had meant that he envisaged war with the Soviet Union as inevitable. He claimed that his actions were defensive, his intentions peaceful, but he was a habitual liar.

Hitler calculated correctly that occupying Czechoslovakia in March 1939 would not provoke the British and French to declare war but he knew invading Poland would. When Hitler made his early morning visit to Paris after German troops had entered the city on 14 June 1939 he believed he was invincible. The scale of his triumph took his incipient megalomania onto a new plane.[53] On 29 July 1940 at a meeting with General Alfred Jodl, head of the Wehrmacht Operations Staff, he decided to invade Russia in less than a year, in May 1941. He told his senior military leaders on 31 July. Hitler believed by the end of 1940 that the United States would be ready to enter the war on Britain's side by 1942.[54] Yet he was still sufficiently cautious to issue a specific order to the German military to avoid taking any provocative steps which could involve the US going to war earlier than this. Joseph Goebbels confirmed Hitler's view as late as 14 September 1941: 'The longer a formal declaration of war can be delayed, the better it is for us.'[55] That this still reflected Hitler's views is almost certain in that Admiral Erich Raeder, talking to Hitler after President Roosevelt's 'shoot on sight' speech on 17 September, ruled that 'the Führer requests that care should be taken to avoid any incidents in the war on shipping before about the middle of October'.[56] On 4 December Italy's Foreign Minister, Galeazzo Ciano, noted that involving America was 'less and less liked by the Germans'. Yet his German counterpart, Joachim von Ribbentrop, later telephoned him happy about Japan's attack on the US on the 7th.

By late 1941 Hitler fulfilled all the key features of hubris syndrome. He did not suffer at this stage in his life from any acknowledged medical illness. In particular none of the innumerable attempts to diagnose mental illness had come up with any convincing evidence. He did not suffer from mania associated with bipolar disorder, having had no very obvious depressive illness or manic episodes.

In searching for the moment when Hitler's hubris made nemesis inevitable I believe the critical period is from the moment the Russian counter-attack was launched on German forces around Moscow, at dawn on Friday 5 December 1941,[57] until the afternoon of 11 December, when Hitler announced that in accordance with the terms of the Tripartite Pact of 27 September 1940 Germany and Italy saw themselves compelled, alongside Japan, 'together to carry out the struggle for defence and thereby for the upholding of freedom and independence of their peoples and empires against the United States of America and England'.

Those six momentous days in December 1941 were as significant for Germany as the five days in London in May 1940 (see page 37) were for the peoples of the British Empire and the world. During that period Hitler took the fateful decision that inevitably and inexorably led to his suicide in Berlin in 1945. He gratuitously took on the United States at the very moment that he was failing to capture Moscow. He took this decision despite the clear legal view of the German Foreign Ministry that there was nothing in the Tripartite Pact which obliged Germany to declare war since Japan had not been attacked by the United States. Japan, by launching a surprise attack on the US fleet in Pearl Harbor on 7 December, had ensured that the people of Germany and of Italy, used to formal declarations of war, did not feel any obligation to come to Japan's defence. Yet news of the Japanese attack, according to a diarist, prompted Hitler to say: 'We can't lose the war at all . . . We now have an ally which has never been conquered in 3,000 years.'[58] This was when German soldiers were facing a serious offensive around Moscow and by 8 December, the Soviet 16th Army under General Konstantin Rokossovsky had recaptured Kryukovo, from which he had been forced to remove his headquarters in November.

Roosevelt was under no pressure from Congress or from public opinion to declare war on Germany. Yet indicative of Hitler's mood, that war with the United States was inevitable, was that he went ahead and lifted the ban on German U-boats attacking US shipping on the evening of 8–9 December, an action designed to provoke American public opinion. The Soviets retook Istra on 11 December, the very day which Hitler chose to declare war on the United States. Hitler must have known what was the situation in the battlefields around Moscow. The Soviet news agency Sovinformburo, which had not announced the 5 November counter-attack, by 13 December ensured that every newspaper carried the headlines 'The collapse of the German plan to surround and capture Moscow' and 'Defeat of German forces on the approaches to Moscow'.[59] On 14 December Stalin ordered the removal of the demolition charges from Moscow's factories, bridges and public buildings.

Hitler, who followed what was happening militarily in considerable detail throughout the war, appeared to have blotted out the Russian offensive from his mind during 5–8 December. A military challenge of this significance is a moment at which any but the most hubristic political leader would reassess and consider alternative options and also listen to the advice of experts. Hitler did none of these. He opened a new political and military front with the most powerful state in the world, against professional advice. Of course, it can be argued that his decision was inevitable and had an inner logic to it given his previous strategy. But there was an alternative.

While the Japanese were pressing for a declaration of war Hitler wanted a new agreement with Japan and this could have been delayed until the Russian offensive was fully evaluated. On the morning of 11 December that agreement, which prevented Japan from agreeing a separate peace with the United States, was signed. Ian Kershaw questions whether the decision to declare war was 'a puzzle, a grandiose moment of megalomanic madness', answering it himself: 'There is no puzzle. From Hitler's perspective it was only anticipating the inevitable. Far from appearing inexplicable or baffling . . . given his underlying premises, his decision was quite rational.'[60] The dark nature of his 'underlying premises' came to the fore as soon as the next day, however, when Hitler, addressing the Nazi Party leaders in the Reich Chancellery in Berlin, gave the go ahead for the annihilation of the Jews in Nazi-occupied Europe. Hitler claimed he had prophesied that eventuality in his speech to the Reichstag on 30 January 1939.

Superimposed on Hitler's apparent rationality were most of the elements of hubris syndrome. Hitler had reached the point in his leadership when his judgements, his insights, his perceptions, were all that counted. He had become totally impervious to the views of others and he was making huge mistakes, hubristic mistakes. Hitler's frame of mind in the early 1930s was rational in the pursuit of power; even in power, until the summer of 1940, without this overlay of hubris he would have taken full account of a potential military reversal around Moscow and would have seen the need to continue with his previous policy of avoiding provoking the United States militarily. By late 1941 Hitler was ignoring military and political reality, since he had full knowledge of the American public's deep wish to avoid war. He could have reverted that December to his earlier wish to offer a political deal to Britain, to avoid the United States coming into the war. If he had unilaterally stopped the bombing and offered to talk to Churchill perhaps, asking Roosevelt to use his good offices to bring about a settlement while distancing himself publicly from the infamous nature of Japan's surprise attack, Roosevelt would not have declared war on Germany. Even if Hitler was right that war with the United States was inevitable, he could have bought a few months and it would have allowed everyone in Berlin to focus on the task in hand of reversing the military defeat around Moscow.

It is the distinguishing mark of hubris syndrome that this broader type of thinking, adapting previous assumptions or making a fundamental reappraisal of strategy, is no longer possible. The leader is in the grip of forces of certainty and supreme self-confidence which lead inexorably to nemesis.

The state of Hitler's mental health has been the subject of prolonged debate. Two psychological profiles were commissioned in 1943 by the predecessor of the CIA, the Office of Strategic Studies. The first was written by Dr Henry Murray, a Harvard personality expert, but not made available until 2005;[61] the second was written by Dr Walter Langer, a well-respected psychoanalyst. It too was kept secret until after it had been declassified and turned over to the US National Archives in the late 1960s. It formed the basis of a book published in 1972.[62]

The Murray study diagnosed hysteria, paranoia, schizophrenia, oedipal tendencies, self-abasement and 'syphilophobia', defined as fear of contamination of the blood through contact with women. The Langer study, in the words of the historian Robert Waite, is a 'significant and suggestive interpretation which no serious student of Hitler will ignore'. Psychoanalytical vocabulary was used and there was general agreement between Langer and his collaborators at the time that Hitler was probably a neurotic psychopath bordering on schizophrenia. 'Neurotic' is not a word much used by doctors today and neurosis is not an illness. Schizophrenia as a diagnosis commonly used in those days was often confused with manic depression, now called bipolar disorder. The authors argued that Hitler was not in fact insane in the commonly accepted sense of the term, but 'a neurotic who lacks adequate inhibitions'.[63]

One event in Hitler's life which Langer focuses upon is his reaction earlier to a slight exposure to mustard gas in the First World War, when he appeared for a time to become blind and mute. By inference drawn from other cases,

Langer speculates that this may have been caused by a childhood trauma of Hitler's in having discovered his parents in the midst of sexual intercourse, though Langer is unable to record any specific incident or factual information to demonstrate that this actually happened in Hitler's case. But in any event, more recently Dr Michael Stone, a psychiatrist at Columbia University, has written that the 'suggestion that Hitler witnessed his mother and father having sex, which in those days was given great weight as a source of psychological turmoil', is immaterial since the theory of the causal relationship with psychological turmoil has itself since been discredited.[64] He describes much of the spate of articles written over the last fifty years about Hitler's mental health as 'psychobabble'.

Langer's classification of Hitler's perversion stems from an unreferenced account from Geli Raubal, the daughter of his half-sister, Angela, describing her sexual experiences with Hitler before she committed suicide.[65] We know nothing about whether or not Hitler's relationship with Eva Braun, whom he married in the bunker just before they both committed suicide, had any sexual perversion within it. Sexual perversion is, anyhow, not an illness as such. Erich Fromm's conclusion about Hitler strikes the best balance: 'The most one can guess, I believe, is that his sexual desires were largely voyeuristic, anal-sadistic with the inferior type of women, and masochistic with admired women.'[66]

Another source of speculation to explain Hitler's personality and decisions is his monorchism – having only one testicle. This was widely known and the subject of a satirical song during the war, which continues to be sung. Confirmation of this apparently came at a post mortem conducted by the Soviets on his partially burnt body. Monorchism is distinct from cryptorchism, having an undescended testicle. Hitler did not suffer from any obvious testosterone deficiency. His personal physician, Dr Theodor Morell, prescribed injections of bull testicles in grape sugar later in his life but this was not as replacement therapy. Morell prescribed a bizarre mix of medication: large doses of Dexedrine, pervitin (a form of amphetamine), caffeine, cocaine and huge quantities of Dr Koester's Anti-Gas Pills, which contained small doses of the poison strychnine and atropine.[67] The combination probably made Hitler tenser than he would otherwise have been but the drugs were taken when the war was lost. Hitler's decision-making may have become impaired, but by then the decisions were less important with defeat inevitable.

Earlier, in August 1941, an ECG had shown that Hitler's coronary arteries were closing up and he began to age, having hitherto been in good health despite his hypochondria and insomnia. Slowly Hitler developed

Parkinson's disease,* leading to a tremor in his left hand and a hesitancy in his speech which was noted on 20 February 1943. A trembling in his left leg became very noticeable by 1944. Further ECGs were showing a deterioration in his heart condition. There was no effective treatment for Parkinson's disease in the early 1940s, but it probably did not much affect his key decision-making, which was fixed by his overambitious strategic objectives. Strangely, Hitler's tremor initially stopped after the Stauffenberg plot (named after its leader, a German army officer) on 20 July 1944, when a bomb exploded in an attaché case near to Hitler at his Wolf's Lair HQ. The explosion ruptured his eardrums and disturbed his balance. The most serious effects of the explosion were psychological and Hitler's paranoia became very much worse. But he was still able to assert his authority and by the end of October he was heavily involved in preparing for the Ardennes offensive and still in control of the military.

Following the bomb explosion in July 1944, Hitler began to use cocaine habitually, both as a 10 per cent concentration frequently swabbed on to his nostrils and as a twice-daily inhalation and this, with Dr Morrell's other drugs, did exacerbate his previous behaviour patterns of irritability and sudden impulsive decision-making. By 1945 he was not making decisions anywhere near as effective as he had earlier in his life, but this did not amount to mental incapacity. The pattern of those later decisions was congruent with patterns set well before the deterioration in his health. He remained responsible for those decisions.

There is no convincing evidence that makes it possible for Hitler to be categorised as mentally ill; he should be depicted instead, as indeed he mostly is, as the embodiment of political evil. For all that has been written about his health, it is hard to see that as linked to his decision-making, or to his anti-Semitism, which seems to owe more to living in Vienna when he was young and poor, where anti-Semitism was rife. It was later, while living in Munich after fighting in the First World War, that Hitler developed his hatred of

---

* Parkinson's disease is a degenerative disorder associated with ageing, usually presenting in the second half of life. It has characteristic degenerative changes in the cells of the basal ganglia, located near the base of the cerebral hemispheres in the brain, which are involved in the regulation of movement. There is often no other evidence of brain damage. Commoner in men than women, it is associated with a deficiency in dopamine and initially responds well to anticholinergic drugs such as levodopa. It is characterised by tremor and rigidity. The tremor is more noticeable when the hand or leg is resting and the rigidity leads to a shuffling walk, an unchanging facial expression and a flat voice.

Soviet communism and his vision for Germany as a world power. In any case, to try to attribute the crimes of the Nazi regime solely to the personality of its leader is itself profoundly mistaken. Hitler's appeal during his twelve-year regime of tyranny was not narrowly based, nor confined merely to Nazi supporters. The power which Hitler's charisma and skilled use of propaganda gave him did not allow him to impose his will on a hostile, reluctant mass population; what he did was to cultivate their enthusiasm for what he wanted to do and to manipulate their support. Hitler received from the German people as a whole – millions of individuals – considerable commitment and support. This is often ignored in analyses which focus entirely on his personal characteristics. Tracing how Hitler and Himmler created the 'Final Solution' for the Jews is very revealing. 'There was no blueprint for the crime imposed from above, nor one devised from below and simply acknowledged from the top. Individual Nazis were not coerced by crude threats to commit murders themselves.'[68] It was a collective enterprise, owned by many thousands of people, that was given an impetus when he opened up the Russian front. Fortunately, there were German men and women, brave people some of whose names and deeds will never be fully known, who resisted Nazism from inside the Third Reich.

Had Hitler not shot himself in his bunker and had he instead been captured and brought before the Nuremberg International Military Tribunal, he would have been convicted of crimes against humanity and hanged. Even if the defence case had been made that he was mentally ill and of unsound mind, the expert medical evidence to the tribunal would not have given credence to such claims. That Hitler had an extreme personality is beyond dispute, as is the fact that he came from a dysfunctional family. Whether he was neurotic, a sexual pervert or had psychopathic tendencies may or may not be true, but that is not sufficient to diagnose a medical illness.

Studies of Hitler's mental state will no doubt continue for as long as people remain interested in history. But it is unlikely that such studies will ever relieve him of culpability for his evil crimes. The view of Hitler's biographer Ian Kershaw is that the 1936 reoccupation of the Rhineland left the German people beside themselves with delight and made a significant mark on Hitler. The change that people close to him saw 'was more than ever a belief in his own infallibility. Pseudo-religious symbolism came to infuse his rhetoric . . . in messianic mode, he saw a mystical fate uniting him and the German people. "That you have found me . . . among so many millions is the miracle of our time! And that I have found you, that is Germany's fortune."'[69] Hitler 'became the foremost believer in his own Führer cult. Hubris – the overweening arrogance which courts disaster – was inevitable. The point where nemesis takes over had been reached by 1936.'[70]

Hitler was the main architect of the Second World War. He inspired the genocide of the Jews. 'The Germany which had produced Adolf Hitler, had seen its future in his vision, had so readily served him, and had shared his hubris, had also to share his nemesis.'[71]

Winston Churchill

On 10 May 1940, Winston Churchill became Prime Minister at the age of sixty-five. At last Hitler faced a head of government with the resolve to resist him. In five days at the end of that month, while the troops were being evacuated from Dunkirk and the odds were against a successful rescue, Churchill's judgement saved the world from Hitler. Only a handful of people at the time understood the reality of those five days, brilliantly recaptured by John Lukacs.[72] Churchill, using every political skill in his repertoire, prevented Lord Halifax, the Foreign Secretary, already firmly linked to the policy of appeasement, from responding to a peace initiative brought to him by the Italian ambassador on Saturday 25 May. In wanting to negotiate, Halifax had the support of the French Prime Minister, Paul Reynaud, who was in London. This led to the initiative being referred to in Whitehall, somewhat disingen-uously, as 'Monsieur Reynaud's plan'. What both men failed to realise was the extent to which Benito Mussolini was already committed to war. He told his Foreign Minister, Galeazzo Ciano, on 13 May: 'Within a month I shall declare war. I shall attack France and Great Britain in the air and on the sea.' On 29 May he told his military leaders that Italy would enter the war any time after 5 June.[73]

Halifax, who, only sixteen days earlier, had stepped aside for Churchill to become Prime Minister, was in a very strong position when the Cabinet started discussions. He had a bottom line for the negotiations, namely that the terms could not be 'destructive of British independence'. Halifax was not ready to give up the fleet or the RAF in any negotiations but was prepared to sacrifice part of the Empire, such as Malta, Gibraltar or some African colonies, 'to save the country from an avoidable disaster'.[74] While as Foreign Secretary it was his duty to look for openings for peace, his diplomatic skills were not tempered by the political reality that there was no opening.

What Churchill instinctively and rightly knew was that in any such negotiations Mussolini was a front and that Britain's adversary was Hitler. Once negotiations started at that point in the war, it would have led to an irresistible call for an immediate ceasefire. Then after a ceasefire had been conceded, he, Churchill, would never have been able to restart the war when faced, as he feared, with humiliating terms from Hitler for ending it.

After nine difficult meetings on 26, 27 and 28 May, the War Cabinet* eventually accepted Churchill's position. To his great credit, Neville Chamberlain, after sitting on the fence, supported Churchill against Halifax. In this one crucial act, coming out against his loyal friend, Chamberlain fully justified Churchill's decision to keep him in the War Cabinet. It was also Chamberlain's way of acknowledging that Churchill had been ambivalent, and only rarely straightforwardly hostile, in his attitude to him when Prime Minister. Halifax came round to the majority view in the War Cabinet after a walk in the garden of No. 10 with an ameliorative Churchill, who had also won the support of twenty-five ministerial colleagues outside the War Cabinet with an inspiring speech in a private meeting. It was agreed in the War Cabinet that no questions of peace terms could be raised until the Battle of Britain had been won. But for Churchill that meant, at the very least, not just the air battle but also the naval battle in the Atlantic.

Interestingly, Churchill in all his post-war writings, books and statements never claimed credit for his remarkable feat in winning around the War Cabinet to saying 'no' to negotiations with the Italians. In the second volume of his war memoirs, *Their Finest Hour*, he wrote: 'Future generations may deem it noteworthy that the supreme question of whether we should fight on

---

* The War Cabinet had originally consisted of only five people, three of whom were Conservatives: the Prime Minister; his deputy and leader of the Labour Party, Clement Attlee; the former Prime Minister Neville Chamberlain; the Foreign Secretary, Lord Halifax; and Arthur Greenwood, the deputy leader of the Labour Party. Churchill, after the Sunday Cabinet on 26 May, added the Liberal Archibald Sinclair for the subsequent meetings of the War Cabinet. Sinclair was a reliable ally for Churchill since he had always opposed appeasement. The evacuation of Dunkirk started on 27 May and not until the War Cabinet had determined its line against negotiation did the miracle of the evacuation become clear: 7,000 off the beaches on 27 May, then 17,000 on 28 May and 50,000 a day on 29 May–1 June. The juxtaposition of the Dunkirk evacuation and the War Cabinet meetings is well described with large quotes from the Cabinet meetings in Hugh Sebag-Montefiore's *Dunkirk: Fight to the Last Man* (London: Viking, 2006), pp. 273–321. For Churchill after the war to have revealed Halifax's negotiating stance would have created a political problem since Halifax was the leader of the Conservative opposition in the House of Lords. Also Churchill preferred to retain the redoubtable image of never having even contemplated any negotiations despite it being untrue.

alone never found a place upon the War Cabinet agenda.'[75] Yet these War Cabinet discussions are a magnificent example of democratic Cabinet government at a time of national peril. They also reveal the true character of Churchill. At this time there is no trace of depression, hypomania, hubris or manic behaviour. What one appreciates when reading the detail is a complete politician using reasoned argument and every political skill in his armoury to win a crucial political battle, in an open debate with colleagues.

Soon after the Japanese attack on Pearl Harbor, Churchill left London for the United States by, firstly, overnight train to Scotland on 12 December 1941. He sailed from Gourock next morning on the battleship *Duke of York* and arrived in Chesapeake Bay on 22 December, flying up to Washington to have dinner with President Roosevelt. Not surprisingly, he arrived looking worn out. After midnight he called his personal physician, Sir Charles Wilson, later to become Lord Moran, to find out if he could take a sleeping pill. Churchill was too excited to sleep and Wilson gave him two red barbiturate pills.[76]

On the night of 26 December, Churchill had a mild heart attack in his bedroom in the White House. Later in a book, Wilson revealed how he prided himself, a trifle pretentiously, on upholding his duty to the nation 'at a moment when America has just come into the war, and there is no-one but Winston to take her by the hand. I felt that the effect of announcing that the P.M. had had a heart attack could only be disastrous.'[77] Churchill had told Wilson in the morning of 27 December that he thought that he had strained one of his chest muscles when lifting up a window. Wilson, wisely, never told Churchill that his account of the way the chest pain spread down his arm was the classic description of angina or coronary artery insufficiency; instead he allowed him to believe it was due to lifting the window and let nature take its healing course. To avoid alerting anyone, Wilson deliberately did not call for an electrocardiograph machine. Churchill that morning then got into a fierce argument with General George Marshall, while still in bed and smoking a cigar, on the vital matter of unity of command. Churchill kept up a cracking pace throughout the next few days. He went to Canada by train on 28 December, then back to Washington. He eventually flew to Florida for a holiday on 5 January, where he swam in the sea every day, and returned to Washington by train on 11 January. Then he insisted on taking a flying boat back to England from Bermuda on 16 January, touching down on Plymouth Sound. The Prime Minister had been away for over a month and had spent fourteen days under the White House roof with thirteen dinners with the

President and eight major meetings with their respective staffs. It was a formidable achievement for anyone, let alone someone suffering from angina.

Churchill's health held up fairly well throughout the war. He continued to eat large meals, smoke innumerable cigars and drink copious quantities of alcohol. Alcohol never appeared to do Churchill much harm, though his concentration often lapsed if, after a late dinner, he remained active until the early hours of the morning. Then his mind wandered and his condition strained the patience of the wartime chiefs of staff, as is very clear from the unexpurgated diary entries of the Chief of the Defence Staff, Field Marshal Sir Alan Brooke (later Lord Alanbrooke). 'I am "sick unto death" of these night meetings . . . and the stink of the last one is not yet out of my nostrils!' (November 1943).

Churchill developed pneumonia in December 1943, while visiting north Africa. In March 1944 Brooke wrote about Churchill: 'We found him in a desperately tired mood. I am afraid that he is losing ground rapidly.'[78] As real diaries do, Brooke's reveals his pent-up frustration and makes instant judgements. Brooke has been criticised for expressing this, but the criticism is unfair; the point of diaries is that, if honestly written, they provide important insights. Brooke's and other wartime diaries demonstrate how crucial a factor tiredness can be when making important decisions and how impossible at times Churchill was to those who worked with him. Brooke is also revealing in other ways, a wonderful example being when he describes how Churchill with boyish humour decided to pee on the First World War Siegfried line when visiting British troops in March 1945.

Throughout his life Churchill suffered from bouts of severe depression, as mentioned in the Introduction.[79] His father's family had a history of it. Wilson describes Churchill discussing the black depression which had settled on him when he was young, married and in the House of Commons and how he talked about past suicidal feelings. Churchill told him that he didn't like to stand near the edge of a platform when an express train was passing through, if possible preferring to get a pillar between him and the train, and how a second's action could end everything. He described the feelings as a few drops of desperation.

By the time he had become Prime Minister, Churchill, rather like Theodore Roosevelt when President, had flattened out the violence of the mood swings of his youth. His daughter, writing about his times of depression and deep frustrations, felt that depression had 'been his companion too often in earlier years for him not to know the power of such feelings. But for him the security and loving companionship of marriage had banished "Black Dog" to his kennel.' She added that his writing and painting were 'sovereign antibodies to the depressive element in his nature'.[80] But whether or not it can be said that Black Dog was in his kennel, Churchill still got depressed. His private secretary, John Colville, described Churchill's mood in February, 1944: 'The PM looked old, tired and very depressed.'[81]

The medical issue surrounding Churchill is whether he suffered not simply from depression but from manic depression, or what is now called bipolar disorder. Those who dispute it argue that there is no case of an incontrovertibly manic episode in his life. They are sceptical too of attributing examples of his undoubtedly bizarre behaviour to mania. For instance, some have used his tendency to dictate to a secretary while in the bath – and certainly he was unself-conscious about being in the nude – as diagnostic of mania, but this was quite common in his social class and is not conclusive.

Nonetheless, the testimony of those who worked closely with Churchill does imply a manic as well as a depressive side to him. Oliver Harvey, the private secretary to Anthony Eden, the Foreign Secretary, noted in his diary on 13 July 1943: 'The PM [Churchill] was in a crazy state of exultation. The battle has gone to the old man's head. The quantities of liquor he consumed – champagne, brandies, whiskies – were incredible.'[82] What is interesting here is that Harvey says it is the battle, not the alcohol, which has gone to Churchill's head. And interestingly he uses the phrase 'crazy state of exultation', a symptom which psychiatrists would certainly take into account in diagnosing bipolar disorder.

Yet much more revealing of the exceptional character of the man is the picture painted by General Hastings Ismay, Churchill's military chief of staff, in a letter written on 3 April 1942 to General Claude Auchinleck, in the desert of north Africa. 'The Auk', as he was called, had been recently on the receiving end of Churchill's volatile mood:

> You cannot judge the P.M. by ordinary standards: he is not in the least like anyone that you or I have ever met. He is a mass of contradictions. He is either on the crest of the wave, or in the trough: either highly laudatory, or bitterly condemnatory: either in an angelic temper, or a hell of a rage: when he isn't fast asleep he's a volcano. There are no half-measures in his make-up. He is a child of nature with moods as variable as an April day, and he apparently sees no difference between harsh words spoken to a friend, and forgotten within the hour under the influence of friendly argument, and the same harsh words

telegraphed to a friend thousands of miles away – with no opportunity for 'making it up'. . .

I think I can lay claim to having been called every name under the sun during the last six months – except perhaps a coward; but I know perfectly well in the midst of these storms that they mean exactly nothing, and that before the sun goes down, I shall be summoned to an intimate and delightfully friendly talk – to 'make it up'.[83]

Roy Jenkins described Churchill in the late spring of 1944 as exhibiting a

great fluctuation of mood, with bursts of energy and indeed brilliance of performance intervening in a general pattern of lassitude and gloom, stemming largely from an awareness that none of his interlocutors – Stalin, Roosevelt, de Gaulle – would do exactly what he wished and a growing feeling of impotence to impose his will. He approached victory with much less buoyancy than he had confronted the menace of defeat four years before.[84]

Whether accounts of his 'crazy state of exultation', of his being either 'on the crest of a wave or in a trough', of there being 'no half measures in his make-up' and of 'bursts of energy and brilliance of performance' coexisting with 'lassitude and gloom' provide enough evidence for a diagnosis of bipolar disorder is a point psychiatrists will dispute. But if Churchill did suffer from bipolar disorder there is no evidence that the illness led the War Cabinet into irrational decision-making. It could be said on the contrary that it gave him the inspirational quality to lead the country which in 1940 proved so vital.

In any event, by the last stages of the war, Churchill's decisions were not the vital ones, as Jenkins's account makes clear. Churchill gave the impression at times that he would have had the Allies take Berlin before the Russians but the casualties would have been so great that I suspect he would sensibly have shrunk from the prospect. In any case he knew that the United States, who would have borne the brunt, saw no strategic need.

The descriptions of Churchill as he really was during the Second World War explain a lot. They underline what will become a constant theme in this book, that most heads of government have extraordinary, even abnormal, personalities. They cope with immense stress by transferring some of that stress on to those in their inner circle, whether colleagues or advisers. Also their strengths are often the product of coping with their illness.

Franklin Delano Roosevelt

The most influential political leader during the Second World War and arguably for the entire twentieth century was President Franklin Delano Roosevelt. But what makes Roosevelt's political life story particularly important to this book is that he spent all his years in high government office, four as governor of New York and twelve as US President, in a wheelchair, having contracted polio when he was a young man of thirty-nine. He was paralysed in both legs from the hips down and by the time he beat Herbert Hoover, who had suffered from a depressive illness, for the presidency on 8 November 1932 he had become used to hiding his condition from the public. As President the impression was given, on important occasions, that he could stand up and he even designed a method of taking a few steps to imply that he could walk with just a little support, usually from one of his sons or a body-guard. All of this was perfectly reasonable conduct by Roosevelt because he did not feel disabled and was determined not to appear handicapped. Roosevelt was practically never photographed in a wheelchair. Of the 35,000 photographs in the Roosevelt Presidential Library, only two have him in a wheelchair.

In the early years of his presidency, Roosevelt's health appeared excellent. He was never a bureaucratic politician; doing deals in a smoke-filled room was part of his style. In Madison Square Garden, New York, in the latter stages of the 1936 election campaign, he made a typical, self-confident, hard-hitting and highly partisan speech mocking the Republicans:

> For twelve years this government was afflicted with hear-nothing, see-nothing, do-nothing government . . . They are unanimous in their hate for me – and I welcome their hatred . . . I should like to have it said of my first administration that in it the forces of selfishness and lust for power met their match. I should like to have it said of my second administration that in it these forces met their master.

By the time of his third presidential election, on 5 November 1940, Europe was at war. A desperate Winston Churchill hoped Roosevelt would commit America to the war against Germany. It is easy to assume that it was inevitable that the United States would fight Germany but there was always a deep strand of American reluctance to fight in another war in Europe. During the campaign Roosevelt had felt it necessary to make his 30 October pledge: 'Your boys are not going to be sent into any foreign wars.' Instead of men, Roosevelt offered Churchill money through the Lend-Lease scheme, which he described at a press conference on 17 December 1940, using the simple, though somewhat misleading, analogy of lending your garden hose to your neighbour to put out his fire. On 22 June, Germany attacked Russia. Between 9 and 12 August Roosevelt met Churchill in Placentia Bay, Newfoundland, on board HMS *Prince of Wales* and USS *Augusta* and together they signed the Atlantic Charter. Even then, Churchill still had to wait for Roosevelt to show any sign of a readiness to come into the war. Roosevelt briefed the US press afterwards as having had 'an interchange of views, that's all' and for indirect quotation 'no closer to war'.

Three months earlier, in May, Roosevelt had been diagnosed as having raised blood pressure and being seriously deficient in iron, so much so that he had two blood transfusions and spent the early half of the month in his bedroom. But it was politics, not the health of the President, that was keeping the United States out of the war. Hitler fully realised this.

It was the Japanese attack on the US base at Pearl Harbor, on 7 December 1941, that transformed the scene. Roosevelt described it as 'a date which will live in infamy' and declared war on Japan. On 11 December Hitler declared war on the United States. For Churchill the relief was immense. He knew better than anyone that Hitler would eventually be defeated by American and Soviet power. Churchill's personal contribution to victory would never again be so crucial.

Roosevelt's own health deteriorated during the period 1942–4, though that went largely unrecognised by his personal doctor, Admiral Ross McIntire. Only on 28 March 1944, in Bethesda Hospital, did a 39-year-old naval cardiologist, Dr Howard Bruenn, make the first full hospital-based medical examination of Roosevelt since he had become President eleven years earlier. This was done at the insistence of Roosevelt's daughter, Anna, but against the wishes of McIntire. McIntire should never have been the President's personal physician. He did not have the medical expertise and persistently showed the disadvantages of being a serving naval officer, for whom his patient was also his Commander in Chief. Bruenn found Roosevelt's blood pressure was 186/108; an X-ray of the chest showed a large heart and Bruenn had no hesitation in diagnosing hypertension, hypertensive heart disease, left ventricular cardiac failure and acute bronchitis.[*]

---

[*] On 27 February 1941 the President had had two blood pressure recordings of 188/105 and 178/102, both clearly showing hypertension, but McIntire, who was an ear, nose and throat specialist, said at the time that the President's 'cardiovascular measurements stayed on a good level'. (Ross T. McIntire, *White House Physician* (G. P. Putnam's Sons, 1946), p. 139.) That may have been true for a reading in May 1941, but McIntire should have taken regular readings and at least considered treatments for lowering a patient's blood pressure, although admittedly the treatments available were of dubious value. There is no evidence that he did either.

The bronchitis was the sole instance in which McIntire had been correct. Bruenn later said the President's condition was 'god awful'.

Typically, McIntire was not even ready to accept Bruenn's judgement that Roosevelt had to be given digitalis.* It was only after McIntire had convened three special boards of medical advisers on 30 and 31 March and 1 April 1944 that he reluctantly agreed to its being used, and that was only after Bruenn had threatened to have nothing more to do with the case unless Roosevelt was digitalised, a brave act for a young naval officer.[85]

Though Bruenn continued to treat the President and managed to introduce a low-salt diet and a weight reduction programme and also gave phenobarbitol, he was never asked by McIntire or, even more revealingly, by Roosevelt himself, whether the President should run for re-election in November. Bruenn later said that, had he been asked, he would have answered that it was impossible medically. It is sometimes suggested that Roosevelt should not have been 'permitted' to run, but who permits a President? This President was determined to run.† On 11 July 1944, at a morning press conference, Roosevelt read from a letter he had written to Bob Hannegan, chairman of the Democratic National Committee, saying he would run again as President: 'All that is within me cries out to go back to my home on the Hudson River, to avoid public responsibilities . . . Such would be my choice.' But he claimed there was a war to win, a peace to secure, an economy to be put on solid ground. 'Therefore, reluctantly, but as a good soldier, I repeat that I will accept and serve in the office, if I am so ordered by the Commander in Chief of us all – the sovereign people of the United States.'

---

* Digitalis is a glycoside derived from plants such as foxglove and strophanthus, which has the effect of slowing the heart rate and increasing the contractility of the heart muscle. It has in therapeutic doses saved many lives. Digoxin is given orally for heart failure and atrial fibrillation.
† In August 1944, according to Bruenn, Roosevelt developed classic angina pain. This confirmed his diagnosis of coronary artery disease. McIntire thought the pain was 'muscular'. Roosevelt himself was in denial about the severity of his illness despite knowing that Bruenn was a heart doctor and that he had by then very high blood pressure. At the Quebec conference with Churchill between 11 and 16 September the President's blood pressure was at an all-time high of 240/130. Illness may have explained Roosevelt's rather rare lapse in judgement in supporting the so-called Morgenthau plan for deindustrialising post-war Germany, named after his Treasury Secretary. This 'envisaged returning Germany to its pastoral condition before 1870, eliminating industry by sending everything removable to Russia as reparations'. (Roy Jenkins, *Franklin Delano Roosevelt* (London: Pan, 2005), p. 160.) Roosevelt backtracked once his advisers got at him, showing he was still capable of listening to good advice.

At noon Roosevelt saw his Vice President, Henry Wallace, for lunch to settle a statement they had discussed the day before which had Roosevelt endorsing Wallace. This time the President was evasive, mentioning to Wallace that many people looked on him 'as a Communist or worse'.[86] Perhaps Roosevelt realised that, because of the state of his own health, the choice of Vice President was even more important than usual. That evening Roosevelt met for dinner with some Democratic leaders who opposed Wallace being nominated again. Two names were discussed: the Supreme Court Justice, William O. Douglas, who Roosevelt talked up; and Senator Harry Truman, who was proposed by Hannegan. Roosevelt then wrote on an envelope that he would be happy to run with either. But he could not bring himself to formally dump Wallace and only on the Chicago convention floor, on 21 July, did Hannegan and the other Democratic Party bosses swing the vote to Truman, having adjourned the night before when threatened by a grassroots bandwagon for Wallace. Fortunately, Truman, as President, turned out to be an extraordinary ordinary man. Wallace was a dreamer and America needed and got a realist in Truman.

While it was not right, given the state of his health, for Roosevelt to run again in 1944, it is hard to conclude that a new US President would have made much difference to the actual conduct of the war in those few months between Roosevelt's inauguration on 20 January 1945 and his death on 12 April, aged sixty-three. In Europe, from early 1944, General George Marshall and the other US chiefs of staff, with General Dwight D. Eisenhower as Supreme Allied Commander, chosen by Marshall, had been taking key military decisions. In effect Marshall, with Roosevelt's agreement, had been controlling the lead into D-Day and its follow-up. In early 1945 it was Marshall and the US military who were the most reluctant to race the Soviet Union to Berlin, a view expressed in March by Eisenhower in a telegram to Stalin in his capacity as Marshal of the Soviet Forces. It confirmed that the Allied armies under his, Eisenhower's, command would not try to take Berlin. Field Marshal Sir Alan Brooke in his diaries reveals that he told the British chiefs of staff that Eisenhower 'had no business to address Stalin direct, his communications should be through the combined Chiefs of Staff' and that 'what was implied in it appeared to be entirely adrift and a change in all that had been previously agreed on'.[87] In part, it was a praiseworthy wish of the Americans to save the lives of Allied soldiers based on the judgement that Hitler would insist on fighting to the last man and that Stalin was ready to take Berlin, irrespective of the cost. Even so, it is surprising that Eisenhower wrote without specifically consulting the military and political authorities in London; probably he did not consult them because he already knew that Roosevelt and Churchill held different views. At a two-and-a-half-hour conference in Honolulu on 27 July 1944, which Roosevelt had insisted on attending, even though to do so involved weeks of slow travel, the big decisions already agreed between him and Marshall in Washington were ratified.

Roosevelt then travelled to Yalta in February 1945 to meet Stalin and Churchill. It is still a highly contentious issue whether Roosevelt's health was an important factor in the outcome of the conference. Here the future shape of eastern Europe was settled, involving particularly tough discussions about Poland.

Those in Roosevelt's intimate circle knew it would not be long before the President would be unable to cope with the burden of office. On 8 February, towards the end of the conference, Roosevelt developed pulsus alternans, in which a weak and strong pulse alternate. This is indicative of a very serious heart condition, namely left ventricular failure. Fortunately, after a few days, his pulse reverted. Just before this incident, the President's daughter, who was also in Yalta, had been told about her father's heart condition for the first time, the information coming not from Admiral McIntire but from Dr Bruenn, the young naval cardiologist. She wrote on 5 February to her husband:

> This 'ticker' situation is far more serious than I ever knew. And the biggest difficulty in handling the situation here is that we can, of course, tell no-one of the 'ticker' problem. It is truly worrysome and there's not a heluva lot anyone can do about it. (Better tear off and destroy this paragraph.)[88]

Churchill's doctor, Sir Charles Wilson, was watching the President and, with his experience, was hardly likely to miss what was going on. On 7 February, he recorded in his diary: 'To a doctor's eye, the President appears a very sick man. He has all the symptoms of hardening of the arteries of the brain in an advanced stage, so that I give him only a few months to live.'[89]

There is no doubt that Roosevelt was seriously below par in his health at Yalta in 1945. It has also been suggested by Alen Salerian, a former chief psychiatric consultant to the FBI, that Roosevelt was clinically depressed at the time, but diagnosing this from the medical records is not easy. How fast he was deteriorating is revealed by a retrospective neuropsychological evaluation, published in 2005, in the form of a study of Roosevelt's last speech to

Congress on 1 March 1945. Very rarely for him, Roosevelt delivered the speech sitting down. On several occasions, he lost his concentration and had problems following the prepared text, he mispronounced 'Yalta' as 'Malta' and there were flawed verbal expressions and poor vocabulary when he was diverting from the text.[90]

Yet according to the accounts of those who were actually at Yalta, Roosevelt does not seem to have been unduly incapacitated as a negotiator, despite his very serious ill health. Senior diplomats and politicians who were present, some of them closely involved in the seven plenary sessions in February 1945, have defended Roosevelt's mental capacity by reference to his performance. Charles E. Bohlen, then the State Department's liaison officer to the White House, acted as the President's interpreter. He was certainly no sycophant, but, in 1969, he wrote about Roosevelt's performance at Yalta: 'I do not know of any case where he really gave away anything to the Soviets because of his ill health.' He added: 'He seemed to be guided very heavily by his advisers and he took no step independently.'[91] An interpreter is uniquely placed to see the role of advisers, because often, to assist them and let them know what to expect, they are given advance copies of the speaking notes prepared by officials for the head of government. The American historian Arthur M. Schlesinger Jr wrote to Valentin Berezhkov, Stalin's interpreter, to enquire about Soviet perceptions of Roosevelt's health at Yalta, especially compared with the previous meeting in Tehran, in November 1943. Berezhkov replied that it 'was certainly worse than in Tehran, but everybody who watched him said that in spite of his frail appearance his mental potential was high. Before he got tired, he was alert, with quick reactions and forceful arguments.'[92] He also noted that 'Stalin treated Roosevelt with great esteem'.

It is true that a fitter man than Roosevelt might have taken more initiatives and been more active in the discussions. But Roosevelt, in truth, got what he and the United States wanted – above all, Stalin's pledge to come into the war against Japan within two to three months of the end of fighting in Europe. At the time this was thought to be crucial. It is easily forgotten how costly the war in the Pacific was becoming in terms of US lives. Churchill, understandably, was focusing on Europe but for Roosevelt, Stalin was also important because of Japan. The Soviet Union had a naval fleet in Vladivostok and a border with China. As things turned out Stalin decided to come in only a matter of days before the Japanese surrender in August.

Roosevelt had built an interesting relationship with Stalin through letters, now chronicled in *My Dear Mr Stalin*.[93] Averell Harriman, the US ambassador to the Soviet Union in the last years of the war, felt Roosevelt had deliberately developed a capacity to influence Stalin. Decisions over Poland had been left to Yalta because both Churchill and Roosevelt knew that they were not capable of being resolved in Tehran, when the Polish frontier had been delineated with matchsticks. Differences over the future of Poland had surfaced as early as December 1941, when Anthony Eden met Stalin in Moscow. What is more, in their heart of hearts, both Roosevelt and Churchill must have known that any agreement Stalin signed at Yalta to free and fair elections in Poland, already with changed boundaries, would be very hard if not impossible to enforce. Roosevelt knew, too, that it was Churchill, in a bilateral with Stalin in Moscow on 9 October 1944, who had forged the first 'realpolitik' carve-up over the spheres of influence in post-war Europe, in the hope of excluding the Soviet Union from the Mediterranean. To look at Churchill's half sheet of paper scribbled in the Kremlin today, with Stalin's large tick of approval overshadowing Romania – of which the Soviet Union was to have 90 per cent, the others 10 per cent – is to realise what real personal power between leaders can represent. No wonder Churchill claimed to have said to Stalin: 'Might it not be thought rather cynical if it seemed we had disposed of these issues, so fateful to millions of people, in such an offhand manner? Let us burn the paper.'

'No,' said Stalin, 'you keep it.'[94]

In subsequent criticism of the Yalta agreement there has been a tendency to forget that the Soviet Union, having fought the Germans into the ground and conquered eastern Europe, paid a very heavy price in terms of human life for which it felt it should be rewarded at the negotiating table. It has been estimated that for every Briton or American who died, the Japanese lost seven people, the Germans twenty people and the Soviets eighty-five. Figures differ greatly but another estimate states twenty-seven million Soviets died in the Second World War compared to 405,000 Americans. Russians still believe, with justice, that they made the heaviest sacrifice for the overthrowing of Nazism.

Roosevelt was never a man to be under any illusion about his negotiating partners' strengths and weaknesses. He knew, as he said to Admiral William Leahy, 'it's the best I can do for Poland at this time'.[95] That his health had not turned him into a gullible President able to be taken in by Stalin, is clear from a conversation Roosevelt had on 13 March, two weeks after returning from Yalta. He had called Leon Henderson, a New Deal economist, to his office to talk about Henderson's future role as the American economic chief in Germany. Roosevelt warned him about not doing too much in advance and that while the French, the British and the Americans would abide by agreements, the Soviets would suit themselves. They would abide by agreed protocols, not take liberties where it would show, but anywhere they could escape scrutiny they would go their own way.

The account given by Bohlen, in a conversation with the historian Richard Neustadt, suggests that in late March 1945 the President was still focused.[96] Bohlen said that the President was acutely conscious that Yalta was a test of Soviet intent to preserve Big Three comity after the war, and felt that the point had been reached where Moscow was failing the test. Bohlen further believed that, had Roosevelt returned to Washington in April, he would have joined with Churchill in an Allied refusal to withdraw from the Elbe to their previously agreed zones of occupation. Also, since Roosevelt was due to travel to London in May, after a German surrender, Bohlen felt a tripartite emergency meeting would have been held, substituting for the later Potsdam meeting. With Edward Stettinius installed in the State Department, far more tractable than his predecessor, Cordell Hull, it is clear Roosevelt envisaged playing a bigger, not a lesser, role and his appointment of Bohlen to his personal staff to help assert his authority was not really the action of a man reconciled to dying within a few weeks. Roosevelt's life, ever since his polio, had been one of fighting off ill health and even though his doctors knew his days were numbered it would have been in character for him to plan forward, ignoring his health. There are good grounds for arguing that Roosevelt should not have stood for re-election in November, 1944 but Yalta is not one of them.

Roosevelt's health was the subject of many rumours throughout his life. Even his death caused controversy. It was claimed by some that he had died of cancer of the stomach; others suggest that he had a malignant melanoma.* Yet there should be little doubt about the cause of his death (from a stroke or a cerebrovascular accident brought on by heart failure) since the publication

---

* Daisy Suckley (see below) provides explanations of Roosevelt's so-called stomach ailment. She saw the President frequently in 1944, and on 26 May at the Bethesda Hospital records that the President had an X-ray showing stones in the gall bladder. These gallstones are the likely explanation for the President's supposed attack of acute indigestion on the night of 28 November 1943 at the Tehran conference and for his attacks on 28 April and 1 May 1944, witnessed by Dr Bruenn and treated with injections of codeine. The melanoma story seems to have come from the removal of what in those days was called a 'wen', now referred to as a sebaceous cyst, the size of a small egg, on the President's back. This was something he had had for twenty years and it was removed under local anaesthetic. Possibly a pigmented lesion was also removed from his eyebrow, which some believe was a melanoma.

in 1995 of the diary entries of an unmarried cousin, Daisy Suckley, which clarifies all his wartime illnesses.[97] The President trusted Daisy's discretion and charged her with sorting out his private papers for his library. She and Harry Hopkins, his long-standing close adviser, tried to help fill the irreplaceable gap in Roosevelt's life when the health of 'Missy' Marguerite Le Hand, his super-secretary, broke down. 'Missy' had brought the light and fun into his life which his respected wife, Eleanor, could never bring him.[98]

Daisy was the last person Roosevelt spoke to before he died in Warm Springs on 12 April 1945. With her was Lucy Rutherford, whose love affair with Roosevelt had ended when discovered by Eleanor in September 1918. Howard Bruenn was nearby and saw the President soon after he died. He behaved impeccably throughout his time as Roosevelt's doctor. He waited until 1970 to publish his account of Roosevelt's illness and chose the *Annals of Internal Medicine*, rather than trying to make money out of his patient's history. On Bruenn's death in 1995, his widow placed his papers, including his medical diary, in the Roosevelt Library at Hyde Park, New York.

Joseph Stalin

Comparisons between Adolf Hitler and Joseph Stalin have often been made, sometimes to try to determine which was the greater villain. If the measure is the number of deaths of innocent people each caused, Stalin emerges as the blacker figure. Unlike Hitler's crimes, Stalin's were hidden for decades. On 13 April 1990 President Mikhail Gorbachev had TASS, the Soviet news organisation, admit Soviet responsibility for the massacre of Polish officers in Katyn Forest. In October 1992 Boris Yeltsin revealed a Politburo decision signed on 5 March 1940 by Stalin and Lavrenty Beria, authorising the shooting of 14,700 Polish officers and 11,000 other imprisoned Poles. The massacre was falsely attributed at the time and for too long afterwards to Hitler through a piece of Soviet disinformation.

Yet in qualitative rather than quantitative terms, Hitler is the more evil of the two for, as has been said, Hitler's corruption 'lay in its ends', Stalin's 'lay in its means'.[99] Hitler and Stalin used mass murder, deportations, labour camps and terrible privation as weapons of suppression. In preserving his authority, Stalin would unleash all of these forces on large ethnic groups within the Soviet Union, as, for example, in Grozny in 1944. Stalin, however, was not a racist in the sense that Hitler was in his determination to eradicate the Jews.

The Soviet gulags were certainly a monstrous assault on human rights but they were not the equivalent of the Nazi concentration camps, where death was the objective.

Neither ill health nor mental incapacity can exonerate either man. Stalin's health was in general good. He drank long into the night with friends, but he also worked long hours. His physical health remained robust throughout the Second World War and he held his own during the three crucial wartime meetings with his allies in Tehran, Yalta and Potsdam. Yet in the summer of 1941, watching the Germans advance into the Soviet heartland and knowing he had ignored those who warned him of an impending attack, he appeared to collapse with a mental breakdown. He recovered his nerve and defiantly remained in Moscow as the Germans came within the city's defensive perimeter.

What stands out in Stalin's mental make-up, however, is his extreme paranoia. There are legions of stories about it which may make him seem, to the lay eye, mentally unhinged. After the assassination of Sergei Kirov, in December 1934, Stalin's paranoia increased. One day Stalin was walking with a naval officer past the security guards in the Kremlin, who were now posted at ten-yard intervals along the corridors. 'Do you notice how they are?' Stalin asked the officer. 'You're walking down the corridor and thinking, "Which one will it be?" If it's this one, he'll shoot you in the back after you've turned; if it's that one, he'll shoot you in the face.'[100] Another bizarre and horrendous story was that Stalin had a personal guard shot after the guard had unwittingly had a longstanding creak in his boots fixed, so alarming Stalin when he approached him unheard.

On 18 November 1950 Stalin agreed to arrest Professor Yakov Etinger, a Jewish doctor. This was the first arrest in what turned into the 'Doctors Plot'. Etinger's telephone had been tapped and he had been recorded criticising Stalin; he died while being tortured. In February 1951 Stalin ordered the arrest of more doctors and by then his own hypertension and arteriosclerosis were resulting in minor strokes. His old doctor, Vladimir Vinogradov, became an enemy and the 'plot' was used against Beria and Vyacheslav Molotov. 'Absurd as the details may sound, the Doctors Plot had the beautiful enveloping symmetry of a panacea, one of Stalin's fantastical masterpieces.'[101] One of the effects was that, when Stalin suffered his fatal stroke, no doctor was called to see him for twelve hours, at the orders of the fearful senior political figures around him.

We all have in our make-up a variety of personality traits, whether obsessional, impulsive, depressive, histrionic or paranoid. Only when any one or more of these traits become dominant, and frequently displayed, does that person's behaviour, as in Stalin's case, become abnormal. But paranoid behaviour by itself does not constitute an illness. It becomes clinical paranoia only when associated with mental illness such as schizophrenia or mania, or when it becomes so severe, with suspicion and distrust, that a patient's capacity to function becomes seriously impaired. At an extreme it can become a kind of psychotic state in itself. Paranoia, merely as a personality trait, need not be disabling. In the case of Stalin his paranoia did not flow over into every aspect of his thinking, mental life or decision-making. Pervasive and enduring distrust and suspicion were, however, key characteristics which Stalin possessed throughout his life. He would have been an incomparably better leader if he could have contained it, but then it can be argued that his paranoia allowed him to survive.

In varying degrees most politicians exhibit forms of paranoia. Political paranoia, as distinct from clinical paranoia, 'begins as a distortion of an appropriate political response but then far overshoots the mark. . . . The person is always the underdog, always the victim.'[102] But political paranoia is a label; it is not a clinical diagnosis. The paranoid leader, whether despotic or democratic, is at the centre and everything is self-referenced. He or she tends to be hypersensitive, often self-absorbed and jealous.

The origins of Stalin's paranoia probably lie in his roots in Georgia. Many of his ruthless, brutal features are better explained as those of a 'Caucasian chieftain' rather than deriving from a dogmatic Marxism. In any normal democratic society Stalin, as likely as not, would have ended up in prison. 'Throughout his life Stalin's detached magnetism would attract and win the devotion of amoral, unbounded, psychopaths.'[103] He was the mastermind behind a bank robbery in Tbilisi as early as 13 June 1907, at the age of twenty-nine. He thrived on the secrecy and authoritarianism inherent in Soviet communism and his paranoia was fed by the ruthless struggle for power following Lenin's death in 1924. The systematic murders which started under Lenin gathered even more momentum under Stalin. The 1937 'Terror' ordered by the Politburo led to the arrest and execution of the supposedly most hostile anti-Soviet elements through a system of quotas. Stalin, however, encouraged activists in the regions to outperform their quotas. Indiscriminate executions continued during and after what Russians called the Great Patriotic War of 1941–45. During that war the brutality was massive: at least 200,000 Red Army soldiers were shot by their own people.

Any flinching in combat was dealt with summarily, and surviving prisoners of war were often shot.

Sometime before the victory parade over the Germans in Red Square on 24 June 1945, Stalin had a heart attack, something his daughter called 'a minor stroke'. He was diagnosed as having arteriosclerosis and he was treated. But Stalin by then disliked the medical profession and after the Doctors Plot and as a consequence he allowed Aleksandr Poskrebyshev, formerly a nurse, to become his unofficial doctor, administering various tablets and potions. His temper became worse, as did his paranoia.

Stalin's paranoia was fired by suspicion and there was much for him to be suspicious about. But paranoia need not prevent a leader from holding down his job, taking rational decisions and conducting himself effectively. Stalin defeated his many enemies through a combination of having no conscience yet much cunning. Indeed, Stalin's decision-making, by contrast to Hitler's, seemed to improve during the course of the war, in as much as he eventually let his generals conduct their battles on a freer rein than at the start of the war. Initially, he tried to control everything on the frontline with the help of the Communist Party commissars. This had disastrous results as the Germans came close to capturing Moscow. Fortunately, Stalin had enough sense to change his mind and leave his commanders with more powers of initiative. In this and in other characteristics he demonstrated that he did not suffer from hubris syndrome (see Chapter 7).

The complexity of his personality is brought to life in a remarkable book, *Stalin: The Court of the Red Tsar*. Through letters and memoirs, it gives a penetrating insight into Stalin's personality, and shows why he was admired as well as feared. To this day many Russians continue to regard him as one of their greatest leaders.

Benito Mussolini

The crimes of the European dictators of the mid-twentieth century were so great that many people casually assume that the perpetrators must in some sense have been mad. But in fact only the least of the criminals, Benito Mussolini, the Italian dictator, Il Duce, can be said to have suffered from a serious illness. In 1925 he collapsed, coughing up blood, and X-rays showed he had a severe gastro-duodenal ulcer. Thereafter ulcer pain was ever present. He suffered from increasing insecurity and finally became detached from reality. It is possible that he had bipolar disorder.

Depression did not prevent Mussolini from assuming power in 1922 at the young age of thirty-nine and from exercising it over twenty years, despite periods of nervousness. Mussolini initially ruled as the result of a deal between his Fascists and the Church, the business community, the military and the bureaucratic elite. Gradually he built up a cult of personality which, after victory in the Abyssinian War of 1935–6, put him in the dominant position. He never carried King Victor Emmanuel III for war in 1940, and powerful people were against what many saw as a personal and reckless adventure. Yet by 1940 Mussolini personally ruled Italy. Hubris was evident in every action he took. The Fascist Grand Council, the Senate, the Chamber of Fasces and Corporations, the Council of Ministers: all were window dressing and counted for nothing.

Nemesis struck Mussolini after he decided to invade Greece. He told Hitler at their meeting in Florence that Italian troops had crossed over from Albania on 28 October. Just as the Führer did not tell him in advance of his invasions, so the Duce returned the compliment. 'What passed for dictatorial decisiveness was in reality the merest veneer of half-baked assumptions, superficial observations, amateurish judgement and wholly uncritical assessment.'[104] The Greek war was an unmitigated disaster from which Italy had to be rescued by the Germans.

By late 1942 Mussolini's mental health had caught up with him. He lost a quarter of his body weight over a few months, owing not just to an old complaint of stomach ulcers but also to his deep-seated depression. All the bombast had gone; he had no reserves of courage or strength. In December 1942 he was so depressed he sent his son-in-law, Galeazzo Ciano, to substitute for him at a scheduled meeting with Hitler and he spent most of Christmas and New Year in bed. In April 1943, during a trip to Germany, he had another medical crisis, with stomach pains and insomnia, exacerbated no doubt by the fact that by now Italy was clearly losing the war. He began to appear nervous, talking quickly, and he was losing authority. In July 1943 he was, in effect, imprisoned by his fellow Italians on the island of Ponza, then moved to a naval base in Sardinia and in August to a ski resort. After Italy surrendered in September, Mussolini was rescued by a German SS glider team and flown to Munich. The Germans then returned him to Italy and installed him as the puppet dictator of the remnant Italian Social Republic. He was captured and shot by Italian partisans near Como; his body was flung in the back of a truck and driven to Milan where, on 29 April 1945, it was strung upside down alongside that of his mistress in Piazzale Loreto, where fifteen Italian partisans had been shot in August 1944. Apparently Mussolini suffered from nightmares of a very different death and a characteristically delusional one. Grandiosely, he feared that were he to be captured alive by the Americans he would be taken to the United States and tried in New York's Madison Square Garden 'as if I were a caged beast'.[105] His flight from reality had by then become complete.

★

In 1945 Britain was deeply in debt and debilitated by two world wars. The electorate had few doubts about Winston Churchill's health but they had considerable doubts about his ability to deliver on issues such as housing and jobs. It surprised the world, however, when, before the war against Japan had ended, Britain voted for a Labour government led by the uncharismatic but decisive figure of Clement Attlee. The British electorate had seen Attlee perform well as Deputy Prime Minister in the wartime coalition and they voted for their future, seeing the Labour Party as being better able than the Conservatives to handle the problems of peace. Attlee replaced Churchill halfway through the Potsdam conference. This confirmed Stalin's 'rooted belief that elections when the outcome was not guaranteed were too dangerous to be allowed.'[106] Elections took place within the Soviet empire but resulted only in vast, rigged majorities.

Attlee is widely considered to have been one of the best peacetime British Prime Ministers. He remained personally in good health. Only on 21 March 1951 did a duodenal ulcer temporarily force him to spend time in St Mary's Hospital, in west London. Consequently Attlee missed the crucial Cabinet meetings when the Health Minister, Aneurin Bevan, clashed with the Chancellor, Hugh Gaitskell. Bevan and the others who were threatening to resign visited Attlee in hospital, the stress of which could not have helped his ulcer to heal. On 23 April Bevan resigned, which contributed to Labour's electoral defeat in October that year and the return of Churchill as Prime Minister.

Churchill's decline

Keeping Winston Churchill working as Prime Minister from 1951 was, his personal doctor Lord Moran, formerly Sir Charles Wilson, claimed, his prime responsibility. Churchill had had two strokes in 1949. Then, on 23 June 1953, he suffered a very serious one (see p. 111). Churchill's private secretary, John Colville, was told that Churchill would probably die over the weekend.[107] Churchill, still able to speak without difficulty, had given Colville strict instructions not to let it be known that he was incapacitated. A medical bulletin was drawn up by Moran and the neurologist Sir Russell Brain, which had a reference to 'a disturbance of the cerebral circulation' but this was cut out after discussions with two senior Conservative politicians, Rab Butler and the Marquess of Salisbury. Colville also consulted three of Churchill's friends in the press, John Berry (later Viscount Camrose), Lord Beaverbrook, who he refers to as Max, and Viscount Bracken, who joined the conspiracy of silence and persuaded their colleagues in Fleet Street not to print in their newspapers a word about how severe Churchill's illness was.[108] In fact, Churchill survived, though he was incapable of governing properly for a number of weeks. Churchill's son-in-law, Christopher Soames, a Conservative MP, acted for him even to the extent of repeatedly forging Churchill's signature.[109] It was Churchill who, apparently casually, mentioned in the House of Commons a year afterwards that he had had a 'stroke'.

During all Churchill's illnesses Moran was, quite properly, primarily serving the best interests of his patient. In 1941 his judgement about Churchill's heart attack had been that those interests clearly coincided with the best interests of the country. In 1953 this judgement was not so obvious. Moran cites testing Churchill's memory on 6 July, fourteen days after the stroke: he checked the text from a book as Churchill recited Longfellow's poem 'King Robert of Sicily', getting only half a dozen words wrong against three hundred and fifty. Yet this is not a good test of the brain's capacity to handle new information. Moran quoted a conversation he had with Churchill on 4 April 1955, two days before the Prime Minister was finally due to leave Downing Street:

Churchill: As my doctor, do you think that I ought to have gone before?
Moran: I sometimes wonder how I shall come out of this in fifty years time.
Churchill: You have not answered my question.
Moran: Well, last year when Max and Camrose came to Chartwell after your stroke they asked me what was going to happen. I told them it was guesswork.
Churchill: What do you mean by guesswork?
Moran: How long it would be before you had another stroke. They both said you would never again appear in the House of Commons. I told them I had seen patients more paralysed than you were get quite well. We must wait and see.

> *Churchill:* Do many people get over two strokes?
> *Moran:* They took it for granted you were finished as a politician. I felt from the first you were more likely to snuff it out if you retired.[110]

Later, Moran lost the respect of Churchill's family, particularly his wife, Clementine. She wrote an indignant letter to him in July 1964, when she heard that he was writing a book about her husband's medical illnesses. 'I had always supposed that the relationship between a doctor and his patient was one of complete confidence . . . I do not see how you can justify your present course.'[111]*

Churchill's illnesses illustrate the problem of judging how open to be with the public about the health of incumbent or potential heads of government, especially when the need to maintain public morale is an important factor to weigh. If the British Cabinet had known about Churchill's heart attack in late December 1941, they would have been very worried about the effect on public morale if it had become widely known, generating speculation that he might have to stand down. It's likely they would have wanted to make sure there was as little publicity as possible and to urge Churchill quietly to go away for a rest, letting Clement Attlee temporarily step into the breach. In fact, this is what happened when Churchill developed pneumonia and pleurisy in December 1943 at Carthage. The Cabinet encouraged him to recuperate at Marrakesh and not hurry back. The fact that the United States had come into the war by then and was contributing strongly helped to defuse any crisis of political or public morale. If Churchill had died in 1943 it would have been a blow; in December 1941 damaging; but before then it would have been devastating.

---

* Moran did not reply for some time. Then in January 1966 he wrote to Lady Churchill, a year after her husband's death, when he was preparing to publish, seeking permission to use a photograph. She replied: 'I regret very much that you should write about Winston.' This time Moran replied immediately, citing the eminent historian G. M. Trevelyan on the doctor–patient relationship: Trevelyan, he claimed, had taken the view that everything would eventually become known and had approved and encouraged him to publish, as had Field Marshal Jan Smuts and Lord Bracken. Lady Churchill, after reading Moran's book, told her daughter, Mary Soames: 'It shows Winston in a completely false light.' Soames summed up the family view with the simple proposition: 'Prince or pauper, prime minister or ploughman – a person should be able to repose complete trust in the inviolable confidence of his priest, his lawyer and his doctor.' (Mary Soames, *Clementine Churchill by Her Daughter* (London: Cassell, 1979), p. 253.)

When Churchill eventually left office at the age of eighty, his daughter, Mary Soames, referred to it as 'the first death' he minded so much. His resignation was long overdue and his successor, Sir Anthony Eden, had become visibly impatient to become Prime Minister. Revealingly, Churchill said to his private secretary on his last night in Downing Street with some vehemence, 'I don't believe Anthony can do it.'[112] Prophetic words (see Chapter 3).

2

1953–2007

I dread our own power and our own ambition. I dread our being too much dreaded . . . We may say that we shall not abuse this astonishing and hitherto unheard-of power. But every other nation will think we shall abuse it. It is impossible but that, sooner or later, this state of things must produce a combination against us which may end in our ruin.

Edmund Burke (1729–97)

Dwight Eisenhower

The United States of America and the Union of Soviet Socialist Republics were in 1953 the two most powerful nuclear weapon states in the world. Gradually over the next four decades the United States became the single superpower, but within America a few perceptive commentators began to dread its own power and its own ambition. The presidency of Dwight D. Eisenhower from 1953 to 1961 became a symbol of the United States' growing prosperity and its relative conservatism. Significantly, in view of Vietnam and now Iraq and Afghanistan, one of Eisenhower's last speeches in office was to warn the United States about the dangers of the power of the military-industrial complex within its midst.

Eisenhower's presidency brought into focus two central issues concerning illness in heads of government. One is the question of openness versus secrecy; the other is how to deal with the situation when a head of government becomes too ill to function. On the first, Eisenhower's case provided a fascinating example of how less secrecy and more openness about a medical condition can help retain the confidence of the public.

Eisenhower, however, had not always been so open about his condition. He had enjoyed far from perfect health. In August 1943, when he was Supreme Allied Commander in Europe, army doctors found that he was suffering from high blood pressure and throughout his adult life he had gastrointestinal symptoms with periodic stomach cramps and sudden diarrhoea.[1] Eisenhower recorded in a diary entry dated 4 June 1949:

> I had a severe digestive upset this spring which finally put me to bed on March 21. By the end of the week I was fit to travel and President Truman invited me to use his residential facilities at Key West. I went down there with General Snyder and remained until April 12. On that date he took me to Augusta National Golf Club where I remained until May 12.

Howard Snyder, Eisenhower's personal physician, claims that this episode was gastrointestinal and not cardiac and it was later diagnosed as ileitis or Crohn's disease.* Eisenhower's army cardiologist, Dr Thomas Mattingly, who became his consultant in the White House but was not treating Eisenhower at this time, believed he had a mild heart attack in 1949 and that Snyder covered it up. Mattingly liked and respected Eisenhower but claimed he sanctioned and collaborated in Snyder's deception. Whatever the true diagnosis, the US voters believed Eisenhower was fit and well when he beat Adlai Stevenson to become President in November 1952.

On 24 September 1955, when playing golf in Denver, Eisenhower, who was a heavy cigarette smoker, developed what he thought was indigestion. Snyder, who was with him, was now seventy-four years old, a long-standing family friend who had been treating Eisenhower's wife, Mamie, for a valvular heart condition for years. On this occasion he handled Eisenhower like a family doctor in a rural practice. When called in around 2.45 a.m. on 25 September because Eisenhower had a pain in the chest, Snyder decided that the President was suffering from a heart attack but did not rush him into

---

* Crohn's disease is a chronic inflammation of the small intestine and/or large intestine and bowel, most commonly the ileum. An autoimmune condition, it may last several years, relapsing and remitting. It is often hard to distinguish from ulcerative colitis, which affects the colon, whereas Crohn's disease can involve any part of the gastrointestinal tract. The affected wall of the bowel becomes thickened and ulcerated but some parts are normal. Prevalence is increasing, with up to 7 of every 100,000 people now being affected. Abdominal pain, bloody diarrhoea and weight loss can be presenting features. Treatment with immunosupressants has made recent advances. Patients with extensive disease may require surgery to remove an affected section of the gut. A serious complication is perforation of the gut, while a more common complication is blockage of the gut; both of these conditions require emergency surgery.

hospital. Instead he gave him amyl nitrate to sniff,* in order to dilate his coronary arteries, and injections of an anti-coagulant to stop clotting of the blood with morphine to settle him and ease any pain. At 7.00 a.m. he told the President's press secretary, in order to reassure him and the wider public, that Eisenhower had indigestion. Eisenhower did not wake up until 11.00 a.m. and it was past midday before Snyder called the military hospital to bring over an ECG machine, which showed that the President had had a heart attack with a thrombosis of the coronary artery.[2] At 2.00 p.m. Eisenhower was taken to hospital.[3] Some might say this coolness of approach bordered on foolhardiness. Others might see in it the best qualities of a family practitioner. Another explanation would support the accusation of an earlier cover-up, in that Snyder had no doubt of the diagnosis, having nursed Eisenhower through a heart attack in 1949, and hoped that by not admitting him to hospital or ordering an immediate ECG he could keep this attack quiet as well.

On the morning of 26 September, when Eisenhower's illness became public knowledge, the Dow Jones financial index dropped 6 per cent, a paper loss of $14 billion, the largest decline since the 1929 crash and a fall that exceeded reactions both to President Kennedy's assassination and to the shooting of President Reagan.[4] The panic lasted for only a short time and Eisenhower's general demeanour helped greatly. A few weeks later he was photographed on the roof of the hospital in a wheelchair with the words MUCH BETTER THANKS embroidered on his shirt.

Eisenhower was the first head of government to end the cycle of secrecy and cover-up. He adamantly ruled out any return to Washington until he said he was strong enough to walk into the Oval Office and get back to work, saying that no one wanted a disabled President. Quite openly, Sherman Adams, his chief of staff, kept the Executive branch busy and the Vice President, Richard Nixon, sensibly showed no signs of itching to get hold of the reins of power.[5] Eisenhower arrived back in Washington on Veterans' Day, 11 November. He told the waiting crowd: 'The doctors have given me at least a parole, if not a pardon,' and the public loved him for his honesty. He went to his farm at Gettysburg and then down to Key West for twelve days

---

* Amyl nitrite used to be used to treat angina or pain in the heart due to an insufficient blood supply causing ischaemia of the heart muscle. It is a volatile liquid formed by the action of nitric and nitrous oxide on amyl alcohol. Drug abusers use it to produce a 'high' and it is called by them 'poppers'. The treatment of choice for angina is now glyceryl trinitrate, given in a tablet beneath the tongue.

from 28 December to 8 January. The detailed records of his stay show that he combined government business with recuperation.

On 29 February 1956, after the doctors told him that he had made a complete recovery, Eisenhower decided to run for a second term as President. Yet on 6 June, he had another attack of ileitis, affecting the small bowel, with painful spasms. He was admitted to the Walter Reed Hospital and the surgeons, after some hesitation, successfully operated for small bowel obstruction as a complication of Crohn's disease. By 21 August Eisenhower was fit enough to fly off for a vacation in San Francisco. Despite his sixty-five years he looked in good health again. He now began to profit from having kept the public well informed about his illnesses and the fact that what his doctor had said had been truthful. The American public, as a result, never felt they had been misled and wanted him to run again.

During his second term, on 25 November 1957, Eisenhower, while working at his desk, had the third major illness of his presidency. It started with giddiness and a passing weakness of his right arm and hand; then he had difficulty in speaking and finding the correct words. It was thought that he had had a transient ischaemic attack involving the left hemisphere of his brain, but the fact that he retained a slight but permanent speech defect points to his having had a stroke.* This time, much less detail about the incident was released to the press. At one point Eisenhower told close aides that he was contemplating resignation.[6] In the end, though, he saw through his term in office to January 1961 and lived for almost a decade afterwards. He had another bad heart attack in the summer of 1965, however, and also became depressed. Other heart attacks followed and he died from heart failure in March 1969, aged seventy-eight, nearly fourteen years after his Denver heart attack.

Eisenhower had been troubled for some time about what happened if a President was too ill to make the right decisions. At a meeting of his Cabinet in February 1957 he suggested the formation of a special committee to decide on a procedure for the transfer of power and in April of that year his Attorney General proposed to the Senate a constitutional amendment requiring the Vice President to obtain a majority in Congress before being able to take over

---

* A stroke, otherwise called a cerebrovascular accident, involves sudden brain damage either from an interruption in the blood supply to the brain, usually by a blood clot, or from a bleed into the brain as a result of a ruptured blood vessel. It is commonly associated with atherosclerosis, where the arteries are furred up.

executive power. This foreshadowed the Twenty-Fifth Amendment (see Chapter 8). On 3 March 1958, before that amendment had been passed, a memorandum of agreement between Eisenhower and Nixon allowed the President both to declare and later to terminate a period during which power would pass to the Vice President. It also allowed the Vice President, after such consultation as seemed appropriate, to declare the President disabled. It had no force in law but it concentrated minds in Congress, making them understand that something had to be done.[7] The Kennedy administration was not keen to give the issue a high priority and did not want to specify procedures in the Constitution, preferring a Senate proposal to leave Congress to establish such procedures as it thought necessary. Probably John F. Kennedy wanted to have as little public discussion about the health of the President as possible given his own cover-up.

Eisenhower conducted himself well in office throughout his two terms. He was an underestimated President when he left office but since then he has won increasing recognition as his record of keeping the United States out of any overt military engagements overseas has been favourably compared with that of his successors. As regards his health, he realised that the past habit of presidential cover-up had to stop and that secrecy over illnesses was not necessary for Presidents to win the support of their electorate.

Lyndon Johnson

The illnesses of Eisenhower's successor, John F. Kennedy, are examined in detail in Chapter 4. When he was assassinated in 1963 he was succeeded by his Vice President, Lyndon Johnson, a controversial, larger-than-life Texan who held office from 1963-69. Questions about Johnson's health had begun to be asked even before he became Vice President and they continued throughout his presidency. On Saturday 2 July 1955, while driving to the Virginia estate of the Brown and Root construction company, with which he had a long association,[8] Johnson, then Senate majority leader, started to have a serious heart attack. He had been working at a frenzied pace. There had been warning signs which he had ignored, despite, or perhaps because of, his lifelong fear of a heart attack. He was driven to Bethesda Naval Hospital, sedated for forty-eight hours and given a 50:50 chance of survival. He was prescribed complete rest. At the age of forty-six he was being written off from ever being able to challenge for the presidency. There was even some doubt whether he would be able to stay as leader of the Senate. Johnson fell into a deep depression, a common side effect following heart attacks, although violent mood swings, with clear-cut depressive episodes, had always been part of Johnson's character. He left the hospital on 7 August. On doctors' orders he had to stop smoking and drinking coffee. He had also been told to lose weight and without nicotine, caffeine, calories, sex or the Senate, he had nothing to satisfy himself. Suddenly, he started to read books and to tell people, somewhat unconvincingly, that it was wonderful to 'have time just to sit and think'. According to his biographer, Robert A. Caro, when Johnson went back to his ranch in Texas, he 'fell into a despair deeper even than his despair in hospital', sitting for hours, 'staring at nothing, and saying nothing'.[9] Eventually we may learn more about what, if any, drug treatment for depression Johnson was given then and during the years he was President.

Johnson was intensely ambitious and unscrupulous. Clark Clifford, who knew well all the US Democrat Presidents from Truman to Carter, described Johnson as 'the most complex man I ever met; he also may have been the most difficult' . . . he could be 'astonishingly devious' and 'a terrible bully'.[10] But he understood political power. Dean Acheson, formerly Truman's Secretary of State, wrote to Clifford that Johnson presented 'an unbelievable combination of sensitivity and coarseness, of understanding and obtuseness'. Yet Clifford believed that, had it not been for Vietnam, Johnson 'would have been one of our most illustrious Presidents'.

Johnson tried to stop the momentum for Senator Kennedy at the July Democratic convention in 1960 and described him to the *Chicago Daily News* as a 'little scrawny fellow with rickets'. India Edwards, who was very close to Johnson politically, claimed at a press conference at the convention that Kennedy had Addison's disease.* A 'reliable' source had apparently told her that he had been present at a governor's mansion during a Kennedy campaign stopover and that Kennedy, as a result of forgetting his cortisone, had lapsed into a coma until a state trooper had been able to get some to his bedside that night.[11] This claim was widely seen as a dirty trick from the Johnson camp but according to Edwards, Johnson himself lashed out at her for implicating him in the allegation. While Kennedy appeared not to blame Johnson for this attack on his health, his brother Robert did blame him and never forgave Johnson. From the start Robert Kennedy resented his brother having offered

---

* See footnote in Chapter 4, p. 142 on Addison's disease.

the role of Vice President to Johnson and found it difficult to accept Johnson as President after his brother's assassination.[12]

Two volumes on Johnson's life, *Lone Star Rising* and *Flawed Giant*, have many stories but the one I find most revealing of his wheeling and dealing nature involves Kennedy's father, Joe, saying to him that if Johnson put his son Jack on the Foreign Relations Committee, Joe would never forget the favour for the rest of his life. Johnson recalled his reaction:

> Now I knew Kefauver [Estes Kefauver, a Tennessee senator] wanted the seat bad and I knew he had four years seniority on Kennedy. And I would have preferred showing preference for Tennessee over Massachusetts. But I kept picturing old Joe sitting there with all that power and wealth feeling indebted to me for the rest of his life and I sure liked that picture.[13]

Whether Johnson called in this promise in order to become Kennedy's vice presidential candidate we may never know. Joe Kennedy was a powerful influence on Jack, far more so than Robert. Joe Kennedy would have been attracted to having Johnson on the ticket, calculating that Texas was a state that had to be won; and he would not have worried about alienating those Democrats who disliked Johnson.

The assassination of President Kennedy reignited interest in a constitutional amendment covering illness in a President. It was realised that Kennedy might have survived but been seriously disabled, and there were worries about Johnson's own health, after his serious heart attack eight years earlier. The Twenty-Fifth Amendment was agreed in July 1965 and ratified by the necessary thirty-eight states on 10 February 1967 (see Chapter 8).

It is interesting that in 1965, when Johnson had an attack of acute cholecystitis, affecting the gall bladder, he consulted Dwight Eisenhower about his illness and Eisenhower recommended openness and pointed out the advantages of candour. Johnson, normally obsessed by secrecy, took his advice, told the Vice President and then the Cabinet, and went into Bethesda Naval Hospital for the removal of his gallstones and gall bladder. He also had a stone in his ureter removed. Then twelve days after the operation, on 20 October 1965, he had a famous photograph taken for the press showing a long scar over his stomach.

After that operation Johnson experienced post-operative depression bad enough that he wanted to draw up papers to resign from the presidency.[14] This story has never had much publicity but its source was very close to the Johnson family. He was dissuaded from resigning by the few people who knew and even forty years later this dramatic episode is shrouded in mystery. There were other episodes of paranoid instability and irrationality but this is the only known report of him wanting to step down before he finally decided to do so in 1968. Johnson also had a family history of alcoholism, debt and hypersexuality, which strengthens the arguments for the suggested diagnosis of bipolar disorder, which is an inheritable illness. Given the subsequent history of Johnson's time as President, it is hard to deny that it would have been better for him and for the handling of Vietnam if he had resigned in the autumn of 1965 and Hubert Humphrey, his Vice President, had taken over.

Already in the late spring of 1965, alarmed at what he perceived to be the President's 'increasingly irrational behaviour',[15] Richard Goodwin, his principal speech writer and someone who had been in constant touch with the President for three years, began to study medical textbooks and talk confidentially with professional psychiatrists. Unbeknown to Goodwin, his friend Bill Moyers, perhaps the President's closest young confidant, took the same course and talked independently to two psychiatrists.

> In all cases the diagnosis was the same: we were describing a textbook case of paranoid disintegration, the eruption of long-suppressed irrationalities. As for the future, it was uncertain. The disintegration could continue, remain constant, or recede, depending on the strength of Johnson's resistance, and, more significantly, on the direction of those external events – the war, the crumbling public support – whose pressures were dissolving Johnson's confidence in his ability to control events, that confidence which was his protection both against the buried cauldron of nonrational suspicions, and his fear of being left alone and helpless in a hostile world.[16]

In 2006, the review of biographical sources of American Presidents that diagnosed Theodore Roosevelt as suffering from bipolar-I disorder classified Johnson likewise during his Presidency, with a high likelihood of the diagnosis being correct. It is not surprising, given Johnson's suspicious character, that any information about his mental condition is hard to find. He would probably have instructed his doctors not to leave any paper trail because, being paranoid, he would have feared any revelation about his health. There is little doubt that Johnson had clinically significant depressions throughout his life. The review of the available literature led these psychiatrists to interpret Johnson's coarse and volatile behaviour as reflecting the opposite pole, mania, to that of his depression. Johnson had a habit of speaking of 'my air force' and had an unshakeable belief in his entitlement as President to lie.

President Johnson's early time in the White House was, in terms of legislative social reforms, particularly on civil rights, outstanding. He used all his formidable skills honed in Congress to assemble majorities which no President before or since has been able to achieve. As his presidency continued it became ever more dominated and indeed haunted by the war in Vietnam. Goodwin explained:

> The results of this narrowed focus were devastating. Within government reasoned argument, the exchange of divergent views, critical appraisal of fundamental policy, came to a halt . . . power alone can check power, and if the restraints, not of men but institutions, are dismantled, then democracy is in mortal danger. I have worked with many powerful men. They were all convinced that their goals were righteous, that their sole objective was the public good; and they all resented obstacles to their will.[17]

The strains and anguish over Vietnam meant Johnson went through long periods of stress and during the period 1965–7 his conduct clearly changed. One of his most able biographers, Robert Dallek, wrote that Johnson's 'paranoia raises questions about his judgement and capacity to make rational life and death decisions'. Also he admitted that 'determining psychological incapacity may be impossible'. He then went on to question: 'Who then is to say when a President has passed the bounds of rational good sense?' Nevertheless, Dallek concluded: 'Certainly in Johnson's case, for all the cranky nonsense he espoused about his enemies, he remained largely in control of his faculties and more than capable of functioning as President.'[18] It is true that the war in Vietnam would have been an extremely testing challenge for any President. What was required was the capacity at least to consider rationally and calmly the withdrawal of US troops; this was something that Johnson, with all his self-doubt and paranoia, was incapable of doing. He chose instead incremental increases in troop levels and bombing activity, less than the generals wanted, more than his critics could support.

In 1967 Johnson underwent a highly secret operation for surgery on a skin cancer on his left ankle. Admiral George Burkley, who had been a key figure in the White House dealing with Kennedy's illnesses and was now Johnson's physician, denied all speculation. The operation was confirmed only in 1977, well after Johnson's death from a coronary thrombosis (or heart attack) in

1973. In October 1967 Dr Willis Hurst warned Johnson's wife, Lady Bird, of his great concern over the state of her husband's health and though she wanted to tell him that the decision had already been made that the President would not run again she did not feel free to do so.[19] This implies that she felt her husband's mind had been made up to resign before 1968. Congressman Henry Gonzalez from Texas, a good friend of Johnson's, said: 'He told me to my face that the reason he didn't run again was that several doctors had told him he wouldn't last another term.'

In the run-up to the 1968 presidential election, the Democratic Senator Gene McCarthy polled dramatically well in the New Hampshire primary, damaging Johnson's chances of re-election. Four days later Robert Kennedy announced his candidature, posing an even greater challenge to Johnson. A few weeks later the President announced on television that he would not stand again.

There were a myriad of different views about Vietnam and about Johnson. The President's gregarious, larger-than-life personality seemed to have had the effect of widening, not narrowing, the division of opinion within the United States. Amongst some politicians there was admiration for his incomparable ability to fix deals; amongst others a palpable hatred. Some even managed to combine the two feelings. Fortunately Johnson eventually had enough insight to realise that his own departure from the scene would be a way of healing the very divisions to which he had himself contributed.

The politicians, Dulles, Kennedy, Rusk, Johnson, MacNamara, Nixon, Kissinger and Ford, all in their different ways contributed to what America lost in Vietnam, something which Barbara Tuchman puts in one word: 'virtue'. The first folly was 'continuous overreacting: in the invention of endangered "national security", the invention of "vital interest", the invention of a "commitment", which rapidly assumed a life of its own, casting a spell over the inventor'. A second folly was 'illusion of omnipotence'; a third folly was 'wooden-headedness' and the 'Don't-confuse-me-with-the-facts' habit. The US government's 'grossest fault was under-estimation of North Vietnam's commitment to its goal . . . matched by overestimation of South Vietnam . . . A last folly was the absence of reflective thought.'[20] Every one of these was on display in the invasion of Iraq. Agonising over the choices he faced with regard to Vietnam, often in public, was a feature of Johnson's style, but there was not the supreme confidence in his own judgement which is so characteristic of the hubristic leader.

Harold Macmillan

At almost the same time that Lyndon Johnson became US President in 1963, Britain's Prime Minister, Harold Macmillan, was leaving office because of ill health. Macmillan had succeeded Anthony Eden as Prime Minister when Eden resigned in 1957, ostensibly from ill health too, although also because of his responsibility for the Suez fiasco. Macmillan had presided over a period of apparent economic prosperity. In October 1963, however, during a Cabinet meeting, he developed urinary retention, an extremely painful condition, usually due to prostatic obstruction. He was advised by a surgeon to have an immediate operation.

Macmillan appears to have understood that he was likely to have cancer of the prostate and so began to think in terms of resigning. He always had a tendency to fear the worst about his health. His long history of hypochondria was perhaps related to his having suffered serious wounds in the First World War. But his own physician, Sir John, later Lord, Richardson (who taught me medicine at St Thomas' Hospital and was a reassuring and conscientious doctor), always believed that if he had not been away at the time but had been able to see the Prime Minister before the surgeons did, he would have given him a more optimistic prognosis. Macmillan would not then perhaps have started to feel the need to resign. In fact there was no cancer, just a benign hypertrophy of the prostate. A few months after the operation his health was restored. Charles de Gaulle, less than a year later, had the same operation but remained in office.

Macmillan claimed, initially, to have regretted his resignation but in his memoirs he admitted that it had been time to leave. In truth, he had lost his political touch, as was clear earlier in the year when the Profumo sex scandal shook his government and Macmillan, unusually, performed poorly in the House of Commons. Although he had a fine intellect, he was a classic example of an actor politician; not for nothing was he sometimes called the 'Old Poseur'. When things were going well he was cartooned in the left-wing *New Statesman* journal as 'Supermac' and he never lost the epithet.

Macmillan refused to take either a peerage or a knighthood from the Queen. But on his ninetieth birthday he agreed to accept a hereditary title and became the Earl of Stockton making a whimsical and humorous speech accusing Margaret Thatcher, the then Prime Minister, of selling off, in her privatisation programme, the family silver. He died in 1986.

Charles de Gaulle

General de Gaulle, arguably, became the *de facto* head of government of the French Republic in 1940 during his broadcast from London to the French people known as 'L'Appel du 18 juin'. Next day, he broadcast again and this time claimed to be speaking in the name of France. During the first few years of the war, at a time of great stress, he suffered from serious depression. One depression occurred only a fortnight after his broadcast, following the sinking by the Royal Navy of French naval vessels in Mers-el-Kébir with the loss of 1,297 French lives. Another came after the Dakar debacle, when de Gaulle's presence failed to persuade the French forces loyal to Vichy to surrender to the Free French. De Gaulle later wrote that he actually contemplated suicide. A flagrant challenge to his authority by Admiral Émile Muselier and the refusal of the British to put the admiral under close arrest prompted another bout. De Gaulle also became very ill with malignant malaria, but nobody was told, neither the Free French commanders or politicians nor the British. He was nursed back to health on the outskirts of London by his wife.[21]

As the prospect of victory grew, so did de Gaulle's self-confidence, but he was always prone to dramatic gestures. His first resignation from office took place on 19 January 1946 after the Constituent Assembly, which chose him as President in November, deprived him, he felt, of the personal power he thought necessary to revive France. He was returned to power at the age of sixty-seven after his self-imposed exile in Colombey-les-Deux-Églises on 1 June 1958 by a vote of 320:224 in the Assembly. He negotiated for peace in Algiers, created the Fifth Republic, withdrew France from the integrated command structure of NATO and vetoed Britain's application to join the European Community. All this time his health was considered good.

De Gaulle began to suffer from an enlarged prostate in early 1964 but tried to put off an operation. With his surgeon, who was also a friend, he managed to keep secret the catheter in the bladder, even during a tour of Mexico in March. On 15 April, with very few people knowing, he went into the Hôpital Cochin in Paris and was operated on next day for a prostatic adenoma, a benign growth of the prostate gland. Rumours of his hospitalisation spread and a statement, handwritten by de Gaulle the day before, was released to the press. A copy had also been sent in a sealed envelope to a senior official at the Élysée Palace with the words: 'Not to be opened until after my death. But you will give me back this note the day after tomorrow, if as I expect, everything goes well.'[22]

On 4 November 1964, de Gaulle, having recovered well, announced he would stand again for the post of President. On 5 December he was forced by François Mitterrand into a second round. After some hesitation, a hurt and indignant man fought on and won on 19 December by 54.6 per cent to Mitterrand's 45.4 per cent.

At a press conference on 4 February 1965, ten months after the operation, de Gaulle was asked: 'How is your health, *mon Général*?' 'Quite good,' came the reply. 'But don't worry, one day, I shan't fail to die.' At the age of seventy-five de Gaulle had embarked, unwisely, on a second seven-year term as President. A warning sign of political trouble ahead came in March 1967 in the Assembly elections, when his Prime Minister, Georges Pompidou, won only a slender majority. In May 1968, France was in a deep political crisis triggered by student revolt, and an ageing de Gaulle was quite unable to understand the forces the students had unleashed. By 25 May, the President, feeling he could no longer control the situation, was telling his Minister for Youth and Sports: 'It's all over.' He was in a state of 'profound gloom' and at a Council of Ministers' meeting on 27 May he presided but 'his heart and mind was elsewhere'.[23] He seemed totally indifferent to what was going on around him, barely listening to the conversation. His old depressive mood had returned.

Then on 29 May, de Gaulle embarked on a strange venture. He decided that evening to fly with his wife, their son, Philippe, and his wife and three children to the headquarters of the French armed forces at Baden-Baden in Germany. Opinion is divided as to whether de Gaulle's bizarre behaviour was due to his own disarray or to clever tactical manoeuvring. The two people best placed to judge – Pompidou and General Jacques Massu, the commander of French forces in Germany – believe he was in disarray. The President had been sleeping very little during the crisis and, as his biographer, Jean Lacouture, put it, he was undergoing an old man's 'failure of nerve'.[24] When the crisis was over and de Gaulle returned to Paris, certain of the support of the French Army, he explained himself by saying: 'For the past twenty-four hours, I have considered every eventuality.' But on 1 June he confided to Pompidou: 'For the first time in my life, my nerve failed me. I am not very proud of myself.'[25]

De Gaulle, like Neville Chamberlain, became seriously ill only after he left office. But it is reasonable to question whether his decision-making had, for some time, been affected by his age. When the strikes and student riots developed it was Pompidou who acted decisively and bought off the strikers.

Even so, when the crisis was passed, and the parliamentary elections won on 30 June, de Gaulle was happy for Pompidou to resign and appointed Maurice Couve de Murville as Prime Minister. But if anything, this rupture enhanced Pompidou's standing and enabled him to make it clear that when the time came he would run for the Presidency. Thereafter, for the first time, de Gaulle had an obvious successor in waiting. De Gaulle made another misjudgement in calling a referendum for Sunday 27 April 1969 on regional reform and the composition of the Senate. The referendum was lost by a little under 47 per cent to slightly over 53 per cent. Soon after midday on 28 April a short official announcement was made, on behalf of de Gaulle: 'I am ceasing to exercise my functions as President of the Republic. This decision takes effect from noon today.'

De Gaulle was not a man to stay in power when the people, whom he had charged with the fate of France in a national television address two days before, were no longer following him. He retired to his home in Colombey-les-Deux-Églises. On 9 November 1970, while playing patience, after feeling a sudden pain in his back, he collapsed. His wife was beside him at the card table. He had experienced a rupture of the abdominal aorta, probably associated with atherosclerosis.* De Gaulle's funeral took place in the local church, at his express wish, without the President of the Republic or any foreign heads of state being present and without speeches, music or fanfare. As André Malraux said, 'It was the funeral of a knight.' But de Gaulle had, like many a knight before him, fought one battle too many. He would have been wiser in late 1964 to have announced that he was stepping down, eschewing a second term on grounds of age, and in so doing not risked his place in history as the greatest French leader.

Georges Pompidou

Pompidou was elected to succeed Charles de Gaulle on 15 June 1969. At the beginning of his period in office he was a highly effective President. One of his achievements was to lift de Gaulle's veto on British membership of the European Economic Community and to work with the Dutch and the British Prime Minister, Edward Heath, to bring it about in 1973. But by August 1972

---

* 'Arteriosclerosis' is used for any of a number of conditions affecting the arteries and most frequently is interchangeable with atherosclerosis, where fatty plaques develop on the inner walls. As the body ages, so do the walls of the artery and the muscles that make up the wall. The wall can become weakened by this process and split or burst. This is a life-threatening condition which can sometimes be cured by emergency surgery.

Pompidou was feeling weak and was lacking energy. His doctor ordered a series of tests, including a bone marrow test and X-rays. These confirmed that he had a progressive cancer involving the bone marrow. The nature of this illness was never revealed before his death, even though his face filled out when he was on high doses of steroids, as was particularly visible in early 1974. He died on 2 April of that year from myelomatosis,* having been for many months in considerable pain, particularly when walking. In Paris, despite speculation, very few officials in the Élysée knew of Pompidou's condition and he did not tell even his wife until after a trip to China in 1973. François Mitterrand's decision (taken when running for the presidency) that there should be the utmost transparency about his health was influenced by Pompidou's death in office. But it was completely reversed when, as President, Mitterrand himself became ill (see Chapter 5).

Willy Brandt

Georges Pompidou's period in office coincided almost exactly with Willy Brandt's as Chancellor of the Federal Republic of Germany, West Germany. Brandt had spent the war years in Norway. He never had the slightest taint of association with the Nazis. He won immense personal prestige as a defiant mayor of Berlin during the crisis of 1961, when the tensions of the Cold War were being felt acutely in his city. In the late 1960s, as leader of the Social Democrats (SPD), and as Foreign Minister for three years in the grand coalition his party formed with the Christian Democrat Chancellor, Kurt Kiesinger, Brandt realised that West Germany had to change the policy of the long-serving post-war Chancellor, Konrad Adenauer, to refuse to recognise the communist German Democratic Republic (GDR), commonly referred to as East Germany, in any shape or form.

By the late 1960s any appeal that communism might have had in western

---

* Myelomatosis is a malignant disease of the bone marrow with two or more of the following:
  a.   excess and abnormal plasma cells in the bone marrow;
  b.   an appearance of holes in the bones when X-rayed;
  c.   abnormal gammaglobulin in the serum, which can be myeloma globulins, Bence Jones protein or macroglobulins.
A plasmocytoma is a single tumour in the bone marrow. If there is more than one tumour it is called multiple myelomatosis. Radiotherapy and chemotherapy are used in the treatment and the prognosis varies considerably, depending on the exact type of cells involved.

European eyes had been greatly tarnished by the Soviet invasion of Hungary in 1956 and then of Czechoslovakia in 1968, and also by the increased contact between eastern and western Europe, particularly East and West Germany. What Brandt realised, and then championed as Chancellor from 1969 to 1974, was that West Germany could not rely only on initiatives from the United States, the UK or France for ending the divisions of Europe and that it had to develop a strategy of its own. This strategy, of which Brandt was the architect, was known as *Ostpolitik*. It amounted to what Brandt's chief adviser, Egon Bahr, called 'change through rapprochement' and it meant slowly and steadily normalising relations. For example, in 1969, a mere half million telephone calls were placed between West and East Germany. Twenty years later it had become some forty million. Telephone contact between the two halves of Berlin was negligible in 1970 but had reached ten million calls by 1988.[26] West Germany's relations with the Soviet Union and other eastern European countries improved steadily too under *Ostpolitik*.

What is perhaps not given sufficient recognition outside Germany is that it was Brandt's personal emotional make-up which fuelled his *Ostpolitik*. This was well illustrated when he visited Warsaw as Chancellor. After formally laying a wreath at the grave of Poland's unknown soldier, Brandt went to the memorial dedicated to the Jewish ghetto of the city and its dead. In his autobiography he wrote of his tortured emotions:

> I did what human beings do when speech fails them. Even twenty years later, I cannot say more than the reporter whose account ran, 'Then he who does not need to kneel knelt, on behalf of all who do need to kneel but do not – because they dare not, or cannot or cannot dare to kneel.'[27]

There is little doubt that on occasions that same emotional character left Brandt vulnerable to depression. His depressions were periodic – about twice a year – most often in the autumn, when the days became shorter, and he would stay in bed for two or three days, incommunicado to everyone, even his wife. His personal staff called the episodes 'influenza'. When he returned to work he was not apologetic about his absence but seemed to regard it as quite normal. There is no evidence that these depressive absences impinged greatly on his work in any of his public offices. Brandt's distinguished biographer, Peter Merseburger,[28] told me in personal correspondence that he doubts whether Brandt received medical treatment for them.

On 24 April 1974, having flown back from Cairo after meeting President

Anwar Sadat, Brandt was met at the airport by the leader of the Liberal Party and Minister of the Interior, Hans-Dietrich Genscher, who told him that Gunther Guillaume, one of Brandt's advisers in the Chancellery, had been arrested and had admitted to being a spy for East Germany. Brandt's political vulnerability was clear. Soon stories started to appear about his womanising, though this was no secret to those who had known him in both Berlin and Bonn. A report from the Federal Criminal Investigation Office expressed fears that, at his forthcoming trial, Guillaume might mention what were euphemistically called 'painful details'. This raised the dilemma that these details would, if mentioned, make the federal government look ridiculous or, if not mentioned, mean that the GDR government would have a means later of humiliating the Brandt Cabinet and the SPD.[29]

On 6 May, Brandt decided to resign, citing his own 'negligence'. In his autobiography he wrote:

> Did I have to resign? No, it was not imperative, even though the step appeared to me inevitable at the time. I took political responsibility seriously, and perhaps too literally . . . I will admit that intrigue affected me, and it would have been strange if the distress occasioned to my family had not troubled me.

He mentions having had to go to bed with a stomach upset picked up in Egypt, having had pain from two molars extracted by his dentist the week before his resignation and feeling 'groggy'. Brandt also wrote in his autobiography that 'there was also talk that I entertained the idea of suicide: a gross exaggeration of the fact that I was very depressed.' Brandt finished his description of what he calls the Spy Affair, concluding: 'In the physical and mental condition of my later years I would not have resigned; instead I would have cleared up the whole affair as far as possible.'

In his excellent play *Democracy*, about Brandt's last few weeks as Chancellor, Michael Frayn depicts Brandt as indecisive, though Merseburger believes that he was generally decisive on important political questions. It is probable that Brandt's admitted depression contributed to his resignation. But by this time the big challenges of his political life were behind him. And it is hard to argue that the resignation damaged Germany's political development. His successor, Helmut Schmidt, who had argued against Brandt resigning, was better suited to handle the economic difficulties that had resulted from the 1973 world oil price rise and he followed, with the exception of defence, most of Brandt's foreign policy. In retirement Brandt made a distinguished contribution to

German and Third World politics and he is another example of why a history of depression should not be an automatic disqualification to someone becoming a head of government.

Richard Nixon

In the year that Pompidou and Brandt came to power, Richard Nixon was sworn in as US President. He was, as someone once described him, a 'pathological loner'. It is not possible to say with certainty whether, during his time in the White House, Nixon was psychotic[*] but it is clear he came very close to it.[30] There were clear instances of Nixon's abnormal behaviour over the invasion of Cambodia, well before the Watergate crisis erupted and he faced the threat of impeachment. For example, the distinguished journalist James Reston reported:

> Between 9.22 p.m. on 8 May and 4.22 a.m. on 9 May 1970, Nixon made 51 telephone calls to members of his Cabinet, his staff, magazine editors, Foreign Service officers, newspaper reporters, repeating calls to one or the other, talking about his family, his grandparents, the civil war – sort of a sleepless, compulsive nightmare of talk – after which, to the consternation of the Secret Service, he got into his car at dawn and drove to the Lincoln Memorial to argue with the startled young people who had come to Washington to demonstrate against his invasion of Cambodia.[31]

An interesting study of Nixon was made by Dr Arnold Hutschnecker, who treated him from 1951, initially in New York when he was a general physician. He continued to treat Nixon when he became Vice President in 1952, but in 1955 Hutschnecker's approach became increasingly focused on psychotherapy and Nixon worried about adverse publicity. Thereafter there were a number of discreet meetings between the two men but Nixon only saw Hutschnecker twice in the White House. One of those visits came after he decided to announce the invasion of Cambodia. Ushered in without signing

---

[*] Psychosis is a general term for a group of diseases where the person loses contact with reality, but may be so disturbed that they are unaware that they are ill. Depression, paranoia and alcoholism, all of which Nixon had, are not of themselves psychotic conditions, though they can develop into a psychosis.

the visitors' log at the gate, Hutschnecker encountered none of the old intimacy with Nixon. Two days later Henry Kissinger thought Nixon was in fact 'on the edge of a nervous breakdown'.[32]

Nixon and Hutschnecker met for the last time in 1993, when Nixon asked him to sit with the family at his wife's funeral. Hutschnecker became an exponent of psychiatric screening for political candidates while making it clear that he had seen Nixon only as a physician, not as a psychiatrist. He wrote an article on leadership types in *Look* magazine on 15 July 1969, and it gives a useful insight into the complexity of Nixon's personality. Hutschnecker argued that the Nixon who, after losing the 1962 election for governor of California, had famously said 'You won't have Nixon to kick around any more!' should be classified a strong excitatory type of leader. But the Nixon who he claimed had calmly handled the North Korean plane incident in April 1969 might have become a 'controlled, adjusted personality, moving with strength through negotiations towards peace'. There is, however, a different view of how Nixon reacted to this incident, in which on 14 April a US spy plane was shot down, with the loss of thirty-one crew. The diary of Nixon's chief aide, H. R. Haldeman, claims he first wanted a 'strong reaction' and held back only when his aides advised prudence – 'suppressing his instinct for a jugular response', according to Kissinger. Kissinger's aide Lawrence Eagleburger talked of Nixon as 'ranting and raving, drunk in the middle of a crisis'. At another time a drunken Nixon reportedly said to Kissinger, 'Henry, we've got to nuke them.'[33]

Hutschnecker believed that leaders can change and pointed to Abraham Lincoln as an example of someone who had changed. By contrast, Professor James David Barber, of Yale University, argued at the sixty-fifth American Political Science Association meeting, on 3 September 1969, that after the age of fifty US Presidents do not change. I am not convinced. James Callaghan changed on becoming Prime Minister in 1976, losing the 'chippiness' in his character and becoming a bigger personality and a wise leader. The jury is still out on whether Gordon Brown will change as Prime Minister. Barber was perceptive about Nixon, however, when saying that 'it is the isolation, the lonely seclusion adopted consciously as a way of deciding that stands out in Nixon's personal relations style', and he classified him as an 'active negative type' of President, whereas Truman had been an 'active positive type' and Eisenhower a 'passive positive type'. America has for many years been studying the personality of political leaders, using techniques of content analysis of speeches, interviews and their texts; an interesting review article by

David Winter, one of the leaders in this field, concludes that in such an enterprise 'a certain sense of humility is necessary and becoming'.[34]

The facts of the Watergate scandal, which brought Nixon down, can be summarised briefly because they are so well known. On 17 June 1972, five men were arrested and later found guilty of attempting to burgle the Democratic Party election headquarters in the Watergate apartment block. We now know that on 20 June Nixon had first begun to discuss their arrest – though there was an eighteen-minute gap in the Oval Office tape recording made of this first discussion. Fatefully, Nixon started to become intimately involved as a co-conspirator in the cover-up. On 1 March 1974, the Federal Grand Jury in Washington indicted seven people, four of them close to the President. Two of them, Haldeman and John Ehrlichman, could not have been closer as political aides; John Mitchell was an old friend, besides having previously been Nixon's Attorney General; and Charles Colson was an important White House aide. Eventually, on 15 June 1974, a finding was made public that 'there is probable cause to believe that Richard M. Nixon (amongst others) was a member of the conspiracy to defraud the United States and to obstruct Justice'. Impeachment proceedings began in July and Nixon resigned in August. Previously, in 1971 Nixon had authorised in relation to the leaked Pentagon papers an attempt to break into the Brookings Institution and into the office of Daniel Ellberg's psychiatrist, when Ellberg was thought to be responsible for the leak.

It remains a mystery whether the Republican Committee to Re-Elect the President was authorised by Nixon to bug the Democrat headquarters. They must all have known that he was heading for a decisive victory (he won in forty-nine of the fifty states) on 7 November 1972. Still less is it clear why Nixon should have involved himself in the cover-up. Nixon's own definitive comment did not come until 13 April 1977, when in his television interview David Frost extracted from him: 'I let the American people down, and I have to carry that burden with me for the rest of my life.'

In his play *Frost/Nixon*, based on the interviews, the playwright Peter Morgan has the liberal intellectual James Reston say:

> Aeschylus and his Greek contemporaries believed that the gods begrudged human success, and would send a curse of 'hubris' on a person at the height of their powers, a loss of sanity that would eventually bring about their downfall. Nowadays we give the gods less credit. We prefer to call it self-destruction.[35]

Was a loss of sanity, drink or hubris the cause of Nixon's destruction? There is no doubt that after winning re-election he developed many hubristic features. There were certainly those who doubted his sanity in his last eighteen months in office as the arm of the law grew ever closer, as his circle of intimates grew smaller and he became even more of a loner. The Speaker of the House, Tip O'Neill, who saw him during the Yom Kippur war of October 1973, wrote: 'President is acting very strangely.' In December, Senator Barry Goldwater wrote: 'I have reason to suspect that all might not be well mentally in the White House. This is the only copy that will ever be made of this; it will be locked in my safe.' The Joint Chiefs of Staff were told by the Defense Secretary, James Schlesinger, a politician full of common sense, not to carry out any decisions of the President involving military matters unless all five of them agreed. Also they should check with him first. So great was Schlesinger's concern about Nixon's mental stability that he also demanded that under the National Security Act all military orders from the President should be transmitted through him as Defense Secretary.

There were reports of Nixon being close to a nervous breakdown and being frequently drunk. His drinking was not simply social and in retrospect senior psychiatrists have classified it as alcoholism.[36]Admiral Elmo Zumwalt, Chief of Naval Operations, met President Nixon on 22 December 1973 in the White House.

> While not a 'drunken wreck' . . . he did present the very disturbing spectacle of a man who had pumped his adrenalin up to such a high pressure that he was on an emotional binge. He appeared to me to be incapable of carrying on a rational conversation, much less exercising rational leadership over a nation involved in a score of complicated situations, embarked on dozens of hazardous enterprises.[37]

Nixon's paranoia, his dislike of Jews and his foul language are all evidenced in the hours of tape recordings made in the Oval Office. So too is his readiness to use money to pay people off and to corrupt the electoral process. In 1973 Nixon had told a meeting of Associated Press editors in Florida, in the context of an Internal Revenue Service investigation of his income tax returns from 1969 to 1972, that 'people have got to know whether or not their President is a crook'. Clearly he was. But his presidency was a strange mixture of the venal and the brilliant. And it would seem that despite the paranoid temperament, the anxiety depression and his alcoholism, this deeply conflicted man just managed to hold on to his sanity. Nixon's personal physician was Dr Walter Tkach. His son, Dr John Tkach, wrote to Robert Dallek in December

2005 that his father's medical records would be sealed for seventy-five years in the Nixon Library and went on that 'there are some things about the Nixons that are so confidential I shall never reveal them'.[38]

Nixon did manage to function in his last few months as President, though, staggeringly, he was not involved, presumably because he was drunk, in a tense moment in the middle of the night with the Soviet Union over the war in the Middle East. In this episode, which took place on the evening of 24 October 1973, Leonid Brezhnev nearly sent a Soviet airborne force to the war zone and US forces were put on increased alert. This non-involvement was possible only because Nixon was buttressed by General Alexander Haig, coming back into the White House, and by Henry Kissinger, as Secretary of State, projecting an image internationally of business as usual. Haig called the end of the Nixon presidency 'one of the most dangerous periods of American history' and said that lawful change of leadership 'was not a foregone conclusion at the time'.[39] He feared improper action by Congress, not the military.

There is no case where vital US national interests were damaged by Nixon's medical condition. But what did suffer was people's trust and belief in politicians and politics, not just in the United States but in democracies around the world. Without the mechanism of impeachment for holding a President to account, Nixon would never have resigned and his persistent abuse of the office would never have been revealed. The danger is that much of this has been forgotten and instead, under successive Presidents, Nixon has been rehabilitated to an extent and credited with major foreign policy initiatives. This is particularly so with regard to reopening American relations with China, after a gap between 1949 and 1971, and travelling to Beijing to meet Chairman Mao. Yet Nixon's abuse of power should never be forgotten. Alcoholism is also a serious medical condition for any political leader to have had. It is discussed further in Chapter 7, pages 320–1, in relation to George W. Bush.

Mao Zedong

The brutality of the dictatorship of the Chinese Communist leader Mao Zedong has led some people to ask the same question as is often asked about Hitler: was he mad? His ruthlessness and lack of regard for human life are indisputable. The 'Great Leap Forward', which he instituted in 1958, involving the collectivisation of agriculture and the restructuring of the Chinese peasantry into people's communes, led to the death of an estimated twenty-seven million people during the ensuing dislocations, violence and famines.[40] It was certainly one of the most savage political acts of the twentieth century. And aside from the human cost, the economic effects were devastating. Between 1958 and 1962 agricultural output dropped by 28 per cent and light and heavy industrial production by 21 per cent and 23 per cent respectively. Later, during the Cultural Revolution, launched in 1966, there were purges and mass killings and much of China's rich cultural and intellectual base was destroyed.

Mao was ruthless in purging any opposition and there is no doubt about his early total disregard for people's lives. Violence was the way to smash the social order. As early as March 1927, in a report of a visit to Hunan published in the Comintern journal, Mao wrote with sadistic pleasure about personally witnessing some brutal scenes, claiming that he felt 'a kind of ecstasy never experienced before . . . It is wonderful . . . One or two beaten to death no big deal.'[41]

It is, of course, perfectly possible for someone to be sadistic, ruthless and callously indifferent to human life without being mentally ill, but in Mao's case there is some evidence of mental illness, though too little is known to allow a firm diagnosis to be made. As well as being seriously paranoid, bearing grudges, imagining he was being poisoned and spying on his colleagues, he is judged to have probably suffered from depression throughout his life. Periodically Mao spent months in bed, ill with worry, according to his doctor.[42] It may be, however, that depression was only part of the story and that his underlying illness was bipolar disorder. The reason to suspect this is that he was able to bounce back from his undoubted depressive periods with a vigour that may well be evidence of the manic phase of bipolar disorder. For example, after the burst of activity of the Great Leap Forward he seems to have sunk into relative inactivity, allowing himself by 1960 to be marginalised by other members of the Communist hierarchy, including Deng Xiaoping. Yet Mao was able to spring back to launch the Cultural Revolution six years later. Periodic bursts of activity, which turn out to be ill thought through, are the frequent accompaniment of bipolar disorder.

As regards his physical health, in September 1934 Mao developed cerebral malaria, which responded to massive doses of quinine and caffeine.[43] In January 1946, at Mao's request, Joseph Stalin sent a KGB doctor, Melnikov, to examine him at a time when he was thought to be ill. Melnikov found nothing more than mental exhaustion and nervous stress, terms in those days often used for depression. Mao became seriously ill in the 1970s with congestive heart failure and retention of water in his lungs and legs. In October 1971, when Henry Kissinger made his second trip to Beijing to prepare for President Nixon's historic visit, Mao was bedridden and suffering again from depression.[44] Yet prior to Nixon's visit on 21 February 1972, Mao's health dramatically improved and he stayed well in the immediate afterglow of what was seen in China as a foreign policy triumph. The Americans made 'an unwitting contribution [to Mao's recovery] as well: oxygen tanks and a respirator that had been sent on ahead in case Nixon fell ill, were moved into Mao's bedroom'.[45]

But the improvement was short lived and Mao's health started to decline again. By 1973 he was having difficulty in speaking and needed oxygen much of the time. His mind, however, remained clear at times and in October 1974 he appointed Deng First Deputy Prime Minister and automatic successor to Zhou Enlai. Towards the end of Mao's life he had to give up swimming, his favourite pastime, and some have indicated this was owing to early signs of motor neurone disease. He died from a heart attack on 9 September 1976, having been diagnosed two years earlier as suffering from Lou Gehrig's disease, a rare progressive nervous disease paralysing the throat and respiratory system.

Harold Wilson

Harold Wilson was Britain's Prime Minister when Nixon came to power and he had regained the office by the time Nixon left. Wilson is one of two recent political leaders – the other being Ronald Reagan – who, after leaving office, were diagnosed as having Alzheimer's disease.[*] The case studies of these two

---

[*] Alzheimer's disease is the commonest form of dementia, characterised by a progressive loss of intellectual and social function. It is named after a German physician, Alois Alzheimer (1864–1915), who wrote a paper on the condition in 1906. It is in its early stages characterised by a loss of short-term memory. It involves the degeneration of brain cells, mainly located in the temporal and frontal lobes of the brain. There is an occasional disorientation in time and space, and a deterioration in intellect and behaviour over varying periods of time. Eventually the patient's walking is often affected and they become immobile and die after a period of care in bed. Much research is being done and neuroscientists are hopeful of making significant advances. There is a proven genetic basis involving three specific genes in many cases. Examination of brain tissue shows plaques containing the protein amyloid outside the cells in the cortex, the outer layer of the brain. Also changes occur inside the neurons or nerve cells where neurofibrils twist around and thicken to form neurofibrillary tangles. Alzheimer's is a disease of the elderly, being rare before the age of sixty, whereas it has been calculated that 30 per cent of those aged over eighty-four have some signs of the disease. Treatments are undertaken but most only claim to be able to slow down the spread of the disease. In 2006 4.5 million Americans had the disease and if nothing changes dramatically in the treatment that number will have trebled by 2050. For a summary, in layman's terms, of current research being undertaken into Alzheimer's disease see 'Puzzling out the truth', *Economist*, 29 July 2006.

leaders bear upon an important issue in this book – the mental capacity of heads of government.

Harold Wilson's first period as Prime Minister ran from 1964 until 1970 and he was re-elected in 1974. He stepped down on 16 March 1976. To most members of the British Cabinet, and to the country as a whole, his decision to leave office came as a complete shock. He had, however, in late December 1975 alerted two of his likely successors, James Callaghan and Roy Jenkins, that he was going to retire. While still in opposition in 1973, after a minor incident involving his heart, Wilson had decided and promised his wife that if he became Prime Minister again he would remain in the job only for a short period. His overriding objective was to call a referendum on Britain's staying within the European Economic Community, later the European Union, and to personally ensure a 'yes' vote. His tactic was to renegotiate the terms of entry to the EEC and claim that the new terms made all the difference as to whether Britain should stay or leave. Although it is highly debatable whether the new terms, in reality, were much of an improvement on the old, the political trick worked brilliantly and Wilson and Callaghan, the then Foreign Secretary, succeeded in swinging Labour voters behind membership. The 1975 referendum endorsed membership by a margin of two to one. This result put Edward Heath's major achievement in negotiating UK entry into the Community somewhat in the shade for a few decades. But historically Heath will be given considerable credit.

In retrospect, Wilson's decision to retire was an enlightened one. He had become weary of having to deal with what then seemed like Britain's endlessly recurring political and economic problems and his government reflected his own weariness. He did not have the will to cope with the impending financial crisis and by stepping down avoided the inevitable negotiations with the International Monetary Fund in 1976. Yet at the time there was endless political speculation as to why Wilson had resigned. Some of it was ludicrously fanciful. It was suggested he was involved in a financial scandal, even that he had been a Soviet agent. In fact the reason for his resignation was probably much simpler: he had become more and more worried about his health. Talking to him informally in and around the House of Commons over the previous nine years, I had become well aware how important his photographic memory was to him. But it had now begun to desert him. Philip Ziegler, his biographer, described the effect on him of the deterioration of his memory. For Wilson, 'to slow up, to be at a loss for words or to grope for a statistic was not merely galling, but a blow to his confidence'.[46] Nevertheless Wilson was and remains the only Prime

Minister who stepped down voluntarily without any pressure from his party. What pressure there was came from his wife and his doctor.

By 1980, four years after resigning, Wilson's health was not good. He developed cancer of the bowel that summer and had three operations. A doctor recorded the clinical detail that while his memory of years gone remained excellent he could not remember what he had had for breakfast that day,[47] a classical early sign of Alzheimer's. Though Wilson's last book, *Memoirs: The Makings of a Prime Minister 1916–1964*, was published in 1986, his mental function had begun to decline some years before and the deterioration was continuous and severe.

Wilson died on 24 May 1995. The lesson of his experience is that even mild memory failure, if progressive, should be taken by a head of government and his medical advisers as an indicator that it is time to consider retiring.

Edward Heath

Elected in June 1970, having won the Sydney–Hobart yacht race less than six months before, Edward Heath was fit and well through his period in No. 10. What was surprising was his own decision to call the February 1974 general election, during a miners' strike when electricity supplies were reduced, on the rather bizarre issue of 'Who governs Britain?'. This decision has led some doctors to question in retrospect whether he might have been suffering from the early effects of hypothyroidism in the last year he was in office, despite it not being diagnosed until six years later. It is not unusual for hypothyroidism,*

---

* Hypothyroidism results from underactivity of the thyroid gland. The gland secretes two hormones, thyroxine and tri-iodothyronine, which control the metabolic activity of the body, expressed in the measurement of the basal metabolic rate (BMR). In hypothyroidism the BMR is reduced. It starts between the ages of thirty and sixty, and it can develop very slowly into a general sluggishness, where intellectual functions slow up, physical energy is reduced and patients start to gain weight. The commonest cause is the auto-immune destruction of the thyroid, known as chronic thyroiditis, sometimes called Hashimoto's disease. It is relatively common and more often found in females – 14 per 1,000 against only 1 per 1,000 in males. The early diagnosis depends on finding a low level of the thyroid hormones in the blood and a high level of the pituitary thyroid stimulation hormone (TSH), which is raised in a vain attempt by the pituitary gland to increase the activity of the cells in the thyroid, which are damaged, to produce more thyroxine. The treatment is through thyroxine, either isolated from the gland or produced synthetically. In Heath's case his thyroxine T4 blood level – normally within a range of 60–170 – was 32, remarkably low, and his TSH level was increased to more than 50, when it would normally lie below 5. This indicated a phenomenally low level of thyroid activity.

also called myxoedema, to take many years to manifest itself. The signs and symptoms of a general slowing up appear so slowly that the people surrounding the person affected adjust their own assessment of a lowering of performance without realising it, and this adjustment can include the patient's own doctors.

In 1981, Heath, then a distinguished backbench MP, had been diagnosed as having hypothyroidism. He had recently been given thyroxine and probably because of that thyroxine he developed atrial fibrillation of the heart and was suffering from what his doctor called 'rip-roaring heart failure'. He responded well to treatment with replacement thyroid. For some years after he ceased to be Prime Minister in 1974 there had been comments in the press about his somnolence when attending the House of Commons. By 1981 the degree of underfunctioning of the thyroid gland would, his doctors had no doubt, have impaired his political acumen. The unresolved question was for how long had he been impaired. But to postulate that Heath's hypothyroidism was sufficiently severe to impair his cognition some six years before his hypothyroidism was detected is implausible. The best data on this subject comes from the Framingham study, set up to identify cardiovascular risk factors in the population of Framingham, Massachusetts, with retrospective analysis of blood samples from subjects subsequently found to be clinically hypothyroid. The main lesson, however, from a silent disease such as hypothyroidism is to emphasise the value of an independent medical assessment for people in key decision-making roles, since the disease is often missed for long periods by their personal doctors.

Ronald Reagan

When Ronald Reagan first entered the White House in January 1981, at the age of nearly seventy, he looked very fit. He left office, as the oldest US President, eight years later, still very popular. President Reagan was a remarkable man whose qualities were often masked by his deficiencies and vice versa. True to form, his frankness about medical illness surprised many. During the 1980 presidential campaign he talked on a plane to the *New York Times* health writer, Lawrence K. Altman, about his mother, Nellie, who had been senile 'for a few years before she died' from a stroke at the age of eighty. Reagan said he fully expected his White House doctors to check his mental status and pledged to resign if he himself became senile while in office. He asked Altman about senility and Altman explained about amyloid deposits in the brain and Alzheimer's disease, which was not much known about then.[48] It obviously concerned Reagan and he was well aware that with his mother's history and his brother's memory problems he could be affected. The risk of developing Alzheimer's is usually quoted as between 1 in 5 and 1 in 6 if a first-degree relative is affected. Without a first-degree relative affected the risk is between 1 in 15 and 1 in 20 – the perception of the risk is probably higher than the actuarial risk in most people. In the over-eighty age group Alzheimer's exists in about 20–30 per cent of the population. What is unusual is that Reagan was ready to speak about his anxiety publicly before he was elected in November 1980.

Many people had doubted Reagan's mental capacities from the beginning of his presidency. I first talked to him on a one-to-one basis in 1978 in the Foreign Office, soon after his term of office as governor of California had come to an end, and then again in the White House on 3 June 1985. It was very hard to assess his mental capacity at the best of times because of his self-confident ignorance and his charming gift of self-deprecation. Reagan was a strong-willed leader with a limited attention span, but his great gift was his readiness to concentrate on simple presentation and focus only on a few big policy issues, delegating large areas of policy to others.

The average American did not expect Reagan to be immersed in detail and this saved him when it came to the Iran–Contra arms scandal and subsequent cover-up. Reagan shifted his testimony before the presidential commission on the arms shipments and then on 20 February 1987 wrote to John Tower, the former Senator heading the commission: 'The only honest answer is to state that try as I might, I cannot recall anything whatsoever about whether I approved a replenishment of Israeli stocks around August of 1985. My answer therefore and the simple truth is "I don't remember, period".'[49] The public were mainly forgiving. They let the issue drop, with Reagan admitting responsibility but not complicity. His age helped; the public knew that forgetfulness and memory loss, with difficulty in remembering names, are the experience of most people in their older years. They can signify nothing serious, but they can be, and in Reagan's case may have been, the early manifestation of Alzheimer's. As yet, we do not know enough about the early stages of this disease to be sure. The first signs of the mental deterioration associated with Alzheimer's are hard to pinpoint.

The excellent, though admittedly idiosyncratic, official biography, *Dutch*, written by Edmund Morris, draws on the four leather-bound volumes of

Reagan's presidential diary to show that his judgement was not impaired by any falling away in mental capacity.[50] Morris describes these diary entries as 'uniform in style and cognitive content from beginning to end. There was no hint of mental deterioration beyond occasional repetitions and *non sequiturs* and if those were suggested for early dementia, many diarists including myself would have reason to worry.'[51] The diary entry for my meeting Reagan on 3 June 1985 was accurate, except for adding an S to my name.

However, a retrospective study in 1987 compared Reagan's televised debate with President Carter during the 1980 election campaign with his performance as President in the debates with his Democrat challenger, the former Vice President Walter Mondale, in 1984. It showed that Reagan's answers in 1980 were clear and his sentences well formed and understandable, but by 1984 his answers contained many grave errors, and his replies were at times so muddled they could not be understood. Furthermore there were no paragrammatic errors − incorrect uses of articles, prepositions and pronouns − in the Carter debate, but four years later an average of one every 220 words in the first Mondale debate and one in every 290 words in the second. Pauses occurred five times more frequently in 1984 than in 1980 and there was a 9 per cent slowing of Reagan's speech. The psychologist Brian Butterworth, who conducted the study, concluded in retrospect that Reagan had early senile dementia.[52]

It is possible that if it had been mandatory by then for Reagan to undergo an independent medical assessment prior to running for a second term, the risk of an adverse report might have persuaded him and his wife, Nancy, to choose a dignified retirement instead. They both showed themselves to be surprisingly realistic as well as open about health matters. For example, on 15 July 1985 Reagan allowed it to be known that he was suffering from cancer of the colon. It was felt then that he had an even chance that the cancer cells had not spread beyond the polyp, in which case today he would have a 70 per cent chance of surviving another five years. And in 1987 it was also announced that he had had minimally invasive surgery on a benign growth on his prostate − a transurethral resection of the prostate − a common operation for men of his age, something which President Mitterrand also underwent with his malignant prostatic cancer.

There are detailed medical records in the Mayo Clinic which give a picture of Reagan's mental state during the summer of 1990, a year after he left office. He was given the whole range of formal mental and psychological tests following a riding accident and surgery on his brain to remove a subdural haematoma.* Those tests are said to have given no hint of impending Alzheimer's but others carried out in 1993 did.[53] His doctor during the presidential years, John Hutton, has said that 'all parameters for his age absolutely were within the normal range'.[54] This judgement is supported by other White House doctors, although they had done only simple mental arithmetic tests, asking him to subtract 7 continually from 100 and other fairly standard, though crude, questions.

In September 1992 Reagan, out of office, was still able to make a campaigning speech for President George Bush Sr, but that same night he could not recognise his former Secretary of State George Shultz,[55] even though he had seen him at his own home earlier in the day. One of Reagan's White House doctors, who was seeing him for the first time in six months, described him as being distant, which was unusual, since normally Reagan was fully engaged when he talked to someone. At the end of their conversation, Reagan asked him: 'What am I supposed to do next?' and there was a blank look on his face. Looking back the doctor regarded this as the first sure sign of Reagan's Alzheimer's.

Once it was clear that Reagan was indeed suffering from Alzheimer's, he and his wife handled the situation with grace and dignity. On 5 November 1994 Reagan wrote a moving handwritten letter to 'my fellow Americans' telling them that he was one of a million Americans afflicted with Alzheimer's disease. He went on to say: 'In the past Nancy suffered from breast cancer and I had my cancer surgeries. We found through our open disclosures we were able to raise public awareness.' He ended: 'I now begin the journey that will lead me into the sunset of my life.' He died on 5 June 2004, a much respected former President. His wife said he had not opened his eyes for four years.[56]

An argument can be made on general health grounds that President Reagan's forgetfulness should have led to him deciding not to stand for a second term, just as Harold Wilson, who later developed Alzheimer's, should not have stood in the two general elections in 1974. Yet on political grounds

---

* A subdural haematoma occurs when there is an accumulation of blood from a tear in the veins which cross the space beneath the dura mater, which lines the inside of the bone of the skull or cranium, and the meninges, which cover the brain. Blood exudes slowly and it cannot be felt or seen under the rigid bone covering. As the pressure under the cranium builds up the brain is compressed and symptoms such as headache or drowsiness coming hours after a fall on the head are suspicious. The haematoma can be diagnosed best by a CT scan. The surgical procedure is to drill a hole through the cranium and drain off the blood, giving instant relief. If diagnosed in time there is usually no lasting brain damage.

there was a case for both men continuing in office and both had achievements to their name during their later periods in office. After re-election Reagan had his first meeting with the Soviet leader Mikhail Gorbachev, in Geneva in November 1985. This led to nuclear missile reductions and later destruction. In Berlin in June 1987, Reagan, against the advice of the State Department, demanded: 'Mr Gorbachev, tear down this wall.' His simple anti-communist philosophy had a directness and a consistency which over his period in office contributed to the fall of the Berlin Wall and the collapse of the Soviet empire.

Both Reagan and Wilson left politics before obvious signs of Alzheimer's developed. This contrasts with the case of another head of government, the President of Finland Urho Kekkonen, who while in office began to suffer from an undisclosed disease that seemed to affect his brain functions. He was first elected in 1956, and, though never actually diagnosed as having Alzheimer's, he resigned in 1981 after a cover-up of a serious memory disturbance which manifested itself as early as 1978, the year when he was last re-elected.[57]

In Reagan's case, however, it was neither his age nor any illness that was responsible for one of the most dramatic presidential health crises of recent history. At 2.25 p.m. on 30 March 1981, Reagan was shot by the sixth bullet from a pistol fired by John W. Hinkley after it ricocheted off his limousine. The first bullet permanently disabled the White House press secretary, James Brady, who was hit in the head. The bullet struck the President under his left armpit and was deflected by the top of his seventh rib three inches into the lower left lung, where it lodged one inch from the heart and aorta.

It is widely accepted that Reagan's life was saved by the special agent in charge, Jerry Parr, who bundled him into the car to head for the White House but who, once he saw the President cough up blood, told the driver to divert to the nearby George Washington Hospital. This attempt on Reagan's life came very close to killing him and undoubtedly reduced his capacity to handle the taxing job of being President, but he delegated his authority and husbanded his strength.

What was amazing was how unprepared administration officials were for the crisis. They were, for instance, only vaguely aware of the role of the Twenty-Fifth Amendment, which provides for a President, if he is able to do so, to sign a letter temporarily transferring his executive powers to the Vice President. Dr Daniel Ruge, Reagan's White House physician, was with Reagan throughout the afternoon of 30 March. He believed the President would have been capable of signing a letter had it ever been presented to him, despite his heavy blood loss (more than half of his blood volume) before he went under the anaesthetic at 3.40 p.m. to remove the bullet.[58] If Reagan had signed such a letter, George Bush Sr would temporarily have become President. Instead, Bush was advised only that the President was in a serious condition, first by telephone at 2.40 p.m. while on his way to Texas on Air Force 2 and then at 3.04 in a telex from Alexander Haig, the Secretary of State. Haig then made matters worse by making an ill-advised, breathless, appearance in the White House Press Room and claiming, wrongly, to be the Cabinet minister in charge.

While the operation was underway, Reagan's two key advisers, James Baker and Edwin Meese, consulted one of the surgeons, Dr Joseph Giordano. They wanted to know how the President would function after the anaesthetic. The doctor explained that Reagan was not going to be able to make major decisions since all anaesthetic drugs had some effect on the mind and brain and he would also be on heavy-duty pain medication. When asked how long this would last, he thinks he remembers saying a couple of days.[59] On 9 April, ten days after the attack, Reagan was said to be working two hours a day in hospital but this was an exaggeration. On 11 April he left hospital. Those close to him knew he had been 'horribly drained'. In the days that followed, Reagan was able to work or remain attentive for only about an hour a day. He did not work his first full day until 3 June, two months after the shooting.

Yet the morning after the shooting, Meese said: 'It's really business as usual.' Baker claimed: 'The President is fully capable of taking actions.' Reagan's new press secretary, Larry Speakes, said: 'The President will make all the decisions, as he always has.'[60] This was a totally inaccurate account of the President's state of health and designed to mislead. Senator Birch Bayh, who had been a central figure in the design of the Twenty-Fifth Amendment, said later:

> It is characteristic of many White House staffers to consider their own turf more important than the well-being of the country. If you have a president who can't function – and President Reagan was darn near dead – not to turn it over to Bush was totally irresponsible. I think it violated the Constitution. Fortunately, Reagan recovered and the country was none the worst for it.[61]

Reagan himself was to have a characteristically more straightforward approach to what should happen if he became incapacitated not by a bullet but by his own mental decline. In 1987, when his White House doctor,[62] John Hutton, asked him what he wanted done in the theoretical situation that they might need to invoke the Twenty-Fifth Amendment for mental deterioration, Reagan simply said: 'Just go talk to George and Nancy,' meaning Vice President Bush and Reagan's wife. This was a good summary of both the legal position and practical reality. In most circumstances these are the two people who could be expected to be a US President's advocates and informally to convince him if it was time to step down.

Margaret Thatcher

Apart from a detached retina and Dupuytren's contracture, affecting the little and ring fingers, both of which responded to surgery, Margaret Thatcher was fit and well throughout her eleven years as Prime Minister. Yet her career is almost a model case of a political leader succumbing to hubris syndrome. Her early period in office was not hubristic, though there were a few signs that she might be susceptible in the way she divided her colleagues into 'them and us' and was dismissive of consensus. For the first two years she was careful to keep a large number of dissenting voices from the opposite wing of her party in the Cabinet and when challenged by the miners in an industrial dispute she was likely to lose, in 1981, she beat a retreat, albeit temporarily, until confronting them in 1984.

The decisive event which was to change the nature of her premiership was the invasion of the British Falkland Islands by Argentina in 1982. Although few British Prime Ministers would have done as she did and send a naval task force down to the South Atlantic to retrieve a small archipelago of little strategic significance, the decision itself was not hubristic. I know from my own conversations with her during the war that, while utterly determined, she was surprisingly cautious and in private she was more anxious than belligerent. Her 'rejoice, rejoice' statement on the steps of No. 10, following the landing of British troops on South Georgia, is often quoted as an example of hubris, but it was as much relief as exaltation. What was hubristic was to take a marchpast of servicepeople who had served in the Falklands campaign, arranged by the Lord Mayor in the City of London. That role, Thatcher well knew, was properly one for the Queen.

Her success over the Falklands, though, and her inevitable victory in the subsequent general election in 1983, undoubtedly boosted her self-confidence. She began to dispense with colleagues who disagreed with her and to surround herself with those who shared her views. During the year-long miners' strike she was utterly determined, but not hubristic. She planned for the strike with great care, ordered the building up of coal stocks and only then took on the miners' leader, Arthur Scargill. No other British Prime Minister in the twentieth century would have held their nerve and pushed the miners to total defeat as she did. They would have found an excuse to compromise much earlier. But she sensed, correctly, that outright victory was not just possible but necessary. The defeat of the miners was under the existing trade union legislation, not the new legislation she had introduced. It was a defining moment in her prime ministership, arguably signalling the end of the post-war political and industrial power of the trade union movement. The UK's relative economic decline could only have been reversed by decisive leadership in the 1980s, and Thatcher's pursuit of monetary discipline, trade union reforms and privatisation transformed the British economy, ensuring a considerable legacy.

But the very fact that she had succeeded over the Falklands and the miners in the face of conventional wisdom, which would have had her compromise on both, meant that she became dangerously confident about her own judgement and contemptuous of other people's, especially after her third election victory in 1987. Her insistence on introducing a poll tax perfectly illustrates how she was succumbing to hubris syndrome. The tax was almost universally regarded as unfair but she was convinced it was not and ploughed on with the policy. Even a leader as self-confident as Winston Churchill recoiled from such hubris. In preparing the Conservative manifesto for the 1950 election he had cursorily dismissed the complaint of a young member of the party's Research Department, Reginald Maudling, that a particular proposal was unfair; but when Maudling had the temerity to come back with the observation that the 'British people' would regard it as unfair, Churchill paused and remarked: 'Ah! That is a horse of a very different colour!' The proposal was dropped. But the weight of mere public opinion was not something that was going to stop Thatcher in her tracks. Even here, though, she did not manifest that cavalier inattention to detail which is often symptomatic of the syndrome. Her Chancellor, Nigel Lawson, who opposed the tax, makes clear in his memoirs that there were extensive studies conducted about the whys and wherefores of the tax before it was introduced and that colleagues were very fully consulted. But the momentum behind the tax was undoubtedly Thatcher's unwavering conviction that it was 'right'. At a more comical level it started to become clear she was suffering the effects of hubris when she greeted the arrival of her first grandchild with the remark 'We have become a grandmother!'

By 1989 Thatcher's grasp of the realities in which she was operating seemed to be deserting her. When the Berlin Wall came down in November, she refused to recognise that reunification of East and West Germany would come immediately onto the political agenda. An underlying fear of a larger Germany developed into her privately talking emotionally about a Fourth Reich. She warned President George Bush Sr that 'if we are not careful, the Germans will get in peace what Hitler couldn't get in the war',[63] a quite extraordinary remark. The fact that she totally miscalculated the speed of the political imperative that was driving German reunification was one of the signs that her political judgement was being jeopardised by her political prejudices and that her self-confidence was overriding her caution. By then, her contempt for the Foreign Office was allowing her to disregard all diplomatic advice. In this case she undoubtedly damaged Anglo-German relations, but fortunately she did change her mind when she failed to carry her Cabinet colleagues, particularly her Foreign Secretary, Douglas Hurd. More seriously, she alienated and lost Lawson by refusing to acknowledge that in holding on to a personal economic adviser who allowed his opposition to the Chancellor's economic policies to become public knowledge, she was making Lawson's position impossible. She gave credence to the growing awareness that she was now losing her touch by insisting in public that Lawson was 'superb' and 'unassailable' even as she was failing to take the steps that would keep him from resigning. She even professed ignorance as to why he had resigned. Towards the end of her premiership, one of her backbenchers said that she was now 'off her trolley', implying that she ought to be carted off by men in white coats to a mental hospital. One of her own ministers told a journalist that she had become 'mad, completely mad'.[64]

Full-blown hubris became evident when, on 30 October 1990, she returned to the House of Commons after a meeting in Rome of European Union heads of government, where she had issued a series of statements in a press conference on what she would not put up with. The scene in the Commons was well described by the *Guardian*'s political commentator, Hugo Young: 'Returning home, she had not cooled off. True, as quite often happened in the Thatcher decade, the relevant Whitehall officials effected a certain hosing down' so that the text of what she read out was controlled. But in answer to questions,

> it became in its monosyllabic brutality, the rubric of one of her most famous parliamentary moments, leaping with rage, ringing round the chamber, startling

even those who in eleven years had much experience of the Thatcher vocabulary on Europe. 'No...no...no,' she bawled, her eye seemingly directed to the fields and seas, the hills and the landing-grounds, where the island people would never surrender.[65]

Her over-the-top performance that day in Parliament did not go down well with her party's MPs. In my autobiography, I described her as being 'on an emotional high and the adrenalin was pumping round her system as she handbagged every federalist proposal'.[66] In its absolute certainty of view and the uncompromising manner in which it was expressed, her words brought to mind the famous crude headline in the *Sun* newspaper about the then President of the European Commission, Jacques Delors, 'Up Yours Delors'.

One figure whom her performance particularly upset was her deputy, Sir Geoffrey Howe, an enthusiastic European. He had been her loyal first Chancellor of the Exchequer and in many respects architect of the Thatcherite economic policies of her government. Howe had then been Foreign Secretary and was demoted to leader of the House of Commons. Thatcher became increasingly contemptuous of his mild manner and her willingness to scorn and humiliate him publicly in Cabinet embarrassed even her thickest-skinned colleagues. This was hubris in its rawest form. Over the European Union Howe was ready to act. Nemesis followed his resignation speech in the House of Commons, which was all the more devastating because of the modest manner of its delivery. Within a month she had been forced out of office.

The political tragedy for Margaret Thatcher came about because she had pitted herself against her own source of power in Parliament, the Conservative MPs. She had reached a stage where not only was she not listening to her parliamentary colleagues but she appeared to enjoy deriding their views. The Cabinet had been reduced in stature and in quality. Majority opinion in the Conservative parliamentary party was frequently flouted or manipulated. People of substance, who well knew that Cabinet government was a great constitutional safeguard, had allowed this to develop over the years to the detriment of the British democratic system. It was not just because Thatcher was a woman that the Cabinet had been so supine but it was a material factor. With the Cabinet too weak to act, it was left to the Conservative MPs to show their power. A leader who had won three general elections was removed – not by the nation's voters but within the rules of a parliamentary democracy by her own MPs. For those who believe in representative democracy and decisive leadership it was a perfect example of the democratic control mechanisms over a leader's hubris actually working. Her nemesis was the almost inevitable consequence of a democratic leader succumbing to hubris syndrome. She and her friends preferred to categorise it as treachery and referred to it as a political assassination.

Thatcher's replacement followed swiftly against the background of the impending Gulf War. The Conservative party's political fortunes rapidly revived under her successor, John Major, who acquitted himself well during that war. He went on to win the general election of 1992.

The ageing Soviet leadership in the Cold War

It is easy to forget now how dangerous the world still was in the late 1970s and early 1980s. In 1978, for example, General Sir John Hackett, who had become an academic, wrote, along with some other strategic thinkers, a book called *The Third World War*,[67] which was not alarmist but highly credible. It showed how war between NATO and the Warsaw Pact countries could easily start from a small escalation of tension in apparently logical steps in Europe.

Since, under Soviet communist rule, secrecy had become the leitmotiv of Kremlin decision-making, it was not surprising that Western democracies developed a passionate interest in studying the slightest signs of change, including in health, amongst the leaders of the Politburo. In the process was spawned what became virtually a new academic subject – Kremlinology. In 1977, when, as Foreign Secretary, I was due to visit Moscow, I was asked by Maurice Oldfield, Head of the Secret Intelligence Service (MI6), to observe and comment on the health of the chairman of the Presidium of the Supreme Soviet, Leonid Brezhnev. There had been rumours that Brezhnev had been treated for cancer of the throat. However, when I met him in the Kremlin and talked to him for some time I could find no obvious abnormality although my interpreter felt his speech had changed. What was clear to me, however, was that Brezhnev was ageing fast. At a meeting in Vienna in 1979 he was virtually carried in by two huge KGB officers, and he did not even attend the meeting in December that year when Yury Andropov, Andrei Gromyko, Boris Ponomarev and Marshal Dmitry Ustinov made the massive blunder of invading Afghanistan; Brezhnev just signed off on it in his own office.[68] It was symbolic that the fall of the Soviet Empire started with a collective decision taken by a decrepit leadership over a country that had defeated British forces at the height of the British Empire's power.

Brezhnev died in November 1982 and was succeeded by Andropov, aged sixty-eight, the former head of the KGB. Three months after taking office he was needing to have regular kidney dialysis. Less than two years later he too died, having had one kidney removed in October 1983. In February 1984, when attending Andropov's funeral and after shaking hands with the new President, Konstantin Chernenko, at a reception in the Kremlin, I mentioned to a journalist that it was clear to me that Chernenko, then seventy-three, had emphysema. That aside was soon flashed around the world somewhat to my embarrassment – as a doctor rather than a politician – and I spent days extricating myself from the definitive nature of the diagnosis. It was later confirmed that he did indeed have emphysema, but at the time I had based my observation on little more than hearing his wheezing chest. Ever since, I have resisted making a medical diagnosis of any head of government I have met, especially as my medical knowledge has increasingly grown out of date. Chernenko died in 1985, becoming the third Soviet leader to die within three years.

Unlike in large corporations, there is virtually no succession planning in politics. By and large political leaders cling to office for far too long, becoming suspicious of younger potential successors. The Soviet Union had reached the point when its aged leadership, stuck in the status quo, had ceased to be the fount of wisdom and had become resistant to any change. Fortunately, when Mikhail Gorbachev succeeded Chernenko, the Soviet Union chose a young, fit leader, albeit still a Leninist, to become its first President, whereas in East Germany, along with Albania the last bastion of unreformed communism, Erich Honecker was by 1989 old, ill and inflexible. It was a great step forward that Gorbachev refused to call on Soviet forces to clamp down in East Germany as unrest built up, and in 1989 he allowed the Berlin Wall to collapse.[69] But Gorbachev's vigorous health could not prevent the Soviet Union's demise and after its rapid break-up, Russia found itself led by a charismatic and brave figure for whom ill health was a serious problem.

Boris Yeltsin

Boris Yeltsin will go down in history as the first post-Soviet leader of Russia and the man who, notwithstanding Chechnya, presided over a remarkably peaceful transition from Soviet communism. But in his later years in power he had come to be seen by his contemporaries as a leader seriously incapacitated by ill health and drink who needed to be replaced. The degree of openness about Yeltsin's medical conditions and extremely complicated treatment was, given the past history of Kremlin secrecy, extraordinary.

A crash landing in Spain in May 1990, before he had come to power, had left Yeltsin with a painful leg which he dragged slightly from then on. He suffered from lower back pain and cardiac ischaemia or angina,* giving him heart pain. However, Yeltsin's health became a serious problem for the government of the Russian Federation only from 1994 when the nitroglycerine he had been taking, which he initially found alleviated the pain from his heart, stopped working. Yeltsin began to rely more and more on painkillers and alcohol. Politically, he also started to restrict his inner circle, losing the attractive openness of the early years.

Yeltsin had been very clearly drunk in Berlin on 31 August 1994 for a ceremony to mark the departure of the last Russian troops. On that occasion, he snatched the baton from the conductor's hand and conducted the Berlin Police Orchestra himself before singing a Russian folk song. A month later at Shannon airport, Yeltsin failed to leave his plane, despite having the entire Irish Cabinet assembled at the foot of the stairs to greet him. He is widely reputed to have fallen into a drunken sleep after heavy drinking on a return journey from a summit meeting with President Clinton in the United States and Yeltsin later said his officials had not wanted to wake him. However, it has also been claimed that he suffered a serious heart attack on the flight back to Moscow. Publicly it may have been preferable for the rumours of drunkenness to persist rather than knowledge of a heart attack be known. Yeltsin had in fact suffered five heart attacks while in office, it was revealed in 2004. Two of them, in July and October 1995, had been serious. By January 1996 only 10 per cent of Russians said to pollsters they would vote for Yeltsin in the presidential election due on 16 June.

It was surprising, therefore, that Yeltsin won the 1996 election. He did so only after raising a large amount of money from future oligarchs through a 'loans for shares' scheme. The Western democracies turned a blind eye to the corruption of democratic process, which encouraged Yeltsin to brilliantly exploit a lavishly funded media campaign. Yeltsin signed a decree allowing assets still owned by the state to be sold not to the citizens through the voucher scheme, which Prime Minister Yegor Gaidar and his deputy, Anatoly Chubais,

---

* Cardiac ischaemia can be another name for angina and results in changes in the heart muscle due to lack of a proper blood supply. Pain is present but it may not be as acute as in angina.

had introduced for rapid privatisation, but 'through an auction rigged in favour of large banks that then made massive loans to the government. As a result, a handful of financial-industrial groups ended up with some of the largest energy and metal companies in the world at liquidation-sale prices.'[70]

In the election Yeltsin persuaded the Russian people to vote for him by simply pointing out that the alternative was the Communist leader, Gennady Zyuganov. In a defiant campaign speech on 15 February at Yekaterinburg Yeltsin warned the Russian people of returning to the past. He was hoarse and coughing as he quoted Solzhenitsyn's famous words about perishing 'under the red wheel'. In Moscow, wits recalled the old proverb '*Masterstvo propit' nel'zya*' (You cannot completely lose your talent, no matter how hard you drink).[71] Though reducing his drinking during the campaign helped Yeltsin, as did his medical treatment, it was his drive as a politician who had recovered the will to win which probably made the crucial difference. Some of these flamboyant performances may have been helped by his doctors discovering that Yeltsin was suffering from obstructive sleep apnoea and giving him oxygen at night, which could have resulted in a proper sleep, a lifting of depression and greatly increased energy in the day. All we know for certain is that he had been sleeping badly and this improved.

Yeltsin just won the first round against Zyuganov but neither had over 50 per cent and General Aleksandr Lebed, who ran third, agreed to be co-opted by Yeltsin into his team before the run-off. Despite another heart attack in the form of chest pains followed by depression hitting Yeltsin again, on 3 July he beat Zyuganov by a margin of 15 per cent. Yet, by his inauguration on 9 August, Yeltsin was hardly able to walk, had slurred speech and was clearly very ill.

In September 1996 it was announced that Yeltsin would have open heart surgery and President Clinton arranged for him to be seen by Dr Michael DeBakey from Houston. He was found to have hypothyroidism, which is likely to have contributed to his coronary artery disease and to his puffy face, as well as an inability to metabolise excess alcohol. DeBakey recommended a delay for the operation and more preparation and so it was not until 7 November that Yeltsin had surgery – a seven-hour quintuple bypass operation. Chancellor Helmut Kohl told the Americans that two German doctors who had participated in the operation thought that Yeltsin would not last until the 2000 presidential election.

Yeltsin stepped down on 31 December 1999 and his Prime Minister, Vladimir Putin, became acting President and won the election in the spring of the following year. Yeltsin not only survived but went on to enjoy a peaceful retirement, watching Putin win again by a large margin in 2004 with genuine popular support. Yeltsin was the first Russian leader to have a Russian Orthodox burial for over one hundred years when he died from heart failure on 23 April 2007, aged seventy-six.

Critics of Yeltsin's record point to the wars in Chechnya and to the blood on his hands following his ordering of the shelling and storming of the White House in Moscow in October 1993, when some anti-reformist members of the parliament tried to mount a coup. His critics also hold him responsible for handing over so many of the state's assets to the oligarchs. But in defence of Yeltsin, he alone, on top of a tank in August 1991, stopped any reversion to communism. He introduced more freedom, more choice and market reforms which by 2008 had improved the lives of many Russians. President Yeltsin also handsomely repaid President Clinton for his consistent and tolerant support by playing an important role in the 1999 Russian–US diplomatic initiative which brought the war in Kosovo to a diplomatic end without the United States and other NATO countries having to deploy ground troops. Most of all, after the largely peaceful revolution from Soviet communism, overseen by Yeltsin, the possibility exists that by the end of the first quarter of the twenty-first century Russia will develop a stable democracy. It has gone through a necessary phase under Vladimir Putin of greater centralised discipline and a managed democracy. Hopefully, and no one can be sure, Russia will keep a hold on democracy; if so, Yeltsin, whether sick or well, sober or drunk, will deserve great credit from historians.

George Bush Sr

George Bush Sr became US President in 1988, after eight years as Ronald Reagan's Vice President. In May 1991 he had become unusually tired and short of breath while out jogging. He was admitted to hospital and it was publicly announced that he had been diagnosed with atrial fibrillation. He was later confirmed as having thyrotoxicosis,* but was able to continue as

---

* Hyperthyroidism or thyrotoxicosis is revealed by blood tests which show excessive amounts of thyroid hormone, an iodine-containing substance synthesised and secreted by the thyroid gland. Thyroid hormone controls the basal metabolic rate (BMR) of the body and when present in excess, in hyperthyroidism, the BMR increases. The symptoms of hyperthyroidism are many and varied – a faster heartbeat, loss of weight, irritability, sweating, tremor, anxiety, increased appetite and a dislike of external heat because the body is generating too much heat internally.

President, although there seemed to be a fall-off in his performance. The very high polling support after the Gulf War fell away as the wars in the former Yugoslavia developed in the summer of 1991, marked by savage ethnic cleansing. Also people began to wonder whether Saddam Hussein ought to have been removed from power in Iraq, as his attacks on the Kurds demonstrated his defiance of the United Nations ceasefire terms. In a rather lacklustre campaign President Bush lost in November 1992 to Bill Clinton and at one stage in their television debate Bush was seen to look at his watch as if he was bored. There did not seem to be the same vigour and attention to detail that he had displayed over the Gulf War and some saw this as a side effect of his thyrotoxicosis.

President Clinton had no major illnesses while in the White House. It began to be assumed at the start of the twenty-first century that heads of government would, following Bush's openness, be readier to tell the truth about their medical condition. Sadly that did not happen, and we will see in Chapter 7 that neither Tony Blair nor George W. Bush was prepared to be honest with their electors about their medical condition.

Jacques Chirac

In France, nearly ten years after François Mitterrand had left office, it seemed that the lessons from his medical cover-up had still not been learnt. On Friday 2 September 2005, President Jacques Chirac, after a full day of meetings, developed a bad headache and problems with his vision. His Élysée Palace doctor was called and he was admitted to the Val-de-Grâce military hospital that night. This hospitalisation was not reported to the public until the following day, when a medical communiqué was issued describing 'a little vascular accident prompting a slight trouble of vision'. There was no explanation as to whether the problem was primarily in the brain or the eye,

---

Other, more serious, symptoms are an abnormal heartbeat and often atrial fibrillation. Generally the patient feels below par and unwell and notices a dramatic improvement in their own sense of well-being if successfully treated. In Bush's case, because of his age, he was given radioactive iodine therapy; this is given if the patient is over thirty-five. The aim of the treatment is to destroy only part of the thyroid gland, leaving some tissue unaffected and still able to produce thyroid hormone but in a lesser quantity. If well judged this can mean it is not necessary to take any replacement therapy. If treatment is needed it is given in the form of thyroxine tablets for the rest of the patient's life as a replacement therapy.

allowing rumour to build up that Chirac had suffered a stroke, involving the brain. There were no further details, except for the Prime Minister, Dominique de Villepin, revealing that the President was walking on the Saturday. Speculation continued and politicians from Chirac's own party criticised the absence of medical guidance for the public. Outrage was then expressed in the press when it was learned that not even the French Prime Minister had been told of the President's hospitalisation on the Friday night. This was contrasted unfavourably with Chirac's promise in 1995, in the aftermath of Mitterrand's cover-up, to provide 'transparency' in the case of any medical incident involving himself when President. *Le Monde* thundered: 'In France we practice a cult of secrecy which would have done the Kremlin in the former Soviet Union proud.'

Then on 29 January 2007 President Chirac, in an interview with the weekly magazine *Le Nouvel Observateur*, the *New York Times* and the *International Herald Tribune*, totally contradicted previous French policy by suggesting that an Iran that possessed nuclear weapons would not be much of a danger. Next day the same journalists were summoned to the Élysée to be told by Chirac that he had made a mistake. 'It is I who was wrong and I do not want to contest it.' Chirac also retracted his statement that Jerusalem would be razed if Iran launched a nuclear weapon, claiming, somewhat questionably, that a number of third countries could stop an Iranian missile reaching Israel. What was new was that the long-held tradition of French journalism that allowed the Élysée to prepare a heavily edited transcript deleting any inappropriate answers had been challenged, and the journalists frankly reported on Thursday 1 February in the *International Herald Tribune* on the President's state of health, saying that in the first interview

> he appeared distracted at times, grasping for names and dates and relying on advisers to fill in the blanks. His hands shook slightly. When he spoke about climate change, he read from prepared talking points printed in large letters and highlighted in yellow and pink. By contrast, in the second interview, which came just after lunch, he appeared both confident and completely comfortable with the subject matter.

Nevertheless, the President's office denounced the publication of his comments 'as a shameful campaign' with the American media 'using any excuse to engage in France-bashing'.

It was clear after this episode of confusion that the 74-year-old President was in no fit condition to run for a third term in May 2007, and the vain attempt to hold open that option was dropped on 11 March when in a TV address he told the French people he would not seek a new mandate. The truth was that once again a head of government had clung on to office when too old and refused to face the reality of ageing, particularly after losing the referendum he called on the new EU constitution in 2005. On the credit side, Chirac was the first French President to acknowledge France's responsibility for deporting Jews during the German occupation in the Second World War. He also kept France out of the Iraqi debacle from 2003.

Ariel Sharon

The last of the heads of government in the period 1901–2007 to suffer a serious illness was the Israeli Prime Minister Ariel Sharon. On 18 December 2005 Sharon, then seventy-seven years old, had a cerebral vascular incident in his office involving some minor confusion but no loss of consciousness. This came at a crucial time politically, for Sharon was leaving the Likud party to found a new party called Kadima, in which he would fight the general election expected to take place early in 2006. At the time of this first acknowledged stroke it was recognised that undue secrecy would only compound anxiety in the country and so some medical information was released as he was investigated.

Only a few days before, his two personal physicians had said to the mass circulation newspaper *Yedioth Ahronoth* that 'Sharon is healthy' and that their periodic check-ups did not show anything unusual apart from excess weight. Yet despite such an upbeat report all those close to Sharon knew that for at least a year he had been showing signs of physical deterioration. He walked with difficulty, becoming very short of breath. His advisers made certain that he would not have to climb stairs and counted the steps to be taken between conference rooms. He used the small lift to his office and even the walk from it to his desk in front of TV cameras was an effort. He began to avoid detail, sticking to his prepared talking points, although according to aides his intellectual capacity was not affected.[72]

Earlier, in April 2005, two journalists from *Haaretz*, in an interview with Sharon, had asked him about his health. He immediately responded: 'I invite you to see my medical report. This could have a bad effect on other people's health!' They then asked to see the file and felt that Sharon had not expected this request. 'In fact for me this would be quite convenient,' he said. 'I don't know how this is done.' They still insisted that they see the report and Sharon moved in his chair and turned to his spokesman. 'Ah, how do we do this? Are there rules?'

'We'll definitely check,' replied his spokesman.

In an attempt to avoid embarrassment, Sharon declared: 'I'd like to but it's just not the usual thing to do here. Maybe you can ask...' and the conversation petered out.

The journalists reported: 'With this the matter ended. The rules were not found and the medical file was revealed, partially, only after Sharon's first stroke, when the people around him tried to show that he was healthy, fit to serve and be re-elected.' This was the sort of defensive response that for years politicians around the world had been adopting and getting away with.

On initial investigation in December 2005 Sharon was found to have a small hole in the wall of his heart, an atrial septal defect present from birth. It was felt that his stroke had been due to a blood clot forming in or around the hole then interfering with the blood supply to his brain. The decision was made to let him recover and then to operate and seal the hole by using a device inserted through the oesophagus while under partial sedation.

But according to the *New York Times* in January 2006, during this brief hospital stay doctors diagnosed that he also had cerebral amyloid angiopathy, a relatively common condition in the elderly involving weak blood vessels in the brain. The medical dilemma was whether to give blood-thinning drugs to stop a recurrence of the blood clots and accept thereby an increased risk of a bleed from the weak arteries in the brain. It was also announced that the retired general, who was only 5 feet 7 inches tall but weighed 18 stone 8 pounds, had been told he should lose 100 pounds before the operation on his heart.

But before this operation could take place, Sharon suffered the acknowledged complication of his treatment, a serious bleed into the brain. He was operated on twice to remove this blood and relieve the pressure building up on the brain. He was then put into a medically induced coma. He was still alive in hospital at the end of 2007. Perhaps if he had not had anticoagulants initially he might have recovered. It is an inescapable fact that iatrogenic disease, or illness caused by doctors' interventions, is one of the largest categories of illness. Sharon's deputy, Ehud Olmert, was made acting Prime Minister and put in control of the country. Olmert and his new Kadima party won the largest share of the vote in the general election on 29 March 2006 and formed a coalition government, with Olmert formally taking over as Prime Minister soon after the election. It is to Olmert's credit that on 29

October 2007 he announced that several days before he had been told that he had early-stage prostate cancer. It would require a short surgical procedure to treat a microscopic growth that had not spread. He would be carrying on in office and would not require chemotherapy or radiation treatment.

Sharon was not the first Israeli Prime Minister to have been ill in office: Levi Eshkol, Golda Meir and Menachem Begin were too. Begin, after the signing in 1979 of the Camp David accords, became very depressed, precipitated in part by the undeserved criticism he attracted for agreeing to give up every hectare of Sinai to the Egyptians. His depression deepened in 1982 with the death of his wife. In 1983 there was a very critical report blaming him and Sharon, then defence minister, for not doing more to prevent the massacres at the Shatila and Sabra refugee camps in the Lebanon. Eventually when Begin resigned in August of that year his depression had become incapacitating and he lived a solitary and sad life until his death.

Israel, of all countries, with its coalition governments and living under constant military threat, needs a Prime Minister capable of functioning at the top of their capacity. Its head of government faces day-to-day decisions affecting the nation's security, decisions which, though often referred to the Cabinet, sometimes have to be made within minutes by the Prime Minister of the day and where the political consequences of action or inaction can quickly be weighed only by that person, the Prime Minister. Not surprisingly, any question about an Israeli Prime Minister's health is bound to loom large with the public. What is needed in Israel and other countries are compulsory rules for independent medical assessment and formal arrangements requiring the retirement of a Prime Minister when illness renders them incapable of carrying out their duties (see Chapter 8).

Part II

Case histories

3

Prime Minister Eden's illness and Suez

I would never have done it without squaring the Americans and once I'd started I would never have dared stop.

Winston Churchill, 1956[1]

Anthony Eden had a brilliant political career. A member of Parliament at twenty-six, he became, in 1935 and aged only thirty-eight, the youngest Foreign Secretary in the twentieth century. He resigned on 20 February 1938 over Neville Chamberlain's rejection of an initiative from Franklin Roosevelt on Europe. He came back into Winston Churchill's Cabinet in 1940 as the minister responsible for the Army and became Foreign Secretary again in 1941 when Lord Halifax, who Churchill did not trust, was sent to be ambassador in Washington. In 1945, when Churchill lost the general election, Eden became deputy leader of the Conservative Party in opposition. He returned to run the Foreign Office when the Conservatives, still under Churchill, beat Labour in the general election of 1951. In all he served for over ten years as Foreign Secretary.

Debonair and handsome, he was the pin-up of many Conservative women and popular across the party political divide. By any standard of fairness, Churchill, after suffering two heart attacks in 1949, should have retired to let Eden fight the forthcoming general election as leader. But he hung on and on. Eden's frustration at endlessly waiting for the old man to go came through every now and then: it was obviously gnawing away at him, contributing to the tension and temper tantrums, usually in private and over trivial rather than serious matters, that occasionally broke through Eden's charm and amiability.

It was a misfortune not just for Eden, but for international diplomacy in the ensuing years, that on 12 April 1953 in the London Clinic what should have been a routine operation on the Foreign Secretary, a cholecystectomy or surgical removal of the gall bladder, went badly wrong.[2] The operation was undertaken on the advice of Eden's physician, Sir Horace Evans, because of previous episodes of jaundice and abdominal pain and the presence of gallstones. Evans recommended three different surgeons to Eden, all with expertise in biliary tract surgery. Fatefully, Eden rejected them, choosing instead to be operated on by the sixty-year-old John Hume, a general surgeon. In Eden's words, Hume had 'removed my appendix when I was younger, and I'll go to him'.[3]

Hume was so agitated that the first operation had to be put on hold for nearly an hour to allow him to compose his nerves. After what happened in that operation Hume felt he could not lead a second operation, which was led instead by Guy Blackburn, Hume's assistant at the first. This operation has been described as 'even more tense than the first, and Eden was within a whisker of death at several stages of the lengthy and traumatic process'.[4] The generally accepted view, supported by his official biographer, was that Eden's biliary duct was accidentally cut at the first operation and Eden was told that 'the knife slipped'.[5] Another source was blunter, describing what happened in one or other of the operations as a 'schoolboy howler' of surgery in which 'inadvertently [they] tied the bile duct as it comes out of the liver',[6] resulting in the obstructive problems in the biliary tract.*

From the start Churchill, as Prime Minister, involved himself fully if unhelpfully in Eden's treatment, constantly reminding Hume how eminent his patient was and how nothing should go wrong. Churchill intervened again after the London operations when a third operation was proposed, this time in the United States. Evans had asked Richard Cattell, a world-renowned expert in this field of surgery and who was by chance in London lecturing, to see Eden. Cattell insisted that Eden should travel to Boston for the third operation and Evans agreed. But Lord Moran, who, as well as being

---

* Professor Gabriel Kune, a specialist in biliary tract surgery, believes that there was at some stage in the London operations an injury of the right branch of the hepatic artery. This he supposes because at the two reoperations in Boston (see below) there was found to be a high injury of the common hepatic duct very close to the right hepatic artery. Also at the 1970 reoperation the right lobe of the liver was found to be abnormally small, which suggests to Kune that at the time of the bile duct injury the right hepatic artery was also inadvertently ligated and this relative ischaemia, since the liver has a second blood supply from the portal vein, led to the development of both the stricture and the liver lobe atrophy. There is no evidence, however, that Eden's liver metabolism was affected.

Churchill's doctor had earlier been Eden's (once diagnosing a duodenal ulcer), thought Eden's operation could be done just as well in London. Initially, Churchill felt that to go abroad would reflect badly on Britain and, no doubt egged on by Moran, persisted to the extent that Evans and Cattell had to go and talk to him in 10 Downing Street. In the Cabinet Room Churchill spoke of having been operated upon for an appendicectomy on a kitchen table. In persuading him that Eden should go to America both doctors explained patiently that an appendix operation was a relatively simple procedure whereas a bile duct repair operation was of a quite different order in its complexity and skill.[7]

On 23 June 1953, in Boston, Cattell performed a complicated surgical procedure on Eden. On the same day, back home, Churchill suffered a very serious stroke. At an official dinner for the Italian Prime Minister, Alcide De Gasperi, he suddenly became unsteady on his legs and his speech became slurred. Next morning his left arm was paralysed and he could only walk with assistance. He presided over a Cabinet meeting that morning. After the meeting Sir Russell Brain was called in by Moran and he diagnosed a stroke, but there was no aphasia and Churchill walked with 'only a slight trace of unsteadiness'. After the examination Churchill gave Brain an address on foreign policy.

> Churchill discussed the problem of Eden and said that if he, Churchill, gave up control of the Foreign Office and put someone else in, there would be no post for Eden to go to when he got back. It was clear that if Churchill had to resign owing to illness, Butler would become Prime Minister.[8]

Brain then saw Churchill on 26 June at Chartwell, by which time his condition had deteriorated. His speech was more dysarthric, his left hand weaker and his gait more unsteady. Between examinations by Brain on 28 June and 3 July Churchill had had a period when he could not walk but he had started to improve; when Brain saw him on 25 August at No. 10 he noted that the Prime Minister had been very tired after a Cabinet meeting the previous week. It is interesting to note that on 8 June 1955 Churchill, by now having retired, had another stroke, confirmed by Brain, who saw him at Chartwell on 22 June, and yet another on 20 October 1956.

Eden recovered from his operation, returned home and resumed his responsibilities as Foreign Secretary. He was 'then well until 1954 when he experienced fevers and chills on one occasion and in 1955 on three occasions.

None was severe or prolonged.'* It was reasonable for Eden to believe that his post-operative health now allowed him to succeed Churchill as Prime Minister. According to his wife, his doctor, Sir Horace Evans, saw him on 14 February 1955. 'He wouldn't hear of Anthony not being well enough to become PM, naturally.'[9] Churchill finally stepped down on 6 April 1955. Always determined to call an early election, Eden did so and won in May with a majority in the House of Commons up from seventeen to fifty-eight and 49.7 per cent of the overall vote, the highest percentage total won by any party in the post-war age. His victory was brought about partly by what opinion polls had always shown – that Eden was one of the most popular politicians of his era.

The general election was followed by a four-power summit in Geneva in July, which the American President, Dwight Eisenhower, had helpfully agreed could be announced before the election to give Eden a political boost. Churchill had persistently argued for holding a summit in 1953 but Eden and Eisenhower had been reluctant to support the idea, believing that the new Soviet leaders would not be ready for serious negotiations so soon after Stalin's death. Now Eden was able to make his own assessment of the Soviet delegation, led by Nikolai Bulganin and Nikita Khrushchev, on whether progress could be made on the issues surrounding nuclear weapons. In December, Eden reshuffled his Cabinet, moving a reluctant Harold Macmillan from the Foreign Office to the Treasury and appointing Selwyn Lloyd as Foreign Secretary. This ensured that Eden regained control of the Foreign

---

* In November 2003 an excellent review article was published by an American surgeon, Dr John W. Braasch, titled 'Anthony Eden's (Lord Avon) Biliary Tract Saga' (*Annals of Surgery*, vol. 238, pp. 772–5). Braasch had operated on Eden in 1970 and had had personal communication with Cattell, who had undertaken the third operation – a surgical procedure called an end-to-side hepaticojejunostomy using a rubber Y-tube as a stent – in June 1953. Also Cattell did the fourth operation on Eden in America in April 1957. Both men were associated with the Lahey Clinic in Massachusetts and this surgical retrospection is the closest we will probably ever get to what exactly happened. Braasch tries very hard to be fair to all concerned and even quotes a minority opinion written by a retired London surgeon, claiming to be one of the few people who knew the facts, to another US surgeon that while the ligature on the cystic duct had blown following the first operation, which was then evacuated in the second re-exploration operation on 29 April, Eden's 'common duct was not injured at all. When he left for America his biliary fistula had dried up, he was not jaundiced and he was perfectly well.' The letter must have been passed on to Cattell, who was not only arguably one of the great abdominal surgeons of the twentieth century, but also a gentleman, and he did not respond to the several insulting remarks contained in it.

Office. Yet on 27 December 1955 Clarissa Eden wrote in her diary: 'Anthony feeling tired and low all the time. Depressed about the press, about Russia and about Jordan.'[10]

The fateful year of Eden's premiership, 1956, started with a lot of press criticism and a particularly hurtful article which appeared in the Conservative-supporting *Daily Telegraph* on 3 January. It said: 'There is a favourite gesture with the Prime Minister. To emphasise a point he will clash one fist to smash the open palm of the other hand but the smash is seldom heard' and it went on to say that people were waiting in vain for the 'smack of firm government'. This rankled with Eden and it may well have been a factor in making him so determined to act forcefully when, later in the year, the crisis over Suez erupted. Also a few days after the article, Rab Butler, then Leader of the House, said in an interview: 'My determination is to support the Prime Minister in all his difficulties' and then unwisely assented, without any qualification, to the Press Association reporter's loaded question as to whether Eden was 'the best Prime Minister we have'. It was a rather typical Butler equivocation but the headline was damaging to Eden and one which he never forgot.

On 6 February Eden wrote to his wife Clarissa from Government House, Ottawa: 'I am well but was very tired yesterday, so stayed in bed all day.' That is not the behaviour of a fit man. Lack of sleep and tiredness are too often underplayed when trying to assess the effect of people's health on their decision-making. The following month, in a rancorous debate in the House of Commons about the situation in Jordan, Eden uncharacteristically lost his temper and the opposition benches echoed to the derisive sound of 'Resign!'. According to Eden's biographer, Robert Rhodes James, Clarissa wrote in her diary on 7 March: 'The events in Jordan have shattered A. He is fighting very bad fatigue which is sapping his power of thought. Tonight's winding up of the debate was a shambles.'[11] However, her own book, drawing on her diary, says only: 'The events in Jordan are shattering,'[12] with no mention of fighting fatigue. General John Bagot Glubb, the British commander in chief of the Jordanian army, had been peremptorily dismissed by King Hussein, and Eden blamed this on the influence over Hussein of Egypt's President Nasser.

Anthony Nutting, then a junior Foreign Office minister, describes another of Eden's outbursts, with him shouting down the phone: 'What's all this nonsense about isolating Nasser or "neutralising" him as you call it? I want him destroyed, can't you understand? I want him removed and if you and the

Foreign Office don't agree, then you'd better come to the Cabinet and explain why.'[13]*

Nasser

Britain had ruled Egypt from 1882 until 1922, and had strongly influenced its monarchy right up to King Farouk's overthrow by Gamal Abdel Nasser in 1952. Free passage along the Suez Canal was regarded by Eden and his generation as Britain's lifeline. Eden began to develop a personal animosity to Nasser, having met him once in Cairo when Foreign Secretary. On 20 February 1955 Clarissa Eden described General Nasser in her diary, after meeting him at a dinner at the British embassy in Cairo: 'The General is thirty-five, has never been out of Egypt, is rather inscrutable and very polite with indifferent English.' She wrote that later Nasser turned out to have been deeply offended by the whole evening: he felt that Eden should have come to see him as President; he had attended in a suit, not knowing that Eden would be wearing black tie; and 'finally, he was offended by Anthony speaking to him in Arabic'.[14] However, previously Eden had courageously faced up to

---

* There are many accounts, some true, others false, of Eden's irritability. One incident is described involving a Foreign Office lawyer who reported back to Eden on the research he had ordered into the legality of Nasser's action (in nationalising the Suez Canal), saying that it was indeed perfectly legal so long as he did not close the canal to shipping. 'Eden allegedly tore up the report in front of the lawyer and flung it in the lawyer's face.' (Donald Neff, *Warriors at Suez: Eisenhower Takes America into the Middle East* (New York: Linden Press/Simon & Schuster, 1981), p. 278.) Since his own private secretary was almost certainly also present on this occasion it is stretching the imagination to believe that Eden behaved quite like this report. One has to be very careful about assuming that stories like these are true. To illustrate this, the *Times* on 29 November 2003 carried an interview with David Cornwell, better known as John le Carré, who was a master at Eton during Suez. Cornwell said that during the crisis Eden found time on several evenings to climb into the prime ministerial car to drive to Eton and consult his old housemaster about what to do. Two people who knew Eden's movements challenged whether he could have made such visits and his biographer, Richard Thorpe, pointed out that Eden's housemaster had died in February 1956. All received apologies from le Carré and a promise of retraction but even this story may at some stage reappear as fact. Another example is an incident described in Leonard Mosley's book on John Foster Dulles, in which the widely respected military expert and historian Captain R. H. Liddell Hart is reputed to have had a meeting with Eden in 10 Downing Street during which Eden threw an inkwell at him. (Leonard Mosley, *Dulles: A Biography of Eleanor, Allen and John Foster Dulles and Their Family Network* (London: Hodder & Stoughton, 1978), p. 409.) Yet this story appears to be pure fiction, confirmed by Liddell Hart's wife and son, since the men did not actually meet during the Suez crisis.

reality and negotiated the Suez Canal Base Agreement, involving British troops withdrawing, in 1954, which Winston Churchill had disliked and which had been strongly criticised by a section of the Conservative Party. Under it the last British troops left Port Said on 13 June 1956.

As Prime Minister, Eden had been involved in the US–UK discussions over the financing of Egypt's Aswan High Dam on the Nile, an important project for Egypt. President Eisenhower was recovering from ileitis and his Secretary of State, John Foster Dulles, concerned about growing Soviet influence on Egypt, was hardening against supporting the dam. On 17 July the British ambassador was told to say in Washington that the UK was not in favour of withdrawing from the project. Dulles concluded, rightly, that the British were speaking for the record and did not feel strongly. Under pressure from Congress, Dulles announced US withdrawal on 19 July. In London, the President of the Board of Trade, Peter Thorneycroft, went to see Eden to argue for the High Dam and bore the brunt of one of Eden's famous rages. Eden resented Thorneycroft's intrusion, saying that after the American decision the project was dead and that a suggestion to rescue it was monstrous. This was an indication of Eden's volatility. Lord Moran in his diary entry for 21 July wrote: 'The political world is full of Eden's moods at No. 10.' The day before the Cabinet had agreed that the UK would withdraw financial support for the dam.

Then, six days later, Nasser acted. On 26 July, the anniversary of King Farouk's abdication, in a passionate speech in Manshiya Square in Alexandria he announced the nationalisation of the Suez Canal Company. It was in part retaliation for the decision over the Aswan High Dam. By chance, when news of Nasser's speech came through, Eden happened to be hosting a dinner in 10 Downing Street for King Faisal of Iraq and his Prime Minister, Nuri al-Said. The Iraqi advice was to hit Nasser hard and fast. After dinner Eden called in the US chargé d'affaires, so seeking – ironically, in the light of subsequent events – to involve the Americans from the start. He also called in the French ambassador to join the discussion of Nasser's action, along with four Cabinet ministers: Selwyn Lloyd, the Foreign Secretary and an old friend; the Marquess of Salisbury; Viscount Kilmuir, the Lord Chancellor; and the Earl of Home, later to be Prime Minister as Sir Alec Douglas-Home; as well as two chiefs of staff, Field Marshal Sir Gerald Templer and Admiral Earl Mountbatten. The meeting lasted until 4.00 a.m.

Nationalisation, to Eden, was a direct threat to British interests and he began to see Nasser in 1956 as Mussolini in the 1930s. Publicly Eden declared that Nasser should not be allowed 'to have his thumb on our windpipe' and he made it clear he was ready to use British armed forces to lift the threat of Egypt interfering with the flow of ships along the Suez Canal.

In fact, though, Nasser was keen to show that Egypt had no intention of interfering with any nation's shipping and in the event few other nations, apart from Israel, feared this. The threat to world shipping was an issue on which Britain never really managed to mobilise international opinion. Furthermore, in the way he nationalised the company, Nasser cleverly tried to demonstrate that he was not acting illegally. Shareholders were bought out at the price prevailing on the Paris Bourse at the time Nasser's announcement was made. Nor was international opinion much concerned about Egypt's growing links with the Soviet Union. Most importantly, Eisenhower was not prepared to link the seizure of the canal with the danger from the Soviet Union, and he would turn out to be the single most important person in determining the outcome of the Suez crisis.

Eden's immediate decisions after Nasser's speech on 26 July – to prepare for but postpone immediate military action – were understandable given the attitude of the chiefs of staff, who had no enthusiasm for military action. But it can be argued that, if anything, Eden's decisions at this time were too cautious. This contrasts dramatically with the recklessness of his decision-making from 14 October, when his health had become a key factor. The day after Nasser's speech Eden did not immediately embrace Kilmuir's legal view that Britain could base its case to intervene militarily over Suez solely on the claim that Nasser's action was illegal. Nor did Eden take the view of one of his old and close friends, Viscount Cilcennin, then the First Lord of the Admiralty, that if force was to be used, it should be soon, during the summer. Delay was to prove fateful. Later in the autumn, according to Cilcennin, 'Nasser had covered many of his tracks.'[15] Nevertheless, the Cabinet sub-committee established for dealing with Suez minuted on 30 July that the immediate aim 'was to bring down the present Egyptian government'. So regime change was present from the start. Cilcennin also believed that Eden, who had never worked in America, did not understand the effect that the imminence of a presidential election, due in November, would have on the American response to any British action taken against Egypt.

It is not clear when Eden ruled out involving British troops already in Libya, for fear of an Arab backlash. Using these forces in Libya was something which he was still contemplating when Churchill went to see him very privately on 6 August. Churchill left behind a memo which he had dictated in the car and had had typed in a lay-by as he waited *en route* to Chequers, the Prime Minister's country home. Churchill warned Eden with great perceptiveness about just taking over the canal when Nasser's real power base was Cairo; and it is clear he believed that to threaten Cairo and other large towns the British armoured division in Libya would and should be used. The memo from Churchill said:

> The more one thinks of taking over the Canal, the less one likes it. The long causeway could be easily obstructed by a succession of mines. We should get much of the blame of stopping work, if it is to be up to the moment of our attack a smooth-running show. Cairo is Nasser's centre of power. I was very glad to hear that there would be no weakening about Libya on account of the [   ]* Prime Minister etc., but that the armoured divisions, properly supported by air, with any additional forces that may be needed, would be used. On the other side, a volte face should certainly free our hands about Israel. We should want them to menace and hold the Egyptians and not be drawn off against Jordan.[16]

Churchill saw that toppling Nasser would involve attacking Cairo. But the Cabinet believed that with three divisions on the canal it would not be long before Nasser fell from loss of face. Their plan was that British bombing would be designed for purely military purposes along the Suez Canal and would not extend to Cairo with the political purpose of toppling Nasser. Yet this underestimated the forces of nationalism that Nasser had unleashed. He would still control the country from Cairo and would be able to mount attacks on the invading forces. So there was a central weakness in the plan.

On 7 August Harold Macmillan as Chancellor of the Exchequer circulated a 'little note' to the Egypt Committee about his ideas for an invasion which reflected Churchill's views, told to Eden the day before. Eden told Macmillan that he had no business circulating papers without consulting him as Prime Minister – a sign of the tension that had developed between the two men.[17] The British chiefs of staff did not emerge well from the whole crisis, showing neither cohesion nor decisiveness. Throughout they feared a prolonged occupation of Egypt.

On 17 August Eden wrote to Churchill: 'I am sorry to have been away on Monday, but I needed a few hours off. I am very fit now.' He also said: 'Most

---

* Handwritten word, unclear in the original (added while car was in motion).

important of all, the Americans seem very firmly lined up with us on internationalisation' of the Suez Canal. Yet Eisenhower never hid from Eden his opposition to the use of force. On 3 September he wrote to Eden: 'I must tell you frankly that American public opinion flatly rejects the use of force. I really do not see how a successful result could be achieved by forceable [sic] means.'

There was a clear divergence of interest between Britain and the United States throughout the crisis. Britain was concerned not solely with the safety of vessels going through the Suez Canal; the British government wanted to control the canal. Considerations of prestige were also of major importance for Britain, and the government was not able to draw a clear distinction between the question of the canal and that of Nasser's regime. In retrospect, Guy Millard, Eden's private secretary, wrote in 1957 a most detailed private history of this period for the Foreign Office,[18] and came to the conclusion that it had been a mistake for Britain to try to solve the two problems simultaneously. This was a criticism of British policy made by the Americans during the crisis. Britain was not just interested in an arrangement to protect those whose ships used the canal, as envisaged in John Foster Dulles's Suez Canal Users Association initiative, it also wanted a new and different Egyptian government. But, as with the invasion of Iraq in 2003, the UK was not prepared openly to champion regime change; it used the threat to shipping as the excuse, rather as Britain and the United States used weapons of mass destruction as an excuse forty-six years later.

The stimulant 'purple hearts'

There has been much written and said about Eden's behaviour and health over the next three months. Some of it is gossip, some mere speculation, some fact. As to the state of his health during the crisis, his engagement diary shows that he consulted Sir Horace Evans or other doctors on at least ten occasions between the Suez Canal nationalisation and the end of October.[19] He also spent the weekend of 5–8 October in hospital (see below). Eden's own diary entries are virtually non-existent during the Suez crisis. One of the few entries, for 21 August, reads:

> Felt rather wretched after a poor night. Awoke 3.30 a.m. onwards with pain. Had to take pethidine in the end. Appropriately the doctors came. Kling was more optimistic than Horace. We are to try a slightly different regime. Agreed no final decision until a holiday has given me a chance to decide in good health.

The 'final decision' related to the possibility of another operation, the 'different regime' to a change of drug treatment. Pethidine is a morphine derivative given for severe pain. Yet despite having taken it, Eden chaired a Cabinet meeting at noon and had other meetings in the afternoon before seeing his doctors again later that day. On 7 September he commented: 'After fair night. Sleep at least uninterrupted, but not long, 5 hours.' A week later Eden's diary records: 'There were two difficult days in the House. I was quite exhausted by the end of the debate.'

In 2004 the distinguished journalist Lord Deedes, who had been a minister in Eden's government, said on television that during the Suez crisis Eden 'under prescription had, as many did, and still do, barbiturates, I think, to assist rest and sleep etc. and amphetamines sometimes for a little bit of a pick-up' and agreed that these were what are called 'uppers and downers'.[20] Deedes's account was true and contradicts the genuine though mistaken view of Eden's widow, Clarissa, that he was not taking 'uppers and downers'. The historian Hugh Thomas alleges that Eden told an adviser that he was practically living on Benzedrine,[21] though Lady Avon says he was taking it only in the last fortnight before he resigned.[22]

In January 2005, Clarissa Eden, who had said at the time that she felt as though 'the Suez Canal was flowing through her drawing room', kindly allowed me access to her husband's still-closed medical records in Birmingham University's Special Collections Archives. There I found an important letter, hitherto unremarked on, which Evans had written on 15 January 1957. It was an open letter to any doctor who might have to treat Eden while he visited New Zealand shortly after his resignation as Prime Minister. Evans wrote:

> There have been during the past six months several unexplained feverish attacks which could have been virus infections but the most suspect was an attack of a severe rigor, which came on suddenly without any other symptoms. Though it has been thought in the past that all these feverish attacks were incidental, it could be that some, certainly those with rigors, indicate a transient ascending infection in the liver ducts. It is known from recent investigations that there is a back-flow into the common bile duct, there being no valve at its outlet. On the other hand at the last X-ray examination there was no evidence of any dilation in any part of the biliary tract.

Evans then describes Eden's treatment:

> His general health during the past year has been maintained with extensive vitamin therapy – sodium amytal gr 3 and seconal enseal gr 1.5 every night and often a tablet of Drinamyl every morning. These treatments have only become really essential during the past six months. Before his rest in Jamaica the general condition was one of extreme over-strain with general physical nerve exhaustion, and at this time he seemed to be helped by rest, some increase in the sedation and Vitamin B.12 therapy.[23]

This is the first time that medical evidence has been found that Eden was taking dextro-amphetamine,* a stimulant which, combined with amylobarbitone, a sedative, is contained in Drinamyl. This combination, also called Dexamyl in some countries, used to be referred to as 'purple hearts'. Some of the minor side effects of one Drinamyl each morning may have begun to develop in Eden by July 1956. It seems that the dose was increased after the medical episode on 21 August and possibly again in October and contributed to his collapse in November. We do not know exactly how many tablets a day Eden was taking, particularly between 5 October and 19

---

* Amphetamine and its dextro-isomer, dextro-amphetamine, together with methyl amphetamine (methedrine) comprise a group of drugs which act by releasing monoamines from nerve terminals in the brain, noradrenaline and dopamine being the most important mediators in this connection. (H. P. Rang, M. M. Dale and R. M. Ritter, *Pharmacology*, 3rd ed. (Edinburgh: Churchill Livingstone, 1995), p. 637.) They are stimulants which produce a feeling of energy, overconfidence and euphoria. First synthesised in 1887, they were introduced into clinical practice in 1932 and marketed under the name of Benzedrine. This was used in tablet form during the Second World War for military personnel who had to stay awake and amphetamine then became very widely used in the 1950s and 1960s. In 1964, following a press outcry in the UK about their misuse the unlawful possession of amphetamines was made an offence and doctors began to use them much less. Amphetamines act not only on the brain but also on the lungs, heart and other parts of the body after releasing noradrenaline from binding sites. The effect depends upon the amounts used but even moderate doses often produce insomnia, restlessness, anxiety, irritability, overstimulation and overconfidence. Amphetamines do not create energy, they simply use it up. Prolonged use of even a moderate dose is invariably followed by fatigue; this 'come-down' effect is also often accompanied by difficulty with sleeping. Another sequel described after amphetamine use is called the 'crash'. (Martin A. Plant, *Drugs in Perspective* (Sevenoaks: Hodder & Stoughton, 1981), pp. 37–40.) These after-effects may be the result of depletion of the normal stores of noradrenaline and dopamine in the brain. These drugs can only be prescribed in the UK now under Schedule 2 of the Misuse of Drugs Act. Amphetamine plays an important role in the next chapter on the health of John F. Kennedy.

November, when his doctors became deeply concerned about his health, recommending he take a holiday in Jamaica. They could have produced any of the following effects on Eden: insomnia, restlessness, anxiety, irritability, overstimulation and the overconfidence that one sees in my description of hubris syndrome. Malcolm Lader, a professor of clinical pharmacology at King's College London, in an interview on the fiftieth anniversary of Suez, said that people taking Drinamyl become 'disinhibited' and start acting out of character. With larger doses, he said, they can become paranoid and their judgement 'becomes even more impaired – at the most extreme they can lose contact with reality'.[24] Drinamyl is now very rarely used as the medical profession has become more aware of its effect on judgement, energy and mood. It is, I believe, worth the medical profession researching more deeply any amphetamine effect on noradrenaline and dopamine levels in the brain and on brain levels of these substances during a prolonged period of stressful leadership. I touch on whether there could be a neuroscientific explanation for hubris syndrome in Chapter 9.

Clarissa Eden in her diaries denied her husband took Drinamyl until after the invasion:

> It never seemed to me that health was affecting any of Anthony's judgements and this was the opinion of those working for him. I do not remember him being dependent on daily stimulants and I was with him every day and night. Horace, Evans may have prescribed them, but Anthony was not a person who wished to jeopardise his judgement.[25]

She also wrote that 'later, before and after our return from Jamaica, he was taking the prescribed dose of Drinamyl'.

I found no evidence of any reference by his doctors to excessive usage of amphetamine, no record of any clandestine use, nor of any dependence or addiction. Indeed in one letter to a doctor in the Lahey Clinic in March 1971, Eden shows a proper caution about drugs and their interactions on one another.* Against this conflict of evidence, one has to set the fact that doctors

---

* The letter from Eden to the doctor in the Lahey Clinic reads: 'One other question about sleeping pills. As you know, I take Sparine. Is there any harm if I take the equivalent of four little yellow pills or two red ones occasionally at night? Sometimes I find that it is best to take a little yellow one an hour or more before I go to sleep, and another little yellow one as I turn

well know that even the most careful of patients during times of stress feel some initial comfort in upping their dosage of amphetamines to give them a temporary boost of energy and they may not tell anyone, doctors or close relatives, that they are doing this. We also know that Eden took pethidine tablets for pain and there are reports of 'his own self-medication involving injections by his personal detective'.[26]

In the notes which he prepared to read out to his Cabinet colleagues on 9 January 1957, informing them of his resignation, Eden made no attempt to hide his dependence on stimulants. He openly refers there to his having considerably increased his amphetamines, which he calls stimulants, since July. The full text of this is in Robert Rhodes James's biography. The relevant passage reads:

> During these last five months, since Nasser seized the Canal in July, I have been obliged to increase the drugs considerably and also increase the stimulants necessary to counteract the drugs. This has finally had an adverse effect on my precarious inside. Naturally the first thing I asked the doctors was whether I could last out till the summer or Easter at the earliest. They tell me they doubt it, and think I would not last more than six weeks.[27]

In his letter of 15 January 1957, Sir Horace Evans's description of Eden's feverish attacks correspond to the symptoms of cholangitis.[†] Certainly those with rigors, or shaking of the body, indicated a transient ascending infection of the liver ducts, which Evans treated with mild sulphur drugs.[28] The most serious of these feverish attacks took place on a Friday afternoon, 5 October, while Eden was visiting his wife, who was an in-patient at University College Hospital. He suddenly felt freezing cold and began to shake uncontrollably

---

out the light, followed by a red one, should I wake up, say about 2.00 a.m. Alternatively, I may take a red one on going to sleep and one yellow one about 3.00 a.m., should I be lying awake then, and another at 5.00 a.m. if I have not gone to sleep. Both these methods are unusual, one red and one yellow is usually enough for a night, but I do use them occasionally. My local doctor felt that there was no harm at all in such a practice, but I thought that I should check up with you.' (Extract from letter written by Eden to John Norcross at Lahey Clinic Foundation, 24 March 1971.)

[†] Cholangitis is a bacteraemia or septicaemia where organisms similar to those found in the bile duct can be recovered from a culture of the blood. It is a serious and debilitating illness. The brain can be affected, as evidenced by the alterations of the brain's temperature regulation centre and also by a feeling of haziness and difficulty with judgement, recalled by those who have had such a condition, presumably due to organisms and exotoxins which bathe the brain.

with a fever. On medical advice he went to bed in a room close to his wife's and his temperature rose to 106°F, a very high reading for an adult. He was allowed to leave on Monday 8 October, much refreshed, it was reported. But that feeling can be only temporary: the body has been subjected to great strain during such a rigor and needs time to recover. Most people, including his colleagues, were quite unaware of what had happened. Eden carried on work but, as his official biographer noted, 'a sinister bell had been sounded'.

Collusion

The fever of 5 October came just at the time that the Suez crisis was coming to a head. Two days earlier Eden had told the Cabinet that there was 'a risk that the Soviet Union might conclude a pact of mutual assistance with Egypt; if that happened it would become much more hazardous to attempt a settlement of this dispute by force'. He knew too that as the British troop build-up continued in Cyprus and elsewhere there would come a moment when he could no longer hold them in a state of military readiness, and on 5 October in the United Nations Security Council, Egypt complained about both British and French troop movements.

On Monday 8 October, the day Eden came out of hospital, Rab Butler had to chair the Egypt Committee in the Prime Minister's absence. But by Saturday of that week Eden was well enough to speak in the traditional leader's slot on the last day of the Conservative Party conference at Llandudno. The party faithful loved the passage in which he said: 'We have always said that with us force is the last resort, but cannot be excluded. We have refused to say that in no circumstances would we ever use force. No responsible government could ever give such a pledge.'

On the day of his speech he was informed by Anthony Nutting that the French Prime Minister, Guy Mollet, had requested that Eden urgently agree to see emissaries whom he wanted to send over from Paris. On the evening of 13 October, after the Prime Minister had returned to Chequers from the conference, Nutting told him on the telephone about the visit to London by Sir Gladwyn Jebb, the British ambassador in Paris. Jebb had revealed that the French had delivered seventy-five of the latest Mystère fighter aircraft to Israel without it being cleared with the British and the Americans, as the procedures of the tripartite agreement required. Eden asked Nutting whether the French were putting up the Israelis to attack Jordan, a major British anxiety at the time.

Eden had lunch with Nutting on Sunday 14 October and sent a message of congratulations to Selwyn Lloyd in New York, who seemed to be making real progress in his negotiations with the Egyptian Foreign Minister, Dr Mahmoud Fawzi. Then, in the afternoon, Eden held what turned out to be a fateful meeting with Mollet's emissaries, General Maurice Challe, a deputy chief of staff of the French air force, and Albert Gazier, France's acting Foreign Minister. Nutting was also present.* The Challe plan was based on a conspiracy with Israel and was ruinously to become the central policy instrument in Eden's handling of the Suez crisis.

Until this meeting Eden had had no inkling that the French were already deep in collusion with the Israelis over Egypt. Two weeks earlier, on 30 September, an Israeli delegation had secretly suggested to the French their concept of a bogus *casus belli*. The plan was that Israel would invade the Suez Canal Zone, on the agreed understanding that British and French forces would then intervene to separate Israeli and Egyptian forces, posing to the world as peacekeepers between the combatants. The RAF would take out Egyptian planes which might otherwise threaten Israeli territory.

The French had been in close contact with Israel ever since the Suez Canal Base Agreement. Israel felt that the British troop withdrawal from Egypt had made it more vulnerable while France feared Egyptian interference in its massive military and political challenge in Algeria. The French had some 400,000 troops in Algeria and as President Nasser was supporting the insurgents, the French had a clear incentive for getting rid of him. French arms sales to Israel were already stretching the balance of arms provision in the tripartite agreement which France had signed with the US and the UK.

To any Prime Minister, let alone Eden with his vast experience as Foreign Secretary, Challe's suggestion of collusion with Israel would have seemed

---

* It is cited by some as a sign of Eden being in a paranoid mental state that when Guy Millard was preparing to take a record of this meeting, Eden said: 'There's no need to take notes, Guy.' But in fairness to Eden, once a note had been taken, it would have been the normal practice in those days to circulate it widely in the Foreign Office. It would have been almost impossible not to circulate it, at the very least, to the permanent secretary to the Foreign Office and very hard to stop him circulating it to at least a few other senior diplomats and by telegram to the Foreign Secretary in New York. The circle of people in the know, therefore, would have inexorably widened. It was wholly legitimate for Eden at this early stage to decide for himself who should be in the know, but it was an interesting early indication of his belief that action with France might be the way of solving his problem. Millard was adamant in an interview with me that Eden had not had any prior warning that Israel was going to be involved. (GMTV documentary on Eden's health during the Suez crisis, 5 November 2006.)

contentious and a plan that was bound to be fraught with political dangers at home and abroad. In particular, from the moment Israeli involvement was mentioned, Eden should have ruled it out. He knew that Israel was the only nation whose ships were not allowed by Egypt to use the Suez Canal, and which therefore had a direct interest in who controlled it. Eden should have known that if Britain were to invade it would be better done with the French alone and after the US elections. It would still have encountered much international criticism, but there was some merit in claiming that its purpose was to uphold the spirit of the Suez Canal Base Agreement, which Eden had negotiated and to which Nasser had been a party.

The normally cautious, pro-Arab Eden might have been expected on his past record to have ruled out involving Israel from the moment he first heard of it. Though Eden did not formally commit himself to it then, his not throwing it out at the meeting was in itself a decision. His questions left the French in little doubt that he was on board for the concept. Challe sensed that Eden was thrilled, Millard felt he was merely 'intrigued'. Nutting, previously very close to Eden, asked in his book: 'How and why was this mortal decision arrived at? And how and why did the man, whose whole political career had been founded on his genius for negotiation, act so wildly out of character?'[29] A war started in dishonour ended, not altogether surprisingly, in disaster and the man responsible, Eden, was in no fit condition to make such a decision.

It was over these few days that Eden also decided that he would have to proceed on the basis of not informing the Americans of his intentions. He foolishly believed he could keep the Israeli connection within the plan secret from the Americans. In all respects it was a massive misjudgement. This was the truly fateful consequence of colluding with Israel and France and I judge that if Eden had been fit and well he would have realised that such a course contained the seeds of its own destruction. The permanent under-secretary at the Foreign Office, Sir Ivone Kirkpatrick, perhaps the only senior diplomat who favoured military intervention, believed that the Americans would prefer not to know about British plans to use force.

Eden had hoped that a readiness by Britain to proceed with the United States' Suez Canal Users Association Initiative to put the canal under international supervision − something he called 'a cock-eyed idea, but if it brings the Americans in, I can go along with it' − would lead to economic sanctions and then John Foster Dulles would eventually reluctantly support military action.[30] But this, by October, looked extremely unlikely.

Eden decided to tell Lloyd personally what Challe had proposed and Lloyd was summoned to fly back to London, where he arrived on the morning of Tuesday 16 October. Eden authorised Nutting, meanwhile, to talk to only two senior Foreign Office diplomats and specifically excluded the Foreign Office legal adviser, who he knew would say that what Eden proposed to do could not be justified in international law. Instead Eden was now relying on advice from the Lord Chancellor, Lord Kilmuir, who maintained that intervention could be legally justified.[31] But constitutionally the Lord Chancellor is not the legal adviser to the Cabinet – the Attorney General is. Nutting, who was totally opposed to the plan and resigned as soon as it was put into practice, had a quick conversation with Lloyd before the Cabinet, telling him what Eden was up to, and has claimed that Lloyd replied spontaneously: 'You are right, we must have nothing to do with the French plan.' Nutting spoke to him again by telephone after Lloyd's lunch with Eden but found that Lloyd was now in no mood to listen to his pleadings and was flying off to Paris with Eden. The relatively inexperienced Foreign Secretary was not only acquiescing in the Challe plan but was also now saying that his agreement in New York with the Egyptian Foreign Minister on six principles for dealing with the crisis would not be honoured by Nasser.

It was a sign of how reckless Eden had become that he was ready even to contemplate what the French were advocating as the way to defeat Nasser. He swept his Foreign Secretary off to Paris within hours of his having landed from New York without either men having had, as far as one can determine, any formal professional input from the Foreign Office, though Eden could rely on Kirkpatrick's support. This failure to consult was an action quite out of character for Eden. It was but one of many examples of how personalised and unstructured Eden's decision-making had become in 10 Downing Street. Under Churchill during the Second World War the machinery of the War Cabinet had functioned fully, and different departments of state had had their input. Eden himself had always been a stickler for following due procedure.

In a memo signed on 18 October by Lloyd, recording the meeting in Paris on 16 October between Eden and himself, Mollet and Christian Pineau, the French Foreign Minister, and without officials, it is clear that the issue of how the United States would respond if Israel attacked Egypt was discussed and assessed:

> The Prime Minister [Eden] thought that the United States Government would be no more anxious than the French or British Governments to take action under the Tripartite Declaration. The Prime Minister said that during our visit

to Washington in the early part of the year, the United States had made it quite clear that they would have to get authority from Congress before the United States forces would take any part. It was agreed that if Israel were to act before the end of the American election campaign it was most improbable that Congress could be re-summoned or if re-summoned, would give this authority. It was not thought likely that the Security Council would reach agreement on any action to be taken. In any case the Security Council could only pass resolutions and M. Mollet said that so far as the French Government was concerned, they would not be prepared to have Israel condemned as an aggressor for an attack upon Egypt after the way the Egyptians had behaved. The idea was then put forward by M. Mollet that it might be possible for the western powers to intervene to stop fighting in the area of the Canal. It was thought improbable that the United States would be willing to join such action, particularly during the course of the election campaign.[32]

On 24 October Lloyd noted that the previous day, in a meeting in London with Pineau which Eden joined,

> the question of discussions with the Americans was raised. It was not thought that any useful purpose would be served by talking to them as the French and ourselves had talked, owing to their pre-occupation with the election campaign, and the generally unsatisfactory nature of our exchanges with Mr Dulles about US action of any character.[33]

Lloyd's account is important for what it says about the Americans. Clarissa Eden's diary entry for 23 October reads: 'Pineau came here this evening. Anthony went round to Carlton Gardens after dinner. Pineau says the French have now talked Ben Gurion round and he will attack but only if we do so too simultaneously. Anthony says no, only afterwards.'[34]

We now know that at this moment, when Eden was depending so exclusively on his own political instinct, he was in very poor physical shape. Only a week earlier he had had an exceptionally high fever. He was daily taking a mixture of sedatives to sleep and stimulants to counter the effect of the drugs and he had been under prolonged stress since the end of July. But how did the quality of his political instinct and his decision-making seem to his contemporaries, who knew very much less about his exact medical state?

Lord Home, one of nature's gentlemen and someone who would always lean over backwards to be fair, was a supporter of Eden's policy, serving on the Egypt Committee, and he has described Eden's conduct of such meetings.[35] 'They were fairly restless' and the Prime Minister 'was not undoubtedly well. I don't think it probably clouded his judgement, that will be for historians to tell us later on.' Home went on to say the 'meetings were probably not as methodically conducted as at times of lesser stress'. The permanent secretary at the Ministry of Defence, Sir Richard Powell, whom Eden constantly rang up, described him as 'very jumpy, very nervy, very wrought'. He also described Eden as having 'developed what one might call a pathological feeling about Nasser' and as being 'in a state of what you might call exaltation . . . He wasn't really 100 per cent in control of himself. Extraordinary, strange things happened.'[36] Air Chief Marshal Sir William Dickson, chairman of the Chiefs of Staff Committee, speaking in April 1957 to John Colville, used the same word 'exaltation', saying that Eden 'during the final days was like a prophet inspired, and he swept the Cabinet and the Chiefs of Staff along with him, brushing aside any counter arguments and carrying all by his exaltation'. Exaltation is defined as 'a marked or excessive intensification of one's mental state or a delusive euphoria'. Dickson added that he 'had never been spoken to in his life in the way the PM several times spoke to him during those tempestuous days'.[37] The chiefs of staff were very reluctant to have the Israelis as allies.[38]

A bizarre example of Eden's state of mind was when he called in Churchill's then private secretary, Anthony Montague Browne, and asked if he thought Churchill would accept a post in the Cabinet as Minister without Portfolio. Churchill was then eighty-two years old. Montague Browne replied: 'I do not believe he would like the opposite of the harlot's prerogative,' a reference back to Stanley Baldwin's famous jibe at a newspaper proprietor 'wanting power without responsibility, the prerogative of the harlot throughout the ages'. Churchill joked later with his secretary for declining without even asking his opinion. But in truth the joker was Eden in making such a ludicrous proposal.[39]

Guy Millard, Eden's junior private secretary in the Foreign Office during the Second World War, who then served the Prime Minister within 10 Downing Street, was not only present at all his most important meetings on international affairs but would see him late at night and early in the morning, read his notations on documents and listen in to many of his telephone conversations. A Foreign Office diplomat's diary entry of 1 November 1956 on Eden's state of mind in October writes of Eden: 'Guy Millard says he is not mad, but merely exhausted.'[40] Eden was certainly not mad, nor so drugged that he could not carry out his day-to-day duties as Prime Minister. His stamina was in many ways remarkable, particularly after his October fever. But there are many other observations from people involved at the time confirming Eden's volatile behaviour during the Suez crisis. These accounts are fully compatible with what would be expected of someone taking the stimulant Drinamyl.

They also show Eden acting wholly differently from the way he had conducted foreign policy during the previous two decades and even the previous few months. For example, during the period of disillusionment with Neville Chamberlain which led up to his resignation in 1938, Eden deliberated carefully and consulted widely. It is well documented how, on numerous occasions during the Second World War, he provided stability to Churchill's sometimes wayward decision-making. After 1951 Eden's foreign policy decisions were taken dispassionately and, like the 1954 Suez Canal Base Agreement, where he risked unpopularity with his own party, were explicable in the context of the time. Yet analysing the crucial month of October 1956, one sees an honourable and courageous man, borne down by illness and fatigue, weighing very difficult questions but then making too many mercurial decisions which were not in keeping with his past sober record. In his book *Anthony Eden: A Life and Reputation* the historical analyst Professor David Dutton concluded that 'it is difficult to understand why Eden believed that he would get away with the Franco/Israeli plan and conceal it from the United States unless you believe that his judgement was not what it was at its peak'. He also went on to say that 'all the evidence is that he [Eden] was seriously ill by that stage . . . In the beginning of October he was weak and tired and desperately in need of a rest and probably on the verge of a nervous breakdown.'[41]

The strain on Eden was immense. His Minister of Defence, Walter Monckton, the only senior government figure to come out against the use of force, had remained in that office until 18 October, before being moved sideways. The absence of dissent may explain the fact that the Egypt Committee met thirty-five times between 27 July and 17 October but did not reconvene for its next meeting until 1 November, the day after the RAF started bombing Egyptian airfields.[42] A more difficult opposition to handle came from Admiral Lord Mountbatten, the naval chief of staff (see note in Chapter 8, p. 331). He offered his resignation to Lord Hailsham, then the First Lord of the Admiralty. Hailsham recalls in his memoir, *A Sparrow's Flight*, that he followed Churchill's example in the First World War with the then First Sea Lord, Admiral Jackie Fisher. He told Mountbatten in a written note he was entitled to the protection of a direct order and told him to stay at his post until further orders. Eden was then informed and he confirmed Hailsham's action.

Mountbatten was not an easy colleague. Previously supreme commander in Asia, then Viceroy of India, and a member of the Royal Family, he was utterly charming but there were questions over his judgement. On one occasion, after a dinner for General Alfred Gruenther at No. 10, Mountbatten started to argue on the doorstep against the invasion and, according to Clarissa, he went on 'arguing and arguing until Anthony had to tell him the political side was none of his business'.[43] The then chief of the Army, Field Marshal Gerald Templer, had no time for Mountbatten and thought he was crooked, while Eden had little regard for him. Even after military action had begun, Mountbatten rang Eden, using his privileged access, actually to urge him to stop the invasion force, which was already steaming towards the canal after the Egyptian airfields had been bombed by the RAF. Eden was remarkably even-tempered in rejecting this advice. Nevertheless, however difficult a colleague Mountbatten may have been, he was a serious man who examined the detail of policy and was right politically as well as militarily over the invasion of Suez.

Invasion

On 29 October Israeli paratroopers, led by the then unknown commander Ariel Sharon, were dropped into Sinai. The following day the British and French, as agreed with the Israelis, issued their ultimatum demanding a ceasefire and threatening to intervene if this were not agreed. Gamal Abdel Nasser rejected the ultimatum and on 31 October, Anglo-French military action began.

It seems that by now Eden was calmer. Despite the strain and stress of 30 October he showed coolness when he telegraphed President Eisenhower after the launch of the invasion. Eden's press secretary, William Clark, who opposed it, described the mood of Eden and Selwyn Lloyd: 'The big decisions are over and they seem calm and detached.' On 31 October, when British bombers attacked military bases in Egypt, Lord Home's wife Elizabeth wrote: 'Much impressed by how well the PM and everyone in Government look.'[44] But it seems this was only temporary. Hours before Eden's broadcast to the country on the evening of 3 November, a young BBC producer called David Attenborough was summoned to No. 10. He saw Eden, while resting on his bed with a line of medicine bottles above it, looking tired and ill, so much so that he suggested that the Prime Minister should try and get some rest before the broadcast. In the broadcast Eden laid claim to be 'a man of peace, a League of Nations man, a United Nations man – I am still the same man'.

By this point the view of Eden's own principal private secretary, Freddy Bishop, was that he had 'finally given up making allowances for AE or feeling sorry for him'. It is easy to be overly moralistic about what is done to win in times of war and collusion is certainly not unknown. Also by the time of the invasion Eden and Lloyd were not alone amongst British ministers in being party to the collusion. It has been clear since January 1987, when, under the thirty-year rule, the Eden Cabinet papers were first made public, that the Cabinet were told about the collusion with France and Israel on 23 October. This was the moment for the Cabinet collectively to have challenged that collusion and Eden's judgement. So why didn't they? Why, despite some initial dissent, did they go along with the policy?

The short answer is realpolitik. Any Prime Minister, supported by the Foreign Secretary, has great influence on a Cabinet decision on international affairs. It is similar to but even greater than the power of a Prime Minister, when supported by the Chancellor of the Exchequer, on domestic affairs. In addition, personal ambition and party manoeuvring played a part, especially for Harold Macmillan, the Chancellor. Harold Wilson later described Macmillan's position as being that of 'first in, first out'.

Macmillan was on the face of it fully committed to Eden's policy.[45] He advised Eden after privately seeing Eisenhower at the White House on 25 September that 'Ike is really determined, somehow or other, to bring Nasser down. I explained to him our economic difficulties in playing the long hand and he seemed to understand.' The British ambassador, who had accompanied Macmillan and did not see his note to Eden at the time, later commented that he could see 'no basis at all for Harold's optimism' about Eisenhower's support. But Macmillan did also send Eden a report of his meeting with John Foster Dulles. He told Eden that Dulles had said that while Suez was not playing much part in the election at present,

> if anything happened it might have a disastrous effect. He reminded me of how he and the President had helped us in May 1955 by agreeing to the Four-Power meeting at top level, which had undoubtedly been of great benefit to us in our electoral troubles. Could we not try and do something in return and try to hold things off until after 6 November?

This was much more than a hint from Dulles to delay any action until after the US elections and Eden was also made directly aware of the sensitivity of the US election in correspondence with Eisenhower.* But as October went on neither Macmillan nor Eden ever seemed to weigh the effect on Eisenhower of invading Egypt on the eve of his presidential election. This is very strange since, as democratic politicians themselves, they must have known that almost all political leaders fear losing elections even when they have commanding leads in the opinion polls and they hate any uncertainty in the last few days before polling. For Eden and Macmillan not to have taken it into account was folly. Macmillan at least acknowledged later in his memoirs: 'Perhaps I should have attached greater weight to the date of the Presidential Election.'

It was Macmillan, as Chancellor, who, on receiving messages from Washington on the night of 5–6 November, was the first to realise the error of his judgement about Eisenhower's reaction. The crisis had put huge pressure on sterling and was costing Britain's foreign exchange reserves dearly. Macmillan needed to be able to rely on standby credit from the International Monetary Fund, but that necessitated the United States helping. But he was told that US support for sterling depended on a ceasefire by midnight. This information, along with news of the US Sixth Fleet harassing Royal Navy vessels off Port Said, was conveyed to Macmillan and he at once changed his position on supporting military action.[46]

---

* Eisenhower had received a 'Dear Friend' letter from Eden on 5 October requesting some public announcement in general terms to the effect that the United States Air Force would provide technical information to modify aircraft and would train RAF air crews to carry certain types of US atomic weapons. He had answered on 12 October requesting any announcement be held 'in abeyance', referring to 'a number of sensitive issues, both in our domestic political situation and in our relations with our other allies'. The domestic situation was a clear reference to the elections on 6 November. Eden, after a revealing silence, formally accepted delay on 28 October. On 30 October in a 'Dear Anthony' letter Eisenhower calls Eden 'my longtime friend' but is clearly warning him about Anglo-Franco-Israeli military action and ends: 'It seems to me of first importance that the UK and US quickly and clearly lay out their present views and intentions before each other, and that, come what may, we find some way of concerting our ideas and plans so that we may not, in any real crisis, be powerless to act in concert because of misunderstanding of each other.' Eden wrote that same day promising a further letter but the Anglo-French ultimatum was announced in the media before the arrival of Eden's second letter to Eisenhower. Eisenhower wrote back formally on 30 October 'Dear Mr Prime Minister' and an identical message was sent to the French Prime Minister, Guy Mollet. (Peter G. Boyle (ed.), *The Eden–Eisenhower Correspondence 1955–1957* (Chapel Hill: University of North Carolina Press, 2005).)

Eden's authority, never more brittle than on 6 November, could have been overtly challenged by Macmillan, the one man who could have swayed a Cabinet that had already lost its nerve to disown Eden. But Eden moved first. He summoned the Cabinet to meet in his room in the House of Commons at 9.45 a.m., knowing that he could not expect to maintain a majority in the Cabinet for carrying on with the policy. He said that with the Americans likely to support economic sanctions in the Security Council later that day there was no alternative but to announce a ceasefire. Macmillan, according to one Cabinet member, 'was very strong in his warning of what the US would do . . . he put the fear of God into the Cabinet on finances, as Chancellor'.[47]

It was a diplomatic debacle; in Eisenhower's words, 'I've just never seen great powers make such a complete mess and botch of things.' It was a humiliating about-turn caused by France and Britain having run out of friends; this was more fundamental than US pressure on the pound and the threatening letter over Suez from Mikhail Bulganin (who at dawn on 4 November had moved 200,000 Soviet troops and 4,000 tanks into Budapest). That crucial reality of total isolation was about to be demonstrated in the Security Council.

It would have been better from Eden's personal point of view, and for British and French prestige in the Middle East, to have delayed calling the Cabinet together until 7 November, allowing time to take the whole canal while using the veto with the French on any UN sanctions resolution. There was no question that this is what Guy Mollet, the French Prime Minister, and David Ben-Gurion, the Israeli Prime Minister, would have preferred, but Eden felt he had to pre-empt Macmillan and the Cabinet, once called together, was not ready to wait and defy the Security Council.

Later Mollet, meeting on 6 November with Konrad Adenauer, the German Chancellor, was told: 'France and England will never be powers comparable to the United States . . . Not Germany either. There remains to them only one way of playing a decisive role in the world: that is to unite Europe . . . We have no time to waste; Europe will be your revenge.' The Treaty of Rome, the first step to creating the European Union, was signed by the original six continental European countries, with Britain remaining outside, the very next year, 1957.

Cover-up

No hint of collusion with Israel was given to the House of Commons during the actual military operation and that was justifiable. What was bizarre and an indication that Eden believed the cover-up could be made to hold for much longer was his decision to send two diplomats back to Paris in an attempt to gather up and to destroy all the copies of what was later called the Protocol of Sèvres,[48] after the suburb of Paris where the meetings had taken place. Selwyn Lloyd had attended the initial meeting at Sèvres but the second meeting had involved a senior diplomat, Patrick Dean, and Lloyd's private secretary, Donald Logan. Guy Mollet, and David Ben-Gurion, who had attended both meetings, agreed to total secrecy.[49] Eden should have known, however, that in democracies there can never be perpetual secrecy. The French and the Israeli leaders, who resented the British Cabinet's decision to halt the advancing troops down the canal, and had no guilty consciences about the military operation, were never going to keep it secret.

It was also a wholly unrealistic view of Eden's that any cover-up could be kept from American intelligence for much longer than a few weeks at best, more likely a few hours. In fact the CIA claimed to have known about the operation at all stages, though there is some evidence to doubt this. On 29 October, when it is claimed John Foster Dulles first heard about the Israeli attack, he suspected French, but not British, involvement. It was only after the announcement of the French and British ultimatum that Dulles saw through the veil of camouflaged intent[50] and asked John Coulson, the British chargé d'affaires, next day how the Egyptians, who were being attacked, could be expected to give up their own territory and submit again to occupation. Coulson cabled Lloyd, saying: 'What rankles the most is what they believe to be deliberate concealment on our part, if not an actual plot with the French and Israelis.'[51] More realistic than Eden, Christian Pineau told the United States about the facts of their collusion while Eden was still pretending to the Americans that no collusion had taken place, compounding US anger.

Given that Eden had known Dwight Eisenhower for over a decade, it was a major misjudgement of his character to believe that he would not react to being misled on such a vital issue by someone he had previously trusted. Eisenhower, not unreasonably, felt betrayed by Eden's behaviour. And the truth, as the then British ambassador later said,[52] was that Eisenhower, not Dulles, made the major choices in US foreign policy. Lord Home criticised Eisenhower for demonstrating his hostility by sailing the US Sixth fleet alongside the British invasion force,[53] but like many he was underrating the toughness that underlay 'Ike's' friendly personality.* Eden, for his part, reserved his venom for Dulles, referring to him as 'tortuous as a wounded snake, with much less excuse'.[54] But Dulles was a scapegoat: the US viewpoint was explicit throughout.

Eden's continued attempt to cover up diminished his standing, and when he said in the House of Commons on 20 December that 'there was not fore-knowledge that Israel would attack Egypt' it was a lie.[55] Lying to the House of Commons was something which Eden had never done in more than thirty-two years as an MP. It was totally out of character and it hastened his departure. On 1 January 1957 Horace Evans was adamant Eden should resign, otherwise he would eventually kill himself, and another doctor talked of liver damage.[56] In truth Eden resigned on political, not purely health, grounds. Eden told Winston Churchill in advance of his decision. Churchill wrote back the same day: 'It is important that only one reason should be given – health. Policy and spirit will look after themselves. Anyhow one cannot do more than health allows.' In one of his last acts as Prime Minister, Eden dictated a note about his last audience with the Queen on 9 January before resigning the next day: 'I told her that the doctors report which the Queen had seen left me in my judgement no choice but to ask to be relieved of the duties of her First Minister.'[57]

Conclusion

How important was Eden's illness in the debacle over Suez? The historian and former Conservative MP Robert Rhodes James admits that over Suez it is difficult for him 'to be precise about the factors that pushed Eden from an

---

* On 2 November, regarding Eden, Eisenhower concluded: 'It was undoubtedly because of his knowledge of our bitter opposition to using force in the matter that when he finally decided to undertake the plan he just went completely silent.' (Dwight D. Eisenhower, *Ike's Letters to a Friend 1941–1958*, ed. Robert Griffith (Lawrence: Kansas University Press, 1984), p. 176.) Eisenhower emerges from this two-year correspondence with Eden extremely well and his public image as a semi-detached, golf-obsessed President is very wide of the mark. Eden, who had every reason to know this from personal contact, was foolhardy to ignore Eisenhower's view and from the tone of the earlier letters would never have done so before October 1956, by which time Eden had become beguiled by the Israeli option. Eisenhower gave Eden no reason to deceive himself into believing that he, Eisenhower, could afford on the eve of the presidential election to have the Americans see his global authority so openly flouted by the British. Yet, just after being elected for a second term, Eisenhower was more generous to Eden than Dulles. Eisenhower offered to see Eden and it was then Dulles, while in hospital, who persuaded him not to see Eden and Mollet so soon after the ceasefire. In the light of this reaction, had the invasion of the Suez Canal been launched some weeks later, Eisenhower's reaction might have been more muted.

absolutely legitimate position to what was perilously close to being an illegitimate one'.[58] There are some who doubt whether his illness was a particularly important factor. Hugh Thomas has written that a doctor who was seeing Eden as a patient – probably Dr T. Hunt – thought he would not have acted very differently in the Suez crisis if he had been in robust health. I do not believe that comment can be justified when one takes into account my detailed analysis of the timing of Eden's critical decisions against his medical condition. The Achilles heel of the Suez crisis was not military action but the decision to collude with Israel without American support; if Eden had been in robust health, the evidence suggests to me that he would have rejected such a course.

It is undoubtedly true that Eden's belief in the need to take a forceful position derived from his seeing the Suez crisis as part of the bigger problem posed by what he saw as the Soviet threat. That view had nothing to do with his health. Eden saw the Soviet Union and its short- to long-term intentions in the Middle East as an immense threat and his views are clearly expressed in a letter he wrote to a fellow Conservative MP, Irene Ward, on 28 December 1956* and later in his memoirs, *Full Circle*. A private and succinct explanation of Eden's reasons for the initial military intervention and then its withdrawal was given to his former and still very trusted private secretary, Bob Pierson Dixon, when the latter flew up from the United Nations in New York to meet Eden at his request in Ottawa on 25 May 1957. Eden had feared that, unchecked, President Nasser, with Soviet support, would have moved against Israel in the spring of 1957.

Pierson Dixon found Eden

> sure that it was right to have intervened. The trouble was that one could never prove that the situation would have been worse if action had not been taken. He still felt that the issue against Nasser was really the same as the issue against Mussolini – something had to be done to stop dictatorship. To take another example, had we moved against Hitler over the Rhineland there would have been much criticism but it would have been the right thing to do and many

---

* Eden wrote: 'I find it strange that so few, if any, have compared these events to 1938 – yet it is so like. Of course Egypt is no Germany, but Russia is, and Egypt just her pawn. If we had let events drift until the spring I have little doubt that by then, or about then, Russia and Egypt would have been ready to pounce, with Israel as the apparent target and western interests as the real one. Russians don't give away all that equipment for fun. Yet so many seem to fail to see this and give Nasser almost as much trust as others gave Hitler years ago.' (Letter to Dame Irene Ward, Avon Papers, ref. AP20/33/8A.)

millions of lives would have been saved. His calculation was that Nasser and the Russians would have moved in the Middle East (presumably against Israel) about March or April of the following year. Since the troops could not be kept hanging on indefinitely in Cyprus, he had felt bound to take the decision at the end of October to strike before the Egyptians.

On the morning of the ceasefire the President had telephoned to him and said he was glad about the ceasefire and had added that now that we were ashore he supposed that we had all we needed. Sir Anthony had not been able to pursue the conversation since he was off to the House of Commons to announce the ceasefire and had told the President that he would call him back. After lunch he had spoken to the President and suggested that they ought to "get together". The President had agreed, and asked when. Sir Anthony had said, the sooner the better. The President then suggested that M. Mollet ought to come too, and Sir Anthony had agreed to bring him along.[59]

An interesting assessment of the way Eden was using intelligence at the time has been provided by Percy Cradock, a very experienced diplomat, former chairman of the Joint Intelligence Committee (JIC) and someone well aware of how a Prime Minister functions in No. 10. He wrote:

By the Spring of 1956 JIC assessments were not having much influence on Eden. He had by now come to see Nasser as irredeemable; he regarded himself as an authority on the area; and he was already falling into the dangerous practice of selecting the pieces of intelligence that fitted his preconceptions and neglecting the Committee's more balanced overall view.'[60]

If there had been, as there undoubtedly should have been, an inquiry into the Suez crisis, many lessons might have been learnt and might have prevented many of the mistakes made later by Tony Blair over Iraq. The handling of a complex international crisis from No. 10 in both cases, as can be seen by comparing this chapter with Chapter 7, is a recipe for disaster. Both invasions were militarily successful but the aftermath was a political failure. There were, however, crucial differences between Suez in 1956 and Iraq in 2003. Blair was acting in support of a US President; Eden was acting against the clear-cut advice of a US President. Blair was supporting an inexperienced and immature President; Eden was ignoring a proven military commander and level-headed President. By 2008 it had become clear that Iraq was far more damaging to British long-term interests than Suez, and an inquiry must be held into the Iraq War.

Eden's illness was only a factor in determining policy towards nation-alisation of the Suez Canal but it was central to the way that policy was implemented. Robert Carr, an impressive Conservative Cabinet minister in the early 1970s while I was an MP, had been a close friend and admirer of Eden and served as his parliamentary private secretary. I attach importance to his assessment of Eden's physical and mental disposition at the time. He said:

> I find it difficult to accept the judgement that Anthony's health did not have a decisive influence at least on the conduct of his policy . . . he might well have pursued the same basic policy had he been well, but I find it very hard to believe that he would have made such obvious miscalculations in its execution both in the political and the military spheres.[61]

Two well-informed surgeons agree that the sequence of events strongly suggests that illness was an important factor in Eden's decision-making during the crucial months of October, November and December 1956, and one concludes that the Suez Canal debacle was significantly contributed to by the disastrous and tragic consequences of his bile duct injury.[62]

In the light of Eden's rigors and fever of 106°F on 5 October, nine days before making one of the key decisions in the Suez crisis, namely to collude with Israel, I do not think it is sustainable to claim that none of his decisions was affected by illness. We will probably never know what was the exact dosage of amphetamines Eden was taking by then, but some indication of the extent can be gleaned from a remark of Sir Horace Evans. Evans, unlike Lord Moran, was a discreet man and in the tradition of eminent doctors who believe that a patient's secrets go to the grave with them. Rab Butler, who, in Eden's absence, became the acting head of the government on 23 November, writes that he saw Evans (who was his own doctor too) in the drawing room of No. 10, probably on 19 November. Evans rightly felt he had to tell Butler the truth and Butler recalls Evans saying to him 'that Anthony could not live on stimulants any more and that since he was unlikely to relax at a clinic a few weeks in Jamaica had been recommended for recuperation'.[63] In the light of the phrase 'live on stimulants' it is a fairly safe assumption that by October Eden was taking more than one Drinamyl tablet a day. From a review of the medical literature on the subject, it is clear that this would have affected his judgement and decisions, making him more changeable and unpredictable from one day to another, depending on whether he was under greater influence of their stimulant or their sedative actions.

For the good of the country his doctors should have persuaded him to step out of the decision-making process for a time, at least after his high fever. When he returned to No. 10 from hospital that weekend he admitted to Lloyd that he was still 'pretty weak' and at that stage a military invasion of the Suez Canal was far from inevitable.

If Eden had decided to resign on grounds of ill health or, more likely, had told his party conference that he was ill and on his doctor's advice was flying out to Jamaica that night, 13 October, and not, as he did, in November, then the history of the Suez Crisis would have been very different. Selwyn Lloyd's negotiations in New York with the Egyptian Foreign Minister, which Eden and Anthony Nutting considered with a measure of optimism before meeting Maurice Challe at Chequers, would have been given a few more weeks. There might have been no early meeting with Challe and neither a caretaker Prime Minister, for example Butler, nor the Foreign Secretary would have been in any position even to consider a totally new policy such as that proposed by France and Israel, at least until after the US presidential elections on 6 November.

The situation in Hungary might have turned out differently too, if there had been no October invasion of the Suez Canal. By the time of the Israeli attack on Egypt on 29 October, the Hungarian revolution, which had started on the 23rd, was experiencing a ceasefire and Soviet troops, having been repelled, were withdrawing. But on 2 November Nikita Khrushchev flew to see the Yugoslav leader, Marshal Josip Broz Tito, and in the early hours of 3 November Tito agreed it was reasonable for the Soviets to invade Hungary. Khrushchev said to Tito that Suez provided a

> favourable moment . . . This will help us. There will be confusion and uproar in the West and in the United Nations, but much less than there would have been because Britain, France and Israel are waging a war against Egypt. They are bogged down there and we are stuck in Hungary.[64]

Shortly after midnight on Sunday 4 November Soviet tanks penetrated Budapest's outer defence ring. On 5 November, Bob Pierson Dixon sent a telegram to the Foreign Secretary from the UN: 'We are inevitably being placed in the same low category as the Russians in their bombing of Budapest. I do not see how we can carry much conviction in our protests against the Russian bombing of Budapest if we ourselves are bombing Cairo.' (This was a reference to an earlier bomb which had exploded near Cairo's central railway station.)

The Suez debacle had the most profound long-term effect on British and French foreign policy. The French angrily moved towards challenging US hegemony, the British, after their humiliation, towards rebuilding and relying on the special relationship with the United States. In the words of his *Times* obituary in 1977, Eden 'was the last Prime Minister to believe Britain was a great power and the first to confront a crisis which proved she was not'.

Eden, in 1956, was the most experienced international politician in the country. He had courageously resigned over appeasement and had played a significant role in the Second World War Cabinet. To some extent his international influence was in decline because Britain's influence was in decline along with its empire. Guy Millard spoke publicly for the first time on the crisis thirty years later, and gave an insider's judgement on Eden's decisions: 'It was his mistake of course and a tragic and disastrous mistake for him. I think he overestimated the importance of Nasser, Egypt, the canal, even of the Middle East itself.'[65]

Eden in October and November 1956 had to make critical judgements hour by hour, while courageously struggling with a serious illness. In some of these decisions he showed the careful consideration on which his great reputation deservedly rested. Yet in relation to three crucial decisions – to collude with Israel, to mislead the American President and to lie to the House of Commons, even after the invasion – his judgement was seriously impaired and his illness and treatment made the major contribution to that impairment.

4

President Kennedy's health

'How is your aching back?'

Kennedy replied with a smile, 'Well it depends on the weather – political and otherwise.'

Press conference[1]

John F. Kennedy was elected President of the United States in November 1960 with 303 electoral college votes to Richard Nixon's 219, but only a slim majority of the popular vote – 118,574 out of a total of 68,837,000 cast. Yet, in a poll taken after Kennedy's inaugural address on 20 January 1961, nearly three quarters of the American people approved of their new President. Around the world a young, confident voice resonated:

> Now the trumpet summons us again, not as a call to bear arms, though arms we need – not as a call to battle, though embattled we are – but a call to bear the burden of a long twilight struggle, year in and year out . . . a struggle against the common enemies of man: tyranny, poverty, disease and war itself.

At forty-three, the new President appeared full of 'vigah' – a much-used Kennedy word – vitality, charm and humour. He was the first Roman Catholic President, the first holder of the office to be awarded a Purple Heart and the youngest President ever elected. Tragically, he was also the youngest President to die and the fourth US President to be assassinated.

But some were not convinced by Kennedy's charm, nor was everyone enamoured of the Kennedy image from the start. Dorothy Thompson, a journalist, watched Kennedy's inaugural speech, and said to a friend: 'There's something weak and neurotic about that young man.' This was an unfashionable but perceptive insight, which still haunts rational assessments of Kennedy's presidency.

Across the Atlantic, older leaders occupied the seats of power. The Soviet Union's General Secretary, Nikita Khrushchev, was sixty-six, as was the

British Prime Minister, Harold Macmillan; President Charles de Gaulle of France was seventy; India's Prime Minister, Jawaharlal Nehru, was seventy-one; the Israeli Prime Minister, David Ben-Gurion, was seventy-four; Pope John XXIII was seventy-nine; and the German Chancellor, Konrad Adenauer, was eighty-four. Yet all of these men were in better health than Kennedy.

Few people arrive at positions of authority without some secrets. As he was sworn into office, Kennedy was living with one very big secret: he had deliberately misled the American people about his health, which was far worse than the public had reason to suspect. He had Addison's disease,* which left him dependent on hormone replacement therapy to live and, he believed, dependent on secrecy to win and hold the presidency. During his election, a bag containing some of his medical secrets had gone missing, and Kennedy knew that if this information had leaked during that critical period, the shock of the cover-up and the reality of his illness would have likely meant losing the election to his Republican rival, Vice President Nixon.

But, even more worrying, there is no sign that, as he dedicated himself to his country's service, the President ever contemplated changing his lifestyle. Kennedy made no move to appoint any of the country's leading physicians as his doctor, nor did he appear to try to curb his recreational drug use – or if he tried, he failed. Instead, Kennedy focused on using the power of the presidency to keep his medical condition secret and to project an image of himself as a normal, healthy, happy, family man, an image which was far from reality.

At the start of Kennedy's presidency I was still a medical student in London and, like many young people around the world, held high hopes for him. It was impossible not to be aware that we were living in dangerous times. The

---

* Addison's disease is also called chronic adrenal insufficiency and hypocortisonism. It is a partial or complete failure of the adrenal gland, first described by Thomas Addison in 1855. Most doctors nowadays take Addison's disease to mean the auto-immune failure of the adrenal cortex. Debilitating symptoms can develop very slowly in childhood and build up into and beyond adolescence, as happened with Kennedy, or the disease can present as an acute emergency, with most of the patient's normal functions collapsing. It represents a deficiency of adrenocortisol hormones, namely cortisol aldosterone and androgens. It occurs in 1 in 25,000 of the population. Formerly closely associated with tuberculosis, fewer than 20 per cent of cases are now due to that disease, while 70 per cent are due to auto-immune damage. Occasionally it can be caused by a secondary growth or metastasis from a carcinoma such as the bronchus or from the removal or damage to the pituitary gland, attached to the base of the brain. The treatment is with replacement of the deficient hormone by hydrocortisone.

Cold War was in full force, focused at that time on the communist threat to cut off Berlin and on the ever-escalating nuclear arms race between the Soviet Union and the United States. Part of this was the Cuban missile crisis, for which Kennedy's presidency will be remembered.

On Monday 22 October 1962, Kennedy publicly broke the news that missiles capable of striking the United States had been found in Cuba. A hundred million Americans tuned their televisions to his address, as many millions more listened around the world. At the time, unbeknownst to the Kennedy administration, the Soviet Union had 162 nuclear warheads in Cuba and four submarines trailing US naval vessels near the island. Each submarine carried torpedoes with nuclear warheads and had the authority to launch them, despite being out of communication with its Soviet base.[2] The Cold War was dangerously close to becoming a nuclear war. In Khrushchev's words, it was 'a time when the smell of burning hung in the air'.

In the Kremlin, Khrushchev awaited Kennedy's speech and considered using the nuclear warheads in Cuba, should Kennedy announce a US invasion of the island. Khrushchev was deliberately challenging Kennedy's authority close to American shores, in an area which the US government had clearly defined as a zone of American influence since the Monroe Doctrine of 1823.

As Kennedy addressed the nation, the Soviets had drafted instructions for their commander in Cuba, General Issa Plicv, 'to put all his forces on the alert'.[3] The 41,000 Soviet troops in Cuba would have been totally outnumbered in any US invasion, and the only potential salvation for the Soviet forces was the presence of Luna, the Soviet short-range missiles with nuclear warheads. Tentatively, a set of instructions was drawn up to authorise the use of Luna. Fortunately, the Soviet Defence Minister, Marshal Rodion Malinovsky, persuaded his colleagues to delay instructions for the deployment of Luna and to send an order to the Soviet forces in Cuba banning the use of any nuclear weapons. Malinovsky was wise enough to fear what might happen if Washington intercepted a message delegating the authority to use tactical nuclear weapons before any invasion took place. Moscow also sensibly gave instructions not to fire the nuclear-tipped R12 cruise missiles, which had a range of 1,100 miles, without a direct order.

It is no exaggeration to say that the fate of a large part of the world lay in Kennedy's and Khrushchev's hands over those tense days in October 1962, and, apart from the initial provocation, the Soviet Union handled the situation with considerable constraint. President Kennedy also deserves immense credit for his handling of the Cuban missile crisis. It was measured, at times nuanced, but also resolute and determined, and, regardless of the 'ifs' of hindsight, Kennedy's strategy of open confrontation worked. Yet, in light of his performance during this crisis, I have always been puzzled by President Kennedy's mistaken series of decisions in relation to Cuba only one year earlier during the Bay of Pigs fiasco. Why did he plan for and support the launching of an attack on Cuba by 1,500 anti-Castro Cubans on 17 April 1961? Even more importantly, why was Kennedy's Vienna meeting with Khrushchev in early June 1961 such an abysmal failure?

The Bay of Pigs was, in the words of the historian Theodore Draper, 'one of those rare events in history – a perfect failure'. The Vienna summit with Khrushchev, which followed, was arguably an even more serious debacle, for which Kennedy alone was responsible. The simple and most obvious explanation for this series of failures is inexperience on the part of Kennedy and his team. But that, I believe, does not sufficiently explain things. While judgement and wisdom are acquired skills, Kennedy's errors of judgement in his first year in office were not just those of inexperience. I believe they had their roots in his overall medical condition. While previous investigative reports and doctors' accounts of Kennedy's illnesses have been met with great resistance and disparagement by people who served under him, we now know, particularly through the work of the biographer Richard Reeves, that the majority of these disclosures were true.[*]

In these pages, I hope to provide fresh insight into the disjunction in Kennedy's decision-making abilities from the Bay of Pigs to the Cuban missile crisis. I believe that a key, and as yet neglected, factor in the puzzle is the very marked difference in Kennedy's medication and general medical condition between much of 1961, when he was in poor health, and early spring of 1962, when his health greatly improved.

---

[*] The physician John R. Bumgarner wrote a book titled *The Health of Presidents*. The first two sentences of his chapter on Kennedy read: 'It is with a great deal of dread and reluctance that I approach this chapter. Several talented investigative writers have been frustrated by the obscuring mask which surrounds and bars any approach to the true Kennedy.' Four outstanding contributions have helped to unravel the truth about Kennedy's illnesses prior to Robert Dallek's authorised writing about Kennedy's health: Richard Reeves, *President Kennedy: Profile of Power* (New York: Simon & Schuster, 1993); Herbert S. Parmet, *JFK: The Presidency of John F. Kennedy* (New York: Dial Press, 1983); Michael Beschloss, *The Crisis Years: Kennedy and Khrushchev 1960–1963* (New York: Edward Burlingame, 1991); Seymour M. Hersh, *The Dark Side of Camelot* (Boston: Little, Brown, 1997).

The Bay of Pigs fiasco

Kennedy had taken a number of different positions over Cuba and Castro prior to his election. In October 1959 he said, implausibly, that if the Eisenhower administration had given the fiery young rebel a warmer welcome in his hour of triumph, especially on his trip to the United States, he might not have gone over to the communists. But by October 1960, with the election in full swing, Kennedy was outbidding Richard Nixon in suggesting that some of the anti-Castro forces, both inside and outside Cuba, deserved American aid, provoking Dean Acheson, the doyen of Democratic foreign policy, to warn Kennedy that his campaign rhetoric was locking him into an untenable position for the future.[4]

Following an American presidential election, an incoming President receives two months of briefing by the outgoing administration before their inauguration. It is a sensible system which gives the President-elect time to evolve into more of a statesperson and quietly put aside some of their political electoral rhetoric. Kennedy's presidency was no different. On 18 November 1960, Kennedy had a major intelligence briefing with the CIA's director, Allen Dulles. When the subject of a possible invasion of Cuba (where Fidel Castro had taken power the previous year) was broached, Kennedy said he needed to consider the issues, but Dulles warned there was not much time. On January 19 1961, just before his inauguration, Kennedy held his second meeting with the outgoing President, Dwight Eisenhower. Amongst vitally important topics, Eisenhower mentioned that because of Castro's plans to promote communism in Latin America, the United States was helping Cuban anti-Castro guerrilla forces and training a group in Guatemala.

Immediately after the election, Kennedy in private sometimes appeared fairly open minded on Cuba, and he did not even rule out a rapprochement with Castro. A week before the inauguration, Adlai Stevenson, due to become the US permanent representative to the United Nations, sent Kennedy a report from a Chicago union leader who had just returned from Cuba emphasising that while freedoms had been lost, the people in the country largely supported Castro and that press reports out of Havana were unreliable. At around the same time Dulles briefed Kennedy fully on the CIA plan to infiltrate Cuba and topple Castro, and Kennedy told him without prejudice to continue the planning.

On 22 January, Kennedy, as the new President, met with his Secretary of State, Dean Rusk; his Defense Secretary, Robert McNamara; the Attorney

General, his brother Robert; the Chief of the Defense Staff, General Lyman Lemnitzer; and Dulles. Dulles estimated that there were only two months before something would have to be done about the Cubans under US training in Guatemala. Rusk warned that any direct US intervention would have enormous implications.

By February, Kennedy's advisers were split. The CIA and the hugely influential Richard Bissell, the agency's director of plans, saw an invasion touching off a civil war which would allow the United States openly to back the anti-Castro forces. But the State Department foresaw very grave consequences in Latin America and in the UN. Bissell shared President Kennedy's love of Ian Fleming's James Bond novels. Tall and handsome, he described himself as a 'man-eating shark' and was the sort of Ivy Leaguer whose advice the President and his brother instinctively wanted to follow.[5] The well-respected intellectual and historian Arthur Schlesinger, who had been asked by Kennedy to come into the White House, was against the invasion. He wrote Kennedy a memo saying: 'However well disguised any action might be, it will be ascribed to the US. The result would be a wave of massive protest.' He also warned the President that the operation might trigger defections and uprisings.[6] On 11 February 1961 Kennedy held a seminar in the White House to discuss the Soviet Union with Averell Harriman, George Kennan, Charles Bohlen and Llewellyn 'Tommy' Thompson, the US ambassador in Moscow, who had returned specially for the meeting. The sense of the seminar was that there should be nothing approaching a summit with Khrushchev, but Kennedy was clearly impatient for a meeting and on 22 February he wrote hoping that they would meet before too long for an informal exchange of views.

It was strange that the President, so skilled in press relations, could believe throughout the next few months that the invasion would be deniable. It was an example of both overconfidence and wishful thinking. But Kennedy and some of his advisers appeared to fear that if he cancelled the operation, the Cubans then training in Guatemala would return frustrated to the United States, publicly reveal his decision and depict him as having lost his nerve.[7] Kenny O'Donnell, a political adviser and someone personally very close to Kennedy, was concerned – as he said later in a tape interview – that scrapping the invasion would make Kennedy look like an 'appeaser of Castro', as if 'Eisenhower made a decision to overthrow Castro and [Kennedy] dropped it'. This machismo argument, the CIA believed, would weigh heavily with Kennedy, whose policy positions and personality as the incoming President it had studied with some care. The CIA sensed that he had been holding back from making a commitment over Cuba, and it calculated that it was best to push for an early decision and to play up the potential for the media presenting a contrast between a decisive Eisenhower and a weak, indecisive Kennedy.

The early plans Eisenhower had seen were different in important respects from the one Kennedy eventually approved. The first CIA plan presented to Kennedy was a naval landing at the coastal town of Trinidad under the hopes that the population of the town would join the US-trained Cuban forces. Feeling this 'too spectacular' and too much like a Second World War invasion, Kennedy wanted to land at a different place and project the appearance of an infiltration by guerrillas in support of an internal revolution. Yet his rejection of heavily populated Trinidad in favour of the remote Bay of Pigs made a mass uprising much less likely. And it was the view of the Joint Chiefs of Staff that the absence of a Cuban uprising would make it unlikely that the invasion would succeed. This was something which Kennedy felt, afterwards, should have been made clearer to him. He had perhaps unwittingly also effectively ruled out the option of guerrilla fighting in the mountains, which were now some 80 miles away across swamps and jungle.

The CIA accepted Kennedy's rejection of the Trinidad option without protest (though without approving it), since its first priority was to achieve presidential authorisation, believing that once committed, no President would allow the mission to fail. Kennedy, however, soon gave an indication of how differently he saw things when, on 12 April, someone suggested in the planning process that they could send US troops in to back up the exiles. Kennedy exploded:

> Under no circumstances! The minute I land one Marine, we're in this thing up to our necks. I can't get the United States into a war and then lose it, no matter what it takes. I am not going to risk an American Hungary. And that's what it could be, a fucking slaughter. Is that understood, gentlemen?[8]

Though, seemingly, Kennedy's position against the use of any US forces could not have been clearer, experienced people in the CIA and the military felt that there was sufficient ambiguity in his position that he would choose to win by using US troops rather than to accept defeat. Writing about it much later as a historian rather than as a contemporary participant, Arthur Schlesinger cited Dulles saying that he recognised his mistake: 'I should have realised that, if [Kennedy] had no enthusiasm about the idea in the first place, he would drop it at the first opportunity rather than do the things necessary to make it succeed.'[9]

Given that Kennedy, when facing defeat, did not choose to continue military action, the claim that his machismo was his dominant – or even only – emotion cannot be sustained. In fact, Kennedy's position throughout the Bay of Pigs period wavered to and fro. At some moments such as, for example, after he had spent Easter weekend in Palm Beach seeing a lot of his father, Joseph Kennedy, he was gung-ho to invade. At others he wanted assurances that he could stop the invasion at any time.

Torn for some time between his lust for action and intellectual reasoning for restraint, Kennedy to some extent overcame these conflicts before the invasion by compartmentalising the issue and carrying on with other business. On 28 March, Schlesinger asked Kennedy: 'What do you think about this damned invasion?' Kennedy replied, wryly: 'I think about it as little as possible.'[10] This was two weeks after having effectively signed the plan off, with the proviso that all US ships were to be clear of the landing area by dawn and that he could cancel even up to twenty-four hours prior to the landing.

In mid-March, the National Security Advisor, McGeorge Bundy, warned Kennedy that 'there is unanimous agreement that at some stage Castro's Air Force must be removed . . . My own belief is that this air battle has to come sooner or later, and that the longer we put it off, the harder it will be.' But on 28–29 March, Kennedy instructed the CIA to tell the Cuban Brigade leaders that 'US strike forces would not be allowed to participate in or support the invasion in any way', thus ensuring that the action could only succeed if there was an uprising from within Cuba. Yet the CIA and the military still misjudged the President's determination not to use US troops. It was Chester Bowles, a senior diplomat in the State Department, who, fearing this very scenario, opposed the invasion and, unbeknownst to the President, told Rusk the invasion should be scrapped.

At the end of March, Kennedy consulted the former Secretary of State Dean Acheson about the plan. Acheson did not think highly of Kennedy and asked: 'Are you serious?' When Kennedy admitted that he was supporting 1,500 invaders against Castro's likely deployment of 25,000 defenders, Acheson retorted: 'It doesn't take Price-Waterhouse to figure out that fifteen hundred aren't as good as twenty-five thousand.'[11] Senator J. William Fulbright, the powerful Democratic chairman of the Foreign Relations Committee, was also briefed and strongly criticised the whole concept.

The National Security Council met on 4 April, with Fulbright in attendance, and he denounced the whole operation as both 'disproportional and immoral'. But it must have been hard for those present to have given due weight to Fulbright, who was a politician from outside the administration. Not surprisingly perhaps, the meeting approved the invasion. Tellingly the Joint Chiefs of Staff carefully qualified their position once again, by saying that – if the CIA's assumptions were correct – the plan was feasible militarily. The CIA's assumptions were of course by then totally wrong and the military sensed that, but they were not ready to challenge the momentum towards action.

Yet Kennedy went ahead. Why? He was driven in part by domestic political considerations, determined to demonstrate his toughness and not to be seen as a weakling in comparison to Eisenhower. His brother Robert was also urging him to act decisively, brutally and savagely against Cuba. As the Attorney General he was motivated by a deep hostility to Castro and he later became involved in plotting to assassinate him. One of Kennedy's younger advisers on Latin America, Richard Goodwin, described the atmosphere at the meetings on whether to invade Cuba: 'Beneath the uninformed acquiescence, there was also arrogance – the unacknowledged, unspoken belief that we could understand, even predict, the elusive, often surprising, always conjectural course of historical change.'[12] Furthermore, in the early months of 1961 the election campaign was still very fresh in the minds of both the President and his brother. Everything seemed to be going their way. The President's style and mood were clearly more cavalier in 1961 than they would be eighteen months later.

On Saturday morning, 15 April, eight B–26s flying from Nicaragua bombed three Cuban airfields, but destroyed only five of Cuba's thirty-six combat aeroplanes. An aircraft with Cuban markings also flew from Nicaragua to Miami, to give the appearance of being a defector. It landed in Miami with bullet holes in its fuselage and it was claimed that it had flown in from Cuba. In the UN that same day Adlai Stevenson derided allegations that the United States was involved as being 'without foundation' and said the planes that had bombed the airfields were Castro's. The man responsible for the whole covert operation in the CIA, writing later about watching Stevenson defend the deceitful scheme and feeling a chill through his body, asked if anyone had bothered to tell the US ambassador at the United Nations of the deception involved in the air strike. Stevenson should have been fully briefed and not told that there would not be any American participation. Understandably

Stevenson was furious when he discovered he had deliberately not been informed of the true position. Had he known the truth he could have chosen his words with more care. After treating Stevenson with such contempt, Kennedy had to personally pacify him to stop him from resigning.

A second B-26 air strike was planned for the morning of 17 April, the day the American-trained Cuban exiles stormed the beaches. This air strike did not take place, since Kennedy grounded the aircraft even though the CIA warned him that a failure to hit the beachhead from the air would be disastrous. Later, on 3 May, in giving evidence on the operational plan to General Maxwell Taylor's committee, which had been established by Kennedy to find out what had gone wrong, Robert McNamara said: 'There was one important modification that the chiefs never knew about and one about which they all felt strongly. This was the decision to cancel some of the D-Day air strikes. This decision was made at the only meeting which neither I nor the chiefs participated.'[13] This was, in effect, a damning indictment of the manner in which decisions were being made in the White House. The Taylor committee, including Robert Kennedy, went on to conclude the obvious, that no paramilitary operation of such a magnitude could ever have been conducted in a way that US support for it could have been plausibly denied.

By Tuesday 18 April, there was no evidence of an internal uprising in Cuba and the Cuban government's air force had sunk the exiles' principal supply ship. The White House did not know what to do. As the Chief of Naval Operations, Admiral Arleigh Burke, put it: 'They are in a real bad hole because they had the hell cut out of them.' Kennedy was unsure of what to do, and the CIA, Burke and Bundy now all wanted US carrier planes to shoot down Castro's aircraft. An angry Burke said that the navy had 'just been told partial truths'.

The common misconception that Kennedy ruled out using American combat forces at all stages is incorrect. Kennedy did authorise Burke to send a message to Admiral Robert Dennison to 'prepare unmarked naval planes for possible combat use' and also to prepare to evacuate anti-Castro units. But Kennedy's agonising continued until, at a meeting from midnight until 3.00 a.m. on 19 April, he authorised another message to Dennison that six unmarked US jets should fly over the beaches to defend Cuban Expeditionary Forces from air attack. But they were not to hit any Cuban targets on the ground or to go looking for a fight. Kennedy must have known that this would have been an ineffectual limited intervention. It was meant to coincide with a Cuban émigré air drop, but due to a timing error never took place. By 1.00 p.m. on 19 April the Joint Chiefs of Staff concluded that there was nothing left to do but evacuate. Only fourteen anti-Castro troops were rescued and 1,189 surrendered.

In short, the Bay of Pigs episode was a total disaster. Afterwards, US public opinion was slightly assuaged by Kennedy's acceptance, as President, of sole responsibility. The Kennedy team's masterful manipulation of the short-term media reaction triumphed, and the President's wit was well tuned with attractive self-deprecation, as he told reporters: 'There's an old saying, victory has a hundred fathers, and defeat is an orphan.'

In private Kennedy tried to pin the blame on others, at one point saying that if Fulbright, the person who had predicted this mess, had attended more of his meetings, he would have been converted. But Kennedy was misleading himself, for it was not just the advice in the meetings but the way he, Kennedy, convened and handled those meetings that determined the outcome. On the invasion, Goodwin wrote: 'In retrospect, it could be seen for what it was – not a mere miscalculation but an absurdity.'

Kennedy had been most unwise to rid the White House of the military structures he felt had been too readily established by Eisenhower, without putting anything else in their place.* The Taylor committee reported: 'Top level direction was given through ad hoc meetings of senior officials without consideration of operational plans in writing and with no arrangements for recording conclusions and decisions reached.'[14] Eisenhower, in a meeting with Kennedy after the failed invasion, appeared to be genuinely incredulous that Kennedy had not mastered and challenged the actual detail of the plan before approving it. From the evidence of how he conducted himself in office, Eisenhower would never have automatically gone ahead with any plan, but once approved he would not lightly have let his plan fail.

One excellent study of the fragmentary and somewhat biased accounts of these gross miscalculations in and around the Kennedy White House believed that decision-making showed the symptoms of 'group think', a tendency to seek concurrence at the expense of seeking information, critical appraisal and

---

* Soon after taking office Kennedy peremptorily abolished the Planning Board and the Operations Coordinating Board of the National Security Council. To Eisenhower these were institutional brakes and he was concerned when they went. Eisenhower's Defense Secretary criticised Kennedy over the Bay of Pigs for casual directives overruling formal machinery. More damagingly, Kennedy's one Republican Cabinet member, the Secretary of the Treasury, Douglas Dillon, said that the loss of these checks and balances was the chief reason for the Bay of Pigs fiasco (see Tony Blair's ill-advised changes to the security and defence decision-making structures in Chapter 7).

debate. The concurrence-seeking tendency in this case was felt to have manifested itself by 'shared illusions . . . group solidarity . . . complacent over-confidence'.[15] President Kennedy said afterwards: 'All the mysteries about the Bay of Pigs have been solved by now, but one − how could everybody involved have thought such a plan would succeed. I don't know the answer, and I don't know anybody else who does.'[16]

There is an answer. Firstly, not everyone involved thought the plan would succeed, even in the CIA. Secondly, Kennedy should have known that, from the Secretary of State right down the chain of command, there is a deference given to a US President because of his role as Commander in Chief, regardless of his level of experience. His advisers were also very sensitive to the fact that Kennedy did not like being second-guessed. Richard Goodwin watched Robert Kennedy chew out another critic of the invasion, Chester Bowles, while the President sat calmly by. Goodwin's impression was that 'Bobby's harsh polemic reflected the president's own concealed emotions, privately communicated in some earlier, intimate conversation. I knew, even then, there was an inner hardness, often volatile anger, beneath the outwardly amiable, thoughtful, carefully controlled demeanour of John Kennedy.'[17] But while Kennedy had some hubristic attitudes, he did not suffer from hubris syndrome. He was in some respects too cynical and too humorous to allow himself to be intoxicated by power in that particular way. His self-confidence was also checked by a genuine curiosity and intellectual need to assess alternatives. In short, he was neither as decisive nor as macho as often projected, and his mood changes were often a reflection of what drugs or combination of drugs he was taking.

The intermittent nature of Kennedy's questioning and challenging of advisers, the way he personally changed the CIA's operational plan without consulting the military, the fact that he seemed unaware that he was seriously circumscribing US support by calling off the second air strike − all of these cumulatively led to the Bay of Pigs fiasco. There is no escaping the evidence that Kennedy's decision-making concerning Cuba was flawed over the first three months of his presidency.

One of the most serious consequences of the Bay of Pigs was that the fiasco made Nikita Khrushchev contemptuous of Kennedy, telling his staff that the young President lacked a strong backbone and would not stand up to a serious challenge in the Caribbean or elsewhere. But when that challenge came eighteen months later Kennedy was not the same man. He had taken on board criticisms of his method of working and ensured things were very different.

The characteristics of the executive committee which he set up to help him were 'at the opposite pole from the symptoms of groupthink'.[18]

But the change was not simply administrative; nor was it simply the result of the President's traumatic learning experience at the Bay of Pigs. The deeper change lay in his medical condition and in the way he was being treated for it. The stark difference between Kennedy's inept handling of the Bay of Pigs and the consummate way he handled the Cuban missile crisis can be fully understood only by taking into account his very different states of health during those two momentous events.

Medical history

Not all Kennedy's medical records still exist but I have studied those in the Kennedy Library, particularly as they relate to the period 1961–2.[19] Secrecy over his health has not helped Kennedy for it has hidden the overriding feature of Kennedy's health record, which is his courage in overcoming a combination of ailments which to most people would be totally debilitating.

The facts reveal that Kennedy's health was unstable from an early age. He was a sickly child,[20] spending two months in hospital in 1920 for scarlet fever just before he was three years old. In 1930, at the age of thirteen, he lost a substantial amount of weight and failed to grow. An appendicectomy in 1931 for abdominal pain did not relieve his symptoms and in 1934, aged seventeen years, he went to the Mayo Clinic for a month and was diagnosed as having colitis, though some saw it as coeliac disease. The clinic, with the Nobel Prize-winning Dr Edward Kendall and his colleagues, was at the forefront of research into cortisol or hydrocortisone, its synthetically produced form. Though Kennedy may well have been a guinea pig in beginning treatment with cortisone for colitis in 1937 to reduce the inflammation, it may be that he was thought, even then, to be showing signs of hypoadrenalism.* Either way this pioneering treatment, purchased by his domineering father, was given

---

* Hypoadrenalism can also result from a patient's long-term use of steroids. This hypoadrenalism stems from the administered steroids circulating in the bloodstream at levels which suppress a hormone, ACTH, which is produced by the pituitary gland. The loss of this pituitary hormone means that cells in the adrenal gland are destroyed. Another way for the adrenal gland to be destroyed is if the patient suffers from tuberculosis, which was the likely cause of death for the novelist Jane Austen. Deep pigmentation or tanning of the skin is associated with all forms of hypoadrenalism, though that largely disappears with hormone replacement therapy. Pale,

to very few. This was the same hard paternal hand that arranged a lobotomy or leucotomy, cutting nerve fibres in the brain, on Kennedy's sister Rosemary, without even consulting his wife, which led to Rosemary spending the rest of her life in special care.

Kennedy's back problems, which dogged him throughout his adult life, began, it was claimed, after a car accident at Harvard in 1938. Some have suggested that this back pain might have been due more to the steroids he was receiving, which produced the well-known side effect of osteoporosis. Probably both contributed, with the osteoporosis coming later.

In August 1943 PT-109, a small naval torpedo boat Lieutenant Kennedy was commanding in the Pacific, was rammed in the dark by a Japanese destroyer in a strait between two of the Solomon Islands. The boat was sliced in half, killing two crew members and leaving the eleven others, including their captain, to make a five-hour swim to a small island. When the destroyer hit, Kennedy was thrown violently against the deck of the PT boat and many of his subsequent ailments were dated from this incident, particularly his bad back. Kennedy encouraged this belief since he did not want anyone to focus on the fact that he had hidden his previous poor health record. In this case Kennedy's hiding his medical information was to his credit, so that he could serve his country in the Second World War. Unfortunately, medical cover-up became a lifelong habit.

Kennedy was diagnosed on 23 November 1943 as having a duodenal ulcer but this too may have been a side effect of his steroid therapy. His back pain continued and after examinations in different hospitals Kennedy had an operation at the New England Baptist Hospital on 23 June 1944, under a surgeon from the Lahey Clinic. The surgeon found not a ruptured disc, as had been expected, but on microscopic examination abnormally soft 'fibro cartilage with degeneration'. This was unlikely to have been the result of any previous physical injury but was probably a side effect of the steroids. He was also described then as having 'diffuse duodenitis and severe spastic colitis', an inflammation of his intestine. In October 1944 Kennedy was injected with procaine into the left sciatic nerve and this gave considerable relief. This

mottled patches on the skin called vitiligo are often present when there is auto-immune failure of the adrenals. It is conceivable that Kennedy had hypoadrenalism in 1947 because of the steroids he had been taking since 1937 and that this was therefore a secondary effect. But in favour of him having Addison's disease from an auto-immune illness is the fact that he had hypothyroidism as well, which was treated with testosterone, pointing to multiple endocrine failure. Also the fact that his sister Eunice was later diagnosed as having Addison's disease suggests a genetic predisposition.

started a pattern of procaine injections to relieve the pain in his back.

Although one naval doctor believed, correctly, that many of Kennedy's symptoms were due to a long-standing illness, the retiring naval board declared on 27 December 1944 (influenced perhaps by his hero status), that Kennedy's 'present abdominal symptoms started' after 'he spent over 50 hours in the water and went without drinking water for one week'. He was placed on the navy's retirement list as of 1 March 1945 as being permanently incapacitated, 'the result of an incident of the service . . . suffered in [the] line of duty'.

From 1945 to 1947 Kennedy continued to suffer from stomach and back pain and at one time looked jaundiced, something which was put down to a recurrence of malaria, which he had first caught in 1944.

Kennedy was first diagnosed as having Addison's disease in London in 1947 by the physician Sir Daniel Davis. He was already a Congressman for the eleventh district in Massachusetts. He may have been suffering from a milder form of the disease for ten years before he was admitted to the London Clinic, having started to take cortisol tablets first in 1937. Kennedy had all the classical signs in 1947: nausea, vomiting, fever, fatigue, inability to gain weight and with a brownish-yellow colour to his skin. He may, for some reason, have stopped taking his cortisol tablets.[21]

After the diagnosis of Addison's disease in London, Kennedy was given less than a year to live. He was so ill during the sea voyage home from England in October 1947 that he was given the last rites. He continued to have headaches, chest infections, stomach aches and urinary tract infections and in 1951, while visiting Japan, he had another Addisonian crisis. Notwithstanding this chronicle of illness, Kennedy managed in 1952 to beat the Republican Senator Henry Cabot Lodge Jr in Massachusetts. In July 1953 his back was bad enough that he went into George Washington University Hospital.

On 12 September 1953 John Kennedy married Jacqueline Bouvier, but in April 1954 an X-ray at the Lahey Clinic showed that his fifth lumbar vertebra had collapsed and by May he was on crutches. On 22 October 1954 after an extended metabolic work-up with a team of endocrinologists a three-hour operation took place on Kennedy, when a metal plate was inserted to stabilise his lumbar spine. All went well initially but on the third day, having developed a severe infection, which was not responding to antibiotics, he went into a coma. A further operation took place in New York in February 1955 to remove the steel plate and the screws into the bone because of a persistent infection following the operation. The public, particularly the voters back in Massachusetts, were aware that he had had these operations on his back but still they were never told about his Addison's disease.

In 1955 an article called 'Management of Adrenocortical Insufficiency During Surgery' was published in a surgical journal.[22] Case 3, we now know, was Kennedy.* The article did stimulate some enquiries into whether this might be him and this was actually alleged in one press report. A strong denial was issued that the article referred to Senator Kennedy but it would not have been hard to demonstrate that it was in fact about his operation. In some ways it was strange, given Kennedy's worries of any publicity about his Addison's disease, that he gave his consent to publish. No doubt he was given an assurance that it could not be traced back to him, but the article stated that 'this patient had marked adrenocortical insufficiency'. This demonstrated how inaccurate it was to refer to his illness as mild in the 1960 campaign. Though the last rites were again administered to Kennedy in 1954 this was primarily because of his post-operative infection. During both of these operations skilled medical care ensured that no Addisonian crisis developed.

The two back operations in 1954 and 1955 were a considerable test of Kennedy's courage and patience and he used the experience to write a book about historical figures who had demonstrated outstanding courage.[23] The more one knows about Kennedy's health problems the more one admires his physical fortitude.

Medical cover-up

Most Americans had no idea when electing Kennedy that he was anything other than what he looked – a young, healthy candidate for the presidency. In his television encounters with Richard Nixon, Kennedy appeared extremely

---

* In the report Kennedy is described as an anonymous 37-year-old patient requiring elective surgery for a back injury on a programme of desoxycorticosterone acetate pellets of 150 mg implanted every three months and cortisone in doses of 25 mg daily given orally. Knowing that in 1954 Kennedy was already on such large doses of steroids calls into question the later claim in the 1960 report of his doctors, on the eve of the presidential vote, that his ACTH stimulation tests were considered normal in 1958. For such a test to be meaningful his doctors would have had to stop his steroids for some time before the test. To do so, given the dosage and the fact that he had been on them for more than twenty years, would have been a brave step to take for a small diagnostic return. At Kennedy's post mortem, examination of serial sections of perirenal fat pads revealed no gross evidence of any adrenal cortex or medulla, just a few individual adrenal cortical cells diagnostic of severe Addison's disease, probably idiopathic and certainly not tuberculous in origin. An endocrinological examination should have been made at the autopsy.

fit, relaxed, suntanned and full of energy, in contrast to the haggard, pale, sweaty, half-shaven face of Nixon.

All through the Democratic primaries and the 1960 presidential race, the Kennedy campaigners flatly denied that their candidate had Addison's disease. The reason why is clear. Senator Kennedy was himself in denial, as illustrated in a conversation with his doctor, Janet Travell, which she recorded in her book:

> *Travell:* Senator, I think a series of reviews in the medical journals and popular magazines should be written right away. People don't realize how the outlook has changed in Addison's disease.
> *Kennedy:* But I don't have it, Doctor.
> *Travell:* That's right, Senator. You don't have classical Addison's disease. But the language is changing, too, and doctors disagree maybe because they aren't talking about the same thing.
> *Kennedy:* Doctor, you'll never educate all those Republicans.[24]

In an oral history interview with biographer Theodore White, Pierre Salinger, Kennedy's press secretary, confirmed that Senator Kennedy's denial still existed, even about his drug therapy, at the Democratic National Convention in July 1960:

> *Salinger:* John Connelly and India Edwards held a joint press conference in which they said that John F. Kennedy had Addison's disease. It was decided that the Senator himself wouldn't dignify the press conference by giving a response. I had put out a statement for the doctor [Travell] in which it was categorically denied that he had Addison's disease. Of course, this was a rumour that had gone through all the period of the time that I had known him, which persisted all during his presidency, and which would come up every once in a while. The fact of the matter is that he did have a deficiency which some doctors would diagnose as Addison's disease, but which the doctors who were caring for him would say was not Addison's disease. In other words, it was similar in character.
> *White:* Yes.
> *Salinger:* But it was not Addison's disease. It was not fatal; it was not going to be fatal; it was under control; it had always been under control; it was going to stay under control. I don't remember that it had any—
> *White:* Did you talk to him about this yourself?
> *Salinger:* Yes, I did.

White: What did he say? What did you say to him that he said?

Salinger: I can't tell you the exact conversation, but I remember telling him that he had been accused of having Addison's disease. And he said: 'I don't have Addison's disease.' I said: 'You're accused of taking cortisone.' And he said: 'Well, I don't take cortisone. I did take cortisone, but I don't take it any more.'[25]

All this was playing with words, for cortisol, synthetically produced, and cortisone, naturally occurring, were in effect the same thing. Yet Kennedy's state of denial about taking cortisone had been unfortunately reinforced by Travell saying, in a telephone conversation with Sargent Shriver, Kennedy's brother-in-law: 'Of course, he does take some relatives of cortisone, but in the way he uses them, in physiological doses, they're not *drugs*.'* Once again a political leader and his personal doctor were dissembling before the electors and stretching the truth to the point of lying. The line did not vary thereafter when campaigning against Nixon. Two days before polling day, a statement from Travell was issued by Robert Kennedy:

> John F. Kennedy has not, nor has he ever, had an ailment described classically as Addison's disease, which is tuberculous destruction of the adrenal gland. Any statement to the contrary is malicious and false . . . In the post-war period he had some mild adrenal insufficiency and this is not in any way a dangerous condition. And it is possible that even this might be corrected over the years since ACTH stimulation tests for adrenal function was [*sic*] considered normal in 1958. Doctors have stated that this condition might have arisen out of his wartime experiences of shock and malaria.

---

* Shriver was married to Kennedy's sister Eunice. In a telephone conversation with Travell, he said that at a news conference in Los Angeles supporters of Senator Lyndon Johnson had raised the question: is Kennedy fit?

> *Shriver:* It's that rumour about Addison's disease, they claimed he's living on drugs – cortisone. Bobby replied that he doesn't have Addison's disease and he doesn't take cortisone. *Travell:* Well, that's right, Jack hasn't taken cortisone in years. Of course, he does take some relatives of cortisone, but in the way he uses them, in physiological doses, they're not *drugs*. Bobby can say that those hormones are natural constituents of the body and they're given prophylactically to make up for some deficiency of his adrenals when he's under stress. Jack feels so well that his doctors are not inclined to stop them now. (Janet Travell, *Office Hours: Day and Night – The Autobiography of Janet Travell, M.D.* (New York: World, 1968), p. 331.)

By using a very narrow definition of Addison's disease, namely, an insufficiency of the adrenal glands caused by tuberculosis, this campaign medical statement was creating a calculated and knowingly misleading diversionary tactic. It was, as one writer described it, undoubtedly one of the most cleverly laid smokescreens ever put down around a politician and a travesty of the truth to say that Kennedy's post-war adrenal insufficiency had been 'mild', especially when, in 1947, he had been very seriously ill to the point of being given the last rites.

Cortisol, a synthetically produced drug, was first made in 1935. Before the 1930s, 90 per cent of patients with Addison's disease died; since 1950 most have had a normal lifespan.* It is important to remember that, when untreated,

> psychiatric abnormalities are present almost without exception in patients with Addison's disease. The commonest changes are those which might be expected in persons suffering from chronic physical exhaustion – depression, emotional withdrawal, apathy and loss of drive and initiative. There are sometimes sudden fluctuations of mood, or episodes of marked anxiety and irritability.[26]

Only after the November 1960 election did Robert Kennedy agree to give a little more information on the President-elect's health in an interview, but in a very controlled way. An article in the February 1961 edition of *Today's Health*, published by the American Medical Association, was also reported by newspapers including the *New York Times*.[27] It mentioned that Travell and Dr Eugene Cohen, a New York endocrinologist, had drawn up a statement on 21 June 1960 giving some very sensible information about Addison's disease,

---

* Several groups of medical researchers contributed to the discovery in 1935 of cortisol, including Dr Edward C. Kendall from the Mayo Clinic, who in his Nobel Prize lecture in 1950 said that the precise chemical was first synthesised by Merck in 1944. The most eminent expert in the United States on Addison's disease in Kennedy's time was Dr George W. Thorn at Harvard University, who Kennedy, interestingly, did not consult, probably not wanting it to leak out in Boston that he was seeing him, given his association with Addison's. In a book published in 1950 Thorn explained how mortality rates improved. (George W. Thorn, 'Metabolic and Endocrine Disorders', in T. R. Harrison (ed.), *Principles of Internal Medicine* (Philadelphia: Blakiston, 1950), p. 598.) Prior to the 1930s, before there was any specific treatment, 90 per cent died. Between 1938 and 1946, when extracts of the whole adrenal gland, adrenal cortex and imperfect hormone replacements were used, 50 per cent died within a five-year treatment period. Between 1950 and 1955, with oral corticosteroid adrenal hormones, mortality rates dwindled away so that if replacement treatment was well conducted a normal lifespan could be anticipated.

pointing out that the term covers different grades of adrenal insufficiency and that replacement therapy was so successful that surgeons hardly hesitated to remove both adrenal glands as a treatment in a number of conditions. It added that women with Addison's disease were bearing children without difficulty. If this forthright approach had been continued when Kennedy was President it would have been possible gradually to educate the public and remove much of the prejudice and fear surrounding the diagnosis. Openness about Kennedy's illness would have allowed the truth to emerge and the dissembling to stop.

Americans have had to wait over four decades for the truth to slowly emerge. Honesty and responsibility in government requires public awareness of when the medical conditions or the treatments given to our head of government have the potential to impair judgement. For that we need, at the very least, a disclosure of medical illnesses, something we clearly did not have with Kennedy.

But it was not only the American people who were kept in the dark about the health of their president. Given the tight secrecy surrounding Kennedy's medical condition, none of even his closest aides knew how ill he really was nor the extent or type of his medication. Had they known they might have been more questioning of his judgement in the early part of his Presidency. A privileged few – his wife, his brother Robert and his father – knew most of what his doctors knew. In her memoirs, Travell, who followed Kennedy after his election victory to become his first White House personal physician, mentioned the President once saying to her that if she could not contact him about his health, 'Ted Sorensen [Kennedy's close adviser and speechwriter] is the only person here who is fully informed about my health. Discuss it with no-one else.' Travell confirmed that the course of restricting all information to only a few continued after the President's death.[*]

Travell was, anyhow, a very surprising choice as the President's White House personal physician. Undoubtedly an expert on myofascial pain, a term used to describe chronic pain and dysfunction of the skeletal muscles, she was not a general physician of distinction and she did not deal with Kennedy's Addison's disease. Primary responsibility for this lay with Cohen. A feature of Kennedy's case was his use of specialists, deliberately compartmentalised, so no one doctor had authority over the whole of his care. Travell consulted

---

[*] In the Kennedy Library there is a file dated 6 December 1963 recording the 'ruling' by the Attorney General, Robert Kennedy, who continued in that post under President Johnson, that all correspondence which dealt with personal medical matters should be regarded as a 'privileged communication' and should not go to the central files in the federal archives.

frequently on the telephone and in person with Cohen, particularly about when and by how much to increase the dose of steroids when Kennedy had infections. Her expertise was in treating Kennedy's back and her particular technique involved flooding procaine or novocaine, through a syringe, into his lumbar muscles. Procaine is a synthetic substitute for cocaine and even when diluted, some was very likely to be absorbed into Kennedy's central nervous system. Procaine's effect on the central nervous system would have included lack of concentration, inattention, tiredness, mood changes and a mixture of indecisiveness and impetuousness, anxiety and restlessness, all noticeable at times early in Kennedy's presidency.*

The President, to ease his back pain, sometimes took five hot showers a day in the White House, swam in a warm swimming pool and used a rocking chair. Over the years he had many procaine injections into his lower back. Controversially, Travell used these injections as often as three times a day and sometimes even more frequently – five or six times has been mentioned. Some of his other doctors became increasingly worried by the summer of 1961 about her repeated use of procaine injections, and in her clinical notes there is evidence of progressively greater use from July until October. Travell, as is obvious from her oral history given on 20 January 1966 in an interview with Theodore Sorensen, was devoted to the President and his family. In that interview she gave some interesting specialised medical details.†

---

* Travell used a large syringe attached to a long, thick needle and her technique involved using the needle to stab into muscle spasm areas and discrete spots or trigger points; this was initially very painful but the pain eased when the spasm stopped, allowing the muscle to relax. Also if procaine was used, not just saline solution, there would have been a local anaesthetic effect. Procaine is a synthetic substitute for cocaine which was discovered in 1905. Cocaine was isolated from the leaves of coca, a South American shrub, in 1860; as a local anaesthetic it is mainly confined today to ophthalmology and minor nose and throat surgery. The tendency of procaine to produce unwanted central nervous system effects is one reason for its replacement in clinical use by agents such as lidocaine and prilocaine, whose central system effects are much less pronounced. (H. P. Rang, M. M. Dale and R. M. Ritter, *Pharmacology*, 3rd ed. (Edinburgh: Churchill Livingstone, 1995), p. 672.) Travell also prescribed corrective shoes, because Kennedy's right leg was 5/16ths to 3/8ths of an inch longer than his left. She puts this difference down, in her Kennedy Library oral history, to Kennedy being born with the left side of his body smaller than the right, not as something secondary to the surgery on his back. This may have given Kennedy a residual muscle weakness in childhood, which he compounded by wearing a corset for his back after his car accident at Harvard.
† Over the years Travell had worked with two endocrinologists in treating the President and she reveals that in 1955 Kennedy had thyroid insufficiency with a low basal metabolic rate of -20, high cholesterol of about 350 and borderline protein-bound iodine. This pointed to his Addison's disease being auto-immune in origin. He was given a new thyroid preparation, tri-iodothyronine,

In the White House, however, she was never given the trust or the authority by the President to get on top of all the different medication (including self-medication) that was accumulating in his body, having been prescribed by different doctors or just given to him by friends or acquaintances. We know from her, though, about some of the drugs he was taking during the first six months of his presidency in 1961. Her written records at the time show that 'stomach/colon and prostate problems, high fevers, occasional dehydration, abscesses, sleeplessness and high cholesterol accompanied Kennedy's back and adrenal ailments'. Doses of so many drugs were being administered that an ongoing medicine administration record was kept,

> cataloging injected and oral corticosteroids for his adrenal insufficiency; procaine shots to painful 'trigger points', ultrasound treatments, and hot packs for his back; Lomotil, Metamucil, paregoric, Phenobarbital, testosterone, and Transentine to control his diarrhea, abdominal discomfort, and weight loss; penicillin and other antibiotics for his urinary infections and abscesses; and Tuinal to help him sleep.[28]

On 19 March Travell refers to a Demerol derivative being given as treatment, it appears, for his irritable colon but presumably in small doses.

What was the effect of all this treatment at the time when decisions over the Bay of Pigs were being taken? As part of his necessary replacement therapy for Addison's disease Kennedy had to have testosterone. We know in most patients that this produces varying blood testosterone levels. With high blood testosterone levels and his accompanying steroid treatment Kennedy was probably pushed at times in a 'macho' direction, and at times when the effect of the drugs had worn off into downbeat moods.

As the invasion date approached it was a time of great stress for Kennedy, when the replacement drug therapy of anyone with Addison's disease would automatically be tested. Additional stress means it is not easy for a doctor to judge at all times the appropriate replacement dose of steroids and testosterone. This was particularly so when the President was also being treated for two spells of urethritis in the month before the invasion, since infections often need higher dosages of replacement steroids. Dr William Herbst, a urologist based

---

eventually settling on 50 micrograms a day. Also in 1957 Kennedy had a post-operative abscess on his back, possibly a stitch abscess, infected with a virulent coagulase positive *Staphylococcus aureus*, which was drained and responded well to streptomycin.

in Washington, had been treating Kennedy since 1953 for a 'burning' feeling as he passed water and 'prostate tenderness'. Kennedy had also been treated for a series of venereal diseases since 1940. In 1961 the diagnosis was non-gonorrhoeal urethritis, an inflammation of the urethra, often due to chlamydial infection.[29] Herbst was called to see Kennedy on 14 April 1961 and he started treating it with an anti-spasmodic, Transentine.

How did President Kennedy's health stand up during the actual Bay of Pigs invasion on 17–18 April? The answer is that he had constant and acute diarrhoea and a recurrence of his urinary tract infection. Undoubtedly this was part of the reason he appeared totally demoralised in defeat. The President was given 600,000 units of procaine penicillin intramuscularly for his urinary infection on 17 April, the day of the Bay of Pigs invasion. He had had a similar flare-up in his chronic urethritis three weeks earlier, for which he was also treated. For anyone in good health, this infection and treatment would have left them feeling below par but for Kennedy, having Addison's disease, the effect was likely to be greater.

On the evening of 18 April Kennedy got so overwrought that he stopped mid-sentence and went out in the dark by himself for almost an hour, walking in the Rose Garden. The following morning Pierre Salinger found him crying in his bedroom. Jackie Kennedy told her mother-in-law that he had been practically in tears and that she had never seen him so depressed except after his operation on his back. Kenneth O'Donnell thought he was as close to weeping as he had ever seen. It was at this time that Robert Kennedy wrote him a prophetic memo: 'If we don't want Russia to set up missile bases in Cuba, we had better decide now what we are ready to do to stop it.'[30]

Chester Bowles described Kennedy at a Cabinet meeting on 20 April as 'quite shattered' and talking to himself and interrupting conversations with an out-of-context remark: 'How could I have been so stupid?'[31] He could not sleep and described the whole episode as the worst experience of his life. He was constantly on the telephone to his father. This was not the behaviour of a fit, resilient Commander in Chief, nor that of a man suffering from depression. It was instead the behaviour of a man physically unwell, buoyed up by a variety of drugs but then brought to a low ebb by failure. Kennedy was not used to failure, for hitherto he had been 'on a roll' from the time he had become a Senator.

It is also worth noting that on 29 April 1961, as the Pentagon Papers show, President Kennedy agreed at a National Security Council meeting that clandestine actions should be taken in Vietnam. Army special forces left a few weeks later for South Vietnam. Some believe this was the critical moment in the escalation of the Vietnam War. The day before he had had sex with a mobster's mistress in Chicago (see p. 187). Kennedy was certainly not well placed physically or emotionally to make such a far-reaching decision.

Max Jacobson, Vienna and Khrushchev

Within weeks of the Bay of Pigs fiasco, President Kennedy faced his first summit meeting with the Soviet leader, Nikita Khrushchev, in Vienna. On 16 May, two weeks before the meeting, McGeorge Bundy, the National Security Advisor, wrote a very revealing memorandum to Kennedy which is sometimes referred to as the 'I hope you'll be in a good mood when you read this' memo. It was about how he should have been preparing to meet Khrushchev.

> We can't get you to sit still . . . The National Security Council, for example, really cannot work for you unless you authorise work schedules that do not get upset from day to day. Calling these meetings in five days is foolish and putting them off for six weeks at a time is just as bad . . . Truman and Eisenhower did their daily dozens in foreign affairs the first thing in the morning and a couple of weeks ago you asked me to begin to meet you on this basis. I have succeeded in catching you on three mornings for a total of about 8 minutes, and I conclude that this is not how you like to begin the day. Moreover, 6 of the 8 minutes were given not to what I had for you but what you had for me from [Bundy went on to list queries from journalists and others] . . . Right now it is so hard to get to you with anything not urgent and immediate that about half of the papers and reports you personally ask for are never shown to you because by the time you are available you clearly have lost interest in them.[32]

This is an indication of how restless and hyperactive, to little purpose, Kennedy had become. It was during this period that Kennedy resumed taking medical treatment from Max Jacobson, a doctor nicknamed 'Dr Feelgood' by his New York patients, who he had seen during the presidential election campaign. Jacobson was certainly no ordinary doctor, but someone who had built up a reputation amongst a particular type of ambitious, often rich, achiever who can be found in most of the big prosperous cities of the world and who want doctors to give them extra energy. Some want improved sexual performance and general help to pursue a lifestyle that requires them to be pepped up. Jacobson earned his 'Dr Feelgood' reputation by dispensing amphetamines, as 'pep' pills and in vials for intramuscular injection. He is known to have injected between 30 and 50 milligrams of amphetamine intramuscularly into his patients, and sometimes to have given even larger doses. Selected patients were also taught to inject intravenously amphetamine in liquid form, more often at that time referred to as 'speed'. He would also commonly supply his patients with injectable vials to be self-administered.

Jacobson's licence to practise as a medical doctor was revoked in New York in April 1975 and an application for it to be restored rejected in 1979 on evidence taken from him starting around February 1966. We know a lot about how two patients in particular were treated between 1961 and 1968 from a 1975 report.[33] The report, which I have read in full, shows that self-administration of injectable amphetamine supplied by Jacobson was commonplace and the description of the effect of those injections is 'elation' or 'euphoria'.

During an interview with Jacobson in 1969 agents from the Bureau of Narcotics and Dangerous Drugs had 'noticed he had needle tracks on his hands. He admitted that he injected himself with 25 grams of methamphetamine (speed) every two or three days.' Presumably the bureau meant milligrams, not grams, injected intravenously.* Jacobson died in 1979.

The first report of Jacobson treating President Kennedy came in the *New York Times* only in 1972,[34] though the reporters felt they had to put in a rider that it could not be said with certainty that Kennedy had received amphetamines. Slowly, despite denials from Kennedy supporters, more and more information has emerged. Robert Dallek's biography of Kennedy, published in 2003, has a special significance because he was granted access by the Kennedy Library trustees, three long-time family associates, to medical information which they had previously withheld. Dallek confirms that Kennedy 'had injections of painkillers and amphetamines' from Jacobson.[35]

---

* Doses of 400–500 milligrams of amphetamine have been given intravenously to patients and the individuals have survived. Also one person has been described as having survived 15 grams injected intravenously over a 24-hour period, but death has been recorded in another patient following the rapid injection of 120 milligrams intravenously. (Edward M. Brecher, *Licit and Illicit Drugs: The Consumers Union Report on Narcotics, Stimulants, Depressants, Inhalants, Hallucinogens, and Marijuana - Including Caffeine, Nicotine, and Alcohol* (Boston: Little, Brown, 1972), p. 288.) The bureau, in addition, reported that officials of the National Multiple Sclerosis Association had apparently labelled Jacobson 'a quack and a charlatan'. (Information concerning Dr Max Jacobson, FBI records, 18 August 1972.)

Kennedy had been first introduced to Jacobson shortly before the televised election debate with Richard Nixon in 1960 by Charles Spalding, a close friend from the early 1940s. In an interview Spalding describes how he 'went to see Max. I guess it was speed or whatever he gave us' and after taking a shot Spalding said he had visited the Kennedys. 'I was hopping around, they said: "Jesus! Where do you get all this energy?" After seeing Max, you could jump over a fence.' Spalding's former wife, Betty, said he would 'take a shot, get flushed in the face. His eyes would get a glazed look – the whites would look full of mucus and be fixed – and his mouth would get dry.'[36]

A revealing chapter on Kennedy's condition is included in Jacobson's unpublished memoirs, from which his medical claims can be analysed. The treatment of stress was one of Jacobson's specialities. After his first consultation, in September 1960, Kennedy is described as saying that his muscle weakness had completely disappeared and he felt cool, calm and very alert. Jacobson did not describe the treatment he gave but it was probably the intramuscular injection Jacobson most often used on patients, called XAM, a compound he himself made up containing amphetamine and steroids. Jacobson did not mention giving Kennedy any vials for self-medication to take away with him although that was his normal practice.

Several weeks after the presidential inauguration Jacobson had a phone call from Janet Travell enquiring about his treatment of stress. She confirmed his question that this referred to the President and he claims he gave her detailed information over the phone but that she bluntly refused his offer to send the same information in writing and a sample of his XAM formula.

The next contact Jacobson described with the White House was three months later, on 12 May 1961. He was telephoned and asked to fly down to West Palm Beach to see the President. When he arrived, Jacobson claimed, Kennedy was very concerned about Jackie's condition following the delivery of their last child and her subsequent chronic depression and headaches. The President, knowing that Jacobson was treating her, wanted to ask whether she could endure the strain of a forthcoming trip to Canada and more importantly the trips to Paris, Vienna and London that followed. Jacobson treated Mrs Kennedy and claimed he got rid of her migraine and her whole mood changed. No mention is made of Jacobson treating the President on this occasion or giving him any vials for self-medication.

President Kennedy visited Canada from 16 to 18 May. He seriously hurt his back while digging to plant a small oak tree and began to be photographed actually using crutches. Strangely, Travell in her clinical notes of 19 May made no mention of Kennedy's back pain, but said 'he is tired'. On 20 May she recorded that he felt all right. Her next entry, on 25 May, recorded that she undertook two infiltration treatments with intramuscular procaine at 8.30 a.m. in three sites and at 8.00 p.m. in two sites and a further entry on 28 May noted that she carried out the same treatment at Kennedy's summer home, Hyannis Port. She had in her medical papers a chart outlining a male torso front and back. The sites were marked where she had infiltrated muscles in four places.

Travell's overall medical notes, which I have seen, are shocking in their inadequacy in recounting the President's treatment, quite apart from the scruffy nature of the scraps of paper they are written on, with no book entries or formal files. There may well have been, therefore, other treatments given to Kennedy by her which were not recorded or for which the records have been lost or removed.

Jacobson described his receptionist telling him of a call from a Mrs Dunn in Washington on 23 May. 'Dunn', he claimed, was their code name for a call from the President's office. This clearly implies that a close arrangement for liaising between his office and the President's secretary in the White House had already been established. Jacobson flew to Washington with the photographer Mark Shaw, who owned a two-engined Cessna aeroplane. Reservations had been made for him at the Sheraton Hotel and he was collected next morning by a White House car. He claims he treated Jackie Kennedy and then went to see the President, who was lying on his back in his bed, following the effects of his tree-planting in Canada.

Jacobson's treatment was not only to relieve the President's local discomfort but also, in his own mind, to provide Kennedy with additional strength to cope with stress, almost certainly an injection of amphetamine with steroids. Yet 'it has been observed that Addisonian patients are unusually sensitive to the mood-elevating effects of steroids'.[37] Nevertheless, Jacobson often supplemented the amphetamine he gave with heavy doses of steroids, garnished with vitamins, even at times adding ground-up bone marrow, placenta, electric eels and whatever other solubilised particles he perceived to be beneficial.[38] The steroids Jacobson gave would therefore have been in addition to the doses already being given as part of the President's replacement therapy. It has been alleged, but not proven, that the FBI uncovered five vials Jacobson had left at the White House, which on analysis revealed high concentrations of amphetamines and steroids.

The President was able to walk around after this treatment in May 1961 and Jacobson claimed he told him that he felt very much better and asked if he would come with him to Europe the following week. Kennedy also commented that his secretary had had no bill for his visit to Jacobson's office in New York earlier in September. This account suggests that the last time Jacobson had treated him had been in September 1960, but it does not rule out the possibility that Kennedy had been self-administering drugs supplied by Jacobson on that occasion. On balance I think it best to assume that Jacobson had not treated Kennedy with amphetamines or given him self-administering vials during the Bay of Pigs crisis. But in the run-up to and during the meeting with Khrushchev in Vienna, Jacobson was in constant attendance on Kennedy and gave him frequent injections.

None of Jacobson's therapy was ever coordinated with any of the President's other doctors and there is no mention of Jacobson or his treatments in Travell's clinical notes.*

A senior Secret Service agent, according to Larry Newman, an agent who joined the presidential detail in the autumn of 1961, 'knew what the guy [Jacobson] was doing and tried to keep him away' from the President and the First Lady. 'We didn't see them [shots] administered or know the schedule of when Kennedy gave himself other shots', said the agent, 'but I was aware that during the waking hours . . . it was every six hours.'[39] Though the use of amphetamines in the early 1960s was not as strongly controlled as it is now,

---

* Jacobson was, for instance, administering 5 cubic centimetres of gamma globulin intramuscularly to increase Kennedy's resistance to infections every four to six weeks between May and October 1961, seeing him once a month for this purpose. But we also know from Travell's records that she was administering gamma globulin. The double dose would not have done much harm but the worrying fact was that she did not know about Jacobson's treatment. Double dosages of other drugs such as steroids certainly did matter and did have damaging consequences. Jacobson's amphetamine and steroids injected intramuscularly continued. The combination made Kennedy feel better for a time but, as is well known, neither cocaine derivatives nor amphetamines create energy; they give a temporary boost followed by a feeling of let-down. The 'speed' effect produced by amphetamines given intravenously was also becoming well known by then in America. Selling injectable amphetamines without a prescription or on the basis of a forged or telephone prescription from a user posing as a physician was increasing. In 1962 federal, state and local law enforcement agencies were trying to stop such practices. When the injectable amphetamine scandal broke, Abbott Laboratories in 1962 withdrew Desoxyn ampoules from the market and in July 1963 Burroughs Wellcome similarly withdrew Methedrine ampoules from distribution through retail pharmacists. Amphetamines were kept only for hospitals. But illicit factories called 'speed labs' took the place of pharmacies. (Edward M. Brecher, *Licit and Illicit Drugs: The Consumers Union Report on Narcotics, Stimulants, Depressants, Inhalants, Hallucinogens, and Marijuana – Including Caffeine, Nicotine, and Alcohol* (Boston: Little, Brown, 1972), pp. 282–3.)

no serious doctor would have given anything like these sizes of dose to a patient with Kennedy's medical history.

We know that by the summer of 1962 Robert Kennedy was very worried about Jacobson's relationship with his brother and had the FBI analyse the substance Jacobson was injecting. 'Inconclusive lab tests, however, allowed Jacobson to continue treating Kennedy through at least the fall of 1962.'[40] From at least 24 May 1961, Jacobson was intensively treating Kennedy in the White House, in Paris and then in Vienna and London, in all of which places he gave Kennedy injections of amphetamine and steroids. It would no doubt have appalled Kennedy's White House doctors that such injections should have been given to the President at all, let alone in the run-up to a vitally important two-day meeting with Khrushchev, scheduled to start on 3 June in Vienna. Kennedy dismissed criticism of the treatment Jacobson was giving him by saying: 'I don't care if it's horse piss. It works.'[41]

But did it work? The cumulative evidence points to the repeated amphetamine injections from 24 May as having had very damaging consequences for President Kennedy's performance in Vienna. We know that no single doctor 'was in overall charge'[42] and the claim that 'Kennedy was more promiscuous with physicians and drugs than he was with women'[43] was probably true and not indicative of moderation.

Jacobson claimed that when he saw Jacqueline Kennedy on the morning after his visit on 24 May, she showed him a vial of Demerol, a synthetic morphine-like painkiller she had found in the President's bathroom, presumably for self-injection.* To Jacobson's credit he took strong objection to the President taking this and said that it was highly addictive – which it was – and would interfere with his own medication. Jacobson was making a distinction between drugs that cause physical withdrawal symptoms and addictive dependency and amphetamines, which 'only in about 5 per cent' of cases do users move on to full-blown dependence.[44] No one apart from the President knew how long he had been taking Demerol, apart from its oral use for an irritable colon in March. It is not unreasonable to believe that he had been having injections during the Bay of Pigs crisis. Mrs Kennedy asked Jacobson if he would try and stop the President from using it. He claimed he raised the issue directly with Kennedy, concerned that it would affect the President's thinking.[45] Later that day Mrs Kennedy told Jacobson that a Secret

* Demerol or meperidine hydrochloride has today a special precautionary note attached to its use in cases of Addison's disease.

Service agent had given Kennedy the drug and had since been dismissed. It was one more revelation of the strange cocktail of drugs which were being taken by the President, not known about by any of his White House doctors.

Jacobson, not Travell, became in effect the President's personal physician for the next few weeks. Indeed Travell did not know that Jacobson was travelling to Paris. After four days of treating Kennedy in Washington, Jacobson returned to New York and flew with his wife on Air France to Paris, but not before he gave the President another treatment in Air Force One at what was then called Idlewild airport in New York, later to be renamed after John F. Kennedy. In Paris, Jacobson claimed he saw the President every day at the Palais d'Orsay, reserved for visiting dignitaries. Kennedy's visit to Paris was the prelude to meeting Khrushchev in Vienna. President de Gaulle thought it was foolish of Kennedy to be meeting Khrushchev but said: '*Tenir bon, tenir le coup.*' Hold on, be firm, be strong. Wait them out. One day, communism will fall of its own weight. De Gaulle wrote privately of his visitor: 'Enjoying the advantages of youth, but suffering the drawbacks of a novice.'[46]

Khrushchev

Kennedy was keen to know more about Nikita Khrushchev and he was presented with a 'personality sketch' of him before he arrived in Vienna, prepared by the CIA. It described Khrushchev's frame of mind, drawing from conversations and stories told by him at diplomatic receptions and other places where he opened up to Western diplomats. One story from which they drew was from a Ukrainian writer, Volodymyr Vinnichenko, whose book *Talisman* Khrushchev had read when he was young. In the story there is a half-educated Jew with whom Khrushchev associated, saying: 'That little Pinya – that's me.' The CIA took the story as indicating a 'consciousness of his humble origins', a 'sense of personal accomplishment' and 'confidence that his vigor, initiative and capacity are equal to his station'. But Khrushchev's perceptive biographer William Taubman from the same story questions the CIA interpretation: 'If Khrushchev really saw himself as Pinya (as a poor little Jew, no less, in a land in which anti-Semitism ran deep) his doubts about himself were more profound than he ever admitted.'[47]

Some twenty American psychiatrists and psychologists were asked by the CIA in 1960 to report. They noted Khrushchev's 'depressions and vulnerability to alcohol' but focused on his 'hypomanic' character.[48] Taubman cites a psychoanalyst's listing of hypomanic characteristics as almost perfectly describing Khrushchev:

> Elated, energetic, self-promoting, witty and grandiose . . . overtly cheerful, highly social, given to idealisation of others, work addicted, flirtatious and articulate while covertly . . . guilty about aggression toward others, incapable of being alone . . . corruptible and lacking a systematic approach in cognitive style . . . Grand schemes, racing thoughts, extended freedom from ordinary physical requirements such as food and sleep . . . constantly 'up' – until exhaustion eventually sets in.[49]

Khrushchev's wife Nina said of him: 'He's either all the way up or all the way down.'

It was fortunate for the world that given this personality, Khrushchev was not made to feel embarrassed during the missile crisis, so that near the end of the crisis, on 28 October 1962, he had 'a sense of satisfaction. It took time for the whole truth about the way he and the Soviet Union had been humiliated by Kennedy to sink in and this contributed to Khrushchev's final unravelling.'[50] By the time Khrushchev was ousted from power in October 1964 his personality had so deteriorated that his 'behaviour was almost surreal: stubbornly persistent in futile policies, seemingly blind to his disintegrating political base, recklessly unresponsive to the growing conspiracy against him'.[51] Leonid Brezhnev accused him of treating colleagues 'rudely' and said that he 'ignored others' opinions' and was 'distracted' in a state of depression. He had either developed bipolar disorder or still had hypomania, but of a very advanced form. I am reluctant to say he had developed hubris syndrome while in office because of the history of depression. On 14 October 1964 he was removed by the collective leadership of the Presidium, although it was described as 'retirement'. After his unexpected fall from power Khrushchev suffered a very serious and persistent depression. He died on 11 September 1971.

The Vienna meeting

Max Jacobson claimed that he flew in Air Force One to Vienna while Janet Travell was in Air Force Two. He went immediately to the US ambassador's private residence, where the summit was due to take place. It is possible from Jacobson's description that an injection of amphetamine and steroids was given intravenously there since he stressed that the atmosphere was tense and that he was called to see Kennedy immediately. He claimed that Kennedy said to him: 'Khrushchev will arrive momentarily. The meeting may last for hours. I can't afford any complications with my back.' An injection containing amphetamine was then administered to the President. We do not know for sure whether it was given with steroids into his muscle as usual or whether methyl amphetamine was given into a vein. Jacobson recalled treating Kennedy in the White House in November 1961, when the cellist Pablo Casals gave a concert, and that Kennedy had asked for a repeat of the 'Vienna treatment'. This implies that the Vienna treatment was different and probably an intravenous injection.

But Kennedy was misinformed over the timing and Nikita Khrushchev did not arrive until forty-five minutes later. Kennedy ran down the steps to meet Khrushchev as if to demonstrate his vigour and health, in contrast to the rather portly 67-year-old Soviet leader. Jacobson may well have given the amphetamine intravenously in order to act quickly and, if so, it would have had a greater impact on Kennedy in the sense of a 'high' and a greater 'low' perhaps coming before the end of the meeting.* Put another way by Robert Dallek: 'As the day wore on and an injection Jacobson had given him just before he met Khrushchev in the early afternoon wore off, Kennedy may have lost the emotional and physical edge initially provided by the shot.'

The first meeting with Khrushchev, on 3 June, went badly wrong and even Kennedy blamed himself for its failure. He acted totally out of character and the experienced Sovietologist Llewellyn 'Tommy' Thompson, then ambassador to Moscow, seated behind Kennedy, told his State Department colleagues that he was shocked that Kennedy just sat there taking one shot

---

* Quite apart from the combination of amphetamines and steroids, injections of steroids alone can produce behavioural effects, with very high doses producing manic or psychotic symptoms. High doses can give a feeling of energy and well-being and increased physical and sexual appetite. Even with all the recent advances, doctors treating Addison's disease have difficulty in setting the right doses of steroids. Eugene Cohen, Kennedy's endocrinologist, at this stage in all likelihood knew nothing about Jacobson's arrival on the scene, and was therefore completely in the dark as to the dosage of steroids he was giving the President. Most endocrinologists at the start of the twenty-first century believe that in the past patients were given too high a dosage. The most widely accepted regime now would be 10 milligrams of hydrocortisone in the morning followed by 5 milligrams at lunchtime and 5 in the evening. Some would choose to give prednisolone or cortisone. What is clear is that Kennedy, when Jacobson was treating him in addition to Cohen, was receiving much more. This is demonstrated by photographs of Kennedy during his presidency showing some fullness and puffiness in the face; this is associated with Cushing's disease, where there is overproduction of cortisol.

after another from the Russian.[52] After that first meeting Kennedy raged that Khrushchev had treated him like a little boy and one of his own note takers at the meeting, Charles Bohlen, said of his President: 'He's a little bit out of his depth, isn't he.'[53] George Kennan, one of the great post-war American diplomats, thought the President had seemed tongue tied and totally unsure of himself. Criticism of this kind was unusual, for Kennedy did not normally come across in this way. It was almost certainly brought on by the drugs Jacobson had given him.

Next day, the conversation on West Berlin became ugly when Khrushchev said: 'The USSR will sign a peace treaty with the German Democratic Republic.' Kennedy asked if this peace treaty would block access to Berlin, and Khrushchev said yes. The gauntlet had been thrown down. 'Force would be met by force,' Khrushchev said. 'If the US wants war that's its problem.' Ending the meeting Kennedy said: 'Then, Mr Chairman, there will be war. It will be a cold winter.'

Kennedy knew he had not handled the meeting well. This is the view of David Reynolds in an assessment of the summit, who picks out Kennedy's failure 'to change tack and get out of the ideological argument on that long first afternoon'.[54] When James Reston, the *New York Times* Washington bureau chief, an experienced journalist, asked Kennedy ten minutes after the finish in a personal meeting how it had gone, Kennedy replied: 'Roughest thing in my life,' and said: 'He savaged me.' He went on: 'I think I know why he treated me like this. He thinks because of the Bay of Pigs that I'm inexperienced. Probably thinks I'm stupid. Maybe most important, he thinks that I had no guts.' Reston thought that Kennedy was practically in shock, repeating himself, blurting out things he would never say in other circumstances.[55] But little of this appeared in the *New York Times*. Reynolds describes the summit as a 'surreal meeting'.[56] It is impossible to escape the conclusion that Jacobson's injection had played a substantial part in Kennedy's performance and that this had a profound effect on Khrushchev and Soviet policy.

The coming storm

The President and his party left Vienna for London to meet Prime Minister Harold Macmillan. Max Jacobson claims he treated Kennedy that evening in the home of Prince Stanisław Radziwiłł, the husband of Jackie Kennedy's sister, Lee. He also claims he saw him there next day and flew back to the

United States with him in Air Force One the following day, treating him on the plane.

At their first working session on 5 June it was obvious to Macmillan that Kennedy was in pain from his back, tense and fatigued; rather than have the scheduled formal session, he took him to his own room to have an informal chat – just the two of them – from 11.30 a.m. to 3.00 p.m. over sandwiches and whisky. Kennedy told Macmillan how surprised he had been by the brutal frankness of the Soviet leader.

David Ormsby-Gore became close to Kennedy as a young man in pre-war London. Kennedy's sister 'Kick' had married a cousin of his, Lord Hartington. Kennedy asked Macmillan at their first meeting in Key West to appoint Ormsby-Gore as the British ambassador to Washington, who became a great success. Later, as Lord Harlech, he recalled in his oral history meeting Kennedy in London, who was 'obviously in great pain at that time because his back was extremely bad'. Harlech said that Kennedy's meeting in Vienna 'had been a most disagreeable interview, that Khrushchev obviously tried to browbeat him and frighten him. He had displayed the naked power of the Soviet Union and this had all been extremely unpleasant and quite unlike what he had hoped their first meeting would be.'

Macmillan described Kennedy's reaction to Khrushchev as being 'rather stunned – baffled would perhaps be fairer' and 'impressed and shocked'.[57] Kennedy, he felt, saw Khrushchev as a 'barbarian'.

Kennedy went on to complain about the way the press had treated him and Jackie in Vienna and said to Macmillan: 'How would you react if somebody should say: "Lady Dorothy is a drunk!"?' Kennedy laughed when Macmillan cracked back: 'I would reply: "You should have seen her mother!"' Kennedy enjoyed his relationship with Macmillan and vice versa, despite their different ages and attitudes to many things, not least women. Macmillan on another occasion had no such quick rejoinder when, after talking about nuclear questions, Kennedy casually said: 'I wonder how it is with you, Harold? If I don't have a woman for three days, I get a terrible headache.'

In his brutal, belligerent way, Khrushchev later declared that Berlin was like 'the testicles of the West: every time I want to make the West scream, I squeeze on Berlin.' Yet we now know from the archives that Khrushchev did not want war, but stability and recognition for Walter Ulbricht's East Germany. Kennedy for his part knew after this meeting that he would face a challenge from Khrushchev.

Vienna was perhaps the turning point for Kennedy personally. After the Bay of Pigs he was privately blaming the failure on others; after meeting Khrushchev he knew the failure was his and his alone. On the flight back to Washington he apparently found solace in a quotation from Abraham Lincoln:

> I know there is a God – and I see a storm coming;
> If He has a place for me, I believe I am ready.

Yet the Kennedy that arrived back in Washington on 6 June was certainly not ready mentally or physically to face any such storm in that summer of 1961. He was becoming reliant on Jacobson's amphetamine injections. He had also refused Jacobson's offer to step aside, made, Jacobson claims, because he had sensed Dr Travell's hostility to his presence as one of Kennedy's doctors. The severity of the President's back trouble was admitted to the press on 8 June, who were told he was on crutches and was going to Palm Beach to rest. Kennedy received his first ultrasound treatment for muscle spasm that day but Travell's notes make no mention of any procaine injections into his muscles and I saw no prior notes for the days she was travelling with the President in Paris, Vienna or London. For the next three days Kennedy had no engagements but on 12 June, propped up in bed and smoking a cigar, he held a meeting on monetary policy. Meanwhile, on 10 June Khrushchev released to the world the aide-memoire he had given Kennedy and on 12 June in Geneva the nuclear test ban talks were effectively killed off by the Soviet delegation. Back in Washington on 16 June, the President, unable to walk up the stairs, had been lifted onto Air Force One by an airport cherry picker, normally used for work on aircraft engines.[58]

On 20 June the President had a sore throat, and by 22 June Travell describes the President as having his sickest day in the White House with a fever spiking at 105°F, because of a streptococcus infection. There are detailed chronological notes, probably made by a nurse during this period, from which it is clear that the President was not at all well and he was treated with 'large doses of penicillin' and cold sponge baths. Yet the press corps at the White House was only told of a temperature of 101° by Travell, whose bland statement said: 'There is no serious concern about the President's health.' On 28 June, Kennedy, now much better, spoke to the press, charging the Soviets with wanting 'to make permanent the partition of Germany' and adding: 'No one can fail to appreciate the gravity of this threat.'

The political pressures post-Vienna on Kennedy were still considerable and generally he rose to the challenge but Berlin was a crisis area that had been long planned for and the President could rely on the extensive contingency planning. On the night of 12–13 August East German security forces put up barbed wire barriers to block people fleeing to West Berlin and the Soviets resumed nuclear testing. Kennedy's view was that 'a wall is a hell of a lot better than a war'. Having spoken out firmly, he called up reserves, rushed additional forces to Europe, made clear a firm intention to defend West Berlin and sent his Vice President, Lyndon Johnson, to the city. Kennedy also asked Congress for an extra $3.25 billion for the defence budget. The crisis froze that autumn but dangers lurked in East Germany and in other Warsaw Pact countries behind the newly built Berlin Wall. Not until 1989, when the wall was eventually knocked down and Soviet communism itself began to crumble, did the Berlin situation cease to be a persistent cause for concern.

In August 1961 Kennedy complained of feeling 'tired', 'groggy' and 'sleepy'. Dr Jeffrey Kelman, a physician who retrospectively reviewed his medical records said: 'He was tired because he was doped up'[59] to dampen down the pain. In addition Travell was injecting him with more procaine, some claim five or six times a day,[60] and there were the amphetamines Jacobson was injecting. Jacobson claimed he was staying in Massachusetts on 28 August when he was asked to drive over to Hyannis to see the President, who he described as nervous and irritable before he treated him. Jacobson referred next to being in the White House on 18 and 19 September and to treating Kennedy in New York on 25 September for a hoarse throat prior to addressing the UN General Assembly.

In the autumn of 1961 Kennedy's back condition was so serious that his naval doctor in the White House, George Burkley, felt he might soon be unable to walk and would end up in a wheelchair.[61] Kept well out of sight of the press, the President could walk down the stairs of a helicopter only one at a time, a humiliating situation for a man who liked to project an image of strength and virility. But to his credit, and unlike President Wilson and Roosevelt's naval medical advisers, Burkley, though still only a naval captain, took a tough line in demanding outside medical opinion.

Together with Dr Cohen, Kennedy's consultant endocrinologist in New York, he confronted Travell with an ultimatum that if she did not invite in Dr Hans Kraus, a proven expert on back pain, to treat the President, they would both approach him for his authority to do so. Cohen had used Kraus to treat pain in the muscles of other patients with Addison's disease and also those with thyroid deficiency and had immense trust in him. Both Cohen and Burkley felt that Kennedy's medical condition was deteriorating so fast that they feared he was heading for a life of limited activity and dependence on narcotics.

Travell tried to oppose involving Kraus, using the knowledge that Kennedy was fearful of allowing another doctor into the White House, which might alert the press to his real state of health. But, more importantly, Travell herself feared that if Kraus, a specialist in her own field, came in she would be pushed out. But she failed. Kraus was brought in on 17 October and from that point Travell was progressively downgraded. Burkley in effect displaced her as Kennedy's physician in the autumn of 1961 though this was not announced until a year later.[62] He became an admiral and went on to look after President Johnson. Travell continued to serve nominally as one of the doctors in the White House until 1965.

What was needed in October 1961 was for Kennedy's medical treatment to become more rational and more disciplined. It was essential, above all, to modify and control his multi-sourced medication starting with Travell's procaine injections, which had become ever more frequent.* It would take many months, building back his confidence and his strength, before the President was ready for the impending 'storm'. But at least a serious regime of medical treatment for his back began in October 1961, a year before the Cuban missile crisis. It was only partially successful because Kennedy took longer to face up to his other big medical problem: Jacobson's injections of amphetamines and steroids.

Dr Kraus

It is fascinating to trace the actual steps which some of Kennedy's doctors started to take, in the latter half of 1961, to bring his medication under control and improve the treatment for his back while he wrestled with the Berlin crisis. On 17 October Hans Kraus, a small, athletic and blunt man who had once been the trainer of Austria's Olympic ski team, and was a legendary rock climber, examined President Kennedy. He found Kennedy's muscles so weak that he could not do a single sit-up yet so taut that his leg muscles felt like 'piano wires'.[63]

---

* Travell's back charts for 25, 29, and 30 June seem to indicate that she gave injections of 10 cubic centimetres procaine at 0.5 per cent dilution into muscle sites, particularly because of grumbling discomfort, in Kennedy's left buttock but not in his back region.

In his detailed clinical notes,[64] which I have viewed in the Kennedy Library, Kraus reports that when Kennedy bent over to try and touch the floor, his fingertips could not reach closer than 20 inches. By 20 November, after exercise treatment, they could reach 11¾ inches. Kraus told the President: 'You will be a cripple soon if you don't start exercising. Five days a week. And you need to start now'. Kraus also demanded absolute control and he wrote: 'I would like to work with this patient three times a week . . . training could accomplish much.' Kennedy was worried that reporters would start writing about his health again if he had a new doctor. Eventually it was agreed that Kraus's visits to Kennedy should be publicly explained as a health upgrade with more regular exercise for the President.

A sign that some people were still sniffing around for medical information on President Kennedy came when Kraus's medical office was broken into soon after he started to treat the President. There was very little information on paper in his office and what there was had been placed in an unmarked file which remained undiscovered. When told about the break-in, the White House immediately took precautionary steps, one of which was to stop Kraus's telephone line being easily tapped. The White House's prime suspect for who was responsible, interestingly, was not the Republican Party but the FBI under J. Edgar Hoover. Previously both Janet Travell and Eugene Cohen had had their consulting rooms entered into clandestinely during the 1960 campaign.

Kraus made thirty-three visits in the fourteen weeks between 17 October and 24 January 1962. Kraus treated spasms primarily by massage, not by injection, which Travell favoured. When Kraus did use injections, his chosen trigger point technique had little in common with Travell's, as it involved injecting the whole of the muscle with saline solution, and only rarely, for comfort, when the pain would not respond to anything else, with procaine or lidocaine. In future it was agreed that Travell's procaine injections were only to be given under the direction of Kraus. In addition, with any extensive injection technique by Kraus came a three-day structured physical therapy protocol.

Heat massage and exercise began to achieve results for the President. However, over Christmas 1961, Kennedy suffered a relapse in Palm Beach. Travell tried to assert her dwindling authority and convened a medical team for a consultation, telling the press who was being invited to it. She omitted Kraus's name from the list. Kraus, who had in fact been invited and was present, felt the President had gone back on their agreement that he would be in complete control. So he spoke directly to Kennedy, in front of Travell, saying: 'I won't treat you again if she touches you.'[65] Kennedy nodded his assent. On one later occasion when Travell gave a procaine injection, not authorised by Kraus, he flew down to see the President and offered to resign if this continued. Kennedy promised it would not happen again.

President Kennedy's health was beginning to show real improvement. By January of 1962 Kraus and George Burkley saw him having a better month than at any time in the previous year. At the end of February they described the previous four weeks, 'medically speaking', as the 'most uneventful month since the inauguration; since the 1960 campaign, for that matter'. And in April they pronounced his general condition 'excellent'.[66] On 16 March 1962 Dr Wade, Kennedy's orthopaedic surgeon, and Kraus examined the President.* The President's back treatment was, at long last, in strong and competent hands and the better results were well appreciated by him and others. Reading between the lines, Cohen emerges as the key medical figure, commanding the respect of other doctors and negotiating directly with Kennedy the delicate question of what to do with Travell. Cohen was the sort of senior, distinguished doctor who should have been the President's personal physician, in overall charge at the White House, from the start of Kennedy's presidency in January 1961.†

By May 1962 all that needed to be done to fully control Kennedy's medication was to get rid of Max Jacobson. In November 1961 it had been Cohen who had written to the President, warning him in particular about the

---

* In March Wade found that the X-rays showed 'no increase in the lesion in the left sacro–iliac region'. Kraus found that Kennedy 'could sit up without effort and he could perform knee bends without effort'. In Burkley's clinical notes in March there is a reference to his concern over Travell still calling herself Kennedy's personal physician and giving another procaine injection, which she had at least reported to Burkley, who worried about 'the continued menace of having the needle so available'. On 2 April 1962 Kraus is reported as believing that another of her procaine injections could have been avoided and Burkley records: 'Dr Travell feels because Dr Kraus did not raise the roof, that he is in accordance with her precipitant use of injections.'

† Dr Russell S. Boles, who was consulted on the President's gastrointestinal problems by Travell, wrote to her next day: 'I found Gene Cohen delightful and also very helpful to work with.' On 9 May 1962 Cohen wrote to Kennedy: 'I spoke with Dr Travell today stating that the Medical Department was being further strengthened under Dr Burkley's supervision and that this placed her in an embarrassing situation.' Cohen then made six specific points to Kennedy, amongst which were first, 'There is really little for her to do now'; second, 'She served a purpose in getting things going for the first year'; and sixth, 'She would be then ready to leave her position as the Personal Physician to the President in August'. By May Travell was slowly given reduced access to Kennedy and she was only kept on in the White House to ensure that she did not reveal Kennedy's health secrets to the public. It was feared that if she was forced out, she would have been tempted to talk publicly about the President's medical condition, although this did not happen when she published her memoirs in 1968.

injections that he was receiving from Jacobson,[67] but Kennedy ignored that warning. Secret Service files and the White House gate log substantiate that Jacobson visited Kennedy as President no fewer than thirty-four times through to June 1962, when he ceased to visit the White House. Jacobson's treatment of the President, however, continued outside the White House for some months after. Jacobson claimed to have seen Kennedy frequently during the Cuban missile crisis, implying that he did so when the President flew out of Washington to New York and Chicago. We also know that Kraus spoke trenchantly to Kennedy in December 1962 in relation to the injections Jacobson was giving him, saying: 'If I ever heard he took another shot, I'd make sure it was known. No President with his finger on the red button has any business taking stuff like that.'[68]

This all points to Jacobson still seeing the President during the Cuban missile crisis, but less frequently than he claimed. The unresolved question is how many injections of amphetamine and steroids Jacobson was still giving Kennedy and in what quantities. The answer, I suspect, is nowhere near as many as during the periods when the President's back was really painful and certainly considerably fewer than, for example, he was giving at the time of Kennedy's Vienna meeting with Nikita Khrushchev. Kraus's dynamic personality and the rapport he had established with Kennedy probably meant that the President took account of his warnings. He once demonstrated to Kennedy rock-climbing techniques on a wall next to the White House swimming pool, jamming his fingers into the cracks and hanging from them and walking up the wall. This was just the sort of man that Kennedy admired.

Yet the President went on seeing Jacobson into 1963 even if there were fewer injections of amphetamine. A published collection of Mark Shaw, the Kennedy photographer, shows President Kennedy with Charles Spalding, Prince Radziwiłł and Jacobson in Palm Beach in February 1963.[69] Jacobson claims that he saw Kennedy in Hyannis Port in July 1963 and flew to Florida to see Kennedy on 3 November at West Palm Beach but does not mention whether any treatments took place. It may be that Jacobson's injections had become by then more of a recreational drug for Kennedy than something on which he relied on a regular basis for the relief of acute pain and stress.

No doubt there are many people who claim to have contributed to one of Kennedy's most famous lines, '*Ich bin ein Berliner*', spoken when on a visit to the Berlin Wall on 26 June 1963. One of those people was Jacobson, who was at least fluent in German. He perhaps exaggerates his relationship with

Kennedy when he describes him, after the assassination, as 'a very dear friend and a great man' but there is little doubt that he was far closer to the President and his wife than has ever been admitted by the keepers of the Kennedy image.

The Cuban missile crisis

The 'storm' came for Kennedy a year after his prediction, arriving in the shape of Soviet missiles photographed in Cuba on 16 October 1962. Fortunately the President's back condition had improved substantially by then, as had his whole medical treatment. He was ready for the challenge.

From the start of the missile crisis, President Kennedy knew the Chiefs of Staff wanted immediate massive air attacks and an invasion of Cuba. Kennedy was, however, determined to take his time and not to let the chiefs become the dominant source of advice. The President as Commander in Chief was now a very different person from the crying, emotional man after the Bay of Pigs failure in April 1961 or the shattered and shaken man that flew back from Vienna in June of that year. Kennedy was now in control of himself as well as his Cabinet and his Chiefs of Staff.

Theodore Sorensen, who was unaware of the Bay of Pigs operation and was not involved until it was over, produced in his book *Kennedy* both candid criticism and intellectual justification from the President's viewpoint for what had gone wrong. He pointed out five fundamental gaps between what Kennedy approved and what he thought he was approving. In that same book he gave total praise for the handling of the Cuban missile crisis. Yet writing some two years after Kennedy's assassination, Sorensen, who knew most about Kennedy's medical condition, never questioned how much his health or medication could have affected any aspect of his decision-making, let alone comment on the marked difference in his health between 1961 and 1962.

Sorensen, who is a highly intelligent and sensitive man, will hopefully have written a more personal account to be published at some future date, because he spent much time close to Kennedy. He did, for example, write about how, when Kennedy was a Senator, they criss-crossed the country together campaigning in 1957 and 1958, sleeping in countless hotels and motels – some shiny, some shabby – and frequently on planes as they went from $100- to $5-a-head Democratic dinners. Yet perhaps Kennedy did not allow even such a close adviser as Sorensen to know many aspects of his private life, or details of the drugs he was taking. Kennedy always kept separate the many facets of his life and personality. Maybe Richard Neustadt's comment on Kennedy's relationship with Sorensen, 'Never have two people been more intimate and more separate', is correct. But even so, Sorensen's personal insights would have value now that all those years have passed.

Sorensen does admit that after 18 April 1961 things changed for Kennedy. 'In later months he would be grateful that he had learned so many major lessons – resulting in basic changes in personnel, policy and procedures – at so relatively small and temporary cost.'[70] I do not believe that the cost of the Bay of Pigs was so temporary, but it did leave behind many lessons to be learnt and Kennedy was always a quick learner. Richard Goodwin, reflecting after a much longer period than Sorensen, thought it

> absurd to pretend that the Bay of Pigs was somehow a blessing in disguise, an inexpensive lesson in the limits of new acquired presidential power. The first adventure of the New Frontier had been a failure, and not an ordinary failure, but one that reeked of incompetence, of naïve and therefore dangerous militance; one that weakened the new President's pretension, so eloquently proclaimed just a few months before, to leadership of the free world.[71]

Kennedy knew after this blunder that he could not leave the use of force just to the professionals and also that force was a blunter, less trustworthy, instrument than he assumed.

In marked contrast to his handling of the Bay of Pigs, President Kennedy imposed a disciplined caution on the decision-making surrounding the Cuban missile crisis through the setting up of the Executive Committee of the National Security Council (EXCOMM). These meetings of fourteen or fifteen people, established only in October 1962, were an innovation. Kennedy – who had never until the Cuban missile crisis used his Cabinet for major decisions – arranged for it to meet, often without him attending any part of the meeting, to thrash out options in some twenty-seven meetings over thirteen days. Robert Kennedy and Sorensen were both fully involved from the start, unlike over the Bay of Pigs. By October 1962 there was also a more knowledgeable and confident Secretary of Defense, Robert McNamara. In 1961 McNamara had fully supported the Chiefs of Staff on the Bay of Pigs, but in 1962 he felt sufficiently certain in his own judgement to consistently oppose the Joint Chiefs' advice over the Cuban missile crisis.

When Kennedy held his first meeting on the morning of 16 October he outlined four possible military scenarios. First, an air strike to wipe out all known missile sites. Second, a 'general air strike' to attack Soviet MiG-21 fighter jets and all SA-2 missile sites. Third, an invasion of Cuba. Fourth, a blockade of the island. Kennedy made it clear that 'at least we're going to do number one, so it seems that we don't have to wait very long'. Fortunately, he soon had doubts about the first scenario because of General Taylor's appraisal of an air strike: 'It'll never be 100 per cent, Mr President, we know.' The President was therefore flexible from the outset, with few signs of having to prove himself or having to demonstrate toughness, as with the Bay of Pigs.

In the early days of the crisis, consideration was given to making private diplomatic representations to Khrushchev. Sorensen tried to draft what he called an airtight letter to be carried by a high-level envoy from Kennedy to Khrushchev, saying that only if Khrushchev agreed in his conference with the envoy to order the missiles to be dismantled would US military action be withheld, while US air flights would oversee their removal. But whatever sweeteners Sorensen put in the letter, it still read like a justification for a pre-emptive strike and an ultimatum which Khrushchev would reject.

Another drawback of private representation was that Khrushchev could have ordered immediate action, even while meeting Kennedy's envoy, perhaps by halting all traffic along the autobahn and canals into Berlin. This would have instantly widened the conflict out from Cuba and given Khrushchev a wider geographical scope within which to conduct subsequent negotiations.

From 18 October onwards Kennedy appeared to have concluded that the only way of playing Khrushchev was to put the challenge onto the world stage. It was a risk but a calculated one, and it was always a grave provocation for Khrushchev to have chosen to challenge Kennedy in Cuba, so close to the United States. In a book on decision-making called *The Politics of Defence*,[72] published in 1972, I thought that Kennedy had been unwise to negotiate by public ultimatum but, wiser myself now, I think he made the correct choice. Kennedy also veered away from the air strike course to the marine blockade, a much more flexible option.[73]

Once private diplomatic representation had been ruled out as the principal mode of negotiation, Kennedy wisely authorised vitally important 'back channel' negotiations, to be conducted secretly in parallel through his brother Robert. In these discussions the offer of withdrawing US missiles in Turkey was introduced.

Khrushchev had decided to put nuclear missiles in Cuba on 24 May 1962 after having asked rhetorically, in April: 'Why not throw a hedgehog at Uncle

Sam's pants?' His motives had been orientated not towards war but more to supporting Marxism-Leninism in Cuba and in Latin America. Letting Americans know what it felt like to have enemy missiles pointing at them had been only a secondary motive. The USSR faced US missiles from bases in the UK, Italy and Turkey, but the US Jupiter missiles in Turkey had not been a determining factor for Khrushchev.[74] Nonetheless it was very helpful in terms of handling the Russian military that he learnt privately on 27 October that they would be withdrawn. Kennedy knew that it is wise never to corner one's adversary in international diplomacy without leaving a face-saving line of retreat.

The former US ambassador to Moscow, Llewellyn 'Tommy' Thompson, predicted in EXCOMM that Khrushchev would take Russian missiles out of Cuba if 'he is to be able to say: "I saved Cuba: I stopped an invasion."' This convinced Kennedy, and McNamara believed it was possibly the single most important decision in the entire crisis on the US side to offer Khrushchev this political lifeline over the Turkish missiles. Given the stakes at that supremely dangerous moment, it was one of the most important decisions in the entire Cold War.[75]

President Kennedy's decision to use sea power in the form of a naval quarantine as the least provocative and most flexible method of exercising the military power of the United States over the Soviet Union ensured a successful outcome. As the first Soviet ship, the *Bukharest*, approached the point of armed interception, 500 miles off the Cuban coast, the world held its breath. In the United Nations Adlai Stevenson, the US permanent representative, was challenging the Soviet ambassador to answer his questions on the missile sites and said he was prepared to wait for his answer 'until hell freezes over'. On 25 October the *Bukharest* was boarded by US forces and, its cargo inspected, allowed to proceed. Another vessel under Russian charter was boarded on 28 October, the day Khrushchev agreed to dismantle the missiles in Cuba, crate them up and return them to the Soviet Union.

By using the naval quarantine Kennedy was able to apply graduated pressure on Khrushchev. Even so on the afternoon of Saturday 27 October, the day an American U-2 spy plane was shot down over Cuba, Kennedy faced up to the prospect of taking early military action. He authorised his brother Robert at 7.15 p.m. to ring up and fix a secret meeting with the Soviet ambassador, Anatoly Dobrynin, which took place half an hour later in the Attorney General's office.[76] Dobrynin was told: 'There is now strong pressure on the President to give an order to respond with fire if fired upon.' Robert Kennedy went on: 'If we start to fire in response, a chain reaction will quickly start that will be very hard to stop,' and he promised that the United States would 'give assurances that there would be no invasion of Cuba' and said it would need 'four or five months' to remove the missile bases in Turkey. Dobrynin was warned that 'the greatest difficulty for the President is the public discussion of the issue of Turkey'; the US Jupiter missiles in Turkey would go but the Soviets were warned that if this was revealed then the pledge would become null and void.

When this private message was spelt out to Khrushchev, having already called the Soviet Presidium together to authorise a 'retreat', he immediately dictated a letter accepting Kennedy's terms. This was deliberately broadcast on the radio so as to reach the United States immediately. Kennedy immediately responded to this broadcast, ignoring in the process Khrushchev's earlier letter. The Joint Chiefs of Staff were not told about Robert Kennedy's private session with Dobrynin on 27 October. Only the President and his Secretary of State, Dean Rusk, knew that they had privately agreed between themselves that if by Monday Robert Kennedy's mission had failed, then U Thant, the UN secretary general, would be urged to propose a Turkey-for-Cuba missile trade which Kennedy would publicly accept, a trade which Stevenson had already been advocating.[77]

The following day Khrushchev wrote very privately to Kennedy about the Jupiter missiles, mentioning his first letter of that same date:

> In my letter to you of 28 October which was designed for publication I did not touch on this matter because of your wish, as conveyed by Robert Kennedy. But all of the offers, which were included in this letter, were given on account of your having agreed to the Turkish issue raised in my letter of 27 October and announced from your side, in his meeting with the Soviet Ambassador that same day.[78]

This back-channel secret diplomacy worked well. We know also that Robert Kennedy had been in regular communication with a Soviet secret service agent for some time on other matters, so that there was a record of successful private diplomacy already in the pipeline between the two leaders.

The crisis was over. Robert Kennedy always believed that if seven of the thirteen men in the Cabinet Room had been President of the United States, the world might have been blown up. So it might have been if President Kennedy had been in the same medical condition in 1962 as he was through most of 1961.

One of the many roots from which Robert Kennedy's contempt for Lyndon Johnson grew was his belief, expressed in an oral Kennedy Library interview, that if Johnson had been President in 1962, there would have been a disaster. As EXCOMM's members left after their final meeting, none of them knowing how the crisis would end, Robert Kennedy and Ken O'Donnell were taken aside by Johnson, who now objected to the President's plan, having never opposed it in all their meetings, and having in fact at times made some sensible interventions. The Vice President is alleged to have said: 'All I know is that when I was a boy in Texas and walking along the road when a rattlesnake reared up, the only thing you could do was to take a stick and chop its head off.' Robert Kennedy never forgot that brief exchange for it confirmed for him all Johnson's weaknesses as a leader at the point of decision.[79]

During the crisis Kennedy still had severe health problems but his back was far better than in the summer of 1961. He had 'his usual doses of anti-spasmodics to control his colitis; antibiotics for a flare-up of his urinary tract problem and a bout of sinusitis; and increased amounts of hydrocortisone and testosterone as well as salt tablets to control his Addison's disease and increase his energy'.[80] Afterwards, on 10 November 1962, Kennedy had, on medical advice, an additional 10 milligrams of hydrocortisone, a sensible additional dosage at a time of stress. Also 10 grams of salt were given him before he made a television address on the dismantling of the Soviet missile base in Cuba. His gastroenterologist, Dr Russell Boles, at his wife's request, dropped antihistamines for food allergies because she had felt he was getting depressed and instead gave Kennedy Stelazine, 1 milligram a day, for 'mood elevation' as she had suggested. But after two days that was stopped. Whatever treatment Kennedy may or may not have had from Jacobson in October 1962, his demeanour and personal concentration were very different to what had been on display at his meeting with Khrushchev in Vienna and his decision-making a vast improvement on what had happened over the Bay of Pigs. Caution and firmness, but not recklessness, were Kennedy's outstanding features during the Cuban missile crisis.

Personal recklessness

While Kennedy can be acquitted of recklessness in his political life it is not so easy to do so in his private life, with regard to recreational drugs and certain women. When allegations were first made about his use of powerful recreational drugs, they were easily brushed aside by the President's former aides. But today the evidence, exposed particularly in a recent book on Frank Sinatra, makes it highly likely that Kennedy was a recreational user of mood-changing drugs, both before and during his presidency. The allegations include 'a claim that he used cocaine during a visit to Las Vegas in early 1960, experimented with marijuana and LSD with a lover in the White House, and – with his brother-in-law Peter Lawford – gave amyl nitrate to a woman to see how it affected her sexual experience'.[81] This represents a degree of irresponsibility that only one other US President, Nixon with alcohol, has ever come near.

Womanising is not a disqualification for being President; nor is lying about it, as President Bill Clinton's failed impeachment proceedings showed. But Kennedy's sexual recklessness with two particular women cannot be ignored. Most Americans would not have been too censorious about Kennedy's affair with Marilyn Monroe had it leaked out while he was alive. Yet conducting an affair with Judith Campbell, when Kennedy was well aware that she was the girlfriend of the infamous Mafia figure Sam Giancana, was political foolhardiness. Kennedy was the head of an administration pledged to clamp down on organised crime. At a one-to-one lunch with the head of the FBI, J. Edgar Hoover, on 22 March 1962 Kennedy was warned off seeing Campbell but did not stop telephoning her until August 1962.

On 3 July 1963 Hoover again tried to restrain President Kennedy, this time from seeing Ellen Rometsch. The problem with Rometsch was that she had grown up in East Germany and was believed to be a spy, having allegedly worked as a secretary for Walter Ulbricht, the head of government. She had made repeated visits to the White House, where she attended naked pool parties and had sex with Kennedy. She had been introduced to the President by the Senate secretary, Bobby Baker, who was well known for making call girls available for Senators.

Both the Rometsch and Campbell affairs raise questions not about Kennedy's womanising but about his risk-taking with national security during his Presidency. Hoover told Robert Kennedy about his brother's affair with Rometsch and Robert arranged to have her deported on 21 August to West Germany. Hoover told senior Senators that an FBI investigation had shown no evidence that Rometsch was a spy or a visitor to the White House, a blatant lie and an example of the way in which Hoover ingratiated himself with President Kennedy and later President Johnson in order to stay head of the FBI.[82]

The key question is: to what extent was Kennedy's personal sexual risk-taking, even to the point of endangering national security, due to a propensity for reckless behaviour inbuilt into his character? Or was it driven by taking testosterone and steroids, part of his replacement therapy, or by recreational drugs such as amphetamines, Demerol or other drugs? The answer is probably a combination at various times of all of these. As the world saw with President Clinton, sexual risk-taking does often fall into a separate compartment. A majority of the public sensibly understand this, judge their leader's competence and claims to stay in office, and decide how to vote as a separate issue. To some extent they accept the sexual activity as a private matter, even going as far as tolerating Clinton's false responses in his deposition, for which he accepted a two-year suspension of his law licence in Arkansas and a $25,000 fine.[83]

Kennedy also handled domestic political issues, not just foreign policy, with more composure and skill as his health improved. By 1963 he was exercising regularly and playing golf frequently, and his back had never felt better.

There is an interesting twist in Kennedy's relationship with his physicians. A young naval captain, James M. Young, became a White House physician in June 1963 and started to describe Kennedy's health in confident terms, claiming that the President was in 'robust health, having no difficulty with his chronic back problems'. Robert Dallek speculated:

> Was Kennedy setting up Young for a part in a 1964 Presidential election campaign when he might want a more fluent medical authority than Burkley to testify to his physical capacity to remain as President? Kennedy's attentiveness to managing his image as someone in excellent health makes such a manipulation highly plausible.[84]

Kennedy promised Dr Kraus, whom he last saw in October 1963, that he would throw away his back corset in the New Year.[85] Tragically, that was a promise he was never able to fulfil and his assassination in Dallas on 22 November 1963 brought to an end a presidency which promised much but had yet so much to deliver.

Conclusion

After Robert Dallek's account of President Kennedy's health was written up in 2002 in *Atlantic Monthly*, a *New York Times* editorial concluded: 'It's hard to read the list of ailments and medications without wondering whether there were times when he may have been too impaired to do the job he was elected to do.'[86] This was not Dallek's view. He wrote that Kennedy's 'medical difficulties did not significantly undermine his performance as president on any major question'.[87] This is a view I do not share.

In my judgement, when Kennedy met Khrushchev in Vienna in June 1961, his presidential performance was seriously impaired. A combination of back pain and Dr Max Jacobson's unregulated injections of amphetamines and steroids interacted with his replacement drug therapy of testosterone and steroids for his Addison's disease to cause a state of exhaustion, restlessness and fluctuations of mood that considerably reduced his ability to do the job of President.

As to the invasion of the Bay of Pigs, Kennedy's medical condition is less clear and any conclusions more speculative. It is unlikely that Kennedy was taking Jacobson's amphetamine and steroid injections but he was taking other drugs. I believe that the balance of probability is that Kennedy's decisions over the Bay of Pigs were significantly undermined by his medical condition, treatment and drug abuse.

On well-controlled medication President Kennedy might have confidently dismissed the CIA and military advice in 1961 to give US backing for the Cuban exiles' invasion as not befitting a great nation. In doing so, he would have been fully supported by Senator J. William Fulbright, Dean Acheson and many other significant figures and experts in international affairs. Also Kennedy might have been emotionally steadier, better prepared and positioned to handle more skilfully his Vienna meeting with a belligerent Khrushchev in June 1961. As a consequence Khrushchev would not have left Vienna underestimating Kennedy's resolution and his authority and would not have decided to place nuclear-tipped missiles in Cuba on 21 May 1962. It is ironic that the sequence of events – Kennedy's bad decisions over the Bay of Pigs, his weak handling of the Vienna meeting with Khrushchev and his subsequent anti-Castro and anti-Russian stance – provoked the very crisis which he then so ably resolved in October 1962 and gave him the self-confidence to chart a course for holding out during the Cold War symbolically over Berlin, which led to the eventual reunification of Germany. A recent book on the history of the CIA, *Legacy of Ashes* by Tim Weiner, paints a different picture and challenges the view that 'for many years thereafter, the world believed that only President Kennedy's calm resolve and his brother's steely commitment to a peaceful resolution had saved the nation from a nuclear war'.

It has long been assumed that if the American people had been given the medical facts from the moment Kennedy first ran for President, they would never have elected him. Perhaps that was true of America in 1960 but we will never know since openness was never tried. I have no doubt that today a reservoir of common sense on health means the general public can be trusted by their politicians with medical facts and will place such illnesses in their proper perspective. Certainly well-controlled Addison's disease is not something which should disqualify anyone running for the highest office.

After having decided to run for President, Kennedy should have had the courage to begin a different, more open and indeed more democratic relationship with the public. He would have enhanced his presidency if he had chosen openness about his Addison's disease, particularly given the successful precedent established by his predecessor, Dwight Eisenhower, over his illnesses. Some say openness could never have been implemented given the past history of cover-up. But it would not have required Kennedy to confess that he had been elected under false pretences or had lied to the public. All that would have been required was gradually to shift to a position of openness and bring his own state of denial to an end. It can be argued that Kennedy got away with it – but his period as President was short. Longer exposure could well have meant that his cover would have been blown and that would have done considerable damage to his credibility in office.

Even if he had delayed action until he had been elected, as incoming President Kennedy had the opportunity to choose greater openness and gradually end the secrecy and cover-up over his medical condition. If he had had the wisdom also to appoint one of the very best of American physicians as his personal White House doctor, such a person, with the standing and authority of having been brought in to control all of Kennedy's medical treatment from his different doctors, could have improved the President's health care quite quickly. The President would have also been under immense pressure to adopt a far more disciplined personal approach over his health: to stop taking amphetamine and steroid injections from Max Jacobson and give up experimenting with recreational drugs. A wise doctor would also have been able to persuade Kennedy to use the presidency to create public confidence towards Addison's and many other diseases and make known to a wider number of people the massive changes in medical treatment.

These are the what-ifs of history. Had he made these decisions, John F. Kennedy would have been a great President.

5

The Shah's secret illness

The Iranians had freed themselves from the Shah, America's brutal policeman in the Gulf, only to find themselves living in a graveyard of theocracy, their democratic elections betrayed by men who feed off hatred for America that now lies like a blanket over the Middle East.

Robert Fisk[1]

The fall of the Shah of Iran and the takeover of power in February 1979 by Ayatollah Ruhollah Khomeini predictably proved to be a geopolitical disaster with whose consequences we are still living. I was the British Foreign Secretary at the time. The relationship between Britain, and other Western countries, and the Shah had been a complex one. He was an ally in a region of vital economic and strategic interest to us. But he was also an autocratic monarch attempting to transform and modernise his country in the teeth of opposition from many powerful forces in it. It was clear by 1970 that without some measure of democratic reform, including a move towards a constitutional monarchy, his regime was heading for trouble. What made such a transition very difficult to influence from outside was that, despite the autocratic manner, the Shah was an indecisive man. Also the US and the UK had compromised their commitment to democracy when they ousted the Prime Minister, Mohammad Mossadeq, in 1953.

What only a handful of people knew in 1973 was that the Shah had become a very sick man, having developed a form of chronic lymphocytic leukaemia.*

---

* Leukaemia is an overall term covering disorders where the white blood cells proliferate in a malignant or cancerous way. It is classified according to which white cells are involved, hence the terms lymphocytic, lymphoblastic/lymphatic or myeloid leukaemia. The rate of proliferation determines whether it is classified as acute or chronic. Acute lymphoblastic leukaemia is a disease of childhood which has had a considerable breakthrough in its response to steroid chemotherapy and radiation of the cerebrospinal fluid. The cause of chronic lymphocytic leukaemia is not known. It is twice as common in men as in women and commonly starts in the over-sixties.

He kept this totally secret until he developed much worse symptoms in October 1979, by which time his political and personal fates were sealed. He died from the disease in exile in Egypt on 27 July 1980.

The Shah of Iran, Mohammad Reza Pahlavi, succeeded his father Reza Shah in 1941. Reza Shah had made himself king and established a new dynasty, the Pahlavis, in 1926 but had been forced to abdicate after British and Soviet forces invaded Iran (or Persia as it then was still more commonly called) during the Second World War. When Roosevelt, Churchill and Stalin met in Tehran in 1943 the young Shah was not a very significant figure and they would have been amazed if told then that within less than thirty years he would emerge as the most dominant ruler in the Gulf region.

The Shah's indecisiveness was first revealed during the coup of 1953, in which his Prime Minister, Mohammad Mossadeq, was overthrown. Mossadeq had nationalised the country's oil industry, so alienating the United States and Britain. But he also faced strong opposition within Iran and this made it possible for the CIA and MI6 to engineer his overthrow. In retrospect the UK and the US would have been wiser to concentrate on influencing the nature of a Mossadeq-led state, pushing for proper democracy and helping to avoid infiltration by the Soviet-backed Communist Party. A more enlightened British leadership within the Anglo-Iranian Oil Company could also have contributed to a more stable solution by anticipating the need to share the rising oil revenues with the Iranian people.

During the coup, the Shah was not only extremely nervous but he wavered and, at a critical moment, thinking the plan was failing, took flight in a small plane to Iraq with Queen Soraya. While in Baghdad he talked to the US ambassador. The British ambassador, Sir Francis Shepherd, sent back a revealing dispatch to London describing what the Shah had said to the Americans, and this gave a clear intimation of the Shah's attitude for the future: 'He had then decided that as a constitutional ruler he should not resort to force as that would lead to bloodshed, chaos and Soviet infiltration.'

The Shah had no idea where to go next, but eventually flew to Rome. There he lived in a hotel without money and able to exert little influence. The Americans managed to stiffen him to assert his constitutional rights and denounce Mossadeq's actions as illegal. The streets of Tehran were full of Mossadeq's supporters and communists from the Tudeh Party but the CIA paid for and mobilised counter-demonstrations. These pro-Shah crowds encouraged the army to come out in favour of the Shah and overthrow Mossadeq. When Mossadeq was put on trial he blamed the British, and what they called Operation Boot, for his overthrow. So the UK gained the reputation of being the master planners, though in fact the Americans did most of the work, but without the same scrutiny of their role, in what they called Operation Ajax.

The Shah, however, thought his return in 1953 owed everything to his people, asserting: 'I knew they loved me,' a myth with which he reassured himself. Thereafter the Shah was haunted by his exile and decided to build up a fortune outside the country in order to safeguard his future. It was also, he felt, necessary to inaugurate his own national intelligence and security organisation, called SAVAK from its Iranian name, *Sazeman-e Etteia't va Amniyat-e Keshvar.* He chose the CIA and Mossad, not the British MI6, as his principal advisers on this. It became a ruthless centre for widespread torture and repression.

The Shah's continued success owed much to his decision in July 1962 to appoint as Prime Minister Assadollah Alam,[2] to whom he gave two principal objectives: to quell the mounting opposition to land reform and to push forward the so-called White Revolution. A national referendum in January 1963 endorsed a six-point programme of social reform. In the spring of 1963 Alam crushed the opposition of tribal chieftains in Fars and he undermined the loyalties of ordinary tribesmen by sweeping away the archaic traditions of tribalism. Protests continued in Tehran and Qom, egged on by a local leader, Ruhollah Khomeini. Alam crucially bolstered an indecisive Shah when he urged that the government must hit back. 'But how?' the Shah is said to have asked. 'With bullets, Your Majesty,' Alam replied, adding that he would assume all blame if it failed. On 5 June 1963, under Alam's personal command, the riots were quelled within hours.

Initially the Shah decided to have Khomeini executed but it was thought unwise to make him a martyr. Instead a reluctant clergy was put under political pressure to make him an ayatollah. Khomeini was then pushed out of the country, first to Turkey and then to Iraq. This ushered in more than a decade of successful rule by the Shah, at least judged by material progress. But his stress on building a secular state and his commitment to the emancipation of women were anathema to Ayatollah Khomeini and a growing number of clerics. The Shah's father had been a reformer and, just as Atatürk had championed the abandonment of the veil in Turkey, so the Shah's mother, Queen Tadj ol-Molouk, and her two daughters, Princess Shams and Princess Ashraf, had gone out in public without a veil for the first time in January 1936.

In 1971 the Shah was largely responsible for the Tehran Agreement, which substantially increased Iran's oil revenues. It was in the aftermath of this, however, that the flamboyance and extravagance of his court began to develop. A grotesquely extravagant party was held at Persepolis in October 1971 to celebrate the 2,500th anniversary of the Persian monarchy. This seems to have been the moment when the Shah lost touch with both reality and his people. Hubris was much in evidence, but his self-confidence was more apparent than real. A tented city was put up for the visiting royals and VIPs, using the most expensive Parisian suppliers: Maxim's prepared the food, Lanvin the uniforms, Porthault the linen. *Son et lumière* celebrated Cyrus the Great, while the prophet Mohammed and Islam were ignored.

By the start of 1974 the Shah was the single most important influence in the Middle East. Broadly, his interests were compatible with the interests of the Western democracies, and the United States, Britain, France and others encouraged him to exert influence over a region extending beyond the Middle East. Iran was a member of the defence organisation CENTO (the Central Treaty Organization) along with Iraq, Pakistan, Turkey, the UK and, later, the USA. The Shah was also a strong supporter of the free flow of trade within the Gulf. Yet he was also very conscious of having a long border with the USSR and always maintained a private channel of communication to Moscow.

The Shah's military might inside Iran was built up to underwrite his projection of power in the region but it was never focused on internal security. That was left to SAVAK. The United States and Britain were pleased by this assertion of regional dominance because the Shah was beginning to fill a perceived gap left by the Royal Navy's withdrawal from the Gulf. In 1941 Iran's armed forces numbered 90,000. By 1978 they amounted to 350,000. In December 1971 Iranian troops landed at Abu Musa and the Tunb Islands in the lower Gulf, asserting their claim to the islands. By 1973 the Shah was talking in grandiose terms of the era of the 'Great Civilisation' and boasting that Iran had joined the ranks of the industrialised nations. He sent Iranian troops to help the Sultan of Oman. Henry Kissinger, then US Secretary of State, accepted and, what is more, encouraged the Shah in his self-appointed imperial role as guardian of the Gulf. The Shah knew he could have sophisticated US aircraft and missiles under the condition that he did not pursue the development of nuclear weapons.

The Shah was neither a pawn nor a puppet of the United States. He forced the pace in OPEC, arguing in the October and December meetings in 1973 for price rises. In a 1976 interview with *US News and World Report* he warned that if the US attempted to challenge Iran's natural and legitimate strategic interests in the Persian Gulf, Iran could 'turn that whole region into an inferno for the US'.

In the 1970s good relations with the Shah were, I believe, correctly judged to be an essential part of American and British foreign policy even though some in Britain retrospectively believed that the Shah in some unspecified way should have been abandoned. Economically, by the 1970s, the Shah's favour was very important to the United States and Britain. The British desperately needed to offset the oil price shock by selling an increased proportion of its industrial output to Iran, and the Shah helpfully agreed to purchase British Chieftain tanks.

In 1977–8 the American and the British interest lay in guiding the Shah towards developing a democratic monarchy whereby his son could be his successor but as a constitutional head of state, with power wielded by democratically elected politicians. As the Western democracies watched, they thought they saw in the Shah the image of a decisive, determined monarch. But it was an illusion. The crucial fact which we should never have allowed to slip our memories was the extent to which, in 1953, the young Shah had demonstrated his indecisiveness.

By early 1975 the Iranian economy was getting into serious trouble. The frenetic industrial and building activity which the Shah had stimulated in Iran, following the oil price hike, meant that inflation was gathering momentum. Soaring rent prices in Tehran were drastically lowering living standards. The Shah was aware of the problem but chose not to deal with the underlying inflation and instead embarked on an anti-profiteering initiative. This angered the bazaar merchants, who correctly guessed that it was an attack on them. Ominously, the economic difficulties started to push the bazaar merchants towards the mullahs, the religious leaders of the Shiite faith. By 1976, inflation was running at more than 20 per cent and corruption was rampant. A palpable malaise was creeping into Iranian society.

On 26 March 1976, the Shah and Queen Farah celebrated the fiftieth anniversary of the Pahlavi dynasty. On that day, Farah later wrote, she felt something changed between the people and the monarchy. 'I could feel it in my bones like a sudden icy wind. There seemed to be an intangible shadow over the harmony and the confidence between us.'[3] She describes how, for the following months, the Shah began to instruct her and her son Reza in the affairs of the country. They received the chiefs of staff, conferred with the Prime Minister and other ministers and saw representatives of the institutions and Parliament. Reza was not that far from his twentieth birthday, the requisite age to ascend to the throne or become regent. The Shah, however, still envisaged his son ruling the country as he had, and there was no hint then of him encouraging his son to share, let alone hand over, executive power.

A secret illness

The basic medical facts about the Shah's illness have been known for some time but it was not until Farah Pahlavi published her memoir, *An Enduring Love*, in 2004 that the full facts were revealed. She published large extracts from three long letters from Dr Georges Flandrin to his professor, Dr Jean Bernard. Both French doctors helped treat the Shah and Flandrin continued until the Shah's death. The letters were written in 1987 to provide a factual record of the Shah's medical history. In this chapter I have drawn extensively on them, in many cases using Flandrin's own words with his permission.

In 1974 an Iranian doctor, Abbas Safavian, who had been advising the Shah, telephoned Bernard in Paris, asking him to come to Tehran and bring Flandrin, his 'head of laboratory', with him. Bernard was the head of the Institute for Research on Leukaemia at the Saint-Louis Hospital in Paris. He was a distinguished specialist in blood diseases who had been President Georges Pompidou's doctor and so Safavian knew he could be trusted to keep a secret. Safavian made it clear that they would have no contact with local medical people and that they would have to bring with them any equipment they thought necessary. Bernard and Flandrin cancelled their outpatient consultations and two days later, on 1 May 1974, flew out to Tehran for the first time.

The Air France plane left from Orly airport and, just before boarding, as they were trying to guess the reason for this mysterious request, Flandrin said to Bernard rather sheepishly: 'What if it is a practical joke?' Bernard dryly replied: 'In my experience, practical jokes don't come with first-class tickets!' At Mehrabad airport in Tehran two cars with flashing lights were waiting for them at the foot of the gangway, and they were taken to the government reception lounge, where they were welcomed by Safavian. Safavian was a French university-aggregated professor and dean of one of the faculties of medicine in Tehran, of which he later became rector. Safavian and Flandrin had worked together under Professor Gilbert Dreyfus at the Hôpital de la Pitié.

In the Hilton Hotel Safavian explained that they would be examining Assadollah Alam, the Minister of the Court. Bernard already knew about his health problem, as another French professor, Paul Milliez, had sought his advice about Alam earlier. But Bernard pointed out, as an aside to Flandrin, that so much mystery seemed out of proportion to Alam's leukaemia, which was a simple and well-known type. They then met Alam, who informed them that, in fact, they would be seeing the Shah.

The Shah spoke in perfect French when he first met the two French doctors. Standing beside him was a small man dressed in a military uniform, General Ayadi, the Shah's general physician. They sat around a table and the Shah explained his problem, telling them that a few months earlier, at the end of 1973, when he was on the island of Kish, he had noticed a curve on his left side below the rib cage, felt it and thought it could be an enlarged spleen. On examining the Shah the spleen was found to be large but it was the only physical symptom. There were no enlarged glands. The Shah was fifty five.

The doctors took samples and under a microscope looked at the blood slides they had coloured with a special stain. It was clear that the Shah was suffering from a chronic lymphocytic blood disease. It was a slightly unusual form of chronic lymphocytic leukaemia because of the enlarged spleen. Ayadi, when informed of the diagnosis, said that the word 'leukaemia' definitely must not be used: as far as he was concerned, the Shah had to be told that everything was fine. For the French doctors that was a lot to ask, since they had just diagnosed a lymphocytic blood disease, which ultimately would become malignant. In addition to that, there would have to be treatment that they could hardly prescribe without some explanation. During this first visit they did not yet have the result of the serum immunoelectrophoresis.* The Shah's medical condition at this early stage did not give serious cause for concern so the French doctors decided to keep their practical recommendations until after they returned to Paris and all the tests had been completed and checked. When they had all the results in hand, they chose to use the term 'Waldenstrom's disease' for the Shah's illness, knowing that it was not the typical advanced form.

---

* In lymphocytic leukaemia there is an increase in the number of lymphocytes, a variety of the white blood cell called a leukocyte. Lymphocytes are found in the lymph nodes, spleen, thymus gland, bone marrow and the walls of the gut. These cells are involved in the immunity of the body. Immunoglobulins are a protein which can be separated by immunoelectrophoresis in the serum, which is the fluid left when the blood cells have been removed. In the case of the Shah at this stage his monoclonal immunoglobulin M peak, characteristic of Waldenstrom's disease, was not pronounced.

When they left the palace after this first visit, their impressions were mixed. Flandrin remembers Bernard saying: 'Tomorrow American doctors will be consulted and they'll be here where we are now.' But Bernard's prediction was incorrect. Bringing Bernard and Flandrin to Tehran was a deliberate and considered choice made by the Shah. He had understood that at the very least his enlarged spleen indicated a blood disease and, realising the possible political implications, had no intention whatever of consulting any American doctors, who he believed would tell the American government. The same suspicion would have applied to the British. It became clear to the French doctors that everything had been organised between the Shah and Alam so that no information would go further than a very tight and trustworthy group.

In the beginning five people knew about the illness: the two French doctors, who had all the information; Ayadi, who had the key facts but was not a specialist; the Shah, who had some information strictly vetted by Ayadi; and lastly, with even more limited knowledge, Alam. Initially, Safavian had no intention of competing with such an influential personality as Ayadi. But the French doctors had stipulated that they would treat the Shah only if he agreed to continue being involved in the process. Later in May 1974, they informed Safavian of the exact nature of the Shah's illness, but they preferred not to do so over the phone so they met him at the American Hospital of Paris in Neuilly for a private conversation. That made six people who knew.

The blood tests were done in Paris on samples with the name and social security number of one of Flandrin's elderly relatives. Once the two French doctors had communicated their conclusions to Safavian, they heard nothing more until September 1974. They were not worried, having deliberately decided not to suggest any treatment and to hold just a watching brief. They were then asked to return to Tehran on 18 September. Interestingly, in the meantime, between 24 and 29 June, the Shah and his wife had been on an official visit to France at the invitation of the newly elected President of the republic, Valéry Giscard d'Estaing, but the Shah personally had no contact with his French doctors.

By the time of their second visit to Tehran in September Milliez had joined the select group of people around the Shah who knew his medical secret. Safavian had thought it reasonable that Milliez, his French mentor, should be involved since Milliez had treated Charles de Gaulle and the King of Saudi Arabia and it was felt he could keep a secret. Now seven people knew and an eighth, while not in on the secret, was aware of why the French doctors were in Tehran. He was someone close to the Shah and Alam who put the doctors up at his sumptuous, out-of-the-way residence on each of their many trips.

It was there, after the second consultation in the palace that Bernard, Flandrin, Milliez and Safavian all met. Flandrin describes them walking in the garden on that sunny Sunday morning, discussing at great length so as to agree on how to handle their patient. Safavian insisted that everything must be kept in the strictest confidence including, to some extent, from the Shah. He feared in particular that the Shah might say something imprudent, as he was prone to talking about his health problems and might inadvertently let someone in his entourage in on the secret. Medically the patient was still in excellent physical shape, but his spleen had grown larger. They decided to begin immediately with the appropriate classic treatment for chronic lymphocytic leukaemia, 6 milligrams of Chlorambucil daily, with the usual monthly blood test check.*

After the French doctors left, the Shah received only a week's treatment before a blood test was ordered by Ayadi. But a week was too short a time to wait before having a blood test. It apparently showed, though this seems very dubious, a significant drop in white cells. There was panic and the treatment was stopped. As a result the French doctors were recalled to see the Shah for a third time, on 18 January 1975. This was in Zurich, as the Shah was skiing in Switzerland. It was only then they learned that the Shah had not been receiving treatment. This consultation took place in the presence of Ayadi, Safavian, Milliez, Bernard and Flandrin. Flandrin had brought from Paris a little Carl Zeiss microscope, a replica of the one he had used in Tehran, dismantled in his shoulder bag. The Shah looked and was fit and told Flandrin about skiing down the Diavolezza trail. Flandrin, a skier himself, admired the feat but was horrified, imagining what a bad fall could have done to someone whose spleen had become as enormous as the Shah's. Treatment was inescapable and Chlorambucil was once more prescribed. On the Iranian side, both Ayadi and Safavian explained that there was no way that they could arrange for blood tests to be done regularly in Tehran and for the whole thing to remain secret. It was decided that Flandrin should come back to Zurich for a few hours to carry out the next blood test as the Shah was staying another month in Switzerland. Having taken this step over monitoring the Shah's progress, Flandrin then went to Tehran on 19 February, and regularly every month thereafter, sometimes with Bernard and sometimes alone. Flandrin's last trip to Tehran was at the end of December 1978.

---

* Chlorambucil is an alkylating agent used in chemotherapy and taken orally. The main side effect to guard against with periodic blood tests is damage to the patient's bone marrow.

The same procedure was followed every time, travelling out of Paris on a Friday on the Air France Paris–Manila flight via Tehran, seated in the front row of the first-class cabin. Arriving usually at night, they were first off the plane and met by the same cars with flashing lights at the bottom of the steps. They left their host's house at dawn on Sunday morning for the palace, returning to the house for a long day's reading and waiting so as to avoid being seen outside, then returning to Paris on the Sunday night flight, to start work again at Saint-Louis on the Monday morning.

Between January and December 1975, the Shah's spleen went back to its normal size and the anomalies in the blood were corrected.* In spite of this improvement, the treatment was maintained at the same dose and frequency, as is usually done in these conditions. In February, 1976 Flandrin was unpleasantly surprised when he felt the Shah's enlarged spleen and saw abnormal cells in his blood. It made him think that the illness had flared up and would already need more aggressive treatment. However, it proved to be a false alarm. It had been decided at the start not to use the name Chlorambucil, which could have given the game away if anyone had seen the label on the tablets and worked out that the Shah was seriously ill. Instead a harmless patent medicine, Quinercyl, sold in the form of white pills very similar to those of Chlorambucil, was named on the package which the Shah used. Flandrin bought these in Paris and took the Chlorambucil in Quinercyl packets to Tehran. They had also agreed to substitute the word 'Quinercyl' for 'Chlorambucil' in their reports. This subterfuge worked all too well because the Shah's valet, thinking that the Shah might one day make a long trip to distant parts, took the precaution of stocking up on this medicine and had bought a supply of Quinercyl in Tehran which for more than two months the Shah had been using, without anyone being aware that it was not Chlorambucil. It was Safavian who, seeing Flandrin so surprised at this early 'flare-up' of the disease, made careful enquiries and, after talking to the valet, understood the mistake that had been made. The real treatment was begun again in April 1976, and by September the Shah had a completely normal blood stain picture.

At that time the demands of secrecy were imposing a particularly heavy burden on Safavian, who, apart from Alam and Ayadi, was the only Iranian to know about the Shah's illness. It seemed obvious to him that some day he

---

* This meant that the monoclonal spike on the electrophoresis tests had totally disappeared from the serum.

would be reproached by the patient's family or by the Iranian people for not having told them the facts. He knew the secrecy had possible political consequences. After he had discussed this subject many times with the French doctors, they decided it was essential to inform the patient's wife. Fearing a foreseeable deterioration of the disease, the doctors wanted the Queen to know, so that she could be psychologically prepared for the inevitable deterioration in her husband's health. Before speaking to her they approached the Shah several times in an attempt to convince him to talk to her himself. But each time he avoided the question. So they agreed to tell her in secret.

Safavian decided the only possible location for such a secret meeting, of which the Shah would be unaware, was Paris. Bernard, Milliez, Safavian and Flandrin met the Queen, who still did not know precisely why they were so keen to see her and why it was so secret. Bernard was the one who gave her the information they had. It was, of course, a hard thing for the Queen to hear. Her husband, who seemed so healthy, had a blood disease which was chronic and would become fatal. In addition to that, her husband knew about his illness and had not wanted to say anything about it to her.

More difficult for the Queen was how to tell her husband that she now knew all about his illness. It was agreed that the only way was for her to ask permission from the Shah to have an 'official talk' with the French doctors, without revealing that she had already secretly met them. She subsequently received permission, and when they were next in Tehran, with the Shah's knowledge, the doctors were invited to meet the Queen. So now one more person was involved in the secret. This circle of people who knew, Safavian believes, expanded no further until as late as October 1979, when a clinical worsening of the Shah's condition occurred in the Bahamas, and especially so in Mexico, prior to the Shah's departure for New York.

Safavian now practises in Paris. In 2005 I met him for two long conversations about the Shah's illness. It is noteworthy that Safavian, Bernard and Flandrin retained the confidence of the Shah and his wife throughout, in spite of the extraordinary circumstances in which they had to conduct themselves. In my judgement, all three handled the Shah's case with great skill.

It has been alleged by an American doctor, Benjamin Kean,[4] who became involved in the case much later, that they had begged the Shah to undergo thorough testing and a biopsy in 1974 and that he had not only refused but had threatened to fire them and find new doctors. The French doctors claim this is not true – firstly, there were no glands to examine at that early stage, and secondly, the Shah did not have that sort of relationship with them. Their relationship was formal, polite and respectful. They say the Shah would never have talked to them in this way.

How serious did the Shah believe his condition to be? His wife recounted how in the winter of 1975 he had told Giscard d'Estaing:

> My problem is that I haven't enough time. I won't be remaining in power for long. I intend leaving in seven or eight years. I will be well over sixty. I would prefer to leave earlier, but my son is still too young. I will wait until he is ready, but I want the essentials to be in place before he takes over. He will have a lot of difficulties in the beginning. It's up to me to bring about the transformation of Iran. I am determined to do it.[5]

No health predictions that could have been given to him by his doctors at this time are consistent with his planning to survive until 1982–3 to pass over to his son. So either he had not been told or he chose to ignore what he had learned. The Queen said she never knew how much the Shah really knew about his illness at that time.

At various times Bernard had tried to bring conversations with the Shah around to his illness, and discuss its possible course, but he appeared not to want to discuss it or to be taking it all in. Then in 1978, at his summer palace, the Shah made a comment, which, in Flandrin's opinion, clearly showed that by now he did understand his situation. At this time, his elder son was in an American air force academy and the Shah said to Flandrin: 'I am only asking you to help me maintain my health for two years, enough time for the Crown Prince to finish the year in the US and spend another in Tehran.'

Reform: too little, too late

In 2005 I had a long conversation with Farah Pahlavi, who carries herself with great dignity and has considerable compassion. She thinks that her husband, once he knew that his illness was bound to deteriorate, began to prepare the country for his son to be his successor. She wrote that the Shah

> repeated many times that his son would not have to govern in the same way as he had; inheriting a country that had finally emerged from its under-development, Reza's task would be to open Iran up to democracy. In the spring of 1977 demands for the liberalisation of the regime were beginning to be more

urgently voiced by the political opposition and by intellectuals and in particular a journalist who later supported Khomeini and the mullahs. In an open letter to the King, the journalist asked him in particular to rule according to the constitution and to give the country freedom of expression equal to that in western Europe and the United States. Shapour Bakhtiar and Mehdi Bazargan also spoke out on the same issue.[6]

Opening the country to democracy would have been a heavy task for any young man to perform. It would have been far wiser for the Shah to have embarked on this transition himself. It is clear to me that if the Shah's illness had been known to Cyrus Vance, the US Secretary of State, and to me, as Foreign Secretary, when we were both in Tehran for a CENTO meeting on 14 May 1977, that would have been the time to suggest to him that he start a process of democratic reform with the aim of creating a constitutional monarchy for his son to inherit. With the knowledge that the Shah was seriously ill, I would have talked to him about the monarchy in Spain, a country which he knew well. Later that same summer I visited Madrid. It was a time when Spain had moved peacefully from fascism to democracy. It had always been envisaged that King Juan Carlos, appointed by Generalissimo Francisco Franco, would rule as a constitutional monarch. The King had accepted this and was later to make his commitment to democracy very clear to the military during an attempted coup. A transition to a constitutional monarchy could have occurred in Iran too. The Shah would have had to be persuaded, by the US and the UK, to advance any timetable towards democracy because of his illness. It was an achievable transition for Iran and it is a tragedy that it never came about, but it had to involve a real transfer of power to the ministers, parliament and people.

Since November 1973, at about the time that he had first become aware of his enlarged spleen, the Shah had envisaged a regency council that would have retained full powers in the hands of his wife until his son was of the age to ascend the throne. In 1977–8, when internal unrest grew, the Shah should have publicly announced that he needed to go abroad to receive specialist medical attention, even though this would have meant slightly exaggerating the state of his health. He should then have set up a very different regency council to the one he had contemplated, one with real power delegated to political leaders, and charged them with starting the process of democratic reform. His absence from the country would have created a different political climate in which the peaceful evolution to a constitutional monarchy might well have been possible.

Instead, with the Shah's illness a total secret, this vital topic was never discussed when I and the Shah's other Western allies assembled in Tehran in May 1977. Rather, we were treated to a display of self-confident monarchical excess of a piece with the extravagance at Persepolis six years earlier. The Shah entertained the CENTO foreign ministers in the Niavaran Palace to a lunch of quite extraordinary lavishness. Even in the Élysée Palace I have never had such a meal. One did not have to be very perceptive to sense a monarch far removed from the people.

The Iran with which I had to deal as Foreign Secretary was a very different country from the one through which I had travelled extensively, as a student, in 1959 on the way to and from Afghanistan, and again as a parliamentarian in 1966. By 1977 it was almost unrecognisable, with hugely increased wealth, power and sophistication. Iran's external position also looked much stronger, as it was then producing nearly 12 per cent of the world's oil and supplying some 16 per cent of Britain's oil needs. BP was obtaining between 40 and 45 per cent of its total oil supplies from Iran. With its vast oil revenues Iran, fortunately, was a major importer of British goods and we were selling about £200 million per annum at 1977 prices of industrial goods, cars and military equipment in addition to 750 Chieftain and 250 Scorpion tanks.

As the Shah grew more autocratic and intolerant, it had become apparent that Britain could easily endanger its relationship with him if he felt it was continuing with what he believed was a long history of intrigue. The UK had chosen, in the late 1960s, not to deploy any of its own intelligence service in Iran, feeling that we had little option other than to rely on SAVAK. In retrospect, it was a mistake, particularly without building up a separate Iranian intelligence analysis unit within MI6 in London. Such a unit would have been a valuable asset at any time and quite crucial in 1977–8. It would also have helped to have had better links with Israel's Mossad.

In the one-to-one talk I had with the Shah in May 1977, we ranged over many regional and global issues. I was particularly keen to persuade him to use his oil power on South Africa with the aim of achieving both an independent Namibia and majority rule in Rhodesia. I had discussed with colleagues whether I should voice our uneasiness over the internal situation in Iran. I was concerned about the human rights abuse taking place and wanted to endorse my anxiety personally. So I told the Shah that, while I did not wish to impose British views on Iran and though his moves towards liberalisation had been well received in Britain, criticism would decrease if the living conditions of prisoners were improved and trials opened regularly to the public. While not belabouring the point unduly, I could have left him in no doubt about the strength of my feeling. There was no adverse reaction from the Shah, either at the time or later.

The meeting reinforced in my mind the image of a powerful leader, not remotely akin to the dithering, indecisive Shah of 1953. I confess that it was this self-confident, assertive image which stayed with me in 1978 while we debated what we should do to bolster the Shah's government. But it was false. People who have a tendency to vacillate very rarely change and underneath he was still indecisive and weak and my big mistake was to fall for the Shah's carefully constructed self-image.

Farah Pahlavi believes the Shah planned to speed up the liberalisation of Iran. In the middle of summer 1977, in order to make it clear to the country that the time for change had come, the Shah replaced the long-standing Amir Abbas Hoveyda as Prime Minister with Jamshid Amouzegar, the secretary general of the National Renaissance Party. Farah describes Amouzegar as 'a brilliant, cultivated man of great integrity'. The problem for Amouzegar and his party was that when it originally came into existence the Shah did away with all semblance of political pluralism. He made himself the centre of all power and became the lightning conductor for all the country's problems. This meant that in 1977 neither the party nor the Shah's talk of liberalisation were taken seriously by his critics.

The Shah found too that dismissing Hoveyda not only did not work but had other side effects. It showed those who had been loyal to the Shah that they could not count on his loyalty in return. The Shah did not trust anyone outside his immediate circle. Like so many heads of government described in this book, the Shah was suspicious, paranoid and, near the end of his reign, severely depressed. He never tried to convince the modernisers that he was ready to move towards a constitutional monarchy, in truth because he was not convinced himself.

The Shah's liberalisation policy, initiated in 1977 as a reaction to the global interest in human rights, virtually coincided with my period as Secretary of State for Foreign Affairs. While it certainly suited my outlook and that of the incoming Carter administration, it was not dictated by us. The apologists for the Shah never cease to blame President Carter for the Shah's downfall. But in fairness, just as Carter's stress on human rights was a reaction to trends of opinion already apparent in the world, the Shah was also reacting to those trends. It was he who opened up Iran's prisons for inspection by the International Red Cross.

The Ayatollah's revolution

In August 1977 the Shah was tolerating his medical treatment well. By October public dissatisfaction was, however, palpable, and in the Goethe-Institut in Tehran readings of literature critical of the regime attracted amazingly large numbers. This was followed in November by students openly demonstrating in Tehran against the Shah before his visit to President Jimmy Carter. In Washington an Iranian student demonstration outside the White House grew so violent that CS gas had to be used, and its acrid fumes drifted across the White House lawn as the ceremonial welcome took place, bringing tears to the eyes of the participants.

On 31 December, Carter, visiting Iran, made a fulsome tribute to the Shah and an absurdly optimistic assessment of the year ahead. In January 1978 an article was published in the daily newspaper *Ettela'at* lambasting Ayatollah Khomeini, accusing him of being an adventurer and a non-believer. The British government felt the Shah must have authorised the placing of this article and that this was crass stupidity. There were riots in the religious city of Qom, where some demonstrators were killed. This was probably the spark that ignited the revolution, the moment when the forces against the Shah gathered momentum, with Islamic fundamentalism in the vanguard.

The entrenched opposition were those who took Khomeini, then exiled in Iraq, as their symbol, while others rallied around the old National Front politicians such as Shapour Bakhtiar and Mehdi Bazargan. The bazaar merchants were more fickle in their opposition but it became very serious when they started to finance the mosques. The largest element of opposition and the least organised were the city dwellers, and they grew restless as inflation rose. All these different sources of opposition to the Shah sensed that his 'Great Civilisation' initiative was coming apart at the seams. This was daily emphasised by a series of power cuts, demonstrating how dismally the planners had failed in making provision for adequate electricity.

Demonstrations followed in Qom at forty-day intervals, a Shia practice in commemoration of the dead. In mid-February there were riots in Tabriz, where tanks were used. In May the rioting continued in Tehran. In June, the Shah dismissed General Nematollah Nassiri, the head of SAVAK. In late July there was unrest in Mashhad. Martial law was declared in Isfahan in August, and the Shah promised further liberalisation, saying that elections for a new parliament, due in June 1979, would be totally free and that legislation would be presented to the National Assembly providing for free expression and assembly. But very few believed the Shah's promises.

The US and UK governments should have concluded that summer that the Shah himself could not be the vehicle for the restoration of law and order and should have joined together in pressuring him to leave immediately. The Shah was by then an empty vessel. There was no effective direction of policy in Tehran from him or the Prime Minister. For example, the Shah should have had technicians in the Iranian army trained long before the crisis, so as to be able to keep the oil flowing if there was a strike in the oilfields. To preserve the flow of oil a contingency plan was needed, and to rely on bringing outside experts into Iran at a time when religiously tainted xenophobia was rising in a crescendo was foolish. In the event, the virtual shutdown of the oilfields came as a shock inside and outside Iran. By the end of October 1978, oil production had fallen from 6 million to little more than 1 million barrels per day.

Had we in addition known of his illness, pressure from Western governments on him to leave could have been strong – but without that leverage he would never go. Faced with him staying in Tehran, one of our major problems was developing a united Western front. Even as late as October, the US administration was still split on such basic questions as whether or not to give the Iranian government crowd control devices. The Shah had already approached the British government for CS gas and we agreed to supply it, feeling that its use would make it less likely that tanks, possibly built in the UK, would open up on the demonstrators. William Sullivan, US ambassador in Tehran, and the State Department opposed supply while Zbigniew Brzezinski, Carter's National Security Advisor, supported it.

In late November the Carter administration made a very strange decision, appointing George Ball as an outside adviser. Brzezinski admits that this was his mistake.[7] Ball was a distinguished man with a long liberal record who had formerly been a political appointment in the State Department. His participation sharpened Brzezinski's internal disagreements with Cyrus Vance over whether the US should back a military intervention by the Iranian armed forces.

Brzezinski was very critical of the State Department's reluctance to press the Shah to assert effective authority and of its procrastination as the Shah's hold on power weakened. He even alleged that by January 1979 'the lower echelons of State on the Iran Desk were clearly cheering the Shah's opponents'.[8] It is clear in retrospect that the estrangement between the White House and the State Department was even worse than I sensed it to be at the time.

On 29 December 1978, while in Algiers attending President Houari Boumédienne's funeral, I was cabled by diplomats in the Foreign Office with a draft telegram for me to send to Vance expressing my opposition to an Iranian military clampdown, as favoured by Brzezinski. I was unconvinced and refused to send the suggested telegram. By then I had ruled out advocating any solutions to the Shah's dilemma. This was a crisis that could be resolved from now on only in Tehran. It was up to the Shah and the Iranian military to decide whether to clamp down. He prevaricated and in effect decided not to. He later wrote in self-justification:

> A sovereign may not save his throne by shedding his compatriots' blood. A dictator can, because he acts in the name of an ideology which he believes must triumph whatever the price. But a sovereign is not a dictator. There is an alliance between him and his people which he cannot break. A dictator has nothing to hand over. Power lies in him, and in him alone. A sovereign receives a crown and it is his duty to pass it on.[9]

So, from my vantage point of London, it seemed that Iran had reached that moment in international affairs when a country has to be left to determine its own destiny. I believed, in a confusing situation, in following the old naval maxim: 'In a fog, slow right down but don't change course.' But even so, even at this late moment at the end of 1978, if I had learned of the Shah's illness, I would have instantly told Vance. The US and UK governments would then have acted decisively to force the Shah to admit his illness publicly, to leave Tehran and to appoint a regency.

As the political crisis in Iran worsened, what responsibility did the Shah's doctors, the only people aware of his state of health, have for letting friendly governments in on the secret? They were hardly unaware of the dire political situation in which their patient found himself. For several months they had had personal experience of the political unrest in Tehran. They had difficulty, on one occasion, in getting back to the royal palace, and were waiting for Dr Safavian in the street, hoping General Ayadi's car would turn up to get them through the picket of guards. On subsequent trips, until the end of 1978, Dr Flandrin found this kind of problem, and others, becoming more and more frequent. Ayadi's withdrawal as the Shah's doctor also resulted in the progressive breaking down of the organisation that had served the French doctors, and the Shah's desire for secrecy, so well. Their visits became more and more difficult as Flandrin no longer had access to the discreet residence where he used to stay. Instead he had to go to a hotel and be confined to his room because of the disruptions, the electricity failures and the street demonstrations, which sometimes bordered on riots.

As for the Shah, he remained as courteous as ever, but Flandrin found the consultation times became briefer and, especially at their last meetings, he could sense the Shah's tension and preoccupation. On the medical level, the discussion was basically concerned with the types of neurosedative that should or should not be prescribed. Safavian was usually, but not always, at Flandrin's side during those consultations in Iran. Flandrin's last trip was at the end of December 1978. He had visited the Shah thirty-nine times, thirty-five of them within Iran. On this occasion, the Shah was almost unrecognisable, visibly suffering from dreadful tension. He could not stop listening to the news on the radio while Flandrin examined him.

At this late stage should the Shah's doctors have suggested to him that he should let the Iranian people know that he was ill? Should the French doctors have reassessed their decision to keep the Shah's illness from President Giscard d'Estaing? The political stakes at that moment could not have been higher. But it is not normal for practising doctors to think like politicians. They are focused on one thing – what is good for their patient. Does it go beyond the boundaries of medicine to ask them to make political judgements in such a volatile and complex situation? And yet doctors are citizens like everyone else; they cannot opt out entirely from the society in which they live. Doctors must be ready to contemplate that they have a responsibility to their own country that goes beyond their responsibility to their patients. The Hippocratic oath is not an absolute. Very rarely there have to be exceptions.

The Iranian doctors could do nothing, but the French were in a different position. Flandrin told me he did not tell his government. I do not know whether either Professor Bernard or Professor Milliez used their distinguished positions in French life to tell Giscard d'Estaing. In any case their attitude to the political situation in Iran, if it reflected that of French newspapers and Paris opinion more generally, would have been more complex and ambivalent than if they had been practising medicine in Washington or London. President Giscard d'Estaing's government gave the appearance of hedging its bets on the Shah and of being in close contact with Ayatollah Khomeini, who by now was living in France. This may have made it less obvious to the French doctors that it was in the French national interest for them to tell the President about the Shah's illness and to break the Hippocratic oath.

In William Shawcross's fascinating book *The Shah's Last Ride*,[10] he wrote that the Shah's doctors were convinced that the French secret service did not know about the Shah's illness, and I have confirmed that that is still their claim. Richard Helms, the former US ambassador to Iran and former head of the CIA, with extensive contacts inside the French intelligence service, said he was convinced from his own enquiries that French intelligence never knew the Shah was seriously ill and confirmed before he died that the CIA did not know either. Further, according to Shawcross, neither Mossad, SAVAK nor MI6 ever knew. I was in charge of MI6 at the time and, for my part, am convinced MI6 did not know.

An American diplomat in 1978 was warned by his Soviet counterpart, with whom he regularly lunched at one of Tehran's restaurants, that the Shah had cancer, but the US embassy apparently dismissed this with the comment: 'This rumour has abounded in many quarters and may be of Soviet inspiration.' Perhaps the KGB did know, but though many KGB records were revealed in the Yeltsin era, this rumour has not, as yet, been confirmed. The then Soviet Foreign Minister, Andrei Gromyko, with whom I discussed the Shah, not surprisingly said nothing to me about his having any illness. There is no public record of East German intelligence knowing and if West German intelligence had known I believe the German Foreign Minister, Hans-Dietrich Genscher, would have told Vance and me at one of our many quadripartite meetings.

But in London in late 1979 the former French Foreign Minister Louis de Guiringaud said to me over dinner, when neither of us was any longer in office, that he had told me of the Shah's illness the year before. I challenged him immediately over this for I knew he was mistaken. No one trained as a doctor would forget information of that import. Had Guiringaud told me, it would have triggered many things in my brain and I would have started to view the Shah as a patient, not just a head of government. But why, other than for vainglorious reasons, should Guiringaud have claimed that the French government, at least by the summer of 1978, did know? He was an honest man and, working together over two years, we had built up a friendship.

An interesting corroboration that the French knew something about the Shah's ill health came from Sir Denis Wright, the former British ambassador to Iran. After he retired from the diplomatic service he served on the board of Royal Dutch Shell. He later revealed in a BBC radio reconstruction of the fall of the Shah that a fellow board member had been a Frenchman, a former ambassador to Moscow, governor of the Banque de France and extremely well connected in Paris. This man had mentioned to Wright that he had heard that the Shah was seriously ill. Wright said he had visited the Shah soon after this conversation but had found no evidence from that meeting of any illness, so did no more to follow up the lead.

Much later Giscard d'Estaing, long after he had been President, was asked at a dinner party in Paris whether he knew about the Shah's illness. He replied: '*Indirectement.*' It is, therefore, possible that the French President and the Foreign Minister knew but did not tell their own intelligence service, perhaps suspecting that it had more links with the US and the UK than it ever acknowledged to its political masters. On balance, I believe this is what happened, though I have no idea how the French President was indirectly told about the Shah. It does explain why Giscard d'Estaing personally decided to allow Khomeini to stay in France during the crisis in Tehran. The head of the French intelligence service was very unhappy about this and it supports the view that it was President Giscard d'Estaing's decision that France might benefit by harbouring him. British interest lay in convincing our friends in the region that we were a loyal ally and did not shift our support for the Shah just because times were rough. In the end I doubt France gained much economically or politically when Khomeini did return to Iran.

The end

On 16 January 1979 the Shah left Tehran, flying to see President Anwar Sadat in Egypt and then on to Morocco, where his illness grew worse. He was seen twice there by Dr Flandrin. He left Iran in the apparent belief that he could control events from abroad but the reality was that by then he could never reclaim the throne. In the nineteenth and early twentieth century, a combination of intellectuals, bazaaris and mullahs had more than once combined to force shahs of the Qajar dynasty into surrendering their powers or abdicating. The Shah had not learned the lesson of history and lost support from all those elements. Most importantly, he underestimated the influence of the mullahs, just as the British and the Americans consistently under-estimated the reach and rapport that Ayatollah Khomeini was building up while in exile. In his memoirs, written when sick and dying in exile, the Shah still insisted on eulogising a hereditary monarchy without apparently recognising that by then the number of monarchs who held executive supreme power was very few. Most countries' monarchies had survived only by retaining little or no executive power and instead representing constitutional continuity and stability.

Khomeini returned to Tehran on 11 February from Paris. The streets filled with masses of people and the once proud Iranian army simply collapsed. On behalf of the British government, I cabled our ambassador in Tehran from the Royal Yacht in the Gulf to formally recognise the new regime, while travelling with the Queen on her visit to Saudi Arabia. The Saudi leaders were very shaken but pleased that Britain had not hedged its bet on the Shah.

Revolutionary committees were established all over Iran, and anyone associated with the Shah's regime was dragged off to prison. The new Prime Minister, Mehdi Bazargan, was powerless to intervene. Summary trials were held, and people publicly executed. The former Prime Minister, Amir Abbas Hoveyda, was tried, sentenced to death and, in a matter of minutes, shot in a prison cell. *Paris Match* published a picture of his body with three revolutionaries, one of whom, full of smiles, was carrying a machine gun; alongside it was a photograph of one of the Shah's family swimming in the Bahamas. The Shah had flown there from Morocco in King Hassan's own Boeing 747.

How much was the Shah's fall due to his illness, and how much due to his politics and personality? Dr Safavian has never spoken publicly but he did authorise me to express his belief that the medical control of the Shah's illness, during the period of treatment in Tehran up to January 1979, was of such high quality that it could not have contributed to the Shah's indecision and vacillation. Flandrin also believes that the Shah's illness did not significantly influence his decisions during the last few years of his regime and that it was not a factor in making him slow to recognise the dramatically growing unrest in his country.

As far as his blood condition was concerned, as diagnosed from the blood slides and other tests, they are of course correct. But the predictable progression of his lymphoid tumour and eventual transformation into a highly malignant cancer, which was then called lymphosarcoma,* must have had an effect on his decision-making powers. The Shah's story is a textbook case of two conditions – stress and cancer – mutually aggravating each other. There

---

* Lymphosarcoma is the traditional term for non-Hodgkin's lymphoma (NHL). An NHL is not easy to classify and a number of different classifications exist. It is more common than Hodgkin's disease. It is usually diagnosed between the ages of sixty-five and seventy. It is not known what causes it, although viral and bacterial infections have been linked to it. High and lower grades of the illness are recognised based on the rate of the proliferation of abnormal lymph cells. Patients present with swollen lymph nodes in the neck, groin, spleen or liver. Radiotherapy is the treatment of choice but chemotherapy may be necessary. Bone marrow transplants are also done.

is some limited scientific evidence that psychosocial factors, including stressful life changes, can be non-specific triggers which allow a focus of already present cancer cells to multiply and spread at a much faster rate than would be expected, as discussed in relation to Neville Chamberlain in Chapter 1 (p. 26). It is highly probable that in the Shah's case there was such an interaction. Flandrin's account of the Shah in his last few months in Tehran leaves no doubt that he was exhausted and under great stress. Visitors describe him as distraught and depressed, asking himself why this was happening to him.

Flandrin was interested in the Shah's personality and what lay beneath the formal image. He had been entertained by Assadollah Alam, the man who more than any other had been able to overcome the Shah's indecisiveness in the past, at his house in the mountains in eastern Iran. Alam had talked a lot about himself and the Shah. On the subject of the Shah's personality, Alam had described to Flandrin some paradoxical traits. 'It's strange to think that this man who has risen to such power could still be naive enough in some ways to trust what people told him.' On the other hand, he had also said that the Shah was 'used to assuming a role since childhood – the King [as he called the Shah] has an amazing ability to completely hide what he is thinking and what he knows'. Proof of this came when Alam had to give the Shah some information that he knew that the Shah had already heard. But the Shah showed not the slightest hint of knowing. Alam ceased to be Minister of Court in August 1977, dying in April 1978. Tragically for the Shah, the man who had made him appear decisive in 1963 was not alive when he needed him most – namely from the summer of 1978, when the Shah's illness was exacerbating his underlying indecisive nature.

Looking back on those years and listening afresh to many people who were around the Shah at the time, I am convinced his downfall could have been avoided only if Western governments had known about his illness. What was displayed in the last few years of his rule were the exaggerated characteristics and traits that had been there in the past. Power was part of his life from an early age and he could not share power, let alone give it up. Indecision was equally part of his life. The medical symptoms from which he suffered in 1978–9, an upset sleep pattern and general fatigue were part of a depression brought on by a natural reaction to being rejected by a significant number of his own people, and also by his underlying illness. It is not possible to separate any of these factors – they all contributed to his downfall. The Shah would never have voluntarily stepped down from power. He would have had to be forced out on grounds of ill health by Western governments.

British ambassadors, like those of other countries, had been watching for signs of instability in Iran for decades. In the 1960s the British embassy in Tehran reported that the collapse of the Shah's regime might or might not be imminent, and it worried about an old-fashioned society being invaded by new ideas and the superimposition of industrialisation on the traditional way of life. Western governments in the 1970s agonised constantly about whether or not the Shah's regime could survive. 'Is the Emperor Fully Clothed?' was the title of a dispatch sent from the British embassy in Tehran in August 1977 to the Foreign Office in London. The real criticism is not of Western governments' skills in anticipating an impending revolution, but of our handling of the Shah. We failed to remember how weak he was before he took on the airs of an autocrat. We were far too deferential. We should have insisted, following our involvement in the fall of Mohammad Mossadeq, that he make real democratic reforms and pave the way for a constitutional monarchy, as Franco had done in Spain. These reforms were necessary not just for his and his heir's survival but also for his country to reject the extremism of an Islamic revolution.

Exile

With the Shah in exile, in the middle of March 1979 Cyrus Vance made what he called 'one of the most distasteful recommendations I have ever had to make to the President', namely that the Shah should not come to the United States. With a similar sense of shame I had sent a note to Prime Minister James Callaghan that the Shah – who never formally applied to come to Britain – should, if he did apply, be politely turned away. There was no honour in our decisions, just the cold calculation of national interest. Given Britain's long history of offering political asylum, it was depressing that all but a few MPs now turned completely against the Shah. On 20 February 1979 I said in the House of Commons that I was prepared for our record of support for the Shah 'to be justified by history'. That was met with mirth and the cutting jibe from one Conservative MP, Sir Peter Tapsell, that 'history may have other things on its mind'. An article in the *Spectator* magazine by Edward Mortimer actually compared the revolution favourably with France in 1789 and Russia in 1917, and predicted that Ayatollah Khomeini was unlikely to impose religious conservatism on the rest of Iranian society.[11] Only a few years later those of us who had been in power in the US and the UK at the time were criticised not for defending the Shah but, by stressing human rights, for having precipitated his fall.

At the end of April 1979, when he was still in the Bahamas, the Shah developed a swollen gland in his neck. Dr Flandrin flew over to see him and diagnosed a lymphoma, aspirated one of the lymph glands and took another bone marrow sample, which showed his illness had deteriorated.* The Shah now knew he was acutely ill and Flandrin recommended much more aggressive treatment, ideally with a spell in hospital to assess exactly the 'stage' the disease had reached. However, the Shah still did not want the truth revealed, saying to Flandrin: 'At a time when they are killing officers faithful to me in my country, I cannot reduce them to complete despair by revealing my state of health.' So the Shah was put on intensive infusions of nitrogen mustard, vincristine, procarbazine and prednisolone with his wife acting as his nurse.

Meanwhile Margaret Thatcher, now Prime Minister, was busy back-tracking on the position she had adopted in opposition of supporting the Shah coming to Britain. In an off-the-record press briefing she had attacked the previous Labour government, saying we should be ashamed for refusing the Shah admission. She also made a private promise to the Shah to reverse the decision when in government. But instead of choosing to announce her change of mind openly, thereby retaining some vestige of honour, she did it clandestinely. She sent Sir Denis Wright, travelling under a different name and passport, to the Bahamas. So, according to William Shawcross, on 20 May it was as Edward Wilson that Wright arrived at the Ocean Club in the Bahamas and it was as Mr Wilson that he was ushered in to see the Shah for tea in his house on the beach. The Shah must have been full of contempt. The shabbiness was further compounded because the British government wanted to be able to say, if asked, that the Shah accepted and understood the decision not to grant him asylum. It was an added humiliation to heap on the Shah, but he apparently accepted the British decision on the condition that we would acknowledge that he had never formally applied to come to Britain. He wrote in his autobiography: 'I have a long-standing suspicion of British intent and British policy which I have never found reason to alter.'[12] In all the circumstances, it was not too harsh a judgement.

---

* The lymph gland showed abnormal lymphoid cells, immunoblasts, which meant that they had acquired an immunity to treatment, although his blood and bone marrow were still fairly normal.

In August 1979 Flandrin flew to treat the Shah in Mexico, where he and his wife had gone after their visas for the Bahamas had run out and not been renewed. He found the Shah's white cell count down, and he therefore reduced the chemotherapy. By September, however, the Shah became jaundiced and Dr Benjamin Kean, a parasitologist from New York, was called in since malaria was suspected. Kean arrived in Mexico on 29 September and diagnosed obstructive jaundice. Flandrin flew over from Paris and together with Kean saw the Shah. Then, according to Flandrin, began a struggle as to who was to control the patient, the American parasitologist or the French oncologist. It was resolved, according to Kean, when, on 18 October, Flandrin officially withdrew as the Shah's physician. It is still not clear why the Shah did not stay in Mexico. Kean was pressurising for the Shah to go to New York and rang Dr Eben Dustin, the State Department doctor. On 19 October 1979, at a weekly breakfast meeting, Cyrus Vance and President Carter discussed whether to admit the Shah to the United States. Vance now changed his mind and argued that the President should admit the Shah. Carter was still very reluctant but Zbigniew Brzezinski, on humanitarian grounds, supported Vance.

The US embassy in Tehran consulted Mehdi Bazargan and his Foreign Minister, neither of whom liked the idea of the Shah going to the United States, but they were ready to strengthen the guards around the Embassy. Still no one in Tehran knew about the Shah having cancer. On 20 October the State Department gave the President the arguments for allowing the Shah into the US and Carter relented. In retrospect, Carter's political instincts, which were against the Shah's admittance, proved more accurate than those of his advisers. The Shah flew in on 22 October to New York Hospital-Cornell Medical Center, where he had his gall bladder removed, but not his spleen. Flandrin (who had always wanted the spleen removed) and the Shah's family became very unhappy with the American doctors. A biopsy of the swelling on the Shah's neck showed that he was no longer suffering from lymphatic lymphoma but lymphosarcoma, a much more lethal form of cancer. An article in *Science* published in 1980 alleged:

> Benjamin H. Kean, the American doctor who attended the Shah in Mexico, misread both the nature of the Shah's illness and the capacity of Mexico's doctors to deal with it. Nothing done by the doctors at New York Hospital or at the Memorial Sloan-Kettering Cancer Center was any trickier than what doctors in Mexico do routinely. There may have been good reasons for admitting the Shah to the United States, but there were not compelling reasons.[13]

On 4 November 1979 the US embassy in Tehran was seized by demonstrators with the sixty-six Americans inside becoming hostages for 444 days. Khomeini had already declared that there was an American plot involving the Shah, and, as many of us had long predicted, he encouraged Iranian students to take action to 'force the United States to return the deposed and criminal Shah'.

On 12 December, after the Shah had been refused permission to go back to Mexico, the White House chief of staff, Hamilton Jordan, came to a US air base in Texas to tell him he could go to Panama. The Shah left the United States on the 15th and the Iranians started extradition procedures. Meanwhile, the doctors argued amongst themselves about the Shah's treatment but there was no doubt that his health was deteriorating. Kean's account of what happened in Panama is quite explicit. The Panamanians were determined to have the Shah's operation at the Hospital Paitilla in downtown Panama City rather than at the Gorges Hospital in the American Canal Zone, and furthermore they wanted Panamanian surgeons to operate. Kean was totally against using Paitilla.

On 23 March 1980 the Shah flew from Panama to Egypt, where fortunately the Egyptians had no such petty reservations about who should operate, wanting only the best treatment for him. Kean, the US surgeon Dr Michael DeBakey and Flandrin all met in Cairo with the Egyptian doctors and agreed that the spleen should come out as soon as possible. During the operation a biopsy was taken of the liver, which showed lymphosarcoma. Kean did not want full chemotherapy treatment to blight the Shah's last days but Flandrin, the Egyptian doctors and the Shah's family felt he should have the treatment. So Kean left on 31 March for the United States and Flandrin began to care for the Shah again.

It was a brave and generous decision of President Sadat to invite the Shah to Egypt. It ignited fundamentalist feeling, already building up in Egypt, and was almost certainly a factor in Sadat's assassination at a military parade on 6 October 1981.

In April 1980 an abortive attempt by US forces to free the Tehran hostages with helicopters ended in a fiasco in the desert. The principled resignation of Vance,[14] who had advised Carter against the mission on military as well as political grounds, followed. Only in January 1981, at the very moment that Ronald Reagan took over from Carter as President, were the US hostages eventually released. The hostage issue did much damage to Carter's reputation.

The Shah died in Cairo on 27 July 1980. His tomb is in the al-Rifai mosque. At the state funeral were the former US President Richard Nixon and the American and French ambassadors. Britain sent its chargé d'affaires. William Shawcross summed the tragedy up:

> The Shah's friend Henry Kissinger was right to call him a Flying Dutchman. His last ride around the tarnished rim of the Western world was a punishment for hubris. He behaved during that forlorn and tawdry journey with both courage and dignity. But his appearance was seen by many of his former friends and allies as a curse.[15]

Postscript

A democratic transition from the Shah's reign in 1978–9 would have avoided a chain of events with profound consequences for the peace of the region. The power of Iran in the region was, within months of the revolution, dissipated and destroyed. If Iran had remained a regional power, there might have been no invasion of Afghanistan by the USSR in late 1979, certainly no Iran–Iraq War from 1980–88, no Iraqi invasion of Kuwait, no 1991 Iraq war to remove Saddam Hussein from Kuwait, and therefore no US troops in Saudi Arabia from 1990. It was the prospect of a US military presence there which infuriated the Saudi Arabian Osama bin Laden. He tried to see the King to oppose the decision but was seen instead by Prince Sultan, the Saudi defence minister. Bin Laden hated Saddam, whom he considered a non-believer though both were Sunni Muslims. Bin Laden had been in Afghanistan through most of the 1980s fighting against the Soviet Union and had become a celebrity in his homeland. He offered to recruit an army of mujahideen to defend Saudi Arabia and claimed millions of Muslims would rally to the cause. Prince Sultan listened for nearly an hour before politely rejecting bin Laden's offer. When the news reached bin Laden that the Americans were coming into Saudi Arabia he denounced the King. In March 1991 he called for the overthrow of the monarchy and in April, fearing arrest, he left Saudi Arabia for the Pakistan border with Afghanistan. The 9/11 attacks in the US on the World Trade Centre twin towers and the Pentagon did not therefore come without warning (see also Chapter 7). The deaths of more than a million Muslims on different battlefields since 1980 has given rise to great ill feeling between Sunni and Shiite Muslims and contributed to the wave of Islamic fundamentalism.

As the world focused its attention on Iran in the wake of the debacle following the invasion of Iraq in 2003, it became very clear how important, once again, Iran is within the region. In late 2007, Iran seemed determined still to defy UN sanctions and proceed with its uranium enrichment programme. After having been invaded in 1980 by Iraq, which was known to be developing nuclear weapons, any form of government in Tehran would have pushed ahead with a nuclear weapons programme. Its determination to continue, after Saddam had been forced out of Kuwait in 1991, was influenced by its Sunni neighbour, Pakistan, becoming a nuclear weapon state despite the Western democracies trying very hard to prevent it. The Iranians knew that Saudi Arabia had helped pay for Pakistan's nuclear weapons and that they could, as a result, acquire such weapons quickly if they wished.

Negotiations will be difficult and it is hard to envisage, following the December 2007 US National Intelligence Estimate that it 'does not know whether it [Iran] intends to develop nuclear weapons', that Russia and China will accept the tougher financial sanctions which the US, UK, France and Germany believe will be needed. Successful negotiations will need the incentive of a genuine offer to lift all sanctions imposed after the 1979 revolution immediately Iran agrees to forgo high-grade uranium enrichment. They will also be more likely if a new, stable, Iraq emerges from the insurgency in which Iran has confidence.

Opinion polls show that most Iranians wish to return to the good relations between their country and the US that date from the Tehran conference of 1943. The deep question is how best to mobilise this opinion. The key issue to address, for those ready to contemplate a US bombing of Iran's nuclear sites, is: will this push the Iranians towards stopping a nuclear weapons programme or, after a pause, will they redouble their efforts? Few now advocate air strikes on Iran in 2008 or 2009. Bombing can affect the balance of fighting on the ground but in the absence of ground forces it can only reinforce diplomacy. When provoked by military attack Iran's fundamentalists are likely to freeze up even more rather than rethink. Had the aftermath of the invasion of Iraq in 2003 been successfully handled, it would be easier now to convince the Iranians to abandon a high-grade enrichment programme. In May 2003 Iran was ready to negotiate, but from 2005 its position seemed to harden. In diplomacy, as in life, failure carries a price; in 2008–9 patience combined with a readiness to embark on a longer period of diplomacy – backed, if need be, by tough and targeted sanctions – is more likely to succeed than a display of limited military force.

6

President Mitterrand's prostate cancer

'Probably there were things Mitterrand hid from himself!' quipped
Georges Kiejman, a longtime associate of Mitterrand.

Ronald Tiersky[1]

François Mitterrand was a politician who always fascinated me. I did not know
him well; few did. I met him first in the mid-1960s, when he presided over
meetings of European parliamentarians in Gauche Européenne in Paris. I
watched his transformation physically from a shabby intellectual to a smart,
aloof leader sporting the red rose of a new era of European socialism. I talked
to him at the Labour Party conference in 1978, in the Élysée Palace on Anglo-
French nuclear cooperation in 1986 when I was leader of the SDP, in the
Élysée again in early September 1992 following my appointment as EU
negotiator for the former Yugoslavia, and a number of times thereafter.

In the first ballot for the French presidency on 26 April 1981, Mitterrand,
the Socialist candidate, came second to the sitting first-term President, Valéry
Giscard d'Estaing. He beat his successor as President, Jacques Chirac, and the
Communist candidate, Georges Marchais. The Communists, who usually
polled around 20 per cent, received only 15.5 per cent of the vote and
Mitterrand polled more than 25 per cent. In the second ballot Mitterrand faced
only President Giscard d'Estaing, who was already under political pressure
from the domestic effects of the second oil price rise in 1979. Giscard
d'Estaing's equivocation in responding to the Soviet Union's siting of SS-20
nuclear missiles in eastern Europe and his alleged personal involvement in the
scandal surrounding gifts of diamonds from Emperor Bokassa of the Central
African Empire had also begun to erode his popularity. On 10 May, François
Mitterrand won the second ballot with 52 per cent of the votes. Taking office
on 21 May, everything seemed possible politically for Mitterrand and he
appeared at the height of his powers, fit and well. Immediately Mitterrand

called for a dissolution of Parliament and won an absolute majority of seats in the French Assembly for his Socialist Party with 38 per cent of the vote.

A state secret

Openness about his health had been a specific commitment of Mitterrand's during the election. He had promised that if he were elected, his doctors would make a statement on his health at six-monthly intervals. Mitterrand had been shocked, along with many other Frenchmen, about the secrecy surrounding President Georges Pompidou and the pitiful circumstances in which he had died of a blood cancer, myelomatosis, with the country unaware of what was happening to its President (see Chapter 2). Valéry Giscard d'Estaing, when running for election in 1974, had also promised regular medical briefings but when in office, for no obvious reason, gave them up. In the summer of 1981 the first Mitterrand health bulletin was issued by Dr Claude Gubler, who had been personal physician to Mitterrand and his family since 1969, in the genuine belief the President was fit and well.

Suddenly, six months into the presidency, after returning from the Cancun summit in Mexico at the end of October, Mitterrand began to complain of having pain in his back and arm, and, more seriously, he also developed a limp. Gubler examined Mitterrand and found he had an enlarged and hardened prostate.* On 7 November, Gubler took the President in his old car, without a police escort, from the Élysée to the Val-de-Grâce military hospital, where he was registered for a battery of tests under an assumed name, Albert Blot. The bone scan carried out as one of the tests made the prognosis very serious. On the evening of 16 November 1981, Gubler was accompanied to the Élysée by Professor Adolphe Steg, a distinguished surgeon specialising in the treatment of the prostate gland. Steg confirmed to Gubler that the bony lesions

---

* The prostate gland is found around the urethra, the tube in males that leaves the bladder and then leads down into the penis. Urine secreted by the two kidneys passes down two ureters into the bladder and thence through the single urethra out of the body. The prostate gland secretes semen which passes down the urethra during ejaculation, usually as the result of sexual intercourse. The gland grows during adolescence and then tends to enlarge further over time, with an incidence of 50 per cent in men aged between forty and fifty-nine and 90 per cent in men over seventy. This is called benign prostatic hyperplasia, giving rise to dribbling of urine and a weak urine stream. Cancer of the gland is the fourth commonest cancer, and is treated with anti-androgen drugs, oestrogens, radiotherapy or less commonly now, surgery.

visible on the X-rays taken earlier were secondary growths from the prostatic cancer. President Mitterrand was told he was suffering from advanced cancer of the prostate gland. The average survival time for a patient whose cancer was this far advanced was three years. There were, of course, rare exceptions but the outlook was bleak.

Steg, according to Gubler's account,[2] did not prevaricate. Earlier, on 13 November, Gubler had told Mitterrand that the results of the tests were not good but he had not used the word 'cancer', and still less that it was disseminated. Steg, however, was blunt. He said to the President: 'My job is not to hide the truth from you. You have cancer of the prostate which is spreading to your bones and this spread is important.' The President murmured: 'I am finished.' Steg replied: 'You cannot say that, let's see, one can never say that things are finished. With Dr Gubler we are going to do what is necessary.' The President interrupted him: 'Stop kidding me – I'm finished.' 'It's true, it is serious,' replied Steg, 'but we are going to commence treatment. You must let us do it. It is important that you are in agreement with everything, if not—' The President interrupted: 'If not, I am finished and you are not giving me any choice.' Steg was even blunter to Gubler. 'Things have started very badly, especially when a cancer of the prostate has begun metastasising.' He went on to say about the prognosis: 'If we do not succeed in arresting it, it's several months.'*

Meanwhile, claims of a serious illness were being denied by Pierre Bérégovoy, Mitterrand's key aide in the Élysée, on the very day that Steg took the full results of the tests to the President. These claims had been fuelled by a four-page story on Mitterrand's hospital visit the previous week, together with photographs, in *Paris Match*.

---

* In 1981 the PSA (prostate-specific antigen) test had not been introduced. This is a test widely used now, on whose efficacy doctors differ. While not being confirmatory of prostate cancer, it is indicative. The PSA measures an enzyme produced by glandular tissue in the prostate gland. Greater amounts are secreted if the gland is increased in size and especially so in the case of cancer. A proper independent medical assessment at the start of Mitterrand's presidency should have included a rectal examination, when a hardened and/or uneven enlarged prostate gland might have been found. There had been no urinary symptoms, however, to trigger such an examination earlier in 1981. At that stage there were also no symptoms to suggest bone metastases, and having a bone X-ray would normally depend on there being some suspicious signs. Had prostatic cancer been found in early 1981, it would have been open to Mitterrand to try to convince his party to let him run for President, explaining to French electors that early cancer treatment had radically improved the prognosis and he was fit enough to lead them. Public knowledge of his cancer, however, would have reduced Mitterrand's chances of defeating Giscard d'Estaing.

Mitterrand now faced a political crisis, not just a medical diagnosis. Only he could resolve it and given his previous promise he might have been expected to choose openness, releasing a short statement that the President had cancer of the prostate and would be having treatment, which would not require hospitalisation. Such a statement would probably have sufficed and he need not have mentioned the fact that the cancer had already gone to his bones, provided there was a firm declaration that he had every intention of continuing his presidential duties. There would have been some controversy, a few articles speculating that he would have to resign, but the majority of French voters would have been ready to give the new President the benefit of the doubt and to wait and see. His party might not have liked it, but a French President, once elected, can survive politically without the support of his party political colleagues.

Instead of openness, Mitterrand chose secrecy. According to Gubler the President immediately said: 'Whatever happens, you must reveal nothing. It is a state secret,' and he added – so that Gubler would be absolutely clear, 'you are bound by this secret.' Some, in retrospect, have claimed that Gubler should have refused to accept the presidential order to preserve secrecy at all costs. But, having been Mitterrand's doctor for twelve years, this would have meant resigning and walking away from the care of a patient at a time of maximum distress. Gubler and Steg felt obliged to accept their patient's demand for secrecy and that in doing so they were serving him. Gubler was forbidden to tell even Danielle Mitterrand, the President's wife, and he did not tell his own wife or children. François Mitterrand told Danielle only in 1991 and she said blithely by way of explanation: 'He simply preserved our tranquillity of spirit.'[3]

Some patients do decide to conceal all information about their illnesses even from their close families. But a democratically elected head of government is not a normal patient. There is an obligation to openness which Mitterrand clearly understood but decided to disregard.

At the beginning Mitterrand himself may have wavered in his determination to keep the news secret, for Gubler claimed that the President must have talked openly to one of his closest aides, Jacques Attali. According to Gubler, Attali wrote a diary entry in December 1981: 'The President tells me he has cancer and that he is condemned.' But then a few days later he wrote: 'The President tells me: "The doctors are imbeciles, they are mistaken. I don't have cancer,"' indicating that Mitterrand had decided, after initially wavering, that his immediate demand for total secrecy was to be adhered to. Neither alleged quotation was present in Attali's published diaries, *Verbatim*.[4]

The ethical and moral dilemmas which Mitterrand's decision posed for Gubler were immense, for it was his name that would be on the six-monthly public bulletin on the President's health. In Gubler's own words:

> I was caught in a trap and plunged into a lie from which I could only escape 15 years later. The lie covered everything. The doctors lied from the time we finished by announcing to our patient his chances of survival were five years, while the prognosis varied from three years to three months if his body did not respond to treatment. The patient had also decided to lie, first to himself, which is quite human, and then to others from the time he had told me in December, to the time I was to prepare the second bulletin concerning his health.

It was in putting out this second bulletin that Gubler crossed an important threshold. The truth is impossible to maintain if the patient's personal doctor is involved in the statement and the patient does not want the truth told. Gubler could have tried either to persuade Mitterrand to abandon his promise to release bulletins, as Giscard d'Estaing had done, or to insist that they could go out from the Élysée only in the name of his press spokesman without attribution to Gubler himself. But it would not have been easy to make this demand given that he had already issued one bulletin in good faith under his own name and many other personal doctors of heads of government had, in the past, issued medical bulletins in their name.

The usual six-monthly bulletins were issued and Gubler increasingly found himself in an impossible position. He would have preferred to make no statements, but his patient wanted them. In the end the wording he chose, he claims, was neither a lie nor a cover-up, just incomplete. But the whole purpose of these six-monthly statements was to convince the French people that there could not be another cover-up of a serious illness, such as was conducted by President Pompidou. Gubler recalls how difficult his position became. In 1982 he was asked by a childhood friend, a doctor and supporter of Mitterrand: 'The President has said that he would hide nothing concerning his health. If he had something serious would you tell?' Gubler replied: 'Obviously,' knowing full well that he was already doing exactly the opposite. In Gubler's words the degree of deception in which he was now involved was very wearing.

In November 1981 Mitterrand started on oestrogen hormone therapy,* which had to be combined with anti-coagulants because oestrogen on its own has the serious side effect of causing blood clots, with 30 per cent of patients dying in the first two years. It started with an intravenous infusion of a very strong oestrogen every day for two weeks and then every other day until the end of February 1982. Laboratory tests were carried out at Val-de-Grâce and checked by a private laboratory under the name of patient Xavier Carpentier. The hormone was so strong it could not be continued in that dosage for much longer than three or four months.

Gubler travelled everywhere with the President. He conducted the treatment himself, carrying the equipment with him, hanging the intravenous drip on a picture hook or a coat hanger so as not to have to hammer a nail into the wall of an embassy or another government's guest house. He then collected the used equipment and disposed of it on his return to Paris. The reason for this was that Mitterrand and Gubler feared international medical espionage. The French believed that Leonid Brezhnev, when Soviet President, had had his hair collected from a comb and analysed to reveal the nature of his drug therapy. This fear sometimes led their deception to take on the elements of farce. There were suspicions that some countries, in looking for medical evidence in visiting heads of government, had gone as far as to collect toilet flushings. Pompidou's condition, they believed, had been diagnosed by a foreign government through the clandestine collection of urine samples. So Gubler would conscientiously check the President's bathroom and flush the toilets after use.

The whole period was, as Gubler wrote, 'eleven years' hide and seek with death'. The imposition of secrecy was, undoubtedly, slightly increasing the medical risks, yet this was the price the patient was ready to pay in order to continue his cover-up. The risks were demonstrated when Mitterrand had a dangerous complication of the treatment, suffering a pulmonary embolus at the end of 1982 which was treated with heparin, an anti-coagulant.

---

* Oestrogen is a natural or synthetic hormone that brings about a change in the walls of the uterus before ovulation, and also the development of the puberty changes in young women, such as growth of the breasts, pubic hair and hair under the armpits and a characteristic appearance of fat rounding out the hips and thighs. Oestrogen is used for treating cancer of the prostate gland. Naturally produced oestrogen is destroyed in the body quickly so for therapeutic purposes synthetic oestrogens are used. Ethinyl oestradiol is the strongest oral oestrogen, some twenty times stronger than stilboestrol, and can be used intravenously.

The Sphinx

President Mitterrand's own cover story was of ignorance about his exact medication, saying these were Dr Gubler's drugs taken for his rheumatism. But such deception was second nature to Mitterrand. His character – on which many books have been, and will continue to be, written – holds the key to understanding his decision to opt for secrecy. He was someone for whom secrecy and subterfuge had been natural companions throughout his career. It is not for nothing that he was sometimes called 'The Sphinx'.

This reputation originated in the way he handled the record of his activities during the Second World War. Towards its end he was involved in the French Resistance, falsifying documents and planning escape routes for prisoners of war. During 1943, under the pseudonym 'Captain Morland' and with Maurice Pinot, the head of the Commissariat, he began to develop a resistance network, Le Mouvement National des Prisonniers et Deportés de Guerre. But then in November 1943, Mitterrand received an award, the Francisque, from Marshal Philippe Pétain, the leader of the Vichy government, which cooperated with the German occupation of France. This was given to praiseworthy civil servants and its award to Mitterrand raised a controversy which was to dog him throughout his career about whether he had earlier been a collaborator with Nazi occupation. Whenever attacked for this, Mitterrand, for years, grandly refused to comment, feeling it beneath his dignity. But as President, in November 1992 he gratuitously snubbed his intellectual critics and lent credence to the collaborationist charge by laying a wreath on Pétain's grave. The act was not wholly without precedence. Presidents de Gaulle and Giscard d'Estaing had respectively ensured that wreaths were placed to mark the fiftieth and sixtieth anniversaries of the ending of the First World War, Pétain having been the head of French forces at the Battle of Verdun. But Mitterrand's action caused a furore, stimulating Jacques Julliard to write:

> Historians will record that the big question that agitated the defenders of the rights of man in France during [an] entire year when Bosnia lived nameless horror, was the placing of a bouquet on the tomb of Pétain, the treasonous former marshal, by the President of the Republic. In France one doesn't stand for any nonsense when it comes to symbols. It is too bad the same isn't true when it comes to realities.[5]

Perhaps Mitterrand felt he knew an inner truth about France, that it does not want the issue of what really happened during the Vichy years ever to be finally resolved. In that sense Mitterrand's ambivalence mirrored the opinion of more than just the generation of French people who were adults during this period. But the extent of his own involvement with Vichy still remains unclear.

In the provisional government awaiting de Gaulle's return in August 1944, Mitterrand, aged twenty-seven, was named for two weeks as the general secretary for prisoners of war. But during the war he had had a difficult meeting with de Gaulle in Algiers, resisting his demand to merge three rival prisoner movements, and he was never asked to serve under de Gaulle. He came into the government under Paul Ramadier in 1947 as the Minister for Ex-Servicemen. From 1947 until 1958 in the Fourth Republic Mitterrand served in eleven governments and was seen as a non-socialist, neo-radical minister, having been elected as an independent deputy in the central department of Nièvre.

His reputation for subterfuge and deception was fuelled by a strange episode which some alleged was a set-up to gain publicity. On 16 October 1959 the press announced that Mitterrand had escaped an assassination attempt. A right wing deputy, Robert Pesquet, charged him with faking it to achieve public sympathy. Mitterrand's parliamentary immunity was lifted so that he could stand trial following the charge but the trial never took place as Pesquet fled the country. The so-called Observatory Affair damaged Mitterrand but largely because, in line with his habit of secrecy, he failed to defend himself.[6]

Equally mysterious was Mitterrand's enigmatic movement from the right to the left in French politics, during which he lived his life behind a smokescreen of his own creation. In 1965 he challenged de Gaulle for the presidency. The result demonstrated his ability to pull together a coalition of the left, as he gained 45 per cent of the vote in the second round. Thereafter he was a politician with a future, nominally of the left but with a somewhat contrived image, a man who wanted to be seen as an intellectual and bibliophile as well as a provincial. He was also described as 'a character from a novel' and a 'procrastinator of Godotesque proportions'.[7]

Until his illness Mitterrand's greatest secret was the existence of the parallel family life he lived with his long-standing companion Anne Pingeot, with whom he had a daughter, Mazarine. This was kept from the French people until it was revealed publicly for the first time in *Paris Match* on 10 November 1994, by which time Mazarine was twenty years old and Mitterrand was six months from finally leaving office.

So by 1981, when his prostate cancer was diagnosed, Mitterrand was very used to being secretive. The most seriously damaging political effect of the secrecy surrounding Mitterrand's illness was the speed with which he moved from being a democratic politician, sensitive to the Socialist Party, the wider electorate and the rights of individual citizens, to an autocratic politician steeped in and surrounded by state power. The democratic influences, which had been part of his life in his rise to power, suddenly became optional; his party, the electorate and the human rights of French men and women became subordinated to one all-pervasive demand – the need to keep his illness secret.

Mitterrand built up an 'anti-terror cell' which was directly answerable to him as President of the Republic and which circumvented the previous ways in which terrorist activity had been dealt with by the French National Police and Gendarmerie, answerable to the Prime Minister and the Cabinet. This cell, under orders which never had a proper legal foundation, undertook the presidential wire-tapping, which was eventually exposed by the newspaper *Libération*.

Mitterrand's insistence on protecting the secrecy of his illness for '*raison d'état*' led to the most massive illegal invasion of privacy in French republican history. On Mitterrand's orders, an unauthorised team of gendarmes tapped the telephones of hundreds of French politicians, journalists, publishers and Parisian personalities. The President justified it on the grounds that he needed to know if any of them were preparing to divulge details of his illness. But this was also, in part, an excuse to maintain the secrecy of his parallel family life and not compromise the security of Pingeot and their daughter, who were secretly housed and guarded at public expense. Mitterrand vehemently denied any phone-tapping when answering a question from Belgian TV interviewers, in 1993. 'The Élysée listens to nothing. There is no tapping here,' he said.

This web of secrecy surrounded Mitterrand's visits to foreign countries. He would arrange two aeroplanes – one for him and the other, arriving a little later, carrying his secret family. Foreign leaders knew, the press probably guessed but little was said or written. Lying became such an element of day-to-day life that it spread into policy areas. We now know, for example, that despite all his denials, in July 1985 Mitterrand authorised the French secret service to sink the Greenpeace ship *Rainbow Warrior*, which was preparing to disrupt French nuclear tests in the Pacific. This was confirmed in July 2005 by Admiral Pierre Lacoste.

A French author, Thierry Pfister, who served as spokesman for Pierre Mauroy, Prime Minister in Mitterrand's first Socialist government, has a highly idiosyncratic and historical viewpoint about Mitterrand's attitude to the truth. He claims that General de Gaulle once shouted: 'Truths! Did you think I could have created a [Free French] government against the English and the Americans with truths? You make history with ambition, not with truths.'[8] Pfister quotes this to illustrate his thesis that for the French mind, lying in politics is the norm and that anyone trying to attach a standard of truthfulness to a politician's behaviour is naive. He goes on to argue that the French, and particularly France's elites, never understood how President Bill Clinton could be impeached. They were terrified by the implications of his impeachment for their ability to keep their private lives secret, particularly their sexual habits. Pfister believes this explained why the French reaction to the Clinton affair, much more than in other democratic countries, was one of ridicule and self-satisfied righteousness. One more reason for a certain disdain for the American way of life.

The harder question to answer is: would Mitterrand have chosen this path of secrecy, mystery and autocracy anyhow, irrespective of his illness? Was he essentially hubristic and attached to the trappings of power and its intoxication? Having watched him before he held power I could not detect any such latent tendencies then and I think illness was the precipitating factor, but like other things associated with Mitterrand, no one can be certain.

The presidential record

Mitterrand proved that heads of government may be ill, their condition serious and their treatment exacting, yet they can still govern effectively. In this they are no different from other people. Cancer treatment has made major advances and patients now tolerate many tough treatments very well. Mitterrand, at this stage, was also only on hormone therapy, which is less debilitating than chemotherapy. Even so, looking back on his political achievement during those years, particularly the first term of his presidency (1981–8), it is amazing how Mitterrand achieved so much.

Mitterrand was an active President in his first term. He spoke in public 1,700 times despite living in fear of losing his voice, one of the side effects of the treatment. He travelled abroad 154 times, made sixty official visits to fifty-five countries, undertook seventy one-day journeys, went to eighteen European Council meetings and attended six summit meetings. Against that record it is hard to argue that he should have resigned in November 1981 and difficult to claim that his illness damaged his decision-making in any significant ways during his first seven years as President.

During his early treatment, with his critics not knowing about his illness, Mitterrand came under considerable pressure from the French right, who despised what they alleged was his new-found socialism and his betrayal of the bourgeoisie. The area they focused their attack on was his initially unsuccessful handling of the economy and his dash for economic growth against the international business cycle during 1981–2. Mitterrand was also under pressure from the left to deliver on his electoral promises, particularly as he had Communist ministers in his government. Later he made a rare *mea culpa*, saying: 'I was carried away by our victory, which intoxicated us. Everyone . . . was predicting that economic growth would resume by 1982. Honestly, I lacked the necessary expertise to be able to contradict them.'⁹ One wonders whether, had he been fitter, Mitterrand would have been readier to take on the left. But, ever the calculator of political advantage, he realised that he could afford a failure in the left's economic recipe early enough in his presidency to enable change. And it also suited him personally to be at peace with the left and attacked by the right in the difficult early months of his treatment.

On 23 March, 1983 Mitterrand changed his economic policies. He raised taxes and kept the franc in the European Monetary System. With the help of Jacques Delors, his Finance Minister, he persuaded the German Chancellor, Helmut Kohl, to revalue the deutschmark by 5.5 per cent. Later Kohl, Mitterrand and Delors, by then President of the European Commission, were responsible for the 1985 agreement on the Single European Act and subsequently the emergence of the single currency in the Maastricht Treaty and the development of the Eurozone. All three were strong believers in European integration and Mitterrand advanced that cause with style and conviction, concluding with narrowly winning the referendum on the Maastricht Treaty in September 1992, which enshrined the euro currency in law.

From the start of his presidency, Mitterrand supported Gaston Defferre, a respected Socialist leader and former mayor of Marseilles, in legislating for decentralisation. After 150 years of Napoleon's Paris-appointed *préfets*, who had hitherto governed provincial France, they reduced the centralised powers of the French constitution. Mitterrand also moved imaginatively with a whole series of policies to advance women's rights.

In my view one of Mitterrand's finest political moments occurred on 21 January 1983, when he addressed the German Bundestag: 'The Soviets with their SS-20 missiles are unilaterally destroying the equilibrium in Europe . . .

I will not accept this and I recognise that we must arm ourselves to restore the balance.' Single-handedly he used the weight of the French Presidency to help bring the German Social Democrats – then in opposition – back to sensible defence policies. Mitterrand's stance helped solidify the transatlantic alliance and finished once and for all Washington's early concerns about how Mitterrand would handle the French Communist Party. The fact that French communism has since been so deftly sidelined owes much to Mitterrand.

In 1982, he robustly supported Britain and Margaret Thatcher over the Argentinian invasion of the Falkland Islands and helpfully revealed secrets about the French Super Étendard aircraft and Exocet missiles which had been sold to the Argentines. Mitterrand was fascinated by Thatcher. He once said to Roland Dumas, his close ally and later Foreign Minister: '*Cette femme Thatcher! Elle a les yeux de Caligule, mais elle a la bouche de Marilyn Monroe.*'* Anglo-French relations were surprisingly good throughout his presidency.

But despite the clear political achievements of his first term, Mitterrand, by any rational medical assessment, should not have stood for re-election in 1988. His decision to do so was driven by the wish to consolidate his political success. He was emerging triumphant from nearly two years of a cohabitation struggle with the then Prime Minister, Jacques Chirac, representing the coalition of the right. Chirac had been imposed on Mitterrand as Prime Minister when the right won a majority in the National Assembly in 1986. Mitterrand was potentially very weak when he lost his parliamentary majority but he confounded the experts who predicted that Chirac would emerge as the presidential favourite. Instead it was Mitterrand who came out of this two-year period of cohabitation appearing to the electorate as both more trustworthy and more sympathetic. He began to define a form of cohabitation with a division of responsibilities that would establish a precedent for the future: broadly, the President would reserve to himself powers over foreign and security policy, with the Prime Minister having authority over domestic policy. As he put it rather grandly, while 'the last word belongs to Parliament on economic and social questions', he would preside above it all as 'a judge arbiter'. Furthermore, 'he who has the ultimate responsibility for the use of our weapons . . . is the head of state'. So he defined his new role: 'There is no question of me becoming a President on the cheap.'

On 22 March 1988, after some hesitation, Mitterrand officially entered the Presidential race. Few doubted by then that he would win. Yet Mitterrand, Dr Gubler wrote, never consulted either himself or Professor Steg, both of whom

---

* 'That woman Thatcher! She has the eyes of Caligula but the mouth of Marilyn Monroe.'

personally hoped he would not run again. Gubler believes that if asked, Steg would have replied that medically he could not predict anything with certainty, but that the risks were very great. Gubler claimed that Steg had given Mitterrand some optimistic statistics earlier, showing that at least half of prostate cancer patients survive for four or five years and that after this, mortality was the same as in the general population. Frequently such patients died of something else. Almost every patient has a capacity to shut out information they do not want to hear and build up that which they find congenial. Mitterrand was no exception. He probably clung in his mind to this one conversation and did not want to give his doctors the opportunity to walk on his dreams of another term as President by asking for their considered advice. A part of him may have actually managed to believe that he had defeated cancer by then and he could now defeat Chirac. In May 1988 Mitterrand very convincingly won on the second ballot by 54 per cent to Chirac's 46 per cent.

For reasons which have not yet become clear, Mitterrand was ready to consider resigning in June 1990, using ill health as the excuse. Gubler gives an account of going to see the President about the six-monthly medical bulletin, and to his great astonishment Mitterrand suggested revealing a part of the truth about his medical condition. Gubler recalls him saying a few days later: 'It is possible that in August I will decide to leave. Under that hypothesis, you must prepare the terrain with regard to my health. If I withdraw we will tell all, but only at that moment. I will telephone you.' Gubler's first draft of a statement about how this might be done had the President admitting to being very tired due to a cause yet undetermined, that he had need of rest and that further medical examinations would follow. The President's key advisers saw this wording as a political 'bombshell' and at their request it was dropped from the six-monthly medical bulletin. Instead what was released was a normal health bulletin to the press. Gubler kept in, however, a slight medical warning by a reference to the President's blood tests showing a high erythrocyte sedimentation rate,[*] sometimes a sign of ill health to come. Gubler later heard that Mitterrand's mysterious contemplation of resignation, which he gathered had never been envisaged for health reasons, was now off.

---

[*] Erythrocytes are red blood cells that absorb oxygen from the lungs when air is sucked in, take this oxygen in the blood to the tissues and carry back carbon dioxide and water vapour, which is blown off from the lungs when a person breathes out. They have a life of about 120 days. The erythrocyte sedimentation rate, or ESR, is the rate at which these cells separate out and settle to the bottom from the blood plasma (the plasma or serum is the straw-coloured fluid portion of blood). In some diseases or infections, the protein in the plasma increases and this means the erythrocytes settle quicker. The ESR is essentially a screening test for inflammation in the body.

Should Mitterrand have been content to serve only one term and step down from public life in 1988? Those who think so argue that he showed poorer political judgement during his second term. In particular they refer to his initial opposition to German reunification after the fall of the Berlin Wall in 1989, a stance which he shared with Thatcher and which initially damaged both Mitterrand and France's relations with Germany. Up to this point, Mitterrand had shown well-nigh perfect judgement in his relations with Chancellor Kohl. Their partnership reached a high point when they clasped hands together at the commemoration of the First World War battle of Verdun on 22 September 1984. Now, for a time, Mitterrand was striking a jarring note with Germany over reunification. He feared that a united Germany would not support, as strongly as West Germany had, his personal commitment to further European integration. Thatcher had a different fear, that of the gathering together of German power. She tried to woo Mitterrand around to speaking out with her against reunification but in the end she failed. Instead he resolved the issue in the way he knew best: he made a private political deal with Kohl. In return for Kohl's support for the euro, which ended the role of the deutschmark and its dominance over the French franc, he, Mitterrand, would support reunification. Up to this point, while European leaders were divided over reunification, it had been the United States under President George Bush who provided the all-important political backing to Kohl.

But against this evidence of declining judgement in his second term it is necessary to set Mitterrand's record over the Kurds, in particular his readiness to champion military intervention. In this he helped break new ground in humanitarian intervention.

The duty to interfere

The invasion of Kuwait by Saddam Hussein on 2 August 1990, was seized on by Mitterrand as an opportunity to exercise his full power in the 'reserved domain' of security policy. He had been struggling to assert himself for some time. Michel Rocard, the Socialist colleague whom he had appointed Prime Minister only with the utmost reluctance, had proved effective and popular. Mitterrand's authority had waned since the presidential election and he wanted to dominate this global issue so he told Rocard not to break his sailing holiday to deal with it. Mitterrand's instinct was to maintain a dialogue with Baghdad but fully to support the Americans in their readiness to use force against Saddam if necessary. Mitterrand was enough of a realist to know that eventually, as President, he would have to accept that if French troops were to fight, they would have to do so under US overall command. He knew this would be anathema to the strongly nationalistic Defence Minister, Jean-Pierre Chevènement, so he discouraged him too from coming back from vacation. It was Mitterrand who ultimately took the decision to contribute French forces under the Americans, later endorsed by the National Assembly by 523 votes to 43. On 14 September 1990, 5,000 French soldiers of the 6th Light Armoured Division were sent to Saudi Arabia along with fifty aircraft, and eventually more than 12,000 French troops fought as part of a 500,000-strong multilateral force. The bombing of Iraqi positions started on 17 January 1991 but the French did not play as central or as large a role as the British, which some in the French military found rather galling. Under attack at home for his dovish position on Iraq, Chevènement resigned on 30 January 1991. In contrast, Mitterrand was decisive and bold. He outwardly showed no trace of any side effects of his illness throughout this period.

But it was over the issue of protecting the Kurds that Mitterrand showed a willingness to espouse a form of interventionism which was at the time quite radical. His wife, Danielle, had for some time been an outspoken defender and advocate of the Kurdish cause. With the Kurdish refugee exodus in the north of Iraq starting in the first week of April 1991, she persuaded her husband to watch TV coverage of their plight. On 3 April, Mitterrand sent Bernard Kouchner, the charismatic Minister for Humanitarian Affairs, made Foreign Minister by President Nicolas Sarkozy in 2007, to Ankara to work through with the Turkish government an acceptable UN Security Council resolution. Kouchner coined the phrase '*devoir d'ingérence*', the duty to interfere. The last thing President Turgut Özal of Turkey wanted was an influx of Kurdish refugees from Iraq into south-eastern Turkey. Yet, to much diplomatic surprise, on 5 April a joint resolution, UNSC 688, naming the Kurds for the first time in a UN resolution, was approved by the Security Council with the Turkish government supporting it. This was crucial in the region. On 7 April the US Air Force started parachuting supplies onto the snow-capped mountains where the refugees were trying to survive in primitive and desperate circumstances.

On 8 April John Major, the British Prime Minister, also won support in the EU for the idea of using troops to protect 'safe havens'. This was to be an area where the Iraqi military and their tanks, armoured cars, planes and helicopters could not go without risking being shot at from the air. London's readiness to push this against Washington's wishes both surprised and delighted the French and Paris did not push its claim to have thought of the idea first. A combined effort by London and Paris eventually persuaded a reluctant President Bush, about to be diagnosed in early May as suffering from hyperthyroidism (see Chapter 2), to introduce a ban on any Iraq government activity north of the 36th parallel. Deploying allied ground troops in northern Iraq was crucial. On 16 April, more than two weeks after the enforced exodus had begun, Operation Provide Comfort was implemented with US, French, British, Dutch, Italian and Spanish troops on the ground in northern Iraq.

In a very small way, by writing to Major in 1991, I had used what influence I had to persuade the British government to intervene to save the Kurdish people and as a result I followed Mitterrand's actions and the growing international debate about the right to intervene very carefully.[10] Hitherto during the Cold War, the UN Charter had been interpreted narrowly and humanitarian intervention had been dependent on the host nation asking for international help. That had been a recipe for ensuring no intervention to alleviate hardship and distress. The approach of Mitterrand and Major changed that and the help given to the Kurds became the first of the humanitarian interventions, backed by military force, that subsequently characterised international activity in the 1990s, in Somalia, Bosnia and Kosovo.

Mitterrand, interestingly in the light of Jacques Chirac's different stance over Iraq in 2003, believed that UN Resolution 688, which called on Iraq to stop attacking the Kurds, and which 'insisted' that Iraq allow access by humanitarian organisations, was the UN's authorisation for military intervention. He said: 'for the first time, non-interference has stopped at the point where it was becoming a failure to assist people in danger.' The United States went one further and argued that Resolution 688 brought the intervention under the earlier Resolution 678, which talked of the use of 'all necessary means'. UN purists argued against such linkage and that Resolution 688 did not specifically refer back to Resolution 678. What mattered, however, was that the Security Council members agreed with the action, making legal interpretation of the resolutions superfluous.

Although Mitterrand showed an admirable enthusiasm for pioneering the '*devoir d'ingérence*' over the Kurds, his record of intervening to 'assist people in danger' elsewhere was much less impressive. Indeed his failures in this regard cast a long shadow over his second term in office. This is especially true in the Balkans. A key question is how much of this was a changed attitude and attributable to his illness.

In December 1991, against their previous views, Mitterrand and his Foreign

Minister, Roland Dumas, collapsed their opposition to the German demand for EU recognition of Croatia before an overall settlement in the former Yugoslavia, which left the British highly exposed. John Major and his Foreign Secretary, Douglas Hurd, immediately followed suit in accepting recognition, also against their better judgement. More wisely, recognition was opposed by the EU negotiator, Lord Carrington, the UN representative, Cyrus Vance, and also by the US government.

A few months later, with the United States in the lead this time, it was decided to recognise Bosnia-Herzegovina, without deploying a preventive UN force with a mandate to restrain the Serbs and the Croats. Predictably this lit a fuse for war in Bosnia. The Bosnian Serbs, helped by Serbs from Serbia itself, started ethnically cleansing large swathes of Bosnia, brutally forcing out Bosnian Muslims and Bosnian Croats from their homes in what Serbs, on often spurious historic grounds, regarded as their own villages or towns. This was accompanied by barbaric killings, rape and the herding of people into camps, reminiscent of Second World War concentration camps. Like many others around the world, I was horrified by the European and American tolerance of these appalling incidents and in early July publicly demanded military intervention. I was surprised and angry that neither Britain nor France was ready to use troops or, preferably, air power to halt the Serbian military's continued odious ethnic cleansing. NATO member governments argued it was impossible to intervene.

Given my public criticism, I was amazed to be asked, in late August 1992, to be the EU's co-chairman of a new conference on the former Yugoslavia even though I knew Cyrus Vance, the UN co-chairman, had urged my appointment. We considered that our prime task, representing the EU and the UN, was to develop a detailed fair peace plan. If this was rejected by the Serbs, then Mitterrand, Major and Bill Clinton, the new US President, would be urged to authorise their troops to enforce it. I knew that neither Mitterrand nor Major was prepared for his forces to engage in a general battle with the Bosnian Serb army unless the United States committed troops as well, though both were already committed to participating fully in the UN's humanitarian intervention. I felt, perhaps too optimistically, that both men's indignation and readiness to use military action against the Iraqis, only a year earlier, to protect the Kurds was a hopeful sign that they might change their mind, though in that intervention the US forces were the strongest element. I was personally keen to transfer from UN to NATO command and supported a NATO-enforced no-fly zone and visited

NATO in December 1992 with the support of the UN secretary general.

I had met with Mitterrand at the Élysée Palace in early September, having previously met Major in London. Mitterrand looked very pale but conducted himself with clear deliberation, calmness and courtesy. He told me that despite my previous advocacy of air strikes against the Serbs I should be under no illusion that France would support any such action. This was no surprise to me, it having been confirmed to me in London a few days before that this was Mitterrand's position by the French Defence Minister, whose own view was more sympathetic to mine. The tone of Mitterrand's response, however, deeply disappointed me but I continued to hope that he would rediscover the enthusiasm he had shown over protecting the Kurds and authorise aggressive intervention in support of the peace settlement Vance and I were determined to put forward as early as possible. Some days later the secrecy over the President's illness came to an end.

The end of secrecy

Mitterrand's illness became public on 11 September 1992, when he could no longer avoid an operation in hospital, to relieve prostatic pressure on the urethra. This pressure from the enlarged prostate gland was stopping him from emptying his bladder, a common but distressing side effect. Prior to the operation, and as a consequence of his prostatic enlargement, he was having to go to the lavatory very frequently. On the eve of his crucial and successful TV debate supporting the Maastricht Treaty with Philippe Séguin on 3 September, Mitterrand had to get up twelve times during the night. When it came to the debate there was only one interval for TV advertisements when he could go to the toilet. Mitterrand demonstrated then, as at other times during his illness, his iron will, courage and stamina.

The operation made the continuing secrecy impossible. Dr Gubler recalls that when the length of the President's illness was revealed to Hubert Védrine, secretary general of the Élysée, he exclaimed: 'You are joking. That you were able to sustain this role for so long!'

After the exposure of his illness following his surgical operation – called an endoscopic resection – Mitterrand returned to laying a medical trail. He spoke publicly about the doctors in 1990 having identified something abnormal, a reference to which he obviously thought he could later refer back, if necessary, if his medical condition deteriorated. Even now that his prostatic cancer was public knowledge the cover-up continued post-operatively. Elaborate steps were taken to ensure that the prostate specimen resected at the operation went for histological testing by a doctor who would report only that the tissue was cancerous. The doctor was deliberately not asked to lie but it was arranged that there would be nothing added in any report signifying that the tissue had signs of being treated with radiotherapy. In the Élysée they wanted nothing on the record to reveal that President Mitterrand had authorised his doctor to release misleading six-monthly medical bulletins for eleven years and that he had previously been treated with drugs and radiotherapy for his cancer. Mitterrand still withheld facts about his condition and continued to order his doctor, who was by then an inspector in the Ministry of Health, to issue misleading medical assessments every six months. In December 1992 the oestrogen hormone tablets were stopped and, as a substitute, chemotherapy was started, at the suggestion of an American doctor. Gubler had no enthusiasm for this treatment, having advised against it.

Was President Mitterrand entitled, in serving the French people, to continue in office? Legally, of course, he was. A directly elected President has a direct mandate from the people and Mitterrand's still had two and a half years to run. But the risk of his becoming incapacitated was far greater during his second term and this indeed is what happened. Mitterrand's health had held out sufficiently for him to win – albeit by a very narrow margin – a 'yes' vote in the French referendum on the Maastricht Treaty on 17 September 1992. That win seems even more remarkable in the light of the subsequent French 'no' vote for the proposed EU constitution in 2005. Once the 1992 referendum was over, Mitterrand had no pressing political reasons for not resigning on medical grounds. Sadly, he was determined to hang on.

What effects, if any, did Mitterrand's illness, now openly declared, have on the conduct of French foreign policy? My direct experience was with regard to French policy towards the wars in the former Yugoslavia from September 1992 onwards. Just before Christmas 1992, the French UN commander in Sarajevo, General Philippe Morillon, and I came close to negotiating a ceasefire. I tried to persuade the UK government to deploy British Warrior armoured vehicles, situated in the Croatian section of Bosnia-Herzegovina, to Sarajevo but my request was refused. Morillon was no more successful in getting the French to consider deploying extra equipment. What we needed were guns of sufficient calibre, preferably with associated radar, to reinforce the ceasefire, with the capacity to fire back at any Serbian heavy weapon violations and counter the fact that in and around Sarajevo the Bosnian government had more ground troops than the Serbs.

In January 1993, the so-called Vance–Owen Peace Plan (VOPP) was announced. Neither France nor Britain was ready to move from purely humanitarian military intervention in Bosnia to an enforcement role until the United States was willing to participate with forces on the ground. One of the reasons for this reluctance was that by February they did not trust American diplomacy, which they believed was opportunistic and playing to the gallery of a pro-Bosnian government faction which wanted the Western countries to fight the Serbs. Many Americans did not recognise the elements of civil war that coexisted with a war of aggression in a highly complex situation dominated by Serbian and Croatian ethnic cleansing. Mitterrand was an enthusiastic supporter of the VOPP and was delighted that in New York I was ready to fight on behalf of the EU against the attempt of the new Clinton administration to sideline the plan, despite its being supported by the EU, Russia and a clear majority of the UN Security Council.

Eventually, in February, the new US Secretary of State, Warren Christopher, gave a somewhat qualified acceptance of working with us on the VOPP and was ready to have NATO plan for its implementation. But most unwisely he ruled out enforcing a settlement, even though for two and a half years this stance would turn out to work against the interests of the Muslim-led government in Sarajevo, which the Americans wanted to support, and in favour of the Serbs.

In order to break the deadlock in negotiations, Mitterrand willingly agreed to a request from Cyrus Vance and me in March to host a meeting in Paris with President Slobodan Milošević. In domestic political terms it was not easy for Mitterrand to invite the Serbian leader to Paris, for the meeting coincided with a critical internal French debate on policy towards the former Yugoslavia, with intellectuals such as Bernard-Henri Lévy defending the Bosnian government and Alain Finkielkraut championing Franjo Tuđman's Croatia. But Mitterrand's readiness to hold the meeting was crucial and his conduct of it showed what a formidable figure he still was.

I was with Mitterrand for many hours on 11 March 1993. Apart from being pale, with the same translucent skin I had first seen in September 1992 and again in December, he seemed much fitter than I expected and appeared to have recovered from his operation. During the afternoon meeting in the Élysée he was in top form: he was well briefed and his interventions were timely and frequently delivered with great emotion, notably when he spoke of Serbia's historical ties with France and when drawing from his own personal experiences. More than once Mitterrand referred to his time as a prisoner of war from June 1940 until December 1941, when he escaped into unoccupied Vichy France. He related how he had been greatly impressed by the resilience of Serb prisoners in a different prison camp across the road under conditions much worse than his own. Mitterrand said that Serbia's current disappearance from the European scene, and the vacuum it left, conjured up the same feelings he had experienced on hearing of the fall of Belgrade in 1941. He then allowed Vance and me to take the lead for much of the time, reinforcing our arguments where appropriate with great effect. He looked to us for guidance in his response, while making clear his full support for our proposals. He described the VOPP at one stage as 'a baby more beautiful than its parents believed'. I was greatly struck by the verve and stamina he showed. One reason for Mitterrand's well-being, of which I was unaware at the time, was that the new chemotherapy treatment had not helped so had been stopped and his original hormone therapy resumed. Chemotherapy, which has a good record of alleviating many cancers, has a disappointing record in treating prostatic cancer.

It was fascinating to watch Mitterrand using all forms of persuasion and argument when dealing with Milošević. France, he said, was one of Serbia's historical friends and did not want to see Serbia isolated or unfairly punished; but Milošević had to face the realities of the current situation and the international climate. If the war continued there would be little even Serbia's oldest friends and allies could do to prevent its further isolation. Even Russia was unlikely to step out of line if the international community called for tighter sanctions, as it was close to doing. It was imperative to get an agreement in the coming days. Milošević was faced with a historic choice. No one was claiming that he could twist the Bosnian Serbs around his little finger, but they looked to him as their 'big brother': he had real authority. Either 'the war continues, the tragedy gets worse, sanctions get tougher', or it is halted, enabling Serbia to rebuild its economy and play its rightful role in Europe. Coming on the heels of Mitterrand's visit to Washington and immediately before his visit to Moscow, the meeting was all the more timely.

Typically, Milošević's parting comment of the afternoon to me after Mitterrand's powerful peroration was: 'Why did he not raise the lifting of sanctions?' Never one to be affected by emotion, he was seemingly not moved at all by Mitterrand's arguments. Milošević was ready to do a deal even though this meant the Serbs withdrawing from 70 per cent of the territory they currently occupied and settling for 43 per cent of the overall land in Bosnia-Herzegovina. Ironically, in view of the Clinton administration's initial criticism that the VOPP was too favourable to the Serbs, by the time of Richard Holbrooke's success with the Dayton accords on 21 November, after many more people had lost their lives or suffered great hardship, the Serbs retained 6 per cent *more* land. Interestingly, the heads of government, including Milošević, returned to Paris on 14 December 1995 to sign the accords in a meeting hosted by President Chirac.

Milošević was not a racist, nor even an ultra-nationalist, though he blatantly used and manipulated nationalistic feeling. Nor was he still a communist. He was a ruthless political leader, hell bent on exercising and retaining power, ready to go to war, to authorise paramilitary killings and the assassination of political rivals. Both his parents had committed suicide, as had a much-loved uncle. There were no obvious signs of mental instability during the times I met him, although occasionally he appeared down, but not clinically depressed.

Nine years after this meeting in Paris, in 2002 Milošević was arrested and brought to trial by the International Criminal Tribunal on Yugoslavia in the Hague. Yet prior to this he had negotiated with the EU, the UN, the US and Russia and had met foreign ministers, prime ministers and presidents without ever showing any apparent concern that he might eventually be brought before the tribunal. An amnesty was never on offer, but he never asked for such a provision to be included in any of the various peace agreements. Arriving at the Hague Milošević was found to have high blood pressure. There followed an inordinately long trial process. It was concluded, after an autopsy, that his death in prison in 2006, before the trial had reached a final comprehensive verdict, was due to a blockage of his coronary artery vessels or heart attack. Just before his death there were well-informed stories that he had been clandestinely taking a drug to block the effects of the medicine to reduce his blood pressure, in order, most believed, to prolong his illness and thereby the proceedings of his trial. Milošević's death, suspiciously in view of this information, took place just before a suicide watch would have been imposed prior to the verdict being delivered.

When I gave evidence as a witness of the court in 2003, and saw Milošević over two days as a prisoner before court, he looked in reasonable health. There was never any question of him using mental incapacity in his defence. He dominated the court proceedings, conducting his own defence cross-examining me and many others, with the aim of defending Serbia, the nation, and only indirectly himself as President. I wondered then whether he would try and commit suicide rather than be condemned as a common criminal. I doubted that his self-delusion was so strong that he did not realise that he would be found guilty on at least the majority of the charges. So perhaps this was a factor in him deciding to interfere with his own treatment and thereby consciously risk his own life. Labelled as a monster or mad in the press, Milošević was neither. He was a bad man ruthlessly wielding considerable power, largely unchecked, for his own power-hungry purposes.

Mitterrand rejoined us that evening during dinner at the Foreign Ministry, the Quai d'Orsay, something which no French President had done for many years. He had obviously decided that if progress was to be made with Milošević, he had to bite the bullet of removing sanctions. He set out France's position in dramatic and unambiguous terms. If the VOPP was accepted, 'then sanctions must and should be lifted as soon as technically feasible'. He admitted that this stance would no doubt be opposed in some quarters, by which he meant the United States. But Mitterrand would put his full weight behind getting others such as Chancellor Kohl to support it. France would 'fight and win the battle to lift sanctions'. Mitterrand had clearly sensed the importance Milošević attached to the lifting of sanctions. He was right because six weeks later, on 25 April, Milošević, in an attempt to evade sanctions, agreed to the modifications of the VOPP acceptable to Bosnian Muslims. Unfortunately, the Bosnian Serbs rejected this in their Assembly in Bijeljina and increased sanctions were correctly applied to Serbia.

That evening in Paris, Mitterrand left Milošević in no doubt about what was on offer, but he also made it clear that there was a real political danger of losing this opportunity. The time for taking a decision was very short. Mitterrand frankly admitted that in a few weeks he would lose his majority in the French National Assembly, and his power would be only 60 per cent of what it was now. It would then be much more difficult for him to deliver over sanctions. It was a bravura performance from a man who within two months would be suffering considerable pain and needing to take painkillers in large quantities. It was in some respects Mitterrand's last big personal intervention in international affairs and a tour de force.

Cohabitation

As Mitterrand had predicted to Slobodan Milošević, the French Socialist Party was heavily defeated in the National Assembly elections at the end of March, gaining only 20.2 per cent of the votes. The Socialist parliamentary group was reduced from 282 to 70, its lowest level since it had been reformed in 1971. Pierre Bérégovoy, the last Socialist Prime Minister of Mitterrand's presidency, was replaced by Édouard Balladur, the candidate of the right.

In his second period of cohabitation Mitterrand played his cards in a very different way, helped by the personality of the new Prime Minister. Whereas when cohabiting with Jacques Chirac there had been a permanent contest for control, with Balladur there developed a civilised partnership. I met Balladur in Paris on 27 April 1993. He was an intelligent man and as Admiral Jacques Lanxade, the French Chief of the Defence Staff, had warned me, he was very precise and cautious over further involving French troops in Yugoslavia. In contrast to his newly appointed Foreign Minister, Alain Juppé, someone very close to Chirac and with a modern, relaxed style in conversation, Balladur's every gesture was carefully calculated and constrained.

Balladur knew from his own experience that it was possible for the French government to continue to function effectively with a dying President provided there was a meeting of minds between the Prime Minister and the President. He had been in the Élysée as general secretary to President Pompidou until his death and had been much moved when at one stage Pompidou, in great pain, said to him: 'Leave me alone. I do not want you to see me crying.' Balladur also knew that Pompidou had been close to resigning before his death, having promised to speak soon to his people, saying: 'I will speak to the French. I have things to tell them.' Yet he never had time to make that speech, dying in office on 2 April 1974.

For Balladur the challenge was to use the office of Prime Minister to build up his authority so that he, not Chirac, would be chosen by the parties of the centre-right to be their candidate for President.* In 1993, Balladur needed all the time that might be available to him. In his book *Deux ans à Matignon* (Two Years in the Matignon), Balladur writes about Mitterrand:

> The President's illness played a significant role on what the French made of me in their minds. I did not know anything other than what he told me. He spoke to me often, sometimes precisely. He knew that he could count on my

---

* For a period during cohabitation as Balladur's poll ratings rose and Chirac's fell, it looked as if Balladur would be the presidential candidate. But in the event, Chirac – using all his party political skills and his position as mayor of Paris – outmanoeuvred Balladur and became the candidate of the centre-right in the presidential election of May 1995.

discretion and that I would not seek to use his physical feebleness to obtain personal or political profit. That would have seemed shameful to me . . . I would add that I would not have been proud of myself if I had attempted to abuse the situation confronting a stricken man.[11]

Mitterrand also cooperated with Balladur in a way that he had not been ready to do with Chirac in the first of his periods of cohabitation. The editor of *Le Monde* wrote on 16 July 1993 that Mitterrand

this time around produced a brilliant theory of the ideal cohabitation based on a simple principle. Not to turn disagreements into conflicts. At most they can serve to express a difference, to launch a criticism, but they should no longer be the weapons of a struggle for power as in 1986.[12]

Balladur spoke of the situation having the virtue of its defects and probably genuinely believed that it represented an element of added strength. The two models of cohabitation showed the strength of the Fifth Republic and demonstrated that de Gaulle's constitutional instrument was more flexible than Mitterrand had ever given it credit for when he was in opposition.

From the viewpoint of the Élysée, Hubert Védrine was correct when he wrote that cohabitation under a government of the right was a blessing for Mitterrand in that it put so much presidential power into the Prime Minister's office. 'It suits us fine. The Matignon people are of goodwill. It would be easy for Balladur and [his chief of staff Nicholas] Bazir to short-circuit us. But oddly they are playing fair.'[13]

Although Mitterrand, in March, had quantified in front of Milošević how much power he would lose during the forthcoming cohabitation of 1993–5, by May 1993 his health had worsened and his power progressively lessened. He would arrive at the Élysée in the morning from his apartment and go straight to bed, where he would stay for most of the day.

Not surprisingly, thereafter Mitterrand played a much reduced role in French foreign and domestic policy-making.[14] From May 1993 he was personally far less engaged on the issues involved in the break-up of the former Yugoslavia, and in those months of April and May 1993 when I advocated, privately and even publicly, moving from negotiation to military enforcement, I could not engage Mitterrand's attention. His focus naturally enough had become his own personal battle against death.

It is impossible to know for certain whether, had he had good health,

Mitterrand would have pressed hard for enforcement of the Athens peace plan, rejected by the Bosnian Serbs in Pale, but the record suggests that he might have done. This was the man who not only had seen the need for a humanitarian intervention to help the Kurds in 1991, but who, in June 1992, without telling any other EU nation, dramatically flew to Sarajevo, at some personal risk, in a successful and brave bid to keep open the airport. The political difficulties of cohabitation would not have stood in his way. Under the terms of his arrangement with Balladur and Juppé he would not have encountered obstruction from them had he wanted to give French support for enforcement, and Juppé would have supported him.* Yet France, the UK and the US failed to support enforcement of three successive peace plans – the VOPP in May 1993, the EU Action Plan in December 1993 and the Contact Group Plan in the summer of 1994.

Yugoslavia was not alone in suffering the consequences of Mitterrand's loss of interventionist zeal. A healthier Mitterrand might have urged Balladur and Juppé to agree in the Security Council to the request of the UN commander General Roméo Dallaire for 6,000 troops to halt the genocide in Rwanda in April 1994. And if France had taken a more committed interventionist stand in the UN, the reluctance of the US and the UK might have been overcome and a larger UN force would have been sent to Rwanda in 1993. The lives of 800,000 Rwandans, who were killed in the violence, could then have been saved.[15]

Within France, Mitterrand was much criticised for arming, training and supporting the Hutu-dominated army of President Juvénal Habyarimana's Rwandan government. In January 1994 Dallaire requested permission from Kofi Annan, then head of peace-keeping in the UN, to raid the Rwandan army's caches of arms but was refused.[16] After Habyarimana was killed in a plane crash in 1994 the Hutu massacre of the Tutsis began. To many critics, President Mitterrand and Prime Minister Balladur appeared compromised and slow to react. The French peace-keeping mission, Operation Turquoise, failed to stop the killing and, the Rwandan Tutsis claim, by then establishing a buffer zone allowed the Hutu killers to escape.

---

* There has been an attempt to portray the government of the right in France as more aggressive militarily in the Balkans than that of the left. (Brian C. Rathbun, *French Party Positions on Humanitarian Intervention* (Washington, DC: Brookings Institution, 2003).) This was not true under Balladur and Juppé. Whether President Chirac made a difference, apart from his more militant early rhetoric, is harder to determine because events moved very rapidly in Bosnia after he became President on 7 May 1995 and it was the massacre of Bosnian Muslims in Srebrenica in July of that year which shocked the Clinton administration into political and military action.

I would like to believe it was Mitterrand's ill health that influenced his policy over Rwanda and Yugoslavia and there is reason to do so. People when ill are often described as risk averse, hesitant to act and readier to let events play out without intervening. Yet, as always with Mitterrand, one cannot be sure. The more one probes his behaviour and motivation, the more one detects a deep-seated ambivalence. It may be that in attributing his later inertia to his illness one is doing no more than giving him the benefit of the doubt.

Dying

The twists and turns of Mitterrand's medical treatment from the time his illness became public have been chronicled in some detail by Dr Gubler, although less so from May 1993, when Mitterrand became seriously ill. He relapsed further in the November. Various treatments and combinations of treatment were tried, as the physicians and surgeons differed as to what was the best treatment. Gubler was, however, no longer the trusted physician confident in his relationship with his patient. Yet the rivalries amongst Mitterrand's doctors and the changes in treatment did not by then make much difference to the decline in his health.

There is one aspect of his treatment, however, which is worth highlighting, especially alongside President Kennedy's reliance for a while on the dubious Max Jacobson, 'Dr Feelgood', discussed in Chapter 4, and that is Mitterrand's use of very doubtful alternative treatments. As Mitterrand's health deteriorated so there was a loss of confidence in the existing team of advisers. As many people are tempted to do in such circumstances, Mitterrand's mistress, Anne Pingeot, began to explore second opinions and alternative treatments. His brother Robert also investigated the US medical scene in the hope that it could provide new approaches and new medicines.

According to the now-sidelined Gubler, a Dr Mirko Beljanski became involved. A former researcher at the Pasteur Institute and a doctor of science, he had built a reputation amongst practitioners of alternative medicine, such as Dr Philippe de Kuyper, who had also been called in to the Élysée. Gubler summarises this particular rivalry, though there were many more, as between himself and Professor Steg of the classical school versus Kuyper and Beljanski of the alternative school. Beljanski's treatments involved using non-toxic molecules extracted from natural products. These molecules were meant to couple with any radiotherapy to protect patients from the side effects of the radiotherapy. Kuyper thought Beljanski's products were the best available and used them on his patients though he refused to confirm whether or not they were used on Mitterrand. The President apparently saw Beljanski at Beljanski's home, in December 1994, despite there being a case before a Saint-Étienne court about the legality of his practice of medicine and pharmacy. After the trial in April 1995, Beljanski's non-profit organisation was dissolved.

While hormone therapy had been reinstated with radiotherapy, various homeopathic and other alternative medicines were also tried. Still Mitterrand's condition deteriorated and he spent a lot of time in bed. In November 1994 Gubler was still accompanying the President to his treatments despite being disillusioned by the increasing rivalry and incoherence of the President's medical entourage. Gubler by now had concluded that the President was no longer capable of carrying out his duties and was not fulfilling the mandate for which the French people had elected him. By December, Mitterrand's voice was affected and he had difficulty speaking. Gubler signed off on the last of his six-monthly medical bulletins, which still did not reveal the full extent of the President's incapacity. Effectively, from then on, Gubler was no longer the President's doctor.

On 8 January 1996, eight months after leaving office, Mitterrand died in his sleep at the age of seventy-nine, having decided himself to stop medication. His doctor at the time, Jean-Pierre Tarot, first called in Pingeot and their daughter, Mazarine, then Danielle Mitterrand and their sons.

A short time after Mitterrand's death, Gubler tried to publish his book about his time as the President's doctor, but it was banned. A complaint from Danielle and their children was lodged with a French court, which later ruled that Gubler's book was a grave intrusion into the family's privacy. The court issued a restraining order prohibiting further sales and levied a fine for every book sold in violation of the injunction. French law had recognised a right of privacy for at least 150 years. In 1970, France gave statutory expression to this right in Article 9 of the Code Civil, which states simply that 'each person has the right to the respect of his private life'. This right survives death and family members may assert a privacy claim on behalf of the deceased. Public figures are no exception.

Weeks after the court order, however, the book was put on the internet in English. By March 1996 it was available from several websites in the United States, but of course accessible to French surfers. When the French website carrying it was closed, American servers became the source for French citizens to read Gubler's views in defiance of their country's privacy law. I first read

Gubler's account on the internet in English and it is that wording which I have chosen to extensively use and quote from, in addition to talking to Gubler directly.

Should Gubler have written the story of the medical cover-up so soon after Mitterrand's death? On balance, I believe he should, but it would have been better if he had written in a medical journal in the first instance with some of the restrictions and constraints, as well as the safeguard of peer review, that cover such publications. Deep underlying questions in medical ethics have been given great prominence as a result of knowing the true facts surrounding Mitterrand's illness. What are the real requirements of the Hippocratic oath, which is still meant to guide doctors' behaviour? Does society value those standards and, if so, what is it prepared to do to help doctors to uphold them? In particular, can we keep the role of the personal doctor as the private adviser to the patient and stop the practice which has grown up in many countries of the personal doctor also being the public voice of the patient? These and other questions will be examined in Chapter 8.

Ultimately, Gubler's decision was vindicated. In May 2004, the European Court of Human Rights held that the decision of French courts to prohibit the distribution of Gubler's book breached Article 10 of the European Convention on Human Rights.

Mitterrand's legacy

One year after Mitterrand's death, in January 1997, I was invited to speak at a two-day seminar in Paris remembering his life, run, in part, by UNESCO. My closest friend in French politics since 1966 had been, and remains, Michel Rocard, a successful Socialist Prime Minister but someone loathed by Mitterrand. Back in March 1993 Mitterrand, in the newspaper Le Figaro, had contemptuously listed his chosen successors in order: Delors, Léotard, Barre, Giscard, Chirac, his dog, Rocard! Mitterrand deliberately and systematically destroyed all his likely Socialist successors, happily passing over to a President from the right, Chirac, whom he always credited with helping him to beat the centrist President Giscard d'Estaing.

So I did not pretend that I was impartial. Yet, after knowing him for thirty years, and well aware of all the intrigue, manipulation and even corruption, I acknowledged there was a grandeur and style about Mitterrand, the man. I admired the way he had conducted himself in his last years with dignity and courage and the manner in which he handed over the presidency in May 1995 while in the terminal stages of a savage illness. It provided for those who watched, within and outside France, an indelible memory that has favourably influenced attitudes to his entire presidency.

On the tenth anniversary of his death, Hubert Védrine said: 'François Mitterrand gave the impression of strength and success. He seduced everyone.' Mitterrand's many opponents are already finding out that when they want to turn the page, in his own words it is 'not a page that is easily torn out'. His dominance as President, his achievements and his remarkable struggle against cancer make Mitterrand still an all-pervading figure in French life.

Mitterrand's overall presidential record is one of considerable achievement within France, for Europe and around the world. Historically he will be remembered for how he handled two periods of presidential cohabitation. And by hanging on to office he achieved his ambition of becoming France's longest-serving head of state since Napoleon III.

France is still digesting the complexities, brilliance, contradictions and ruthlessness as well as the ramifications of his presidency. The habit of secrecy and the laws of privacy regarding politicians are coming under scrutiny. So is Mitterrand's commitment to ever-increasing integration within the European Union, which appears, though it is early days, to be shared by President Sarkozy. On the outcome of that debate depends whether Mitterrand may be, as he said to his biographer, Georges-Marc Benamou, and in the words of the title of a film about him, *The Last President:* the last French President in this world of globalisation and European integration really capable of fully representing France, the nation. Much depends on whether Sarkozy changes direction.

Jacques Attali, one of Mitterrand's closest advisers, said in 2006, while Chirac was still President: 'France today is no longer a truly independent nation, but not yet part of a global European nation. We're in a no-man's land. There is a longing for a monarch and a request for a stronger President.' As for his old boss, Attali was quite clear: 'François Mitterrand was the last King of France.'[17]

Part III

The intoxication of power

7

Bush, Blair and the war in Iraq

Hubris combined with ignorance led Bush the younger to undertake adventures that concealed the more serious problems abroad that ought to have concerned him.

Stephen Graubard[1]

Blair seemed a political colossus, half-Caesar, half-Messiah. Equally, as times became tough following the Iraq *imbroglio*, he became an exposed solitary victim, personally stigmatised as in the 'cash for peerages' affair. Blair discovered, like Lloyd George and Thatcher before him, that British politics do not take easily to the Napoleonic style.

Lord Morgan, on Tony Blair's speech to the 2001 Labour Party conference[2]

The conduct of the US President, George W. Bush, and the British Prime Minister, Tony Blair, in deciding to go to war in Iraq and in handling its aftermath well illustrates hubris syndrome. The evidence for such an interpretation derives not only from the mass of knowledge, now made public, about how these events came about but also, in the case of Blair, from my own personal dealings with him on the subject during the period between 1998 and 2003. This chapter is different from the other case histories (Chapters 3–6), which have the perspective of a greater distance from the period of history they describe.

Tony Blair

Although the war in Iraq was overwhelmingly an American-led enterprise it makes sense to begin by discussing the evolution of Blair's approach to Iraq, since he came to power in May 1997, three and half years before Bush entered the White House. I first met Blair for a serious conversation on 15 July 1996 at his home, when he was leader of the opposition and the issue was whether I was ready to publicly support New Labour. I first discussed Iraq with him on 2 March 1998 in Downing Street and, as a sign of my depth of feeling about Saddam Hussein's regime, gave him a book about the Kurds written by Jonathan Randal, an experienced war correspondent with the *Washington Post*. It reflected my deep concern at the time and why I believed that the handling of the Kurdish position, so long ignored by the Western democracies, had become so crucial. I hoped Blair's chief of staff, Jonathan Powell, would read this brilliant book, as it posed many questions for the future. For example, it discussed how the aftermath of the defeat of the Iraqi forces in 1991 had much to be desired. Randal wrote:

> The American planning was a hodgepodge of naivety and *realpolitik*, more tactics than strategy, seemingly consistent only if its peculiar assumptions were correct. No-one should have been surprised by anything that happened from 2 August 1990 when Iraq invaded and occupied Kuwait to the end of the following March, when Saddam Hussein crushed the Shia and Kurdish uprisings.[3]

I followed up the concerns I had expressed at that meeting with a letter to Blair on 12 November, arguing that there had to be a political strategy involving the Kurds to help topple Saddam Hussein. Blair replied: 'We are not working to bring down Saddam Hussein and his regime. It is not for us to say who should be President of Iraq, however much we might prefer to see a different government in Baghdad.' This exchange encapsulated the UK's particular problem: successive British governments have felt legally bound to use wording on regime change based on a particularly inflexible interpretation of the United Nations Charter. That position needs re-examining.

Following the withdrawal of UN inspectors from Iraq in December 1998 in response to Saddam's non-cooperation, the United States and Britain launched a four-day bombing campaign against Iraqi targets. The military operation was undertaken, as in 1993 and 1996, and again in 2002 and 2003, with the US and the UK claiming the authority of the UN resolutions passed in 1990 and 1991 and in addition UN Security Council Resolution 1205, passed in 1998. Blair asked me to dinner at 10 Downing Street on 18 December 1998, the third evening of the bombing blitz. The main reason for the invitation was Blair's wish to dissuade me from establishing a cross-party organisation later called New Europe, which opposed the UK joining the euro. But we also discussed Iraq at some length. His mood was quite different from what it seems to have been two days earlier when, over dinner with his wife and two close friends, he was reported to be 'distinctly nervous'.[4]

At dinner on the 18th in similar circumstances with our wives I found him relaxed, almost laid back. He had started well as Prime Minister, particularly in handling Northern Ireland, and it looked as if he was set to be a successful premier. There was no undue hyperactivity. He did not excuse himself to get an update on the attacks that had been launched and I found him cool, rational and anything but hubristic. He was ready to discuss the complexity of the relations between the Shiite majority and the Kurds and Sunnis in Iraq in some detail but he was not very knowledgeable about them and he had obviously not yet read Randal's book. We agreed that the situation which allowed Saddam to stay in power was totally unsatisfactory and shared the frustration about UN limitations within which he, Blair, felt formally he had to operate. The United States' Congressional resolution for regime change, called the Iraq Liberation Act, had meanwhile been passed by an overwhelming majority, which President Bill Clinton did not veto. The challenge was Saddam's continuation in power, not WMD, which were only briefly mentioned though we both believed they were still present in Iraq.

The US and the UK dropped more than 600 bombs and launched 415 cruise missiles against Iraqi targets during this action, killing an estimated 1,400 members of Iraq's Republican Guard. The action, which had been targeted on some nuclear facilities, was later assessed as having set back Saddam's nuclear weapons programme by two years.[5] Clinton, though committed to the Congressional resolution calling for regime change in Iraq, was never likely to authorise the full military invasion necessary to achieve this. American public opinion was not ready for military re-engagement on the ground in Iraq. The failed impeachment of Clinton over Monica Lewinsky in February 1999 had weakened his authority to go to the American people and demand action and this may have been a factor also when deciding what to do with the growing threat to the United States of Osama bin Laden and al-Qaeda. The priority issue for military action for NATO, in the year ahead, was Kosovo.

My next conversation with Blair was during the Kosovo crisis when NATO was engaging in air attacks on Serbia. On 16 April 1999, the Prime Minister unexpectedly rang me wanting a long and detailed talk about his anxieties over the deteriorating situation. The Serb military were still largely unaffected by the NATO bombing and he wanted to discuss my publicly stated views that we should from the outset have been prepared to use NATO ground forces. Somewhat unconventionally, I had been attacked by name for these views, along with Henry Kissinger, in an article by General Charles Guthrie, then the UK Chief of the Defence Staff.[6] This was a small but significant sign of an undue politicisation of the chiefs of staff. Clinton's advisers had apparently told the President that Slobodan Milošević would fold if threatened and, when he did not, that bombing would do the trick in forty-eight, then seventy-two, hours.[7] It took eventually seventy-eight days of bombing and, even more importantly, a powerful intervention from Boris Yeltsin for Milošević to agree to withdraw the Serbian armed forces and police. They left reluctantly, never conceding military defeat.

I mentioned to Blair at an early stage that I was speaking from Berlin on an open line. He laughed and said he wanted anyone listening to know about his anxieties. Blair was surprisingly frank and we had an animated discussion. I sensed, however, for the first time a note of exaltation in his voice. Soon afterwards real tension developed between Blair and Clinton about the need to prepare to send in ground forces and on 21 April Blair told Parliament that ground troops were an option.

The following day Blair made a speech in Chicago, in which he tried to identify the circumstances in which Britain 'should get actively involved in other people's conflicts' in defence of our values. Whatever its rights and wrongs, and in large part I agreed with it, what was extraordinary for such an important speech was how little examination of its implications took place in Whitehall. It was drafted by a professor of war studies, Lawrence Freedman, who was himself surprised that Blair made very few changes to his proposed text. The input from the Foreign Office and the Ministry of Defence was minimal.

One damaging side effect of Kosovo, in retrospect, was the mood of self-confidence and personal dominance that began to appear in Blair's handling of foreign affairs. Kosovo was Blair's first test in a big international crisis and unmistakable signs of hubristic attitudes were beginning to emerge. Visiting refugee camps he was hailed as a hero. At one stage, Clinton angrily told Blair to 'pull himself together' and halt 'domestic grandstanding'.[8] He was starting to display excessive pride in his own judgements. Clinton's aides mocked Blair's 'Churchillian tone'.[9] One official who frequently saw him said: 'Tony is doing too much, he's overdoing it and he's overplaying his hand.'[10] One of Clinton's aides suggested Blair 'was sprinkling too much adrenalin on his cornflakes'.

It is worth noting how often this hormone, called epinephrine in the United States and secreted by the medulla of the adrenal gland, is referred to when people discuss manic or hubristic behaviour. But if there is any linkage it is a complex one embraced within the two-factor theory of emotion, where the adrenalin may produce a physiological arousal but there also needs to be a thought process or cognition to interpret the meaning of this arousal.[11]

After my telephone conversation with Blair, I was beginning to appreciate how personalised and very different his style of leadership was from the measured and structured style I had watched James Callaghan adopt as Prime Minister. Blair liked to claim he was following Margaret Thatcher's style of leadership, but this claim was false in many respects, particularly over her precise handling of the Falklands War (see Chapter 2). Unlike him, she had a formidable commitment to a political philosophy and she was renowned for her close attention to detail. But most of all, she was already experienced when she became Prime Minister, having served for many years in governments led by Harold Macmillan and Edward Heath. On taking office Blair was the most inexperienced British Prime Minister since Ramsay MacDonald in 1924, neither having held any ministerial office before entering No. 10. That lack of experience in retrospect was to prove more damaging to Blair's record than I initially thought it would.

Furthermore, Blair had had no formal training or experience in management. He tried to make up for this by talking to management thinkers and seemed, according to an article in *Management Today*, to want to act like a chief executive: 'fast on his feet, flexible in his thinking and able to make quick decisions, often taken on the hoof, in shirtsleeves, on the sofa, coffee latte in one hand, mobile phone in the other, running Great Britain plc as if it were a City investment company'.[12] But the role of Prime Minister is not that of a chief executive and the UK government is not a company making profits for shareholders.

Like Blair, Thatcher had sought to accrete more power in No. 10 but she had worked within the existing Cabinet structures to do so. Even though Thatcher made considerable use of a personal foreign affairs adviser, Charles Powell, then a serving diplomat, the Cabinet Secretary remained a powerful independent figure. By contrast, Blair chose a formalised and progressive destruction of the Cabinet system. He started by appointing a political chief of staff, Jonathan Powell, the brother of Charles. He, however, along with Blair's press secretary, Alastair Campbell, were exceptionally given the powers of a civil servant. This progressively undermined the authority of the Cabinet Secretary. Also collective Cabinet discussion and responsibility were substantially reduced. Later, in 2001, and in the flush of victory after winning a second general election, Blair, with no parliamentary scrutiny, was to change the whole basis of Cabinet government as it related to foreign and defence matters. A system which had evolved during the First World War was swept aside without a single serious objective study. This was not modernisation but hubristic vandalism, for which, as Prime Minister, Blair alone bore responsibility.

The new structure was deliberately designed by Blair to ensure he could exercise over international policy much the same powers as a US President. The Cabinet Office method of handling foreign and security matters had, until then, been designed to service the Cabinet as a whole. From the summer of 2001 onwards, the key officials and their staff on foreign affairs, defence and the European Union were brought into the political hothouse atmosphere of 10 Downing Street in two new secretariats.[13] The No. 10 secretariats were intended to service the Prime Minister alone, politically and strategically. Blair was to do much the same to the Joint Intelligence Committee (JIC), in terms of its working arrangements if not of its formal structure. This new structure in No. 10 was designed to cause the progressive downgrading of the Foreign Office and the Ministry of Defence and their respective secretaries of state. Inexplicably, it was virtually ignored by the press, who had become enamoured of the aura which Blair began to project of a successful Prime Minister.

A few months after the two secretariats were in place in No. 10 the new structure provided the means to project Blair's very personalised response to the 9/11 attacks in New York and Washington.

George W. Bush

George W. Bush became head of government in January 2001 without having previously served in any national government post. It is true that he had been governor of Texas, but Texas is unusual in that its governor exercises much less executive power than those in most other American states. When Bush was elected President he started by saying he would appoint good people, delegate authority and hold them accountable for results – following best practice at Harvard Business School, which he had attended. Such an approach to government is the opposite of hubristic. So too was his characterisation of the foreign policy he promised when running for office: he said he wanted America's stance in the world to be 'strong but humble'.

On 16 February 2001 Bush agreed that US and UK bombers, as part of the ongoing policy inherited from President Clinton's eight years, should hit Iraqi radar and command centres and on 10 August the United States and Britain bombed three Iraqi defence sites. Press comment was low key.

Whether or not Bush really did intend to be 'humble abroad' and not 'engage in nation-building' as well as being a delegating, hands-off leader will remain one of the unknowns of history. But it is clear that after 11 September 2001, or 9/11, that would have been impossible for any American President to do. Initially Bush was shocked, as his face showed when, in a school in Florida, he was first told the news of an aeroplane hitting the World Trade Center in New York. The outrage the American people felt immediately after 9/11 meant that they were ready to abandon the long-standing philosophical guidelines set down by John Quincy Adams when he was Secretary of State in 1821, a warning which the Vietnam experience had seemed to justify. America 'goes not abroad in search of monsters to destroy. She is the well wisher to the freedom and independence of all. She is the champion and vindicator only of her own.' From the moment Bush seized the bullhorn or portable loudhailer in the devastation and rubble on 15 September and said: 'The people who knocked these buildings down will hear all of us soon,' he came to refer to himself as the 'decider'. He was to be a 'wartime President' and he saw his main priority as mobilising America for military action. In doing so his adoption of the phrase 'war on terror' was imprecise, even misleading, but it was understandable in the immediate circumstances, in which he needed to rally his country to face the foe which they felt al-Qaeda presented. The problem was that very soon his self-image became inflated. He promised 'to smoke 'em out and get 'em running' and on 16 September vowed to 'rid the world of evil doers'. This was not just talk, it truly represented his approach. He saw the war as a military war, like the First and Second World Wars. He had not recognised that those wars had gone, at least for a time, and that the wars now were, in the British general Rupert Smith's words, 'war among the people'.[14]

The will to take up arms internationally returned to America after 11 September 2001. Quite rightly, President Bush seized the moment. He chose, first, to take action militarily against Afghanistan and its Taleban government, who had been sheltering al-Qaeda, the agents of 9/11. Other deeply dysfunctional states, such as Somalia and Sudan, had been involved with al-Qaeda before, and Afghanistan's harbouring of international terrorism had made the case for pre-emptive action against it, already a strong one even before 9/11, overwhelming. Once the al-Qaeda attacks on New York and Washington had happened, few doubted anywhere in world capitals that military action against Afghanistan was the correct initial response. It should be remembered too that 9/11 was not, as many people in the world seem to think now, a personal reaction to Bush's policies or actions. Still less was it a direct result of the Arab–Israeli dispute: the planning for 9/11 had started well before, at a time when President Clinton was actively involved in seeking a settlement between the Palestinian leader, Yasser Arafat, and the Israeli Prime Minister, Ehud Barak.

It is easy to overlook the fact that Samuel Huntington's thesis *The Clash of Civilizations and the Remaking of World Order* had been published in the United States as far back as 1996 and that there had been a vigorous debate about Islamic fundamentalism for some years. Al-Qaeda itself claimed that the United States had run away from confronting it on the ground in Somalia in 1993, long before George W. Bush turned up on the world scene.

In February 1993 the World Trade Center had been singled out: a van bomb filled with 1,500 pounds of urea nitrate was driven into the basement and detonated, killing six people. When Ramzi Yousef, nephew of Khalid Sheik Mohammed, a key al-Qaeda figure, was captured in Pakistan and later convicted for his part in the attack, police found a mass of newspaper clippings. This emphasised renown, one of the 'three Rs', along with revenge and reaction, which are the reasons terrorists take such actions.[15]

The US armed forces' presence in Saudi Arabia was highlighted when al-Qaeda killed five American members of a joint military training team there in November 1995.[16] This was followed by the Iranian-backed Hezbollah attacking a residential block outside Riyadh with a suicide truck bomb, killing nineteen Americans. Then a fatwa calling on all Muslims to take part in a jihad to force all US forces to leave Saudi Arabia was announced by Osama bin Laden.

On 7 August 1998 truck bomb attacks organised by al-Qaeda on the American embassies in Nairobi and Dar es Salaam had a horrific impact, to which Clinton responded with Tomahawk missile attacks in Afghanistan and Sudan. This was followed by a telephone call from a laughing Mullah Omar, the leader of the then Taleban government in Afghanistan, to a senior official in the US State Department.[17]

Less than a month before Bush was elected President, in October 2000, al-Qaeda carried out an attack on the USS *Cole* while in the port of Aden. Furthermore, as long ago as 1995 the Philippine authorities had found a plan, in a laptop computer discovered under a plane seat, to fly aeroplanes into major American buildings such as the World Trade Center. It had been devised by

Khalid Sheik Mohammed, who was to mastermind 9/11. He was captured in Rawalpindi by Pakistani security officials in March 2002, and his interrogation revealed details of 'more than' twenty plots against US infrastructure targets. including communication nodes, nuclear power plants, dams, bridges and tunnels, which George Tenet, the then head of the CIA, believes would not have been revealed if he had been treated like a white-collar criminal, read his rights and immediately shipped for indictment in New York.[18]

There should have been more urgent action about al-Qaeda by the Clinton administration, before 9/11. It took from 25 January 2001, when Bush came into office, until 4 September to hold a Principals meeting with the National Security Advisor, Condoleezza Rice, the Secretary of State, Colin Powell, the Secretary of Defense, Donald Rumsfeld, and Tenet on al-Qaeda.

The 9/11 Commission report should have put an end to scapegoating and hindsight as to whether the Clinton or the Bush administration was responsible for nearly 3,000 people being killed by the al-Qaeda operation. Their answer was that both administrations failed. To his credit, in the heightened tension immediately after 9/11, Bush spoke warmly of the many peace-loving Muslims within the United States and tried to reassure them. He also did not repeat the mistake that President Franklin Roosevelt made after Pearl Harbor of using internment, as had been done for Japanese nationals.

Bush and Blair's developing hubris

The undoubted novelty of a terrorist organisation being able to extend its reach to create such devastation in the two most important American cities led Bush, and Blair too, to claim that this meant that the challenges they now faced were unparalleled in human history. It soon became a feature of the way Bush and Blair spoke after 9/11 that the world they lived in had, almost by definition, to be different from the world past leaders had lived in. Their problems had to be somehow greater and more challenging than those of other leaders – a ludicrous claim when one considers the challenges that the Second World War and the ensuing nuclear weapons stand-off in the Cold War posed for the post-war generation of leaders. The language and rhetoric of both men began to take on the ring of zealotry: nuance and qualification became rarer; certainty and simplicity became ever more dominant.

Even though the invasion of Afghanistan was justified, worrying signs of a developing hubris within Bush emerged from the start of the Afghan campaign. In the first place, the longer-term problems of controlling the country after the invasion had been achieved were grossly underestimated from the outset. Furthermore Bush, by focusing on war and military ways of dealing with the new aspects of worldwide terrorism, at the expense of gaining the support of the communities within which they operated, allowed al-Qaeda to gain in strength.[19] The war mentality detracted from other, longer-established, ways of dealing with unstable states and the terrorists they often harbour. The side effects of the new techniques for prisoners, such as those used in Guantanamo, and the practice of rendition have actually served to breed terrorism. The climate in operation around Bush, which disregarded the possibility that the consequences of their approach could actually worsen the problem they were trying to deal with, is a characteristic of hubris syndrome. In defence of Bush and his advisers, there was sufficient genuine concern about existing ways of dealing with terrorism after 9/11 to have many questions re-examined but not to have them pre-empted. Any examination should have been done with other countries and quietly involving responsible politicians. Instead changes were confined to secret agreements between the intelligence community and governmental lawyers and between other nations, allowing no parliamentary scrutiny.*

A warning sign of Blair's developing hubris was the astonishing speech that he gave to the Labour Party conference immediately after 9/11, when he promised the American people: 'We were with you at the first, we will stay with you to the last.' The consequence of Blair's exclusive dependence on his new No. 10 secretariats was to be the lack of objectivity, probity and collectivity which became the hallmarks of his misjudgements and incompetence in handling the aftermaths of the 2001 invasion of Afghanistan and the 2003 invasion of Iraq.

There have, of course, been incompetent Presidents and Prime Ministers before but Blair's incompetence was to be of a very particular sort, and it was largely shared by Bush. It was triggered by three characteristic symptoms of hubris: excessive self-confidence, restlessness and inattention to detail. A self-

---

* Democratic politicians recognised from 9/11 onwards that changes would need to follow. The House of Commons Foreign Affairs Committee asked the UK government in 2007 to recognise that the Geneva Conventions 'lack clarity and are out of date' and urged it to seek a way 'to update the conventions so as to deal more satisfactorily with asymmetric warfare, with international terrorism, with the status of illegal combatants, and with the treatment of detainees'. (Foreign Affairs Committee, *Visit to Guantánamo Bay*, Second Report, Session 2006/07, HC 44.)

confidence that exclusively reserves decision-making to itself, does not seek advice and fails to listen to or is contemptuous of the wisdom of others, particularly if it conflicts with the leader's own viewpoint, is hubristic. If this is combined with an energy that is restless for action and is ready to intervene on the basis of a loose sense of the broader picture rather than the detailed study of all the relevant information, then serious mistakes are almost inevitable. Such was to be the case in Bush and Blair's handling of affairs after 9/11: the misjudgements were those of hubristic incompetence, explored in detail later.

Bush and Blair liked to pride themselves on being 'big picture' politicians who had the insight to realise that the whole world, not just Afghanistan and Iraq, must now be seen anew and in fundamentally different terms after 2001. In fact, the world, as looked at from the perspective of many centuries, did not change fundamentally on 9/11. There was, however, more irrationality and less predictability. Islamic fundamentalists were ready to sacrifice their life as part of committing an act of terrorism, which made bomb-carrying more deadly and a primitive nuclear device in a suitcase conceivable. It took some years for the rhetoric to cool and only in April 2007 did the British government announce formally that it was stopping using the term 'war on terror'.

It was to become a feature of both Bush and Blair that neither showed much attention to process or detail, nor were they great respecters of the facts. The combination was, of course, massively unequal in terms of power, but Blair made up for what he lacked in power in the relationship by his far greater verbal fluency and passionate language. Blair's political importance was that he reinforced Bush's beliefs and prejudices in the period after the invasion of Afghanistan and in the run-up to the invasion of Iraq. It was a form of *folie à deux*. Blair's links with Clinton were also useful to Bush in helping to keep the Democrats 'on board' for war.

Blair had appeared to have an excellent relationship with Clinton when President, but he later said to one of his aides: 'Clinton messes you around but when Bush promises something, he means it.'[20] Experienced officials, however, have questioned whether Blair was deluding himself about his relationship with Bush. They worried about the lack of substance in the Bush–Blair dialogue and about the extent of the mutual posturing. They noted how Margaret Thatcher had nailed Ronald Reagan down in a way that Blair never did with Bush, or how John Major, though only having a short time before the 1991 Gulf War period, afterwards built a relationship of some depth with Bush's father.

Blair's own particular form of hubris was his obsession with presentation and his need to put himself visibly at the centre of events. This had already become evident when a private memo he wrote to his staff in 2000 was leaked. In it he urged them to search around for 'two or three eye-catching initiatives . . . I should be personally associated with as much of this as possible'.[21] The biographer of another Labour Prime Minister, Ramsay MacDonald, wrote of Blair's ten years in office:

> The true origin of his tragedy lies in an intellectual deformation that is becoming more and more prevalent in our increasingly paltry public culture. The best word for it is 'presentism' . . . His fascination with fashionable glitz, his crass talk of a 'New Britain' and a 'Young Country' and his disdain for the wisdom of experts who had learned the lessons of the past better than he had were all part of the deadly syndrome.[22]

The world after 9/11 provided Blair with endless opportunities for such eye-catching initiatives and he indulged in considerable posturing. Following 9/11 he pursued a frenetic schedule. He held fifty-four meetings with foreign leaders, and travelled more than 40,000 miles on some thirty-one separate flights.

Bush, by contrast, was more disciplined than Blair in how he handled his schedule, insisting on having enough time to sleep, and appeared less frenzied and more controlled. The British press were encouraged by No. 10, with its new foreign affairs and defence secretariats, to exaggerate to the British people the extent of the UK's early involvement in Afghanistan. Beyond the UK launching some cruise missiles and a contribution from the SAS. The invasion was, first and foremost, an American operation: in all its major parameters it was led by the CIA, who used dollars to build up the Northern Alliance, and by the Pentagon, using its special forces and air power to tilt the balance of fighting in favour of those Afghan leaders ready to take on the Taleban. But to reinforce the impression of his own central role, Blair flew into Kabul in early January 2002, just eight weeks after the Taleban-controlled capital had fallen to the Northern Alliance. He was chronically short of sleep and despite a recent holiday in Egypt was exhausted, mentally and physically.[23]

Blair tried to keep up the same pace through 2002 and much of 2003. His determination to be at the centre of everything was designed for and highlighted by the British press. US public opinion, however, liked Blair's easy style, and admired his verbal felicity and presentational skills. It therefore suited Bush to build up Blair's importance over Iraq.

Blair summed up his strategy in March 2002 in a letter to the Archbishop of Canterbury, Dr George Carey:

> Bluntly, I am the one Western leader the US will really listen to on these issues. That carries a price. It means that I don't grandstand; I don't negotiate publicly; I don't list demands. It is a v. difficult and delicate line to tread. Of course if I disagreed fundamentally with their objectives, I wd have to say so and wd . . . My objectives must be to pull the Americans towards a strategy that is sensible in Iraq, contemplate military action only in the right circumstances, and broaden strategy so that it is about the wider world, including the Middle East peace process, Africa, staying and seeing it through in Afghanistan.[24]

By now there was little pretence but that British foreign policy was being run from 10 Downing Street, with the Foreign Office being increasingly sidelined. The British ambassador in Washington recorded this: 'Between 9/11 and the day I retired at the end of February 2003, I had not a single substantive policy discussion on the secure phone with the Foreign Office. This was in contrast to many contacts and discussion with No. 10.'[25]

Blair's hubristic preoccupation with wishing to be seen to be at the centre of events, even if he could achieve nothing of substance, was still present at the G8 meeting in St Petersburg in July 2006. When, unknown to Bush and Blair, a microphone was left switched on, the world was able to hear how the two leaders talked to each other. What was most revealing was Blair's offer to undertake a piece of shuttle diplomacy over the Lebanon crisis. Blair made it clear that what he had in mind was that he could 'go and just talk' and that a failure on his part to achieve anything would not damage the proposed later visit of Condoleezza Rice, the US Secretary of State. Blair was happy just to act as her advance man. It is not simply that this was demeaning for a British Prime Minister, as was the way Bush inarticulately brushed Blair's offer aside. More particularly it vividly illustrated how Blair's primary focus had become himself, his personal position and its presentation through 'eye-catching initiatives'. This was more important to him now than the substance and complexities of an issue. It remained with him in his restless pursuit of his personal legacy right up until he left office in 2007.

On 20 September 2001, Blair and Bush met in America and 'when Blair asked about Iraq, the President replied that Iraq was not the immediate problem. Some members of his administration, he commented, had expressed a different view, but he was the one responsible for making the decisions.'[26] It was only after the invasion of Afghanistan that Bush chose to oust Saddam Hussein from power. He told Donald Rumsfeld on 21 November 2001 to prepare an invasion plan 'and get Tommy Franks [commander in chief of US forces in the Middle East] looking at what it would take'. The Bush administration now began publicly and deliberately to link Iraq to al-Qaeda. It also started to convey to the world an image of the United States as a country that would do as it liked and did not need to take other countries into account. International law was treated with contempt. This was Bush's policy every bit as much as that of Rumsfeld and Vice President Dick Cheney. Bush personally began to show a brash readiness over Iraq to break out of all international restraints with scant regard for the consequences.

Perhaps one reason for this was very personal. On 26 June 1993 Saddam's military intelligence headquarters was attacked by Tomahawk cruise missiles. President Clinton was relying for authority for this action on the UN resolutions dating from 1990 and 1991 which declared Iraq to be a threat to world peace. The attack was ordered in retaliation for the discovery of an Iraqi secret intelligence assassination attempt on the life of the former President George Bush Sr and his family when he was visiting Kuwait on 15–18 April. Two women who really mattered to George W. Bush were on this trip, his mother and his wife. It is not hard to believe that the iron entered his soul then in relation to Saddam and he identified him henceforward as an evil person.

I first became aware of the nature of Saddam Hussein in the summer of 1978, when a former Iraqi Finance Minister was assassinated on the streets of London. Saddam was the most powerful man in Baghdad, though not yet President of Iraq. In a very short space of time it became clear to the police and the British intelligence and secret services, MI5 and MI6, that he was personally deeply implicated in the killing.

There have been many articles attempting to analyse Saddam. One profile stated that it was 'this political personality constellation – messianic ambition for unlimited power, absence of conscience, unconstrained aggression, and a paranoid outlook – that makes Saddam so dangerous. Conceptualised as malignant narcissism.'[27] A Swiss physician, Dr Pierre Rentchnick,[28] who was struck by the slowness of Saddam's responses on television in November 1990, talked to two British physicians who were passing through Geneva. They claimed that he was being treated with lithium for bipolar disorder and that he had suffered two depressive episodes, one during Iraq's eight-year war with Iran and the other in the autumn of 1990.[29] Yet at no time during his trial in Iraq did Saddam use mental illness as a mitigating factor in his defence, nor did the Iraqi Special Tribunal show any interest in exploring any mental illness before sentencing him to death by hanging in 2006.

This sentence was passed for the crime of using gas against Kurdish citizens in 1988 in Halabja, where for two days Iraqi jets dropped a hydrogen cyanide compound, developed with the help of a German company. More than 5,000 civilians were killed. Shamefully, the CIA sent out a briefing note to its embassies at the time stating that the gas might have been dropped by the Iranians.[30] With this genocide against his fellow countrymen, Saddam's conduct passed a threshold which challenged the very purposes of the United Nations. The lack of tough, retaliatory, sanctions against Iraq by the Security Council coupled with the world's low-key protests were indefensible, immoral and in clear breach of the 1948 UN Convention on Genocide. It was a great shame in terms of international justice that US opposition to the International Criminal Court in The Hague prevented Saddam from being tried there in a process similar to that for Milošević.

In part, of course, the American and British governments were not too keen to see a trial in The Hague, where their past acquiescence in the Iraqi invasion of Iran would have been exposed. This acquiescence admittedly owed everything to the practice of a form of realpolitik, explicable only in terms of hoping that by helping to keep the war going for eight years the Iranian revolution would burn itself out. But it was deeply misguided, for the zealotry of Iran's religious leaders continued unabated. It would undoubtedly have been in the best interests of the US and the UK to uphold the rule of international law in 1980 and penalise Saddam. The US and the UK paid the price for not doing so when Iraq invaded Kuwait in 1990 and they were obliged to respond. When Iraqi troops went south to the Kuwait–Saudi border, within 60 miles of the Saudi city Dhahran, President Bush Sr was courageous in responding immediately by deploying US forces into Saudi Arabia even though they would initially have been very vulnerable if Saudi Arabia had been attacked by Saddam. Bush was also deft in his handling of the diplomatic initiatives necessary to build a genuine multinational military coalition to ensure that the Iraqi army was forced out of Kuwait early in 1991. It included not just Saudi Arabia, Jordan and Egypt but also Syria.

In the spring of that year, after the ceasefire, the United States, France and the UK imposed a no-fly zone over northern Iraq in a humanitarian intervention to protect the Kurds (a similar zone would be imposed the following year to protect the Marsh Arabs). This is discussed in Chapters 6 and 8. On 24 September 1991 UN inspectors in Baghdad found a large number of documents detailing Iraq's nuclear weapons programme, not at a military establishment but across the street from a major hotel used by foreign journalists.

It is very easy to forget, irrespective of the arguments about when Saddam acted over the UN ban on WMD while continually obstructing UN inspections, how he steadily began to increase his malign political influence in the region. He did this despite, or perhaps for some countries because of, the continued imposition by the US and UK of the no-fly zones. He ruthlessly campaigned against any UN economic sanctions by refusing to let urgent medical supplies reach Iraqi children, while blaming the UN for their absence. Through the 1990s the World Health Organization reported a steep rise in perinatal mortality rates and avoidable illnesses among Iraqi children. In part, as a result, it became increasingly hard to carry support in international forums for the implementation of sanctions. The UN Security Council tolerated Jordan and Turkey's evasion of oil sanctions, rather than facing up to the need to grant them financial compensation. This meant that the US and the UK were undermining their own positions on implementing sanctions. Increasingly, over the years, in a climate of hypocrisy, international political opposition to sanctions against Iraq grew. France had opportunistically withdrawn its military aircraft from policing the no-fly zones, and among Russia, Germany and many other countries there was a growing mood to ignore UN economic sanctions and instead build up commercial relations with Iraq. The US and the UK were able to contain Iraqi aircraft, tanks and helicopters from crossing the line in the north, but in the south the Marsh Arabs were driven out by Saddam and their habitat flooded. The world appeared to want to forget that the US-led multilateral force in 1991 had deliberately chosen not to capture Baghdad and had, for humanitarian reasons, stopped firing on retreating Iraqi forces, relying instead on the ceasefire terms endorsed by the UN Security Council. It is to the shame of the UN structures, and particularly the Security Council, that these UN ceasefire resolutions were consistently flouted by Saddam and that the deteriorating health statistics for children were not properly explained. Everyone on the Security Council knew that health priorities were manipulated inside Iraq by Saddam for political purposes but few spoke out.

In 1996 the Clinton administration could not get permission from either the Turks or the Saudis to use their air bases to attack Iraq when Saddam violated the northern no-fly zone at Arbis. Instead, on 3 September, the United States launched forty Tomahawks to take out an Iraq air defence installation in the southern no-fly zone. But this was 500 miles from Arbis: the inadequacy of the response demonstrated how little Saddam was being contained. He might not have been capable of attacking his neighbours but his crimes against humanity did not lessen throughout this period. And he felt confident enough to defy the UN by refusing to cooperate with its inspectors, charged with monitoring his commitment not to develop weapons of mass destruction. In 1998, the UN inspectors were withdrawn as a result of the non-cooperation. US and UK aircraft were continuously shot at throughout these twelve years. To say that Saddam Hussein in 2002 was being contained is a travesty of the truth.

Despite what Saddam was doing to the Shiites and Kurds in Iraq over these years, there was no readiness in the United States or elsewhere to use military might to topple him from power. The UN Security Council measures failed to alleviate the rise in infant mortality and the deteriorating health and social condition of millions of Iraqis was an international disgrace.

The corruption surrounding the UN's oil-for-food programme was revealed in a report commissioned by the then secretary general, Kofi Annan, and chaired by Paul Volker, the former head of the US Federal Reserve. It was published on 14 September 2005. It showed that Annan was aware of a kickback scheme involving 2,500 companies in the oil-for-food programme 'at least as early as February 2001'. He was rightly criticised in the report for never subsequently mentioning the kickbacks to the Iraqi government in his published quarterly reports to the UN. As examples of the kickbacks, French companies sold Saddam humanitarian 'assistance' to the value of $3 billion, while Russian companies made deals with Iraq to the value of $19 billion in an overall oil-for-food programme worth in excess of $100 billion. That all the Security Council countries knew about the kickbacks is not an excuse for the secretary general and the UN Secretariat remaining silent. The standing of the UN has been gravely damaged by this complicity of the Secretariat. Of course the secretary general has to work with the council members, particularly the five permanent nations, but he also has responsibility for the good name and integrity of the UN. Annan was in many respects a very successful holder of that office, but he should have forced the issue out into the open and made the Security Council face up to the duplicity and criminality involved.

All these actions by Saddam Hussein made it clear not only that the US and UK's containment policy was not working but that Saddam was still doing much harm in his own country and in the region. Military action to remove him was the only alternative, assassination attempts having failed, but this meant the United States being ready to deploy forces sufficient not just to topple Saddam but also to conduct a nation-building operation in the aftermath.

Going to war

After 9/11 the United States developed, once again, the political will to return to Iraq with the numbers of ground forces that had been used in 1991. I felt any existing Iraqi WMD would be better dealt with in the aftermath of toppling Saddam. Along with most others who studied the subject, I believed Saddam was developing WMD but this should not have been allowed to become, the sole reason for justifying an invasion of Iraq. Saddam by then was in serious default of many of the UN resolutions that had been imposed following his defeat.

My wife and I met Tony and Cherie Blair again for dinner at No. 10 on 24 July 2002. It became very clear to me that Blair was going to commit Britain to Bush's Iraq policy and I agreed with him. What was especially noticeable was that, while he had been ready at dinner in 1998 to explore the complex internal politics of Iraq, Blair was now, in marked contrast, totally unwilling to have any detailed discussion about the consequences of invading. I felt that the political difficulties certain to be encountered in the aftermath of replacing Saddam and Sunni dominance needed to be explored dispassionately. So I tried to do so in a 'Devil's advocate' manner, but Blair was wholly dismissive. There were no problems, he seemed to believe, that could not be solved and were not being solved. I mistakenly took this reluctance to discuss as a sign that he considered all this information highly classified, as indeed in a way it should have been, but it was very different from his readiness to discuss sensitive military matters with regard to Kosovo.

Blair's purpose in talking to me about Iraq that evening was evidently not to consult me but to brief me about what he was going to do and to bring me into the personal 'big tent' of supporters which he liked to create around any controversial new policy. It became utterly clear to me that he had made up his mind on Iraq, and that if Bush later authorised an invasion, Blair would ensure that Britain was there with him. I realised that Blair intended me to report from that meeting to my own contacts in the press, on an unattributable basis, that Britain was definitely going to go to war. This I did as, no doubt, did others. Later, when this readiness to plan for war was eventually confirmed in leaked documents, many people were outraged. But in all fairness, neither Bush nor Blair could have done much more to indicate their intentions than by such selective background briefing. It was still months before any invasion could take place. Wars and even the realistic threat of going to war have to be planned for with some secrecy. It takes time, as in the build-up to the Iraq war in 1990–1, to deploy significant armed forces, particularly tanks and heavy weapons.

But my concern about Tony Blair from that meeting was not his support for an invasion, which I shared, nor his wish to get the message out indirectly, which I understood, but the closed nature of his mind. I regret this did not sufficiently alarm me at the time but I was left with the strong impression that Blair was a very different man from the one I had met over dinner three and a half years earlier. Several clear symptoms of hubris syndrome were now manifest over that second dinner. Besides the firm belief in his purpose, which I discussed afterwards driving home with my wife, there was a total confidence in himself and as a new feature a restless, hyperactive manner. His brushing aside of the difficulties that circumstance was likely to throw in his way meant to me that the die was cast in his own mind over forcing regime change. As before, WMD were not a major topic in Blair's conversation; he was focused quite simply on getting rid of Saddam for moral and geopolitical reasons, all of which I supported. But, as my wife said afterwards, he was messianic.

The opportunity to exercise decisive and controversial leadership is one of the strengths of representative democracy and there is a need from time to time for a certain boldness. But representative democracy also demands that leaders' decision-making be open to democratic scrutiny, that they tell the truth and that after making the key decisions they should be held accountable and, if found wanting, be ready to resign from office.

Bush and Blair showed courage in deciding to invade Iraq, and as a believer in the virtues of representative democracy I want heads of government to lead. It is also necessary for such leaders, particularly but not exclusively at a time of war, to push, prod and challenge their diplomatic and military advisers. This view of leadership, well documented in Eliot Cohen's *Supreme Command*, was not followed sufficiently by either Bush or Blair. In Cohen's four case histories he writes of 'Lincoln searching for a general whose concept of the war mirrored his own; Clemenceau attempting to balance contradictory impulses on the part of equally competent military leaders; Churchill relentlessly probing for choices; Ben Gurion determined to grasp the fundamentals in the midst of complexity'.[31] Neither Bush nor Blair seem to have engaged intellectually with the military planning for or execution of the Iraq War.

I am not attracted to conspiracy theories. I do believe, in contrast to many of their critics, that Bush and Blair thought that gas and chemical weapons were inside Iraq in 2003, as did the intelligence services of France, Russia and Israel. I believe they genuinely did fear that these weapons might be used, as gas had been previously used against Iran. They were concerned about the eventual development of Iraqi nuclear weapons. There was also serious discussion in Washington and London on whether Iraqi WMD might be passed on to other Muslim countries, although most experts felt this was unlikely given Saddam's suspicion of and hostility towards all his neighbours. But – and it is a big but – neither Bush nor Blair displayed a sufficient readiness to understand the nature and the complexity of the war they had embarked upon. Both men's strategic aim was regime change, and for perfectly valid reasons. Bush was open about this. Blair felt he could not be as open. George Tenet, then head of the CIA, has confirmed this: 'The United States did not go to war in Iraq solely because of WMD. In my view, I doubt it was even the principal cause. Yet it was the public face that was put on it.'[32]

The nature and the scale of their incompetence seems to me closely linked to their hubris and in Bush's case the overconfidence of his close conservative colleagues, Cheney and Rumsfeld. Blair, by contrast, did not have any close ministerial colleagues. The linkage over Iraq between hubris and incompetence has been repeatedly made by a number of serious commentators.[33] But merely asserting the linkage is not sufficient to demonstrate hubris syndrome. There has to be a detailed examination of the nature of the incompetence and of the incoherence which so accompanies hubris. As in all wars, many straightforward errors of judgement were made. I do not intend to imply by focusing on hubristic incompetence that this was the only source of error but it was a significant part of the total decision-making.

Hubristic incompetence 1: failure to plan the aftermath

George W. Bush had the advantage of having two experienced colleagues, Colin Powell and Dick Cheney, who had been in his father's Cabinet when Saddam Hussein had invaded Kuwait. A major objective for Saddam then was removing the threat of a $30 billion Kuwaiti debt claim on Iraq. This is why he did not just occupy the disputed Rumailah oilfields but took Kuwait City and then provocatively went south to the Kuwait–Saudi border, making a direct threat to the Saudis. Right from the start, on 3 August 1990, at the second meeting of the National Security Council with the President, Saddam's personal position was considered. Powell, who was then chairman of the Joint Chiefs of Staff, asked: 'How individualised is this aggression? If he is gone, would he have a more reasonable replacement?' Brent Scowcroft, the National Security Advisor, said: 'Iraq could fall apart,' and a foreign policy specialist, Richard Haas, said it was 'unlikely that anyone else would have the same cult of personality' to hold the country together.[34] That conversation remained the basis for the 1991 Desert Storm campaign. The United States would remove Iraqi forces from Kuwait but not attack Baghdad.*

A large multilateral force was assembled by President George Bush Sr with significant troop contributions from many countries, the largest coming from the UK, France, Saudi Arabia and Egypt. On 12 January 1991 Congress voted to authorise the use of force, as did the Senate, but in the latter the vote was close: fifty-two to forty-seven, with many Democrats opposing. Military success came initially by bombing from the air for six weeks. This was followed on 24 February by a rapid attack with sophisticated tanks, and a large helicopter assault, followed on 27 February by a ceasefire supported by Cheney and Powell. Later Cheney felt it had been a mistake not to take out Saddam. But this retrospective view is not shared by President Bush Sr, his then Secretary of State, James Baker, Scowcroft or Powell. Against that background, one would have thought that the question of how to handle in detail the aftermath of another invasion twelve years later aimed at deposing Saddam Hussein would have preoccupied George W. Bush. Yet he appears to have believed that having toppled Saddam there would be few problems, since the Americans would be seen as liberators. The harsh truth is that Bush and Blair gravely underestimated the situation, as did General Tommy Franks, who did not take seriously the early signs that Saddam had planned for an insurgency.[35]

The choice for Bush in 2003 after taking Baghdad was either a political fix and an early handover to the Iraqis, allowing a quick exit, or occupation and a programme of nation-building inside Iraq, with an exit postponed until this had

---

* On 7 August 1990, Cheney, then Secretary of Defense, saw King Fahd in Jeddah and sought permission to base US forces in Saudi Arabia. He pledged that after the threat was removed, the forces would be withdrawn and the United States would seek no permanent base in the kingdom. Crown Prince Abdullah, then second in line to the throne and now King, spoke against any US forces coming in. He reflected the views of most of the Saudi princes. He said such a decision would be very unpopular and that there should be consultation with the tribal elders and religious scholars. King Fahd, more alert to the danger, for the first time in his reign made the decision without a consensus to accept US forces. (Christian Alfonsi, *Circle in the Sand: Why We Went Back to Iraq* (New York: Doubleday, 2006), pp. 89, 115–20.)

been achieved. Bush and Blair should have chosen one or the other of these options before the invasion. What happened was that, sensing division among his advisers, Bush postponed any decision until well after the invasion and Blair acquiesced. It was clear from their stance on Afghanistan that Cheney and Rumsfeld, well before the invasion of Iraq, were dismissive of the need for nation-building and reluctant to get involved in it. They and the leading neo-conservatives, the deputy Defense Secretary, Paul Wolfowitz, and a colleague at the Department of Defense, Douglas Feith, 'did not believe the US would need to run post-conflict Iraq'. Their aim was to turn the country over very quickly to their favoured exiles in the Iraqi National Congress (INC) and make a rapid exit. In accordance with that policy Cheney stuck his finger into Powell's chest late in 2003, saying: 'If you hadn't opposed the INC and Chalabi [Ahmed Chalabi, its leader] we wouldn't be in this mess.'[36] The State Department, by contrast, under Powell, favoured nation-building all along. Whatever he did Bush had to decide one way or the other. It was a massive error that Bush left this vital issue of aftermath planning seemingly unresolved, though he did decide that Rumsfeld should handle the aftermath and not Powell.

In Britain we know from the subsequent leaking of many official papers[37] how the aftermath planning issues were presented to Tony Blair and how he seems to have ignored the manifest concerns of his officials. For those interested in analysing the mistaken decisions and incompetent execution of British policy, these leaked papers provide a treasure trove of background information. Sir Peter Ricketts, political director of the Foreign Office, warned on 22 March 2002: 'US scrambling to establish a link between Iraq and al-Qaeda is so far frankly unconvincing.'[38] Stories had been emerging of links between al-Qaeda and Iraq and a particularly persistent story described how the mastermind of 9/11, Mohammed Atta, had met with an Iraqi intelligence agent at a meeting in Prague five months before the hijacking of the aircraft. I believed this story for a time and wrote about it in the *Wall Street Journal*.[39] But it was wrong and disproved well before the invasion of Iraq. Nevertheless, a sign of the loose way intelligence was being used by the White House throughout was that Lewis 'Scooter' Libby, Cheney's chief aide, was described later by *Time* magazine as responsible for assiduously promoting this very story. *Time* called it a 'hard-to-kill Libby favourite'.[40]

In April, Blair went to see Bush at Crawford, Texas, with clear warnings about the invasion path on which he was already, in his own mind, embarking. The Foreign Secretary, Jack Straw, had written to him on 25 March:

We have also to answer the big question – what will this action achieve? There seems to be a larger hole in this than on anything. Most of the assessments from the US have assumed regime change as a means of eliminating Iraq's WMD threat. *But none has satisfactorily answered how that regime change is to be secured and how there can be any certainty that the replacement regime will be better* [emphasis added].[41]

On 21 July an official's note was circulated to ministers ostensibly on Iraq, titled 'Conditions for Military Action'. It warned:

Little thought has been given to creating the political conditions for military action, *or the aftermath and how to shape it* . . . When the Prime Minister discussed Iraq with President Bush at Crawford in April he said that the UK would *support military action to bring about regime change provided that* certain conditions were met: efforts had been made to construct a coalition, shape public opinion, the Israeli–Palestine Crisis was quiescent, and the options for action to eliminate Iraq's WMD through the UN weapons inspectors had been exhausted . . . *A post-war occupation of Iraq could lead to a protracted and costly nation-building exercise. As already made clear, the US military plans are virtually silent on this point* [all emphasis added].[42]

Two days later Blair was warned about the fixing of intelligence in Washington and was issued an even more serious warning than the one Straw gave in March. A Secret and Strictly Personal 'UK eyes only' memorandum dated 23 July 2002 was eventually leaked to the press two years after the invasion of Iraq and it described a meeting attended by three Cabinet ministers – the Prime Minister, the Foreign Secretary and the Defence Secretary – and the Attorney General, but neither Blair's deputy Prime Minister nor the Chancellor of the Exchequer, Gordon Brown. John Scarlett, the head of the JIC, was present, as was the head of MI6, Sir Richard Dearlove, called 'C', who described his recent talks in Washington. Dearlove reported: 'Military action was now seen as inevitable. Bush wanted to remove Saddam, through military action, justified by the conjunction of terrorism and WMD. But *the intelligence and facts were being fixed around the policy* . . . *There was little discussion in Washington of the aftermath after military action* [emphasis added].'[43] Later Dearlove told George Tenet he had objected to the word 'fixed' in the records of the meeting and had it corrected to reflect his view 'about the undisciplined manner in which the intelligence was being used'. He also said that he had had a polite but significant disagreement with Libby over his belief that there were links between Iraq and al-Qaeda.[44] Also at that meeting was the Chief of the

Defence Staff, Admiral Sir Michael Boyce, who said that the military 'were continuing to ask lots of questions. For instance, what were the consequences if Saddam used WMD on day one or if Baghdad did not collapse and urban war fighting began?'[45] Three of Blair's political appointees were also present, Jonathan Powell, Alastair Campbell and Sally Morgan. Thereafter politics, not military strategy, dominated No. 10 as they started to prepare public opinion in the UK for war. Their chosen method was, fatefully, pushing Saddam's possession of WMD to the forefront.

What is clear from these leaked papers is that by the end of July 2002, the Whitehall machine seemed to be assuming that a protracted and costly nation-building option was likely to be forced on them, but, along with the intelligence services, the military were deeply alarmed by the lack of any post-invasion planning in Washington. Yet Blair appeared to ignore the warnings his own people were giving him, and in conversation with me over dinner the very day after the meeting reported above, he was dismissive of any difficulties and trying to give me the impression that it was all being dealt with. This was not ordinary incompetence, it was hubristic incompetence. He was becoming immune to all arguments about the practical difficulties that might ensue, which many people were putting to him. A senior official recalls that when advising Blair about the difficulties ahead, Blair would say: 'You are Neville Chamberlain, I am Winston Churchill and Saddam is Hitler.' It is difficult to conduct a serious dialogue with a leader thinking in this emotional and simplistic way.

This was also Blair's frame of mind when dealing with outside advisers. Charles Tripp, an academic expert on Middle East politics, was called in along with other experts to give advice. He later wrote an account of his meeting:

> At a Downing Street meeting in November 2002 attended by Blair, Straw and six academics familiar with Iraq and the Middle East, two things became clear. The first was that Straw thought post-Saddam Iraq would be much like post-Soviet Russia and could thus be easily pigeon-holed as that strange creature, a 'transitional society'. Either he had been persuaded of this by the recycled Cold Warriors clustering round the Bush administration, or they had failed to inform their 'key ally' of their determination to dismantle Iraq's state and security structures. More ominously, Blair seemed wholly uninterested in Iraq as a complex and puzzling political society, wanting confirmation merely that deposing Saddam would remove 'evil' from the country.[46]

That Blair should be interested only in being reassured that he was fighting evil can be equated with Bush's simple talk of his crusade to rid the world of 'evil doers'.

Unlike in Britain, the unease of the American military was made public by General Eric K. Shinseki, the US Army chief of staff. He told the Senate Armed Services Committee on 25 February 2003, just before the invasion, that, based on his experience of peace-keeping in the Balkans, post-war Iraq would require 'something on the order of several hundred thousand soldiers'. This was the reasoned estimate of a lifelong military man who had lost most of a foot in Vietnam, had led NATO's Peace Stabilization Force in Bosnia, and had commanded both NATO's land forces and the US Army in Europe. The US separation of powers allows for such frankness in Congressional hearings. Traditionally UK service leaders keep their advice to ministers private when appearing before select committees in Parliament. In the light of what happened over Iraq the UK Parliament needs to reconsider this convention.

President Bush and Condoleezza Rice, the National Security Advisor, should have insisted on the White House reviewing the planned force levels after Shinseki's evidence. Instead he was contradicted a few days later by Paul Wolfowitz, who told the House Budget Committee that this estimate was 'wildly off the mark', explaining: 'It's hard to conceive that it would take more forces to provide stability in post-Saddam Iraq than it would take to conduct the war itself and to secure the surrender of Saddam's security forces and his army. Hard to imagine.'[47] For those experienced in post-war conflict it was, on the contrary, all too easy to imagine why more forces would be needed in the aftermath. This was particularly the case for the UK military in view of their experience in Northern Ireland over three decades and in Bosnia-Herzegovina from 1992 onwards.

Apologists for the British policy and for Blair personally over Iraq tend to put all the blame for the admitted incompetence on the Americans. This is to underestimate British knowledge of the region. Britain, unlike America, had been involved in Iraq through most of the twentieth century. By 1918 David Lloyd George had sent more than a million British and Commonwealth troops into Ottoman territory to impose a post-war settlement.[48] Britain had administered Iraq, albeit not very successfully, under a League of Nations mandate from 1920 until 1932, and had remained close to King Faisal and Nuri al-Said, who dominated the country for the next two decades. The British Foreign Office and Ministry of Defence had knowledge and experience and some well-formulated views on the best way of handling the aftermath of any invasion, especially in the light of the mistakes of 1991. But this expertise was never utilised by Blair. A Foreign Office strategy paper, which the State Department was hoping would arrive, their own having been ignored by the Pentagon, never came.[49] The then British ambassador to Washington has written about the 'titanic struggle' for six months to keep Britain 'onside for war' and how 'there was little energy left in No. 10 to think about the aftermath. Since Downing Street drove Iraq policy, efforts made by the Foreign Office to engage with the Americans on the aftermath came to nothing.'[50]

This was the consequence of Blair's taking so much of the handling of the preparation for war into his own hands, sidelining the Foreign Office and ignoring warnings from the military and the intelligence services. Even so, it would still be reasonable to expect that in any real substantive relationship between two heads of government such as Bush and Blair, there would be detailed discussion on all of the key issues, including dealing with the aftermath. But there is little evidence that they ever did discuss them in detail before the invasion. Rumsfeld was formally put in charge of post-war planning by Bush on 20 January. But the planning should have been completed in Washington and in Whitehall months before.

The two leaders met in Washington on 31 January 2003 and some of the leaked content of that important meeting appeared in a book.[51] But much more detail appeared later in the *New York Times*, its reporter having reviewed a memo of the meeting by the Prime Minister's senior adviser, David Manning, in its entirety.[52] Blair was told that the start date pencilled in for bombing was 10 March 2003. It is clear that neither he nor Bush seemed to think it necessary to plan for the possible consequences of Bush's own expectation, stated at the meeting, that the Iraqi army would 'fold very quickly'. Indeed Bush is reported by Robert Draper, the author of *Dead Certain*, as saying: 'The policy had been to keep the army intact; didn't happen,' but he couldn't remember how he had reacted when he found that the policy had been reversed. I was told by a prominent neocon at the time that, far from folding, whole divisions of the Iraqi forces would come over to the allies intact and help maintain law and order. Bush and Blair at their meeting seemed to envision a quick victory and swapped ideas about the post-war Iraqi government, with Blair saying: 'People would find it very odd if we handed it over to another dictator.' Indeed they would have. Yet both men knew that handing over to US-selected Iraqis was still central to Cheney/Rumsfeld/Wolfowitz thinking. When Blair asked about aftermath planning, 'Condi Rice said that a great deal of work was now in hand'. But Bush still spoke of 'the dilemma' of 'managing the transition to the civil administration', making clear that this issue was still unresolved. The Blairites' spin, in their defence, is that the Prime Minister was 'tearing his hair out' that they were not informed. This does not stand up to serious examination. It ignores a series of telegrams from Sir Christopher Meyer, the UK ambassador in Washington, revealed in the BBC television programme *No Plan, No Peace*, shown on 28 and 29 October 2007. It was also a Blair decision to have no one replace Meyer when he came home before the war, leaving the post vacant for too long over a critical period. When Manning was released from No. 10, most of the planning errors had proved disastrous. All the evidence points to the fact that 'post-war planning was no more a priority in London than in Washington'.[53]

With characteristic hubris, neither Bush nor Blair had advisers from defence or foreign affairs ministries at the January meeting, just their own personal staff from the White House and No. 10. The same inner group was used to the comfort of recycling together the opinions and prejudices of their respective political masters in frequent exchanges across the Atlantic – a dangerous phenomenon, well documented by management theorists, called 'groupthink'. Described as a 'personality-determined malaise', the symptoms of this process are well described in the book *On the Psychology of Military Incompetence* and were displayed in President Kennedy's handling of the Bay of Pigs fiasco (see Chapter 4, p. 145). Analysis of past military incompetence produces four most frequently occurring symptoms: 'wastage of manpower, over-confidence, underestimation of the enemy and the ignoring of intelligence reports'.[54]

We now know that Blair was told in early March by Major General Tim Cross that the post-war planning was completely incoherent. 'The plan was, we do not need a plan' was Cross's summary view of what had been going on in Washington. Cross revealed in a *Sunday Times* interview on 21 October 2007: 'As we teased out the issues, Blair listened and questioned. None of it seemed to come as much of a surprise. Indeed it seemed to reinforce what he was starting to pick up from elsewhere.' Cross remembers telling Blair: 'We want to be jolly careful that we don't start this war until we know how we are going to finish it. And I, for one, am far from clear on how we are going to do that.' Cross left Downing Street thinking that Blair 'didn't seem to have the instinct for or understand the scope and complexity of what was going to be needed in the aftermath of an invasion. I don't think he understood what the possible consequences could be.' For Cross the story was a failure of leadership. 'We got it wrong. We underestimated the resources we would need to see the campaign through. We underestimated the time we would need.'

I have heard it privately alleged – but have found no proof of this – that at Blair's final meeting with Bush in the Azores on 14 March, just before the invasion, he was asked by the British military to raise questions about the absence of planning for the aftermath but supposedly he never raised them. So Bush and Blair committed their troops to war with no idea as to how long they would remain an occupying force. As one former covert CIA man put it:

> There was no question we'd get to Baghdad in no time. We better have a plan for when we get there. But we had nothing but four PowerPoint pages. It was arrogant. We used to joke about the PhD club – Wolfowitz, Feith. They knew best . . . We set the conditions for how that happened. This is a self-inflicted mess.[55]

It also meant that one of Henry Kissinger's three conditions for war in Iraq, defined within earshot of the UK ambassador in July 2002, had not been fulfilled. Kissinger said we had to 'arrive in Baghdad with a clear plan for the succession to Saddam. It would be disastrous to begin debating a successor regime after deposing him.'[56]

On 17 January 2003 a retired lieutenant general, Jay Garner, was asked by Douglas Feith to take charge of post-war Iraq and formed the Office of Reconstruction and Humanitarian Assistance. His deputy was Major General Cross. Garner was given no existing plans. It appeared that Feith hoped Garner would turn to Ahmed Chalabi and his band of exiles.[57] When Bush and Blair met on 31 January 2003, they grandly declared that 'failure was not an option'. But both men had already sown the seeds of their combined failure before the invasion started. Brave leaders often sweep cautious advice aside but it was foolhardy for Bush and Blair not to realise that the concerns that had been expressed to them had substance. Not to plan to prevent those concerns materialising was reckless; indeed, it was more than reckless – it was a culpable dereliction of duty. The handling, or rather the non-handling, of the vital issues of planning beforehand and what to do with an occupied Iraq, and also to fail to provide sufficient troops to maintain order, constituted a piece of hubristic incompetence on the part of Bush and Blair which has brought nemesis on hundreds of thousands of people. Their responsibility is manifest – it cannot be shifted on to their subordinates or on to the Iraqis.

In the event it was only after the momentum of a successful invasion was lost that Bush and Rice focused on the detailed arrangements for the transition. Paul Bremer arrived in Baghdad in May 2003 as the American head of the Coalition Provisional Authority with the powers of a viceroy, insisting on reporting to Bush. It had by then been decided to hold off on Garner's public promise of elections within ninety days and an early transfer of sovereignty. Part of Bremer's task seemed to be to sideline and eventually diminish Chalabi's influence. So the nation-building option had, in effect, by then been adopted by Bush but with far too few troops to make it workable, particularly since an insurgency was underway. Bush never explained the cost of war to the American people[58] in the way President Roosevelt did in his 1942 State of the Union address, when he warned: 'War costs money and that means bonds and taxes. It means cutting luxuries and other non-essentials. In a word, it means an all-out war by individual effort and family effort in a united country.' Instead the impression emerged under Bush from 2003 that the United States was not at war – the US Army was at war; the rest of the country was just watching.

Hubristic incompetence 2: Blair's pursuit of a second UN resolution

Seven months before the invasion of Iraq it was the US Secretary of State, Colin Powell, who persuaded Bush to go first to the UN before embarking on direct military intervention. Powell warned Bush, over dinner on 5 August 2002, not to add Iraq to Afghanistan as an American unilateral intervention but to seek UN support. Condoleezza Rice was the only other person present. According to the journalist Bob Woodward, Powell said: 'You can still make a pitch for a coalition or UN action to do what needs to be done,' and he warned of a 'cauldron' in the Arab world that would suck the oxygen out of just about everything else the United States was doing, not only in the war on terrorism, but in all other diplomatic, defence and intelligence relationships.[59] On going to the UN, Powell's arguments were strongly reinforced by Tony Blair. On 12 September, with the crucial paragraph missing from his notes, Bush ad-libbed in his UN General Assembly speech that the United States would work with the UN Security Council for the necessary resolutions, but he had meant to say 'resolution' in the singular. The French seized on this verbal infelicity to push for two resolutions. The following month, in

Washington Congress passed the Authorisation for the Use of Military Force against Iraq. This authorised the President to take action as 'he determines to be necessary and appropriate'.

The unanimous passing in the Security Council of Resolution 1441 on 8 November 2002 was a diplomatic feat, but it was also a political fudge. France, Germany and Russia were still far from being convinced of the case for invading Iraq. The wording of the resolution, however, succeeded in putting increased international pressure on Saddam Hussein and made military action more likely if he did not comply. The extent of the US success can be measured by the response of the French. By 9 December there had developed 'a seeming harmony between the US and French viewpoints'.[60] A French general went to Washington on 21 December to offer between 10,000 and 15,000 troops and 100 aircraft to deploy after the UN Chief Inspector's first report, due on 27 January 2003, which the French expected to be unfavourable to Saddam. On 13 January, President Jacques Chirac sent a personal envoy to speak to Rice with the French ambassador, Jean-David Levitte, who had been at the UN during the negotiations over Resolution 1441. They said they did not want to veto a second resolution and therefore they would prefer the United States, if it felt diplomacy was over, to go to war just on Resolution 1441.

In the immediate aftermath of the unanimous vote in the Security Council, and with Bush enjoying overwhelming support in Congress, it would have been wiser for Blair to have already made clear to Parliament that Resolution 1441 could be enforced on WMD only if Saddam were removed. The reason why this would have been sensible is that it would have enabled Blair to openly make the very important connection between advocating the deposing of Saddam as necessary, in order to enforce compliance with resolutions requiring the removal of WMD, and 'regime change'. The latter could never attract sufficient support within the UN as an objective in itself but by connecting the two it could have won support in the UN and would certainly have widened support and understanding in Parliament.

The interpretation of the UN Charter is the responsibility of the Security Council, which is not a court of law but a collection of member states empowered to act under their interpretation of the charter. Lawyers' advice is but one of many factors to weigh in the balance when negotiating the terms of a UN resolution. Demanding the resignation of a head of government by UN Security Council resolution under threat of action, in the terms of Chapter VII of the charter, can be justified by the Security Council as an action taken to overcome a threat to the peace. A threat to the peace can override the charter's injunction not to interfere in another state's internal sovereignty. Only after 9/11 did such a demand become a practical option in Iraq because of a readiness in the United States to take military action. A UN resolution demanding that Saddam and his chief acolytes step down from power, in order to ensure the removal of all possibility of Iraq developing WMD, and a subsequent UN-supervised election could have been Bush and Blair's first diplomatic response in 2002. It could then have been followed, if the resolution was vetoed or ignored, by invasion. This would have been far better than focusing on WMD alone and could have been justified by Saddam's long record of flouting UN resolutions.

Arguing the necessity of removing Saddam in order to enforce UN resolutions on WMD would have helped Blair with the Labour Party. It would also have had a further benefit: the British military could have been openly involved in detailed planning of the invasion and its aftermath months in advance. Britain would then have been in a stronger position to argue in Washington for larger numbers of troops to be deployed in the aftermath to stabilise the country, control its borders and prevent an insurgency.* The greatest benefit by far, however, would have been that Parliament and the British people would, at last, have been told the truth. Britain was going to war for the combined purpose of getting rid of Saddam and guarantee that this time, unlike in 1991, WMD would be removed immediately, never to return, the human rights of the Shiite and Kurdish people restored and the health services for Iraqi children boosted.

Why did Blair want a second resolution? The case for Resolution 1441 itself providing legality for war rested on the claim that it revived Resolutions 678 and 687, going back to the first Gulf War, and which themselves countenanced the use of military force. This was a controversial interpretation which many people disputed. In the Security Council itself there were always different interpretations of the wording of Resolution 1441, as there had been in relation to the other UN resolutions on Iraq in the 1990s. Also while it was undisputed that the Security Council was required to meet before the start of any military action, there was argument as to whether it needed expressly to

---

* The US and the UK collaborated early over the first Gulf War of 1991, with British military involvement right from the start of planning in the autumn of 1990. Moreover, a British general with much Arab experience, Sir Peter de la Billière, was hugely influential as deputy commander under General Norman Schwarzkopf.

confirm 'material breach by Iraq' of earlier resolutions or to pass another resolution specifically endorsing military action. For the United States, and to a slightly lesser extent for the UK, there was a commitment only to meet 'in order to consider the situation and the need for full compliance with all of the relevant Council Resolutions in order to secure international peace and security'. The American view was that a further decision of the Security Council was not required by the terms of Resolution 1441, taken with the entire series of earlier Security Council resolutions requiring Iraq to disarm. This ambiguity of interpretation was not an accident, nor is it uncommon in the Security Council: it was part of the political reality and the compromises which had enabled the unanimous passing of Resolution 1441 to be negotiated in the first place.

So to those familiar with the workings of the Security Council, in America and in Britain, it was somewhat surprising, to say the least, that Blair was now pushing so hard for a second resolution. Dick Cheney and Donald Rumsfeld were predictably totally against the attempt and even Colin Powell was only supportive because he felt Blair needed it politically. Powell had been told by Bush on 13 January that the United States was going to invade. On 19 January, Bush had, privately and reluctantly, accepted Blair's passionate plea for a second UN resolution. American lack of enthusiasm was understandable because they knew the French were still ready to compromise. At a press conference on 20 January, the French Foreign Minister, Dominique de Villepin, had provocatively and flamboyantly declared 'Nothing! Nothing!' justified war. This was after he became convinced, having met Powell on the 19th, that war was inevitable. On the 21st, Jean-David Levitte again made representations to the Americans. He appeared to want to pull back from Villepin's exposed position the previous day. The French ambassador in London, however, undertook no similar exercise. Levitte suggested that France and the United States should agree as friends to disagree. If there was to be a war France would reluctantly acquiesce in any military action taken under Resolution 1441. It would not itself send troops, but it would not actively support any condemnatory UN resolution of such action, provided that it would not face a second resolution. There was every reason to believe that Russia would accept such a deal and Germany would acquiesce, with China abstaining. In the meeting Levitte was given no encouragement by the United States to think that it would drop the second resolution.

So it certainly was not unambiguously the case that the Security Council had to pass another resolution explicitly authorising war for such a war to be claimed to be legal. Blair's privately stated view, at his 31 January 2003 meeting with Bush, was that a second Security Council resolution would provide an 'insurance policy'.[61] Why, then, did Blair want this insurance policy? Partly because he knew he had not been honest about regime change to the British public and that he was overstressing WMD to overcome the strong dissent within the Labour Party about the legality of going to war solely on the basis of 1441. Naturally any Prime Minister would want to win the support of his party for war and politically it was desirable for Blair to carry Parliament's endorsement on Labour Party votes alone. But to carry one's own MPs is not essential for parliamentary authority.[*] The Conservative opposition in 2003 was steadfastly in favour of the invasion of Iraq, so Parliament's overall support for the war was never in doubt and parliamentary authority for military action, if sought, on Resolution 1441 was always going to be given.

But in the attempt primarily to obtain the votes of more Labour MPs, Blair was pitching himself against hopeless odds and risking almost certain defeat in the Security Council in trying to get a second resolution passed. Furthermore, by so determinedly pursuing it he risked undermining the credibility of the claim that existing resolutions provided legal cover for war. For if that was the case, his critics would and did say, why would there need to be all this effort to get a second resolution?

Bush, after meeting Blair, very noticeably gave only a lukewarm public endorsement of a second resolution, with Blair alongside him at their 31 January press conference in Washington.[62] It is now clear why. For even as Blair was publicly insisting on the importance of a second resolution he himself was privately saying it was not vital. In the leaked memo written by Blair's adviser David Manning, recording his meeting with Bush on 31 January 2003, prior to that press conference, the whole flavour of the discussion between them is one of cynicism over the second resolution still being pursued. Bush is quoted as saying he was determined to invade Iraq and that '*military action would follow anyway*' (emphasis added) even without the second resolution and even if international arms inspectors failed to find WMD. Blair replied that he was 'solidly with the President and ready to do whatever it took to disarm Saddam'. So the second resolution, the very one Blair was causing such damage by pursuing, did not ultimately matter to him anyway. If contempt lies at the heart

---

[*] Blair was content later to carry important education reforms through on Conservative votes and, even more importantly, the replacement for the Trident nuclear deterrent on 14 March 2007.

of hubris it is hard to imagine anything more hubristic. Even so, Bush offered Blair at that meeting the opportunity for them to combine Resolution 1441 with regime change. Bush said: 'At some point, probably when we had passed the second resolution – assuming we did – we should warn Saddam that he had a week to leave. We should then notify the media too. We would then have a clear field if Saddam refused to go.'[63] For some reason this issue was never given prominence. It would have been a dramatic way of achieving regime change and certainly of making it clear before the invasion that WMD and regime change went together. At the meeting Bush predicted that it was 'unlikely there would be internecine warfare between the different religious and ethnic groups' and Blair agreed with that assessment.

In Washington, as Bob Woodward reported, some were not keen to take any French offer to compromise; they thought a clash with France would be a 'liberating moment for the United States and even more so for Prime Minister Blair . . . the whole UN process was hopeless. Bush and Blair could argue that they had gone to the UN and been thwarted by the French.'[64] But it proved to be not a liberation for Blair but a humiliation. By persisting in believing he could secure the necessary votes for a second resolution and not picking up on the French compromise, Blair demonstrated hubris of a high order. The votes were not there in the UN for a second resolution and Blair was told this. But he ignored that advice. He obviously did not trust President Chirac, who had warned him in October that 'while Saddam Hussein could be overthrown, the subsequent consequences would be disastrous'.[65] Blair had also discussed Iraq with Chirac over a long period, and he saw him as protecting France's economic links with that country. It appears that the French offer to abstain in the Security Council was never discussed by the UK Cabinet or even by a smaller number of ministers, although we will have to await the papers being made public or leaked before we can be certain. At the very least Blair should have used Britain's diplomatic links and particularly the well-established Quadripartite mechanism in order to try to bring France and Germany back into a *modus vivendi* with the US and the UK and in effect to give Security Council endorsement to the invasion. This was the time for compromise among the Quadripartite foreign ministers, from the US, the UK, France and Germany.* An agreement, along

---

* The Quadripartite countries had a long history of quietly working out much more difficult questions, originally over Berlin, but also on many other serious areas of foreign and security policy. Quadripartite had, however, progressively lost its clout; some date the start of this to the 1996 Berlin negotiations, when the Americans felt that the European three – Britain, France

the lines which the French proposed, to stick with Resolution 1441 would have demonstrated that the Security Council is a political forum, not a court of law.

Blair's problem with such diplomacy was that it would have meant involving others, particularly his own Foreign Secretary, and that process would have diminished his own hands-on involvement. He preferred to pursue his high-profile arm-twisting exercise on the French and other Security Council members. He therefore pressed on with the pursuit of a second resolution, simply ignoring the French warning that they had already secured the necessary majority of nine votes against the UK and US position in the Security Council.[†]

Unfortunately, Blair became fixed on the need to secure a second Security Council resolution explicitly authorising the resort to war. His belief that he could get such a resolution passed showed extraordinary blindness and a dismissive contempt for those who warned him he could not succeed: he appears to have deluded himself about his own powers of persuasion. His pursuit of the second resolution also demonstrated an astonishing disregard for the damage it would cause to the carefully crafted consensus that had been achieved through the unanimous passing of Resolution 1441. And in addition Blair dismissed compromises that were offered on the way. In short, his conduct over the chimera of a second resolution manifested a monumental incompetence born out of hubris.

The Americans attempted to win around the doubtful members of the Security Council. But Dominique de Villepin went further across the frontier of friendship with his UK and US colleagues and toured Africa, cajoling Security Council members to vote against the second resolution. Buoyed up by the fervour of the moment, Blair failed to pick up in No. 10 that the British initiative was unravelling in New York. Not since Anthony Eden and Suez

---

and Germany – had ganged up on them over EU access to NATO assets. Eventually an agreement was concluded in 2002 as the Berlin Plus Agreement. Quadripartite was, however, the ideal forum for resolving the growing divisions over Iraq. It needs to be revived.

[†] The UN department, now called the International Organisations Department, in the Foreign Office, as distinct from the UK's permanent representative at the UN, would normally produce a written professional assessment about the true state of the likely Security Council voting. Whether it did or it was ever read in Downing Street is not clear. Among the key purposes of that department have been to weigh the views on UN resolutions in the capitals of the fifteen Security Council countries, to test the UK permanent representative's view from New York and to advise the Foreign Secretary and through him or her the Cabinet. If such a professional assessment was written, it is hard to believe that it could have endorsed Blair's belief that a second resolution was winnable.

has a British Prime Minister so misjudged the mood of the Security Council. Eventually, on 8 March, it became apparent even to No. 10 that the French had counted their votes more precisely all along and that the six undecided countries, Angola, Cameroon, Chile, Guinea, Mexico and Pakistan, would not support the second resolution. With a derisory level of support, it had to be dropped.

Sir Stephen Wall, the diplomat inside No. 10 in charge of Blair's relationship with the EU, recalled the moment when, with his press secretary, Blair split the EU asunder. 'I happened to be in the corridor in No. 10 when he and Alastair Campbell were walking down the corridor and they decided effectively to play the anti-French card.'[66] They ignored that Chirac's threat to use the veto was only stated for that evening, '*ce soir*', and they played on incipient British anti-French feeling. It was naked politics but it helped carry the day in Parliament.

The French position was not a principled one, either.* Hence the reasonable conclusion that 'France's government was not so much struggling to save humanity as looking out for Numéro Un'.[67]

Over the second resolution, Blair's failure to achieve a goal that it had always been vain (in both senses of the word) to pursue proved hugely costly. Not only did the effort itself undermine the credibility of the claim, which ultimately had to be relied on, that the invasion was legal without a second resolution, but the futile process shattered what consensus had been achieved over Resolution 1441 and sharpened the divisions within the international community. It also exacerbated the splits between the EU countries on the Security Council, with the French rallying opposition to the resolution while the Spanish and British were shown as incompetent. So much for all Blair's pro-EU rhetoric.

The fiasco over pursuing the second resolution was very much Blair's own. He clearly had delusions about his own capacity to succeed. He was contemptuous of the advice and warnings of others. He rejected a sensible compromise when it was offered. He persisted in spite of reality staring him in the face. And he was utterly cavalier about the risks he was running and the likely costs of failure.

---

* Villepin wobbled as he played to the gallery of world opinion in January and February. He believed that France could hold out only until the middle of March and would then have to support the United States. That position was brutally dismissed by Chirac in February but the President had also been hedging his bets in December and January.

Blair's manipulation of international law and intelligence

On 7 March 2003 Lord Goldsmith, the Attorney General and constitutionally the government's independent legal adviser, sent Tony Blair a memo titled 'Advice on the Legality of Military Action against Iraq without a Further Security Council Resolution'.[68] It was a long, balanced judgment but in places it was clearly equivocal. It said that a 'reasonable case' could be made that Resolution 1441 could 'in principle' revive the authorisation to attack Iraq but admitted that such a case would be challengeable in court.*

On 17 March Goldsmith produced a very much shorter and unequivocal statement which said that 'a material breach of Resolution 687 revived the authority to use force under Resolution 678'. This statement was given orally to the Cabinet and reiterated in Parliament. It was claimed by Blair that the second statement was merely an abbreviated version of the first and he resisted all attempts for the first to be published. In response to the continuing controversy, on 9 March 2005, prior to the general election, Blair said: 'It is being said that the legal opinion of the Attorney General was different from the Attorney General's statement to the House. That is patently absurd.' Yet the Information Commissioner, Richard Thomas, served an enforcement notice in 2006 on the Attorney General, requiring a disclosure statement because Goldsmith's advice on 7 March 2003 was 'significantly more equivocal' than his statement on 17 March. The disclosure statement was published on 26 May 2006. The Attorney General's first formal legal opinion was, to any fair-minded person, long, equivocal in places, but balanced. The second was short and unambiguous in its judgment. The Cabinet should undoubtedly have been made aware of the risks of a future legal challenge. Blair in effect manipulated the Cabinet and the country from 2003 to 2006 on this important legal issue. Such wholly unacceptable conduct was over a decision depicted by the Information Commissioner as a matter 'of such gravity and magnitude as the decision to commit the country to military action'.

---

* As usual, the Attorney General's advice was not made public but, troublingly, nor was it shown to the Cabinet. The Chief of the Defence Staff, Admiral Sir Michael Boyce, was clearly concerned about the legal position and demanded unequivocal reassurance from Goldsmith about the legality of the action to which he was about to commit troops. In fact the International Criminal Court cannot prosecute an illegal war, known as a crime of aggression, for its 'jurisdiction is limited to the conduct of war, not the decision to go to war'. (Philippe Sands, *Lawless World: Making and Breaking Global Rules*, rev. ed. (London: Penguin, 2006), p. 59.) The invading forces operated under the international law of armed conflict.

It was widely believed that Blair had leaned on his political appointee, the Attorney General, to change his advice, although Goldsmith has denied this. A senior Foreign Office lawyer resigned in protest as the war began. Whether or not it is true that Blair manipulated his own Attorney General, it is undoubtedly the case that Blair broke the Ministerial Code of Conduct by denying his Cabinet access to the full, written advice, as the code requires. But Blair's manipulation of the Cabinet was not new. It had been happening for over ten years on domestic issues as well as international issues.

Even more hubristic was the way, before the war, both Blair and Bush were prepared to manipulate intelligence information to suit their ends. On WMD both leaders presented it as being definitive when in fact it was often nuanced and tentative. Blair personally made significant errors in stressing, when the CIA was unsure, the intelligence from the Italians that uranium oxide or 'yellow cake' was ready to be shipped to Iraq from Niger. Blair was also wrong to allow the claim of only a 45-minute warning of an Iraqi missile firing to be hyped up to include British military targets. The missiles were known to be only short range and unable to hit such targets, but nevertheless No. 10 briefed the tabloid newspapers, which reported prominently that this would mean virtually no warning of attacks against British forces in Cyprus and the Middle East. When reporting to Parliament and explaining privately to colleagues, Blair stripped out too many of the caveats that MI6's innate caution had added. In Blair's defence Lord Hutton's report found the intelligence had not been 'sexed up'. Against that fact, it has to be noted that many people who studied the proceedings of the Hutton inquiry came to a different conclusion, based on reading the same evidence.

Politicians down the ages have presented their side of any case in the best possible light, focusing on what is positive and ignoring the negative. Political spin, as it is called, did not start with Bush and Blair. What was new about them was their readiness to spin intelligence matters. Their 'spinmasters', in the shape of Karl Rove and Alastair Campbell, were not only more powerful than similar figures in the past but they were uniquely deeply involved in the domestic debate about Iraq and themselves briefed on intelligence matters. In Blair's case, Campbell was involved in the publication of two dossiers purportedly outlining the threat posed by Saddam. One of them, which came to be known as 'the dodgy dossier', was dismissed by the Foreign Secretary, Jack Straw, as a 'Horlicks' and was withdrawn by the government itself; the other was widely believed to have used tentative intelligence assessments in order to make a compelling propaganda case in favour of war. One Cabinet minister, the former Foreign Secretary Robin Cook, questioned the validity of the interpretation being put on intelligence information and wisely asked for – and received – a personal briefing from MI6. He then resigned and voted against the invasion of Iraq, saying in the House of Commons that he did not believe the intelligence justified it. Also Charles Kennedy, then leader of the Liberal Democratic Party, came out against the whole venture. The vote in Parliament supported the government and Labour MPs' votes on their own gave Blair a majority. But it was gained at a bitter price.

Blair had had trust from all sides of the political spectrum in Parliament until this point, but his manipulation of the facts that day in retrospect gravely damaged that trust. It may have left lasting damage to the very concept of bipartisanship over foreign and security policy. As the facts became better known, Blair's name began to be defaced to 'Bliar' and he could no longer rely on the automatic support that the British Parliament and people traditionally give to a Prime Minister in a time of war. One journalist in particular, a perceptive political commentator in the *Times*, commenting on Tony Blair's mental state, referred to him as 'unhinged', in the serious sense of the word, as early as 29 March 2003[69] and went on to cite a throwaway remark in Parliament that he would ignore Security Council vetos which were 'capricious' or 'unreasonable'.

Bush's hubris after the invasion

Revealingly, an American book on the Iraq War was simply called *Hubris*.[70] On 1 May 2003, George W. Bush, dressed like a Hollywood actor in flying gear, flew onto the aircraft carrier *Abraham Lincoln* off the coast of California and stood on the flight deck to celebrate victory in Iraq, the ship's control tower emblazoned with the slogan 'Mission Accomplished'. It was a hubristic act of a very high order. It was also a contemptuous, if unintended, insult to the troops in the field, who knew all too well the slogan's patent absurdity. Donald Rumsfeld had the sense to dissuade Bush from actually using the phrase in his speech but even so Bush did say: 'In the battle for Iraq, the United States and our allies have prevailed.' Tony Blair never went so far but his early rhetoric was also far too triumphant.

Rumsfeld, for all his faults, was too cynical to suffer from hubris syndrome. In response to the rapid breakdown of law and order in Baghdad and widespread looting, most of which was the result of Bush accepting his advice that there was no need to increase troop numbers on the ground to control the occupation, the Defense Secretary simply said: 'Stuff happens.' It took a playwright, David Hare, to dramatise the deeper significance of this remark.[71]

The scale of the incompetence after the invasion of Iraq will be something over which historians will long puzzle. How could Washington, particularly the Pentagon, be so incompetent on both the political and the military organisational levels? One answer lies in the aloofness and indifference to detail – both hubristic traits – to which many witnesses of Bush's behaviour testify. A candid assessment of these characteristics in Bush's conduct in office comes from a former Secretary of the Treasury, Paul O'Neill, who served from 2000 until 2002. He comments that from the start Bush was 'clearly signing on to strong ideological positions that had not been fully thought through. But of course, that's the nature of ideology. Thinking it through is the last thing an ideologue wants to do.' O'Neill goes on to describe one meeting as 'like many of the meetings I would go to over the course of two years. The only way I can describe it is that, well, the President is like a blind man in a roomful of deaf people. There is no discernible connection.'[72]

Another example involved David Kay, the former UN weapons inspector in Iraq, who had been tasked since 5 June 2003 with finding WMD, He was at Bush's early morning briefing on 29 July, having flown in from Baghdad the day before. He told the President: 'The biggest mistake we made was to let looting and lawlessness break out,' and he went on to warn that they had not found any WMD and might not find any. Looters, by then, had taken 2 tons of unprocessed uranium, 'yellow cake', 194 tons of high-melting-point explosives and 141 tons of rapid detonation explosives.[73] Kay left the meeting almost shocked at Bush's lack of inquisitiveness on WMD, especially when compared with Dick Cheney's detailed probing.

Bush and his war cabinet discussed 'de-Ba'athification' on 10 March before the invasion but while the conclusions lacked specificity, one person at the meeting has said: 'The thrust was clear: treat these people leniently and try to work with them.'[74] But it is claimed that the eventual document forcing de-Ba'athification, issued by Paul Bremer, was shown to neither Condoleezza Rice nor Colin Powell, who believed the policy drafted in Douglas Feith's office did not represent the compromise the war cabinet had agreed. It was a fateful mistake by Rice, then in charge of the National Security Council, to allow this type of document to go out direct from the Pentagon without being checked by her office. The British Secretary of State for Defence, Geoff Hoon, said in May 2007 that to de-Ba'athify was an error. 'I think we felt that a lot of the Ba'ath people were, first and foremost, local government people and, first and foremost, civil servants – they weren't fanatical supporters of Saddam.'[75]

An example of Bremer's viceregal style was the CPA Order No. 2, which he issued eleven days after arriving in Iraq, in which he dissolved the Iraqi army, air force, navy, ministry of defence and intelligence services. On 12 March Bush and his war cabinet agreed to disband the Republican Guard but retain the regular army. Bremer apparently did not consult the State Department, the CIA or Rice on the terms of the order, nor did he mention it to, let alone consult with, Iraqi politicians. This was perhaps the fatal mistake[76] and one which he refused to change.

Nor were US experts in Baghdad consulted. 'By nightfall, you'll have driven 30,000 to 50,000 Ba'athists underground,' the CIA station chief in Baghdad warned Bremer.[77] In the words of one old Iraqi soldier: 'They're all insurgents now. Bremer lost his chance.' In the interview mentioned earlier, Hoon blithely said that he had argued with Rumsfeld against the summary dismissal of Iraq's 350,000-strong army and police forces 'but I recognised that it was one of those judgement calls. I would have called it the other way.' Blair had said in an interview a little earlier than Hoon's, somewhat bizarrely, that it was always envisaged that the Iraqi army would be built up from 'scratch'[78] According to Anthony Seldon,

> Blair had no direct input on de-Ba'athification or the disbandment of the army, content that Manning and Sawers should represent him. One official said: 'His mind was elsewhere. He was not up with the pace of what was happening at this point,' while another recalled: 'I don't think that the Prime Minister felt he had to take any more of a personal interest in stabilising Iraq. He was leaving it all to the Americans.'[79]

These differences of opinion in the UK as to what was intended over the Ba'athists and the Iraqi army are mirrored in US comment indicative of the confusion.

According to Colonel Lawrence Wilkerson, Powell's former chief of staff, in dealing with Iraq Bush was 'too aloof, too distant from the details of post-war planning. Underlings exploited Bush's detachment.'[80] But Bush was never a pawn; he made the big moves, but sometimes without knowing all the positions on the chessboard. He took Powell's advice all too rarely, Rumsfeld's and Cheney's all too frequently, but he was still choosing for himself. Bush's problem was that he had created what Rice called in August 2003 'the dysfunctional US government'.[81] As the journalist Bob Woodward concluded, around Bush 'the whole atmosphere too often resembled a royal court, with Cheney and Rice in attendance, some upbeat stories, exaggerated good news, and a good time had by all'.[82] The reality was that it wasn't just Bush's government that was dysfunctional, it was Bush himself as Commander in Chief.

One of the ironies of the dysfunction of Bush's administration is that the Cabinet committee structure still worked, but only in some areas – usually those where Rumsfeld did not hold departmental responsibility. Rumsfeld could normally only be reined in by the National Security Council or ad hoc meetings of the principals called by Rice to resolve disputes. One area where inter-departmental cooperation worked well on Iraq was over money. Here the US Treasury played the lead role, initially under Treasury Secretary O'Neill and his under-secretary, John Taylor, who stayed until 2005.* So not everything in Iraq failed; in some areas pre-planning worked and Cabinet members worked together. If only the same relationships could have been enforced by Bush between the Pentagon and State Department with regard to security planning in the aftermath, the core issue on which his dysfunctional government failed.

The figure Bush seems most to have trusted and worked directly with was General Tommy Franks, the regional commander for Afghanistan and Iraq, 'a tall, hot-tempered Texan' who openly disparaged the Joint Chiefs of Staff.[83] In his book *Fiasco*, Thomas Ricks, the former senior Pentagon correspondent at the *Wall Street Journal* and now in the same role for the *Washington Post*, describes Franks 'as a product of his Army and his faults reflected those of that institution. The Army went into Iraq with a considerable amount of hubris.'[84]

Bush imbibed that hubris. Speaking like a cocky sheriff in a cowboy movie, he had promised the American people after the fall of the Taleban government in Afghanistan that Osama bin Laden would be taken 'dead or alive'. This was something his wife teased him about, which was a good sign that not everyone close to him was going along with everything he said.

---

* Obtaining money from Saddam Hussein's accounts in American banks, totalling $1.7 billion, Bush authorised 237.5 tons of US banknotes from $1 to $20 to be sent to Iraq on 20 March 2003. They were made available to pay Iraqis in the early days, helping to lift morale. The money was delivered by a fleet of Boeing 747s and distributed by armed convoys to 240 sites in Iraq – no mean feat. It was exchanged for old dinars, which were then dyed, taken away in trucks and incinerated. The new currency was popular and was appreciating even in late 2006. ('We did get the money to Iraq – dollars to dinars', *International Herald Tribune*, 27 February 2007.)

More than seven years later, the head of al-Qaeda had still not been captured and the Taleban had regrouped to fight back. In Iraq, when it became evident that Saddam had prepared for an organised resistance to a successful invasion and that insurgents were about to cause the occupying forces great difficulties, Bush's response was to say: 'Bring 'em on!' He seemed in the early period to give little thought to how to win more support from influential Sunnis, or how to get Iran to influence the Shiite majority. Ignoring the diplomatic route towards Iran in terms of ensuring success in Iraq was very shortsighted.

In May 2003 a secret proposal was sent by Iran to the State Department for a 'grand bargain' with 'full transparency', aimed at assuring the US that Iran would not develop nuclear weapons. The proposal also offered to end 'any material support to Palestinian opposition groups' and turn Hamas and Hezbollah into 'mere political organisations'. Did Bush abort the planned meeting in Geneva without knowing how seriously it had been pursued by his own government's senior officials?[85] Iran was at its weakest point in May and the CIA now recognises they had abandoned their nuclear weapons programme. Yet there were enough signs of a developing Iraqi insurgency to have made it the best moment for the US to cut a deal with the Iranians, sure in the knowledge that once Iraq was a stable democratic state it would be much easier to ensure Iran stayed off nuclear weapons and followed down the democratic path.

This was the compelling logic for starting to develop a dialogue with Iran in 2002 before the invasion of Iraq. It is easy to forget that the Iranians had been helpful to the United States over the invasion of Afghanistan, in helping to mobilise the Northern Alliance, as well as throwing out al-Qaeda operatives from the holy city of Mashhad when they crossed over into Iran in 2002. Given that toppling Saddam was bound to bring the Shiite majority to power in Iraq, the potential for mischief-making from Iran was obvious. Yet Bush and Blair decided that they could deal with Shiites in Iraq while rejecting a wider Iranian dialogue. It is hard to be sure what lay behind Bush's decision, but overconfidence was certainly a factor. His refusal to have any dialogue with Syria was also damaging for the Syrians could have influenced the Sunnis in Iraq. The Sunni–Shiite relationships were bound to be fraught, with a Sunni minority having to get used, in any evolving democratic system, to no longer being the dominating power. By going it alone coalition forces were laid open to insurgents supported and sustained across Iraqi borders with Syria and Iran.

Bush, who started with focused meetings and confidence in the military and the CIA, revealingly, later began to blame them. He said 'Tommy Franks and the generals' had looked him in the eye and had assured him that the Iraq invasion was undertaken with 'the right plan with the right troop levels'. Franks probably believed this when he said it, before his retirement, but even when he said it, it was disputed within the Pentagon among senior military figures. By the summer of 2003, with the insurgency well underway, it was patently not true. Bush also claimed that the head of the CIA, George Tenet, had been extremely bullish, recalling his claim over WMD in Iraq: 'It's a slam dunk case,' a basketball term meaning certain success.[86] Yet Tenet in his account, published in 2007, claims he 'told the President that strengthening the public presentation was a "slam dunk", a phrase that was later taken completely out of context' and had haunted him ever since it appeared in Woodward's book.[87] The 'blame game' had become a feature of the Iraq fiasco by 2007. In a BBC radio interview Lawrence Wilkerson said that he wished he had resigned in 2004 over Guantanamo and that, reading Tenet's book and hearing Tenet give interviews, he was thinking some people in the CIA had 'lied' to Powell before his Security Council meeting on 5 February 2003.[88]

On 24 September 2003 Bush had a private dinner with Paul Bremer and their wives in Washington. On seeing Bremer's organisation chart showing twenty people reporting to him, Bush said: 'Look, I know you went to business school but I went to business school. You've got too many direct reports.'[89] On 27 October, working out with Bremer in the White House gym, Bush asked about Rumsfeld: 'Does he really micromanage?' and seemed surprised when Bremer said he did. Bush must have been one of the few people in Washington not to know this was Rumsfeld's besetting sin. Another sign that the Commander in Chief had no real grip on his administration.

Politically the time for Bush to reconsider his inability to control the insurgency and review his absurdly optimistic predictions was on 12 November 2004, ten days after he had won re-election as President. The second attempt to deal with Fallujah was still underway when Powell saw both Bush and Blair at the White House. Powell said: 'We don't have enough troops . . . We don't control the terrain.'[90] This was also, by then, the view of Bremer. The following month Bush was being cabled by the CIA station chief in Baghdad: 'We face a vicious insurgency, we are going to have 2,000 dead.' A few days later, on 17 December, a US military intelligence expert told Bush to his face about the insurgency: 'It's robust, it's well fed, it's diverse. Absent some form of reconciliation it's going to go on and that risks civil war. They have the means to fight this for a long time.'[91]

Bush and Blair needed to recognise then that they had to change course and decide to deploy more troops. It had profoundly damaging consequences but they did not have it within themselves to face that reality. A characteristic of hubristic leaders is that they do not change their positions, because this means they would have to admit error. Blair would boast that he had 'no reverse gear' to the Labour Party conference; a more absurd claim can barely be imagined. Margaret Thatcher too claimed virtue in 'the lady's not for turning'. Wise democratic leaders change with the facts or change if they are in error. Bush in his wooden-headedness dismissed calls for reinforcements to prevent the now evident descent of Iraq towards civil war and persisted with hubristic talk of 'winning'. It was not until after electoral defeat in the mid-term elections of 2006 that he decided to send a 'surge' of 21,000 extra troops to Baghdad. By then Blair was being pushed out of Downing Street and he never even tried to increase British force levels or to deploy away from Basra.

In relation to the law, Bush's approach began to mirror that of his legal adviser, later Attorney General, Alberto Gonzalez, that the al-Qaeda threat rendered 'obsolete Geneva's strict limitation on [the] questioning of enemy prisoners'.[92] He sought to avoid the constraints of international law on interrogation and detention after a military intervention. Bush believed that 'the war on terrorism ushered in a new paradigm', that the Geneva Conventions did not apply to al-Qaeda and that Taleban prisoners were 'unlawful combatants' who had lost their PoW status.[93] These decisions were heavily criticised.[94] Bush seemed to relish acting unilaterally with little or no consultation with friends or allies. In effect he ripped up long-standing inter-national agreements and announced that America would do as it liked. The resulting damage in Britain to Tony Blair's credibility, let alone America's credibility abroad, can hardly be exaggerated. The treatment of prisoners taken in Afghanistan, prisoners held in Guantanamo, and what happened in Iraq's Abu Ghraib jail when US personnel taunted and abused Muslim prisoners shocked people of goodwill to the United States. It was a double blow to the UK when something similar was done by British soldiers. International criticism then built up over the policy of secret 'rendition' of terrorist suspects to countries whose regimes were prepared to adopt none-too-scrupulous methods of interrogation. Bush's claim that America condemned all torture seemed to many a contemptuous denial of obvious facts. Fortunately after a period the US legal system, when formally appealed to, began to show in 2006 with regard to Guantanamo policy and in other areas a readiness to challenge Bush's assumption of wartime presidential authority over Congressional law and the constitution. An important debate is now underway inside the United States on presidential war powers.

Blair's hubris after the invasion

In Tony Blair's case, the reality of the invasion's aftermath, and the absence of post-conflict planning, in which he had taken so little serious interest beforehand, was made clear to him on 11 May 2003, only ten days after George W. Bush's 'Mission Accomplished' public relations exercise, when John Sawers, the British ambassador to Egypt, who had previously worked in No. 10 and who had been specially sent into Iraq by Blair, wrote a memo entitled 'Iraq: What's Going Wrong'.[95] His summary of the Americans' aftermath team under General Jay Garner was succinct: 'No leadership, no strategy, no coordination, no structure and inaccessible to ordinary Iraqis.' Sawers's clear view was that more troops were needed and he suggested that 'an operational UK presence in Baghdad is worth considering, despite the obvious political problem . . . one battalion with a mandate to deploy into the streets could still make an impact.' Sawers's view about the need for more troops was backed up by Major General Albert Whitley, the most senior British officer with the US land forces, serving in the US headquarters of Lieutenant General David McKiernan. The issue was whether to bring the British 16 Air Assault Brigade, in Iraq but due to return home, to Baghdad. The Sawers memo could hardly have been a more serious communication to a Prime Minister with thousands of troops at risk in Basra, for what affected Baghdad was soon bound to affect Basra too. But what then happened in Downing Street to the Sawers memo?

According to Anthony Seldon, 'When Blair heard of the plan, he gave his full backing. But nothing happened. It ran into the implacable opposition of Michael Walker, who had succeeded [Admiral Sir Michael] Boyce as Chief of the Defence Staff.'[96] The War Cabinet could have decided to redeploy these troops, and if they had done so, it would have been impossible for Bush to refuse to do so as well. Donald Rumsfeld would not have been allowed to 'offramp' the 16,000 soldiers of the 1st Cavalry Division.

This whole vital question of why so few soldiers were in Iraq and Afghanistan for the aftermath, as distinct from the invasion, is still surrounded by military secrecy and much post hoc briefing. It has as much to do with the budgeting process and future force levels debate in both countries as with professional military judgement of what was needed. In December 2006 141,000 US military personnel were serving in Iraq, together with approximately 16,500 military personnel from twenty-seven coalition partners, the largest contingent being 7,200 from the UK. By early August 2007, after the surge, US forces reached a total of 160,000, well below the 200,000 recommended by Shinseki. That week in 2007 was also the one in which the US Government Accountability Office revealed that the Pentagon could not account for 11,000 AK-47 assault rifles and 80,000 pistols supposedly supplied to Iraqi security forces. Few were in any doubt that US-supplied arms were feeding the insurgency, which was overwhelmingly Iraqi Sunni. What foreign fighters there were came mainly from Sunni Saudi Arabia, not Shia Iran, and the roadside bombs were mainly made by Iraqi army-trained engineers from looted explosives, not imported from Iran.[97]

At the end of the 2003 invasion the British cut their forces of some 30,000 in Iraq to 18,000. Within a year this figure had dropped to 8,600 and by August 2007 it was down to 5,500, spread across Basra Palace and the airport. There was no surge in British forces, so well before Blair stood down as Prime Minister the UK was withdrawing while the United States was increasing its forces. Britain would only with notional 'overwatch' forces be with America to the last, as Blair had promised.

By 2007 it was also quite clear that there were insufficient forces in Afghanistan. It was always going to take just as long to stabilise Afghanistan as Iraq, and, once achieved, stability would be very much harder to sustain. Yet even when NATO became involved the Afghan government was not given sufficient support from the Western democracies, whether in development aid or for its security. By early 2006 the Taleban were resurgent in the south. The UK did then increase its NATO force levels but there was no attempt to warn the British people of the probable consequences. Indeed, Blair's Defence Secretary, John Reid, implausibly implied that troops could come out after three years, having suffered no casualties and not having fired a shot.

Britain has a long history of involvement in Afghanistan and had been defeated there at the height of its imperial power. I had ridden over the hills of central Afghanistan as a student in 1959 and even then the USSR was ensconced, with troops exercising in prohibited areas. When the Soviet Union invaded Afghanistan in 1979 it became very vulnerable, and in the 1980s the US and the UK supported the Afghans in their successful fight to throw the Soviets out. In 2006, after savage fighting in the south all through the summer, it was obvious that NATO needed far more troops, helicopters and mobile reserve forces. NATO met in Riga at the end of November 2006 and failed to come up with anywhere near enough extra support, prompting the author of the excellent book *Jihad: The Rise of Militant Islam in Central Asia* to write: 'The situation in Afghanistan is not just dire, it is desperate. The struggle against Islamic extremism will be lost not in Iraq, Iran or even the Palestinian territories, but in Afghanistan.'[98] That was still the situation on 25 October 2007, when NATO countries rebuffed US urging to increase numbers in the International Security Assistance Force, which by then had a remit covering every region of the country, from the then level of about 41,000 troops. It was summed up in a headline in the *Times* of the same date: 'Some won't fight, some can't fight in the snow: the problems that face NATO.'

Sir Jeremy Greenstock, formerly the ambassador to the UN, who was sent from New York to Baghdad to follow Sawers in 2003, later reinforced the significance of Sawers's views, saying, in the days following victory:

> No one, it seems to me, was instructed to put the security of Iraq first, to put law and order on the streets first. There was no police force. There was no constituted army except the victorious invaders. And there was no American general that I could . . . establish who was given the accountable responsibility to make sure that the first duty of any government – and we were the government – was to keep law and order on the streets. There was a vacuum from the beginning in which looters, saboteurs, the criminals, the insurgents, moved very quickly.[99]

On 29 August 2003 another turning point came with the attack on the Imam Ali mosque in Najaf, which killed Ayatollah Baqir al-Hakim, an influential moderate Shi'ite religious leader. Even Blair's hubristic self-confidence over Iraq began to desert him by the end of the year. On 19 October Blair's problems with his heart meant he was rushed to hospital as an outpatient for cardioversion, the details of which are described later.* When the Prime Minister looked tired and strained through 2003 and 2004, those people in and around Whitehall who knew put it down to these additional

---

* Cardioversion or defibrillation occurs when a carefully timed direct-current electric shock is applied to the chest wall using a defibrillator. If the patient is awake an anaesthetic is usually given to put them to sleep before the shock. After the shock the heart rate usually reverts to normal.

stresses. But Blair's self-confidence about Iraq was shaken too. At the annual diplomatic reception at Buckingham Palace, on 4 November 2003, I had another interesting, but shorter, talk with him about Iraq. He insisted on us sitting down together for a serious discussion in the ballroom and ignoring for a time the foreign diplomats circulating around. This was a very different Tony Blair from the messianic leader I had talked to over dinner in July 2002. He was far less sure of himself and he appeared somewhat chastened by events: the inability to find any WMD in Iraq was clearly troubling him. I felt rather sorry for him and tried to cheer him up. But I was, by then, fearful of a debacle and annoyed at his incompetence.

By January 2004 I had become convinced that Blair had permanently lost authority and credibility and should choose an early moment to step down and take another job. I wrote an article in the *Sunday Times* on 4 January entitled 'Self-rule by Blair gives him a Suez crisis'. While still believing that toppling Saddam Hussein was a legitimate policy I suggested that Blair should step down as Prime Minister no later than the expected 2005 general election. I wrote:

> Blair's authority has been severely, probably irreparably, damaged over Iraq, not just in his party but within the country . . . A well-conducted exit would make it more likely that Blair's prime ministership would be well regarded by history. There are other opportunities that lie ahead for Blair, not least perhaps as the next head of the World Bank.

I have had no substantial discussions with him since.

Though subsequently Paul Wolfowitz was appointed, the United States had for some time been interested in the chairmanship of the International Monetary Fund and letting a European run the World Bank. Blair never fully recovered the authority and trust of the British people and Westminster Parliament that any Prime Minister requires when soldiers are being killed in battle.

We now know that from Easter 2004 Blair was under considerable stress, but it was from a matter unrelated to Iraq or his duties as Prime Minister, and over which the press collectively showed great restraint, not reporting on what they rightly considered to be a genuinely private, family matter. Blair had actually decided to step down as Prime Minister around late May/early June 2004. Whether this was because he had simply recognised that his failure meant it was time to resign, because he was depressed or because he was very stressed we do not know; probably it was a combination of all three. Some friends claim he was despondent and that explained his wobbling. He had also suddenly announced after Easter without any Cabinet consultation that there would be a referendum on the EU treaty, after being urged to do so by Jack Straw. Blair was dissuaded from resigning by some of his loyal friends in the Cabinet. It had some parallels with President Lyndon Johnson's wish to resign when depressed in 1965 after an operation and when things were going wrong in Vietnam (see Chapter 2, p. 66). The Chancellor of the Exchequer, Gordon Brown, not unreasonably wanted Blair to step down so that he could succeed him, but he apparently helped dissuade Blair, thinking that it would be better for Blair and for the Labour Party if the Prime Minister stepped down in the autumn, around the time of the annual Labour Party conference.

Blair's heart problems,* which started in October 2003, may have returned at the time of his visit that summer with his wife to the Sardinian home of the Italian Prime Minister, Silvio Berlusconi, but nothing was substantiated. A family friend of the Blairs, Lord (Melvyn) Bragg, the writer and host of *The South Bank Show*, admitted in public later that Blair had been under tremendous stress that summer, saying in September 2004: 'In my view the real stress was personal and family, which matters most to him.'[100] The biographer Anthony Seldon in *Blair Unbound* has Blair friends saying: 'He was generally not very well in 2004.' Apparently his heart could begin to pound and make him feel 'strange and disconcerted'. He twice had pounding attacks during Prime Minister's Questions in 2004.

By the time the Labour Party conference came around, Blair had told his Cabinet colleagues not only that he had changed his mind about stepping down but that he was staying on to lead them into the next election. This he

---

* From the start there was an attempt to present Blair's irregular heartbeat as a relatively benign condition. Even so, many doctors believed he had atrial flutter, which affects about 50,000 people in Britain. In such an attack the atrial heartbeat can go as high as 250–350 beats per minute. After the heartbeat has returned to normal, the patient is left feeling tired and unwell, but not for long. Before or after Blair's 2003 episode a routine investigation for the common cause of atrial flutter would have taken place: for thyrotoxicosis with blood thyroid tests. Apparent weight loss might merely have been due to a regime of exercise and dieting, not thyrotoxicosis. Any congenital heart disease or any specific heart abnormality, given the history of his father's illnesses, would have been looked for, probably with an ECG (echocardiogram) and other tests. A hereditary conduction defect such as Wolff-Parkinson-White syndrome would have been treated with drugs to slow conduction in a special part of the heart called the bundle of Kent. Abuse of alcohol and any stimulant drugs such as amphetamine would also have been excluded as a possible cause of atrial flutter.

made public on 30 September 2004. But he went on to say that that election would be his last. This was not a well-thought-through statement, particularly since he had also bought a retirement house in London, but one made to damp down public speculation about his health. Next day he went into hospital as an outpatient for a procedure known as a catheter ablation,* treatment for his irregular heartbeat. This time the hospital admitted he had atrial flutter. So at a time when the Iraq crisis needed new policies and fresh thinking, once again Britain had a Prime Minister in office hiding his illness, denying the facts and pretending to be fit and well. The more one now knows of Blair's medical condition, the more one realises why he contemplated stepping down. But those who develop hubris syndrome always believe that they are irreplaceable and start viewing any likely successor with contempt.

On 14 July 2004 the so-called Butler report, on failures of intelligence prior to the invasion, was published.[101] Blair was apparently surprised that it was not more damaging, but it was he who had deliberately circumscribed its terms of reference. When a former Cabinet Secretary such as Lord Butler is asked to conduct an inquiry on the committee of which the Prime Minister places a loyal former Cabinet colleague, that Prime Minister knows that criticism will have to be deftly drafted so as to reflect a consensus and thereby fall well short of any call to resign. Nevertheless the Butler report had, unusually, gone beyond its remit into intelligence failings before the war and commented on the nature of Blair's decision-making process, singling out for criticism his personalised sofa-style way of making key decisions: 'We are concerned that the informality and circumscribed character of the government's procedures . . . risks reducing the scope for informed collective political judgement.' Deftly drafted and in Whitehall language deeply damaging. But the Blair spin machine defused the potential fallout.

---

* Ablation involves a catheter being threaded up into the heart, having been introduced into a blood vessel. The tip of the catheter can deliver a radio frequency burn, which destroys cells in a localised part of the heart, often near the tricuspid valve which is triggering the abnormal heartbeat. The procedure in Blair's case was conducted by Dr Wyn Davies from St Mary's Hospital, which reported it as having been for an atrial flutter and claimed it a success. Blair returned to Downing Street that evening but an official 260-word statement issued by Dr Punit Ramrakha, the Prime Minister's own cardiologist, still avoided any reference to a specific heart condition. The procedure is effective 90 per cent of the time and in the UK some 3,500 ablations are carried out a year, for various types of heartbeat disorder. Untreated atrial flutter can help create a clot in the heart which can then disseminate or embolise to block a vessel in the leg, kidney, intestines or brain. It is therefore treated either immediately or within a few weeks, not normally delayed by eleven months.

When Colin Powell quoted, in his ill-advised statement to the UN on 5 February 2003, intercepts about Republican Guard Corps commanders discussing removing the words 'nerve agents', this was mistakenly taken, because of prior Iraqi deceit, as yet more evidence of Iraqi bad faith. Since then it has been confirmed as actually part of an Iraqi attempt to ensure compliance with UN resolutions.[102] Powell has, to his credit, since apologised for his mistaken presentation to the UN. Yet he was correct to say then that 'Saddam Hussein has investigated dozens of biological agents causing diseases such as gas gangrene, plague, typhus, tetanus, cholera, camel pox, and haemorrhagic fever and he also has the wherewithal to develop smallpox'.

In Tyler Drumheller's book *On the Brink*, the former head of CIA operations in Europe calls into question, more than the Butler report does, MI6's and his own government's reliance on a secret Iraqi agent for the Germans. German intelligence was relaying information to the CIA from an Iraqi chemical engineer who they codenamed Curveball. He alleged that Iraqi scientists had a biological weapons programme located in mobile laboratories and this claim was used in Powell's UN speech. According to George Tenet this was done in good faith and he was not warned before Powell's speech, by Drumheller or anybody else, about reports of German or CIA doubts regarding Curveball.[103] German intelligence, however, told MI6 and the CIA that Curveball was an alcoholic and a fabricator and his allegations should not be accepted.[104] Also regarding Blair's key claim that Saddam Hussein could develop a nuclear weapon in 'between one and two years' and that this claim was based on a judgement of the intelligence community, the Cabinet Office has since admitted after a Freedom of Information Act request that it does not hold any such information.[105]

In a devastating intervention in the House of Lords, on 22 February 2007, Butler spoke for the first time as an individual, not as the chairman of the inquiry. He accused Blair of being 'disingenuous' about the intelligence, a word that only just avoids the parliamentary ban on saying that someone has lied:

> Here was the rub: neither the United Kingdom nor the United States had the intelligence that proved conclusively that Iraq had those weapons. The Prime Minister was disingenuous about that. The United Kingdom intelligence community told him on 23 August 2002 that we 'know little about Iraq's chemical and biological weapons work since late 1988'. The Prime Minister did not tell us that. Indeed, he told Parliament only just over a month later that the

picture painted by our intelligence services was 'extensive, detailed and authoritative'. Those words could simply not have been justified by the material that the intelligence community provided to him.[106]

In the run-up to the general election, Blair tried initially to campaign on his own, downplaying the electoral role and importance of Gordon Brown. This strategy was clearly failing in terms of public opinion, particularly with Labour Party supporters, and Brown was quickly brought back with a central role in the campaign, which Labour won, albeit with a greatly reduced majority and with only 36 per cent of the vote. Labour stayed in power with only 9.6 million votes, down from 10.7 million in 2001 and 13.5 million in 1997.* Blair privately recognised that it was virtually a defeat and said it was his fault because of Iraq. But he still clung on to office and, despite a massive reduction in the number of votes and seats, his self-confidence soon returned. He never understood why the country would not 'move on' over Iraq. His hubris revived in 2005, though never becoming as marked as in 2001–3. His obsession about his legacy dominated decisions over the date of his promised resignation. He conveyed the impression that he and he alone, with a unit in No. 10, could put into effect the programme of change his government had embarked upon for education and health, but as over military matters his constant intervention and 'presentism' destabilised these services, demoralised the professional staff and had the effect of reducing the benefits of the substantially increased funds being allocated. 'Deliverology' as developed by Blair[107] had one all-pervasive weakness, the wish to exercise central control

---

* Much to my surprise, two days before polling day, I was approached in a telephone call from someone at the time very close to Blair to publicly endorse Labour. They were no doubt worried about the Liberal Democrat vote and thinking perhaps an endorsement from me might check this. Next day, on Wednesday 4 July, visiting the Temple of Apollo in the Peloponnese, where the concept of hubris had deep roots, I telephoned back and declined to make the endorsement. I did not want a Conservative government, but wanted the Liberal Democrats to do sufficiently well to ensure a greatly reduced Labour majority. I also hoped that such a result might convince Blair to step down as Prime Minister soon thereafter, if need be by invoking his health for the political purpose of explaining his departure so soon after the general election. I discovered later the very same day, on the eve of polling, when it had been proposed I should declare for Labour, a tawdry interview had appeared in the Sun newspaper with Tony and Cherie Blair boasting about his sexual prowess. ('My Tony is fit … and up for it', Sun, 4 May 2005.) Increased sexual drive is associated with manic behaviour but in this case the interview had every appearance of being carefully staged and timed to come out on the last day of the campaign, with no scope for a critical backlash. Blair's conduct in his high office was now well below an acceptable standard.

from No. 10 of services that should be decentralised and are decentralised in every other large nation in the world.

In the years after the 2001 election officials noted that it was commonplace for Blair to announce what his decisions were early on or right at the start of a meeting, not at the end. His former Cabinet Secretary articulated the general problem in December 2004:

> There is too much emphasis on selling, there is too much central control and there is too little of what I would describe as reasoned debate in government at all levels . . . The Cabinet now – and I don't think there is any secret about this – doesn't make decisions . . . All this is part of what is bad government in this country.[108]

An article in the *Financial Times* on 12 September 2006 wrote of 'the seven habits of a highly ineffective Prime Minister', reckoned to be failure to lead a collegiate administration; failure to manage expectations and follow through on ideas; adoption of the 'heroic CEO' model; top-down autocratic style; failure to listen to constructive, well-intentioned criticism; addiction to arbitrary targets and performance measures; and failure to manage a stable and orderly succession. All these habits are symptomatic of hubris syndrome.

No British Prime Minister, not Asquith, nor Lloyd George or Churchill, not even Eden, has made the strategic decisions over war so personally and without systematically involving senior Cabinet colleagues as Blair did. There are important safeguards in the pre-circulation of papers with the views of military commanders and key diplomats in the field being made known to all the participants and this smaller group of ministers reporting regularly to the full Cabinet. This was the way Margaret Thatcher conducted the Falklands War in 1982 and the way John Major took decisions over the Gulf War in 1991. It was not the way in which the Iraq War was conducted by Blair. The full Cabinet essentially acted as a rubber stamp on decisions which Blair and a small coterie of colleagues and advisers took in No. 10 on foreign policy. What was even more unusual was that a somewhat similar procedure was operating for Gordon Brown's decisions on economic policy. This dual arrangement, meekly accepted by the British Cabinet, meant that it was comprehensively bypassed.

Over Kosovo, President Clinton had been a restraining influence on Blair. Over Afghanistan and Iraq, Bush and Blair, working within a very small and closed group of advisers, seemed to ignite each other.

Blair's capacity to delude himself and confidently believe that all will turn out right has often been commented on in other areas of his government's decision-making. This characteristic is compounded by his barrister's training to absorb his brief quickly and speak confidently on its contents. Too often, however, his knowledge on policy and on its execution, whether national or international, was superficial and lacked for detail when probed. This was his downfall regarding Iraq. One retired general, Sir Michael Rose, who was adjutant general of the British army and commander of the UN protection force in Bosnia, went so far as to call for the Prime Minister to be impeached over Iraq because of 'a blunder of enormous strategic significance'.[109] Other senior generals talked more guardedly in public but trenchantly in private.

While still available to the US Congress, impeachment is no longer an option in the UK. Parliament used to be able to bring anyone to trial for 'high crimes and misdemeanours'. Warren Hastings was a famous case: in 1795, after a seven-year trial, the House of Lords gave a verdict of not guilty on all charges. An unsuccessful attempt was also made to impeach Lord Palmerston in 1848. The threat of impeachment is a check on the power of a US President, as shown in the case of Richard Nixon. Its controversial invocation for Clinton's alleged perjury but not his sexual conduct was correct, but Congress pragmatically refused to actually impeach. The power of impeachment serves a useful purpose, reminding a serving US President that they are not above challenge and that there is a higher authority than themselves which can remove them from power in between elections. In the UK that power lies with a parliamentary vote or the overt withholding of support by the Prime Minister's own party. It is, however, rarely exercised while the Prime Minister is more popular than the party.

I argued for an independent inquiry into the Afghanistan and Iraq wars in a debate in the House of Lords on 29 June 2006[110] and called for something like the Dardanelles Commission, established in 1916 following the military calamity in February the previous year. In October 2006, the head of the British army, Sir Richard Dannatt, openly criticised government policy, something not done since the First World War, and a much weakened Blair did not dare sack him. A former Chief of the Defence Staff, General Charles Guthrie, in 2006 publicly called the manner of the UK and NATO deployment in Afghanistan 'cuckoo'. On 31 October 2006 the UK government just managed to hold off a demand for an inquiry into the Iraq War while conceding that it probably would happen at a later date. Further calls for an inquiry were made in a debate in the House of Lords on 22 February 2007.

Blair's contemptuous disregard for the advice of his colleagues, made clear in his treatment of many of his Cabinet ministers since coming to power, not least his Foreign and Defence Secretaries, began to undermine his power base as early as 2003, when it became obvious that he could not secure a second UN resolution. It is claimed Jack Straw went back to Blair with a personal minute on the Prime Minister's return from the Azores on 16 March 2003. On the eve of war, Straw apparently suggested that the UK should offer troops only for peace enforcement after taking Baghdad while giving full political and moral support for the invasion.[111] Donald Rumsfeld had already made it very clear publicly that the United States was happy to go into Iraq on its own without the British. But Straw's advice went against everything Blair wanted for himself and he rejected it. A resignation from Straw at this point would have been devastating, not just to Blair, who would probably have been disowned by the Cabinet, but also to Britain's reputation in the United States for steadiness in crises.

Yet it is not a proper defence of Blair to claim he had no option. The UK did not have to go to war in Iraq. Exceptionally, Blair, under pressure from Straw, put the issue to the House of Commons for a formal vote and won its endorsement. Forty years earlier, Harold Wilson, Prime Minister from 1964–70 and 1974–6, had faced a similar choice on whether to contribute British forces to the Vietnam War. He chose not to, believing he would not have sufficient influence on the handling of that war because of President Johnson's nature. In December 1964 Johnson wanted Wilson to send the Black Watch, a Scottish regiment, to Vietnam, for primarily presentational purposes. He revealed that to be his underlying attitude by actually saying to Wilson that even a few pipers would be better than nothing! Nevertheless, apart from measured criticism in a speech in the White House in February 1968, Wilson supported an American presence in Vietnam and knowingly risked the jibe that he was 'the tail-end Charlie in an American bomber'.[112] In a recorded telephone call to a third party Johnson refers to 'that creep Wilson' and once harangued him on the telephone: 'We won't tell you how to run Malaysia, and you don't tell us how to run Vietnam.' On another occasion Johnson threatened to withdraw financial support for the pound if Wilson did not send troops but Wilson countered by arguing that if the British withdrew troops from Malaysia and Hong Kong the pound would not need supporting.[113] Few politicians or historians, on either side of the Atlantic, have doubted that Britain was right to stay out of the Vietnam War.

An example of the contempt, which often comes with hubris, that Blair developed and displayed for Straw came from the account leaked from Downing Street of a conversation between the two men after the result of the

French referendum which rejected the EU constitution. Straw, who campaigned for a 'no' vote in the UK's 1975 referendum on remaining in the EEC, welcomed the French result and it was reported, after their conversation, that privately Blair turned to an aide and contemptuously remarked: 'Tart!' This remark, made within Blair's closed circle, was given much publicity and, though formally denied, the story was never quashed.[114] Somewhat undiplomatically, Straw also described any military pre-emptive attack on Iranian nuclear installations as 'nuts'. This appeared quite deliberate, as if he feared that Bush and Blair might use the existence of any threat, as part of a negotiating stance over the Iran nuclear enrichment programme, to legitimise their acting pre-emptively. Straw was demoted by Blair in May 2006 and replaced by Margaret Beckett, someone with no experience of foreign affairs. He also appointed a new Defence Secretary. Blair's Defence Secretary during the war, Geoff Hoon, who remained loyal to the Prime Minister throughout, was also progressively demoted by him.

By the time of the Lebanon crisis in July–August 2006, with two new and inexperienced secretaries of state in the Foreign Office and the Ministry of Defence, there was no one with sufficient experience to challenge Blair's refusal, along with Bush, to publicly endorse a ceasefire. It was an extra-ordinary omission. Even in Israel there was and, after the eventual ceasefire, continued to be detailed criticism of the nature of the Israeli air attacks on Hezbollah targets in Lebanon. Not only did they destroy a large part of Lebanon's infrastructure but they had little impact on Hezbollah's capacity to launch missile attacks. Bush and Blair were both party to the well-judged G8 summit communiqué from St Petersburg calling for a rapid deployment of a multilateral force. Had they made an immediate contribution to the deployment of a rapid reaction force to Lebanon it would have ensured an early ceasefire. In a swaggering display at a press conference in Washington on 28 July, they both refused to put the weight of their diplomacy behind such a ceasefire. Almost alone among world leaders, they seemed to believe that repeated Israeli attacks from the air on targets in Lebanon, including houses and apartments in urban areas, would destroy Hezbollah. The informed criticism of Israeli strategy from inside Israel made their high-flown rhetoric about values appear totally cynical. Both the senior diplomats initially put in charge by Blair of his secretariats disowned the policy, Sir Stephen Wall, who had retired, publicly and Sir David Manning, ambassador in Washington, privately. Blair's stance was morally indefensible and also one that was doomed militarily. He then spoke in Los Angeles about an 'arc of extremism now stretching across the Middle East', totally ignoring that it was his and Bush's failure to make a success of the Iraq invasion which had made by far the largest contribution to setting the region aflame. Strangely, it was Lebanon, not Iraq, that triggered the moderate centre ground of Labour MPs at last to say that 'enough was enough'. They forced Blair to recognise that he had to say publicly in September 2006 that this would be his last party conference.

Exactly how disastrous Iraq had become for Blair became clear when the medical journal the *Lancet* in October 2006 published a study from Johns Hopkins University estimating that 650,000 Iraqi civilians had died since March 2003. Typically, Blair's spokesman dismissed the study, saying: 'It was not one we believe to be anywhere near accurate.' Also Bush said: 'I don't consider it a credible report.' Yet we now know that inside the British government the Ministry of Defence's chief scientific adviser said the research was 'robust', close to 'best practice' and 'balanced', and he recommended 'caution in publicly criticising the study'. A Foreign Office official also had concluded that the government 'should not be rubbishing the *Lancet*'.[115]

No wonder the public's respect for Blair and Bush diminished to all-time lows when they could not even openly admit the likely civilian casualty figures. In my view, as a minimum, both leaders needed to have said publicly that they had made mistakes and regretted they had not applied different policies, but were trying nevertheless to help the new democratically chosen Iraqi government end the insurgency. I remain of the view that this human disaster in Iraq, following the minimal casualties during the actual invasion, could and should have been avoided and that it was not inevitable that a civil war emerged in the aftermath of the invasion. The capture, trial and bungled hanging of Saddam Hussein at the end of 2006 was never seen as a vindication by the Iraqis for this immense loss of life.

After the Republican Party lost control of the House of Representatives and the Senate in November 2006 Bush at last began to change some of his stubbornly held policies in Iraq. He sacked Donald Rumsfeld and appointed a sensible successor in Robert Gates. Vice President Cheney became less influential in relation to Condoleezza Rice as Secretary of State. She talked Bush around to accepting a very limited dialogue with Syria and Iran but only in the context of regional conferences called by the elected Iraqi Prime Minister, Nouri al-Maliki. By April 2007 Bush, belatedly, increased US troop levels in Baghdad, while the UK was reducing its around Basra. With a new intelligent US military commander in Iraq, General David Petraeus, a different and better strategy for tackling the insurgency and stiffening the Iraqi army was underway, much of it recommended in the Baker–Hamilton cross-party report. The United States was, at last, trying to win around some in the Sunni resistance movement and isolate al-Qaeda insurgents and others who had come in to exploit the situation and destroy the invading armies.[116] But Bush no longer commanded the respect of many of those who had voted for him in 2004 and his popularity ratings fell, while the Democrats, with a majority in both Houses of Congress, set about trying to influence the electorate on the timing for a withdrawal from Iraq. By the autumn of 2007 there were some signs of improvement in Baghdad and as US casualties eased slightly, public opinion began to shift towards a slower withdrawal and the issue itself began to lose salience with the voters. General Petraeus deserves to be supported as long as there is a chance of Iraqis coming together to restore order and rebuild their country.

Meanwhile for Blair, nemesis in 2007 could not be avoided. The man who had won power in 1997 with a landslide majority of 179 seats was leaving after bequeathing his party appalling results in the May 2007 national elections in Scotland and Wales and local elections in England. While such mid-term election results have often been turned around in the UK, Blair's self indulgent long goodbye, in search of a legacy, damaged all around him. Never before had any British Prime Minister started so well and yet ended so badly. Blair eventually stepped down on 27 June 2007. His successor, Gordon Brown, had an impressive honeymoon and was tempted to call an early election in September. The country seemed readier to 'move on' over Iraq, which voters were not ready to do under Blair. In Iraq, troops were withdrawn from Basra City. Brown, when the opinion polls moved back sharply to the Conservatives, backed off an election. Yet in the UK Iraq as in the US was losing its salience. By the end of 2007 Basra province was under Iraqi control.

Why Bush and Blair were susceptible to hubris syndrome

In a book about Iraq entitled *Imperial Hubris*, Michael Scheuer, the former head of the CIA's Bin Laden Unit, claims: 'Arrogance is not the worst of it for America as she charges forward in the cause of instant democracy. That honor falls to the category of hubris, buttressed by ignorance.'[117] Even one of Tony Blair's most consistent supporters, the journalist Philip Stephens, wrote an article in the *Financial Times* on 14 July 2006 entitled 'Hubris is the thread running through Blair's many travails'. My own personal experience of Blair is that his hubris started to develop in 1999 during the Kosovo crisis and built up over Sierra Leone and through the general election in 2001 until 9/11. With George W. Bush there is a *prima facie* case that his hubris syndrome developed quickly after 9/11. In running for office he appeared more modest in his foreign policy objectives and gave the impression of being more of an isolationist rather than an interventionist.

This leads to the question: why does hubris develop in some heads of government and not in others? I think the answer lies both in the particular external circumstances and in the internal personality of each individual. The cases of Bush and Blair illustrate both factors at work.

With regard to external factors, it has been suggested by the sociologist Daniel Bell that hubris is the condition of the age. 'Modern hubris is the refusal to accept limits, the insistence on continually reaching out. The modern world proposes a destiny that is always beyond: beyond morality, beyond tragedy, beyond culture.'[118] If this is the prevailing zeitgeist then it would be hard for a leader to resist it but I think Bell's generalisation may apply more to the United States than to Britain. It is certainly true that the beyond has always had a deep appeal to Americans, going back to the times when the frontier of the United States was being pushed ever westwards across the continent. Once America's territorial expansion had been completed the frontier became outer space, a new beyond to explore. And a powerful case can be made that this can-do mentality is something to celebrate rather than criticise and is central to American culture, especially its popular culture. The hero intent on ridding the world of evil and being ready to use whatever firepower may be necessary to do so is the staple of Hollywood films and of much American television. America's cult of youth also plays to this paradigm. Problems arise when this exuberance develops into hubris.

As an importer of American culture, Britain imbibes some of it but it is perhaps less pervasive a force than in the United States. Britain's culture is older and more European and its imperial ambitions are very much of the past. Perhaps a more specific factor liable to feed a tendency to the hubristic is the underlying belief in both countries that each has been and remains a force for good in the world. That this may in many respects be true is likely to strengthen its effect of providing a spur to a potentially hubristic leader to become a crusader in a wretched world.

For the United States, the end of the Cold War undoubtedly created circumstances likely to encourage hubris in its leaders, for it emerged as the sole superpower. The absence of a counter-force to oppose it left the US with the heady illusion that it was the 'indispensable nation' and the world was now its to control. This found expression in Bush's new National Security Strategy, launched in 2002, in which the United States reserved the right to take pre-emptive action where it thought fit and to deter 'potential adversaries from pursuing a military build-up in hopes of surpassing or equalling the power of the United States'. As his narrowly defeated rival in the 2000 presidential election, Al Gore, later put it:

> President Bush now asserts that he will take pre-emptive action even if the threat we perceive is not imminent . . . An unspoken part of this new doctrine appears to be that we claim this right for ourselves – and only for ourselves . . . What this doctrine does is to destroy the goal of a world in which states consider themselves subject to the law, particularly in the matter of standards for the use of violence against each other. That concept would be replaced by the notion that there is no law but the discretion of the President of the United States.[119]

Britain's strategic position in the post-Cold War world is obviously far less powerful than America's and so less likely to encourage any latent hubris in its leaders. Nonetheless, its history has left Britain with a world role and a propensity to want to work closely with the United States which facilitates a hubristic posture, as we supposedly 'punch above our weight'. The phrase 'special relationship' has also for some years been too glibly used, fostering a self-deluding sense of British importance vis-à-vis other nations. Yet undoubtedly the shared history and language of the two countries ensures that the personal relationship which many American Presidents have had with British Prime Ministers is different from that with most other heads of government. The net effect is to make it more likely that a British Prime Minister will feel caught up in the momentum of US foreign policy and in so far as that has a hubristic quality, it is likely to spread across the Atlantic. Policies towards Russia and Israel are examples where this relationship is most likely to exist.

As regards any personality traits which might incline a head of government towards hubris, several in Blair stand out very obviously. Firstly, as all his biographers make clear, his early passion was not politics but performing: both at school and at Oxford his interest was on the stage, performing as an actor or a member of a rock band. It appears that he was not led into politics by ideological conviction – he was, at school, a Conservative and he has always struggled to articulate a political philosophy that would root him in the Labour

Party – but politics offered him a very large stage on which to perform. The brilliance and range of Blair's acting repertoire as a politician has been much noted. Politicians, particularly when they are not interested in detail, appear susceptible to narcissism but actor-politicians tend to be especially narcissistic – their political vision tends to have themselves at its centre, commanding the stage with all eyes upon them. Blair prefers to have information on one or, at most, two pieces of paper; he often does not read background material. It is hardly surprising that presentation and spin become so important for such politicians. But such narcissism in actor-politicians makes the hero role almost irresistible. The potential is, therefore, present for this to induce hubris.

A second trait of Blair's personality concerns his view of himself, in that he thinks he is always good. The journalist and author Geoffrey Wheatcroft has argued[120] that this is so strong in Blair that he is a latter-day antinomian – the name given to the sixteenth-century heretics who believed that 'to the pure all things are pure', meaning that whatever they did was, by definition, pure. Someone who believes they cannot act badly lacks the constraint on behaviour which the fear that they might would otherwise impose on them. They believe, particularly, that they cannot lie, so shading the truth can easily become a habit. Again, the link to hubris is obvious: to believe that you are always good removes an impediment to behaving hubristically. In 2003, Blair grandiosely boasted that he personally had 'got rid of four dictators in Kosovo, Sierra Leone, Afghanistan and Iraq'.[121] But the Kosovo operation in 1999 was a NATO operation, reinforced by Russian diplomacy; in Sierra Leone in 2000 Blair did have a personal success with the UK keeping control of its forces while working closely with UN forces; Afghanistan was initially in 2001 a CIA operation, with US Special Forces; in Iraq there was US domination and, despite the UK being the largest coalition partner, Blair did not confront Bush, instead while talking tough always backing down. Few saw more of Blair's relationship with Bush than Colin Powell, but he told Blair's sympathetic biographer, Anthony Seldon:

> In the end Blair would always support the President. I found this very surprising. I never really understood why Blair seemed to be in such harmony with Bush. I thought, well, the Brits haven't been attacked on 9/11. How did he reach the point that he sees Saddam as such a threat? Blair would express his concerns, but he would never lie down on the railroad tracks. Jack [Straw] and I would get him all pumped up about an issue. And he'd be ready to say, 'Look here, George.' But as soon as he saw the President he would lose his steam.[122]

This can be read as weakness, but more likely it represents the missionary zeal of two people bound together by a project of transcending importance for each of them and blind to its complexities.

Linked to this is the nature of Blair's religious beliefs and the particular way he sees his relationship with God. Blair is a very convinced Christian whose Anglo-Catholic faith matters deeply to him. He tends to downplay it publicly since in Britain a politician playing on their religion is definitely not an electoral asset, as it sometimes appears to be in the United States. However, in a television interview on 4 March 2006, and perhaps because he knew he was committed to stepping down as Prime Minister before another general election, Blair abandoned his reservations in talking about his religion and said, in relation to Iraq: 'If you have faith about these things then you realise that judgement is made by other people. If you believe in God, it's made by God as well.' The implication is that the accountability that really matters to Blair is not to the electorate but to God. If, however, he is already convinced of his own goodness, that accountability is not constraining as it would be to the believer aware of his own capacity to sin. The belief in God becomes a spur to hubris rather than a constraint on it.

In Bush's case his addictive personality is discussed later but his religious personality is also important. His born-again Christianity started with a meeting with the evangelist Billy Graham in 1986, at his family holiday home in Maine, while his father was Vice President. He writes in *A Charge to Keep* how that sparked a change in his heart over the course of that weekend: 'Rev. Graham planted a mustard seed in my soul, a seed that grew over the next year. He led me to the path and I began walking. It was the beginning of a change in my life.' Bush sees his God not as a power to keep him in check but as the force that spurs him on. Not surprisingly, a playwright chose to highlight Bush's views as they might have been before he became President: 'I feel like God wants me to run for President. I can't explain it, but I sense my country is going to need me. Something is going to happen and at that time my country is going to need me.'[123] I have no doubt 9/11 was for Bush that 'something'. He once told the Palestinian Foreign Minister: 'I'm driven with a mission from God. He told me: "George, go and fight those terrorists in Afghanistan." And I did. And he told me: "George, go end the tyranny in Iraq." And I did.'[124] Geoffrey Perret, the biographer of many Presidents – among them Ulysses Grant, Abraham Lincoln and Dwight Eisenhower – wrote: 'This is the language of no other Commander-in-Chief in American history.'[125] From James Madison until George W. Bush, US Presidents issued 322 'signing statements' to ensure presidential power and prerogatives, an average of eight per President. Bush's certainty that his presidency is directed by a higher power has meant that in his first six years in office, he produced nearly 800 such statements in defence of his belief in the doctrine of the unitary executive and the claim in an emergency to rule by decree.

In the world of Bush and Blair, God is the force which drives the hero to challenge reality: hubris is not something to worry about and nemesis is no more than the bad luck all heroes are bound to encounter at some stage on their crusade through this vale of tears. They believe they will have their reward in heaven. Kevin Phillips, an American historian who understands Bush's Republican Party, has written: 'Few questions will be more important to the twenty first century United States than whether renascent religion and its accompanying political hubris will be carried on the nation's books as an asset or as a liability.'[126]

Medical health

Both Blair and Bush have both misled the public about their medical condition. On the face of it they have both appeared most of the time to be fit and well. Yet we cannot be certain what drugs or medication, if any, they may have taken while in office. So we cannot know whether any drugs or medication have tilted them towards hubris syndrome. Neither of them has a history which indicates that they suffer from bipolar disorder. So if they do have hubris syndrome it is most likely to be in its pure form, manifesting itself in high office. Their health has been touched on earlier but now needs to be examined in some detail to see if there are any leads which could indicate why they developed hubris syndrome.

Blair's health

On Sunday 19 October 2003 it was leaked to the press that Blair had attended Stoke Mandeville Hospital near to Chequers, his official country home. Only later was this news officially confirmed by 10 Downing Street. Blair was then transferred to west London's Hammersmith Hospital to be treated, allegedly, for only a commonplace increase in his heartbeat. Later that night, when Blair returned to No. 10, it was stated that he had never suffered from heart problems before. But it was also announced that at Hammersmith Hospital he had had cardiac shock treatment, or cardioversion. In as much as a medical condition was named at all, it was referred to as a 'supra-ventricular tachycardia', a term which in this context was ambiguous. It meant either a relatively benign arrhythmia (an abnormality of the heartbeat), or something from a range of arrhythmias not so benign such as atrial fibrillation and atrial flutter, caused when the arrhythmia has its origins above the ventricles.

Some cardiologists were surprised that the Prime Minister had had cardioversion for what was apparently a mere supra-ventricular tachycardia and felt his real condition was likely to be atrial flutter. The suspicion that there might be something more serious about Blair's medical condition was strengthened by Bill Clinton blurting out: 'As soon as I heard what happened I called to check he was OK. We had a talk and he sounded in good shape . . . I've known about this for a long time. He told me about it quite a few years ago.'[127] In a later TV documentary, Tina Weaver, editor of the *Sunday Mirror*, described 'being at a restaurant in Barcelona, days after the Prime Minister's heart scare last October', when Clinton arrived. She said:

> I told him who I was and asked if he had heard if the Prime Minister had had a heart scare. He was very relaxed about it and said, yes, he had and indeed had spoken to him. Then he went on to say he wasn't surprised, it was a condition he knew about and in fact the Prime Minister had told him that he suffered from this condition some years earlier and it was brought on by a combination of too little sleep and too much caffeine.[128]

On 27 October a statement was issued from No. 10 to deal with Clinton's claim: 'The Prime Minister did not have, and had never had, a heart condition, nor had he had this complaint before.'[129] Clinton's claim was also flatly contradicted by Blair on BBC Radio 2. Asked whether he had told Clinton that he had a heart condition, Blair said: 'No, this is the first time this has ever happened to me. I'm told it is a relatively common thing to have happened to you and it is a relatively minor treatment.'[130] We now know from the diary of a senior Cabinet minister, David Blunkett, that two days after treatment, 'Tony told me when I spoke to him on the telephone that he had had the heart problem, on and off, for fifteen years, but this time he had to go into hospital, which was why it became public knowledge.'[131]

On 4 November I talked to Blair at a diplomatic reception. I noted down afterwards that he was clearly very worried and that he had aged very much, deep in his face, the contours of which seemed to have changed. He also appeared to have lost weight. I wondered then if his heart condition had been brought on by increased activity in his thyroid gland, which would have explained his weight loss and hyperactivity, but there is no evidence that thyrotoxicosis was diagnosed.

In December 2003 there were reports of a specialist doctor rushing to No. 10 on a motorbike to treat Blair because he had developed acute stomach pain. Speculation followed in the press that what had provoked this emergency was a suspected appendix, but for cardiac experts there was far more concern that it could have been a dreaded, though fortunately not common, complication of atrial flutter – a blood clot forming in the atrium of the heart and throwing off a fragment to become lodged in a vessel supplying the intestines and cutting it off from its oxygen supply. This would cause acute abdominal pain. Fortunately all this proved to be a false alarm.

The suspicion that Blair was covering up a long-standing heart condition also increased when a journalist working undercover, as a footman, in Buckingham Palace wrote in the *Daily Mirror* on 20 November 2003 that the Queen had asked a page to delay dinner until she had heard that the Prime Minister's treatment was successful. She was purported to have said to the page: 'He's told me he's had similar complications in the past,' reinforcing Clinton's claim. Downing Street responded to this by repeating: 'The Prime Minister does not have, and never has had, a heart condition.'[132] But one book has claimed that an earlier episode had transpired as early as 1997.[133] This may have stemmed from the report in the *Guardian* on 21 November 2003 that 'a well-placed source from the Prime Minister's Sedgefield constituency claimed that the Labour leader suffered palpitations or a similar condition before the 1997 election and had sought medical treatment in north-east England for a heart ailment when Labour was still in opposition though he believed the problem was not serious'.

It was then suddenly announced, on 1 October 2004, that Blair had been taken back to Hammersmith Hospital for a catheter ablation, as a daytime procedure. Blair's doctor described the condition only as an 'irregular heartbeat' but the hospital called it atrial flutter. The likelihood is that the ablation, involving a radio frequency burn in a localised part of the heart, has been completely successful.

There has been speculation that for some years Blair had been on beta-blocking drugs for his heart arrhythmia.* I asked a scientist with long

---

* There has been a widespread use of beta-adrenergic blocking drugs in clinical medicine, mainly for conditions affecting the heart and in particular for abnormalities of the beating of the heart – arrhythmias, palpitations (see also the footnote to p. xvii in the Introduction). In dealing

experience of these drugs whether he knew of any long-term side effects that might predispose Blair to hubris in that the normal alerting mechanism in the body to strain and stress was being damped down. He claimed to have had a similar request from the Foreign Office about Saddam Hussein! His answer was that he could not find anyone who has reported studies on the long-term psychological effects of beta blockers, nor any on their acute psychological effects, but there were plenty of anecdotes. One of his favourites came from a professional concert pianist, who told him how emotionally 'unbalanced his performances used to be before and after the interval, prior to taking beta blockers. Before beta blockers he would play the first half with such passion that, by the interval, he was emotionally exhausted. Going into the second half after a shower and a quick change, he felt emotionally flat. After taking the beta blocker propranolol he found that he could play the first half in better intellectual control; he no longer felt emotionally drained, giving, for him, a more satisfying second half. The result was a more even performance intellectually. He wasn't sure which experience he preferred or whether the audience noticed![†]

with performance anxiety in the arts and sporting fields beta blockers have been successful in reducing autonomic symptoms such as palpitations and tremors, giving as a secondary effect a reduction in anxiety. Some beta blockers, such as atenolol, cross the blood–brain barrier and may have an effect on the central nervous system (CNS), and this has led to reports of a good response for social phobias. (J. M. Gorman et al., 'Treatment of social phobia with atenolol', *Journal of Clinical Psychopharmacology* (1985), vol. 5, pp. 669–77; M. R. Liebowitz et al., 'Phenelzine vs Atenolol in Social Phobia: A Placebo-Controlled Comparison', *Archives of General Psychiatry* (1992), vol. 49, pp. 290–300.) But subsequent studies have shown only limited efficacy. It is problematic whether long-term use of beta blockers reduces the constraining effect on the personality of people under stress who might otherwise experience autonomic symptoms and perhaps some CNS manifestations of tension. Most people in high-stress situations are able to recognise the signs of tension building up and as a result pull back from avoidable stress until such signs reduce, but there is not much evidence from any systematic study of this phenomenon.

[†] Another anecdote about beta-blocking drugs goes back to 1962: when tentatively introducing pronethanol to volunteers, a young junior consultant volunteered to have an intravenous infusion of isoprenaline before and after an intravenous infusion of pronethanol. The volunteers recorded the expected increases in heart rate, pulse pressure, respiratory rate and amplitude and forearm blood flow. During the isoprenaline infusion they noticed that the subject was very uncomfortable, twisting, turning and grimacing. After pronethanol all these reactions, including the body language changes, were abolished. Following the experiment the consultant was asked about the changes in his body language. He said that on the first run he thought he was going to die! Since then he had comforted himself with the simple explanation that afferent information from all our peripheral organs is constantly being collated in the visceral centres in the 'brain stem'. In this case the information from the heart was saying 'full steam ahead to

One doctor wrote to me speculating on the medication Blair might have been taking, that having watched him on television for many years, he had noticed how his receding hairline had moved forward and then, after his announcement of his treatment for tachycardia, had moved back again. The doctor wondered whether Blair might have been taking Regaine for hair growth, which has a recorded side effect of triggering tachycardias. He postulated that when the doctors realised he was on Regaine, they told him to stop using it. Whatever the truth, the likelihood is that it is Blair's personality rather than his heart condition that has contributed to him developing hubris syndrome.

It had become ever more obvious that Blair covered up the true nature of his illness and misled the electorate as to its seriousness. One investigative journalist labelled it deceit.[134] Blair was not the first and will probably not be the last head of government to do this. It was, however, emblematic of his tenure at No. 10 and compatible with hubris syndrome that he should have embarked on a course of deception.

Bush's health

During the last week of George W. Bush's first presidential campaign, the press uncovered that he had been arrested for driving a car under the influence of alcohol at the age of thirty. In case this story leaked out, it had been made fairly clear in unattributable briefings since 1999 that as a young man the candidate had been too fond of alcohol. This was presented as a passing phase of little consequence. Yet it has now been established that for a period Bush was much more than an occasional drinker: he was an alcoholic. Alcoholism is a condition that, once it has manifested itself, demands constant vigilance to ensure alcohol abuse does not continue in total secrecy and with the patient in denial.

Bush claims he has drunk no alcohol since 1987, but there have been rumours in the press to the contrary. On 13 January 2002 he lost consciousness while sitting on a couch in the White House watching a football game. His head hit the floor, resulting in an abrasion on his left cheekbone. The incident was blamed on a combination of not feeling well in previous days and an improperly eaten pretzel. I was contacted by a British doctor who had visited

escape', while the information from the skeletal muscles was saying 'body comfortably at rest'. Apparently respiratory physicians report that some patients needing intravenous isoprenaline for severe asthma can have similar fearful reactions. So perhaps there are decision makers whose reactions to crises can be unknowingly pacified by beta blockers, but this is unproven and an indication that we need more research.

Johns Hopkins University and in talking to a group of young doctors was told that though the President had been admitted to Walter Reed Hospital, a blood sample of his had been sent to Johns Hopkins which showed a blood alcohol level in the range of 200 milligrams. All such rumours have been emphatically denied by the White House and there are no other reported signs of Bush resuming his drinking habits.

Personality was once thought to play an important role in alcoholism, although it is felt to play a somewhat lesser role today as a contributor to addiction. Yet it is obvious that some people's personalities are part and parcel of their addictive habit and influence whether they overcome their addiction.[135] Bush has never made any secret of the fact that he does not read much and claims that he is no intellectual. But that does not mean – as some assume – that he has a low IQ. While he was a 'C' student, which means he had to rely on the strength of his family connections to get into Yale, he graduated from both Yale Law School and Harvard Business School, which is not possible without a fair amount of intelligence. Some who meet Bush one-on-one claim to be pleasantly surprised by his intelligence. Question marks about Bush relate, therefore, more to his inattention, his incurious nature and inarticulacy: in short, signs that his brain functions in an unusual way. His electoral appeal, particularly his victory in 2004, owed something to his image as a 'regular guy'. Asked once if he could speak French he said: 'No, I can't. I can barely speak English.' Humour has helped Bush defuse some of his gaffes and helped him retain support in the 2004 presidential election.

Since he has been President, records of Bush's medical condition have been published every year by his doctors. On only one occasion was there some delay. They reveal little of interest except that he has an abnormally low pulse rate. Yet for some years Bush has been uttering so many malapropisms that besides making him the butt of many jokes, they have focused doctors' minds on whether or not he has a form of dyslexia. His brother Neil is reported to suffer from dyslexia.* There has also been speculation on whether Bush has adult attention deficit hyperactivity disorder (ADHD), a lifelong disorder characterised by overactive behaviour, short attention span and poor

---

* Dyslexia is a difficulty in reading or learning to read. Sometimes called 'word blindness', specific dyslexia affects between 4 and 8 per cent of otherwise normal children. It is three times more common in boys than in girls. There is often a family history. The writer Mark Crispin Miller in *The Bush Dyslexicon: Observations on a National Disorder* (New York: W. W. Norton, 2002) argued that Bush's language is noteworthy 'not merely for its formal incorrectness but for its substantive irrationality'. He quotes any number of examples, some amusing, some revealing.

concentration. Also ADHD is one of four psychiatric disorders, the others being depression, post-traumatic stress disorder and schizophrenia,[136] which commonly co-occur with substance abuse disorders such as alcoholism.*

Armchair psychiatrists, according to one American magazine,[137] have for some time argued that Bush suffers from a classic case of narcissistic personality disorder (NPD). This is a highly complex psychological-behavioural syndrome. The diagnosis of NPD was accepted by the American Psychological Association (APA) as recently as 1990. It is associated with a pervasive pattern of grandiosity (in fantasy or behaviour), need for admiration and lack of empathy. It begins in early adulthood, and sufferers often have an unreasonable expectation of especially favourable treatment or automatic compliance with their expectations. They can also be interpersonally exploitative, in other words they take advantage of others to achieve their own ends. Psychoanalytic studies of George Bush offer deeper insights. Psychoanalysts have often written about political leaders whom they have not treated as patients: Sigmund Freud, for example, wrote a book about Woodrow Wilson using evidence provided by a colleague of Wilson's. Blair has been the subject of an analytical study by a former Labour MP, Leo Abse.[138]

One of the analytical books on Bush is by Dr Justin Frank, who believes that the characteristics of his personality overlap meaningfully with a description of what he defines as a megalomanic state:

> The troubles in Bush's early childhood might have made a megalomanic solution an attractive way to adapt – to cope with, and even triumph over, his circumstances. Both megalomania and mania exhibit three overtly similar defensive characteristics: control, contempt, and triumph. Simple mania involves love and the need to deny dependency or loss of a loved person; megalomania involves hate and a need to triumph over paranoid fears. A manic

---

* In the United States ADHD is commonly diagnosed among children, as many as one tenth of all children in some states, but it often peters out before reaching adulthood. Severe symptoms of restlessness are treated with methylphenidate (Ritalin), an amphetamine-like drug which stimulates that part of the brain which allows for concentration and focus on tasks. ADHD is found with learning disorders such as dyslexia. It also co-occurs with substance abuse, including alcohol, a further reason for speculation in Bush's case. Recent genetic studies in ADHD with reading disabilities point to possible noradrenergic mechanisms in the brain being affected. (Bruce F. Pennington, 'From Single to Multiple Models of Developmental Disorders', *Cognition* (2006), vol. 101, pp. 390–3; J. Stevenson et al., 'Attention Deficit Hyperactivity Disorder with Reading Disabilities: Preliminary Genetic Findings on the Involvement of the ADRA2A Gene', *Journal of Child Psychology and Psychiatry* (2005), vol. 46, pp. 1081–8.)

person wants to repair the damage he's caused, once he recognises it. He feels guilt. The megalomaniac is indifferent to any damage he caused, because he had a reason for his actions; he is without guilt or compassion, and incapable of even thinking about making reparation.[139]

The relationship between such a megalomanic disposition and hubris hardly needs spelling out.

What drove both Bush and Blair into hubris syndrome is not easy to quantify; there are some predisposing factors in their character and perhaps a few medical clues, but nothing that is definite. I believe the syndrome should be studied to find out why it affects some heads of government – and leaders in other fields – but not others. It is not in itself a personality syndrome. It is not a condition, usually, which those leaders affected by it bring to office. Rather it appears to develop when heads of government have been in power for a while.

Part IV:

Lessons for the future

8

Safeguarding against illness in heads of government

> The problem of restraining power has always been the central problem of government . . . Power is dangerous. It grows by what it feeds upon, dulling the perception, clouding the vision, imprisoning its victim, however well-intentioned he may be in that chill of isolation of a self-created aura of intellectual infallibility which is the negative of the democratic principle.
>
> Raymond Moley*

Does illness amongst heads of government really matter? After all, it is often said, somewhat cynically, that we get the politicians we deserve. An extension of that scepticism argues that the malady we should really be concerned about is not so much the illness that may affect individual heads of government from time to time but the one that affects the political system as a whole.

Representative democracy

The problem is that these two 'illnesses' are linked. Bad decisions and incompetent execution mean that the very essence of representative democracy, a political leader's capacity and willingness to lead, is eroded. In its place has emerged consultative democracy, whose leaders see they can have an easier life if they are content simply to allow opinion polls and focus groups to dictate

---

* Moley was a political science professor from Cleveland taken on as a speech writer by Franklin Roosevelt when he decided to run for governor of New York in 1928. On 24 June 1936 Roosevelt had a furious row with Moley over his criticism of the President in *Today* magazine and this marked the end of their friendship.

their actions; a lesser version of this is called triangulation and can be demonstrated as a simpler way both to win and to keep power. Criticism of representative democracy may seem very contemporary after the debacle in Iraq, but we should be careful about embracing consultative democracy. Fifty years ago Walter Lippmann, the celebrated American liberal columnist, perceived that politicians were increasingly governing on the basis of popular sentiment. This alarmed him because he felt that during his lifetime popular opinion had been wrong on many big issues of the day. He wrote:

> It can be deadly to the very survival of the state as a free society if, when the great issues of war and peace, of security and solvency, of revolution and order are up for decision, the executive and judicial departments, with their civil servants and technicians, have lost their power to decide.[1]

He concluded that the 'devitalisation of governing is the malady of democratic states'.

As tests for gauging public opinion have become ever more sophisticated, politicians have learnt to triangulate between different views. Today, fewer leaders than before are elected with a definable public philosophy on which they have campaigned and by which they can be trusted by the electorate to govern. We have developed more fettered democracies, constrained by the power of issue-orientated public opinion, which is not of itself always stable and can easily shift and even turn right around. In such a political atmosphere it has become all too easy for politicians seeking power to choose simply to be led by the dictates of public opinion. The more accident-prone course is for political leaders to develop strong convictions, to argue for them and be prepared to stick to them in the teeth of public opinion. The concept of representative democracy has still never been better expressed than by Edmund Burke to the electors of Bristol on 3 November 1774: 'Your representative owes you not his industry only, but his judgement: and he betrays, instead of serving you, if he sacrifices it to your opinion.' Restoring the reputation of representative democracy means more successful decision-making; incompetent decision-making does great harm to the whole concept. The last century has shown that leaders who wish to exercise their independent judgement achieve poor results when they are ill and as a consequence representative democracy has itself been damaged.

It is a central thesis of this book that indecision or wrong decisions, as a result of illness amongst heads of government over the last hundred years, have been among the factors producing poor government. There has been all too little systematic research specifically focused on heads of government and the relationship between their ill health and poor decision-making.

Medical assessment

One recent general study shows that all doctors grossly underestimate the degree to which the decision-making capacity of their patients is affected by illness.[2] In England, legislation passed in 2005 defines loss of mental capacity as 'an impairment of or disturbance in the functioning of brain or mind' and its list of diagnostic symptoms refers to cases where patients

- are unable to understand information relevant to the decision;
- cannot retain the relevant information;
- are unable to use the information as part of the decision-making process;
- cannot communicate the decision.

The study shows that the lack of capacity to make decisions is common in medical in-patients but that this incapacity is rarely detected by clinicians or relatives, even when the patient is seen frequently. Doctors were found to be assuming capacity unless there was strong evidence to the contrary. History demonstrates that personal physicians looking after heads of government raise the threshold even higher than with their other, less well-known patients, before registering an impairment of decision-making.

As we live longer, cancer and arteriosclerosis have replaced tuberculosis and pneumonia as major causes of death. But initially they can present in the form of mild depression or reduced energy and motivation, which can impair the quality of decision-making, in political leaders as well as anyone else. The World Health Organization now rates depression amongst the top two disease burdens in established market economies. An article published in 2006 found 29 per cent of all US Presidents suffered mental illness while in office and that 49 per cent had exhibited features suggestive of mental illness at some time in their life. These are higher percentages than one would expect when comparing with the general population. Between 1906 and 2006 seven Presidents were judged to have been mentally ill while in office: Theodore Roosevelt (bipolar disorder), Taft (breathing-related sleep disorder), Wilson (major depressive disorder), Coolidge (major depressive disorder), Hoover (major depressive disorder), Johnson (bipolar disorder) and Nixon (alcohol abuse).[3] Mental illness has affected many heads of government in other countries. Some of them have been able to hide their depression from people close to them, and from the public. It should be an acknowledged duty on every political leader who decides to run for office to be open about their true health. To campaign with the knowledge that they are suffering from an illness that could impair their capacity to lead means they do not have the quality of honesty that a nation has the right to expect of its leaders. If the voters are given the facts independently about a candidate's health, it is up to them to determine whether a particular illness in that candidate is a disqualification for office.

Automatic disqualification is not justifiable. There is little doubt that in coping with illness a person's personality may be changed, but sometimes this can be for the better. Franklin Roosevelt's polio is quoted as an example of illness making the man. John F. Kennedy's Addison's disease shows why we should not countenance a particular illness being a disqualification for high office. Repeatedly in this book I have highlighted how political leaders have overcome the effects of their illness, have been disciplined by it and have governed wisely in spite of it. For example, it appears that Theodore Roosevelt and Winston Churchill when head of government suffered fewer depressions and their mood swings were easier to deal with than when they were out of office. Perhaps the huge responsibilities they were carrying for the well-being of others took them out of their own problems.

Nonetheless, even though the relationship between illness and the capacity to govern is not a straightforward one, it is something of which democratic societies need to be more aware. Democratic politicians as diverse as Woodrow Wilson, Franklin D. Roosevelt, Churchill, Kennedy, Johnson, Nixon, Pompidou, and Mitterrand have not trusted their electorates with true factual information about their health. Some leaders kept their illnesses secret for years.

Secrecy

It is argued in Chapter 5 that had Britain, the United States and France known about the Shah of Iran's illness in 1977 or 1978, they could have persuaded or pressurised him to leave the country for treatment in Switzerland, creating the opportunity for a regency council with real delegated power to start a process of democratic reform. This could have forestalled the return of Ayatollah Khomeini and much that has subsequently happened in Iran, for there is no evidence that the bulk of the Iranian people wanted an Islamic-dominated state. The Shah's secrecy over his illness has some similarities to that of the Pakistani leader Muhammad Ali Jinnah, who had advanced tuberculosis diagnosed in 1946, a year before Indian partition and independence. The complete medical secrecy he imposed surrounding his health had the profoundest consequences for the lives of millions of people on the Indian subcontinent.

Admiral Lord Mountbatten, Queen Victoria's great-grandson, was appointed Viceroy of India in 1946 by the Prime Minister, Clement Attlee, and charged with transferring British sovereignty in India to a single, independent nation within the Commonwealth by 30 June 1948. If he could not broker an agreement, he was asked to come up with his own plan. Jawaharlal Nehru, leader of the Congress Party, the grouping that represented all races but was seen as commanding the allegiance of the Hindu majority, told Mountbatten that he and his party would do anything to avoid partition. Jinnah, the leader of the Muslim League, told Mountbatten in unequivocal terms that there had to be a separate viable Muslim state.

Unbeknownst to Mountbatten or to British intelligence, in June 1946 Dr J. A. L. Patel, a Bombay physician and personal friend of the Muslim leader, had taken an X-ray of Jinnah's lungs. For the past decade Jinnah had, according to Patel, lived on 'willpower, whisky and cigarettes'. He was told he had advanced tuberculosis.*

On 15 August 1947, power was transferred to two independent states, India and Pakistan. Yet had Mountbatten maintained Attlee's original timetable for independence by 30 June 1948, it would have become clear how ill Jinnah was in the early part of that year and Nehru and the Congress Party might have

---

* Tuberculosis is an infection caused by *Mycobacterium tuberculosis*. It most commonly affects the lungs but it can involve lymph nodes, kidneys, bones, skin, the intestinal tract and the meninges around the brain. Tuberculosis was common in the first half of the twentieth century, then dropped away with chemotherapy in the 1940s and in the latter part of the last century – but at the start of the twenty-first century it returned with a considerable increase in cases, largely due to drug resistance developing in the tubercule bacillus and the increase in HIV infections. Jinnah had two large pulmonary cavities, and was told that unless he changed his habits, he would be dead within one or two years. Jinnah knew that if any of his opponents learnt this – whether within his own party, among the Hindu leaders or in the British government – they would seek to postpone negotiations on independence. He insisted, therefore, on his doctor maintaining the utmost secrecy. Jinnah also refused to slow down his political activity or to stop smoking. He pushed Mountbatten for a speedy resolution and never showed the slightest readiness to compromise.

been persuaded to focus on reviving the UK Cabinet Mission's proposals of 16 May 1946.*

The immediate loss of life following the partition of India was immense and serious wars between the two sides followed. Later Pakistan split, with East Pakistan becoming Bangladesh in 1971. Today, tensions still remain over Kashmir with the Indian and Pakistani military confronting each other across disputed territory. This is particularly worrying since both countries now possess nuclear weapons. If Jinnah's illness had been known to Mountbatten, Nehru and Gandhi, there might never have been the three countries we see today – two predominantly Muslim, Pakistan and Bangladesh, and India predominantly Hindu but with a very large Muslim minority. Had India remained undivided, it would have contained within its democratic structures virtually the whole sub-continent.

Another interesting issue is when political leaders are secretly kept alive by modern technological means. Generalissimo Francisco Franco of Spain was kept alive by life support machines. He was one of the few dictators to manage the transition to democracy. Illness was not a factor during his long period of rule, except that his own terminal illness came close to damaging a successful transfer of power. The life-saving techniques and machines which surrounded Franco had enabled those around him covertly to perpetuate his life. Then the press broke the conspiracy of silence and Franco's dire condition was described very publicly in grotesque detail in November 1975.† It was no way for an 82-

---

* These proposals suggested a country federated into three sections, A, B and C, which grouped various provinces. This gave Muslims almost complete autonomy in sections B and C, where they predominated, and after ten years a majority vote of any provincial legislature could request its position within its allocated section to be reconsidered. Meanwhile, the central government would control defence, foreign affairs and communications. (Victoria Schofield, *Wavell: Soldier and Statesman* (London: John Murray, 2006), pp. 351–8.) The Muslim League had accepted this proposal on 6 June 1946 but the Congress Party made only a qualified acceptance on 24 June, Mahatma Gandhi having insisted on a Muslim nominated by Congress being in the government. Jinnah was outraged that the Cabinet Mission did not endorse its own commitment to go ahead with the interim government even if the Congress Party had declined to join it, and the negotiations ran into the sand. Returning to the earlier compromise proposal in 1946 or 1947, in the knowledge that Jinnah's health ensured that he would not be alive for long, would have offered an outside chance that partition might be avoided. Jinnah became Pakistan's first President in 1947 and died on 11 September 1948.

† The United Press Agency reported about how four mechanical devices were used on Franco: 'One attached to his chest shocks his heart back to normal when it slows or fades; a pump-like device helps push his blood through his body when it weakens; a respirator helps him breathe, and a kidney machine cleans his blood. At various times in his 25-day crisis, General Franco has

year-old head of government to die and his family stepped in. He had been suffering from diabetes since 1963, a disorder affecting the metabolism of carbohydrates which allows sugar to accumulate in the blood. He also had Parkinson's disease. That history of illness should have meant that he and his political supporters would have made arrangements for the succession long before. In fact these had still not been completed in all their detail when Franco lapsed into a coma. One of the reasons for keeping Franco alive while in a coma was so that his aides could 'ensure that the President of the Council of Ministers, who would have been chosen by Juan Carlos, the new king, after Franco died, would be reliable'.[4] Franco was due to reappoint the existing office holder when his term of office expired on 26 November. Franco's daughter, however, insisted that her father be allowed to die before this date and so his life support machines were removed on 19 November and he died of uraemia on 20 November 1975.*

Ferdinand Marcos became President of the Philippines in 1965 at the age of forty-seven. As early as 1971 he was diagnosed as suffering from lupus erythematosus,† an auto-immune disease affecting the arteries, particularly those of the heart and the kidneys,[5] but it did not affect his ability to govern for some years. Marcos demanded that his aides and doctors keep his condition totally secret. By 1978 he was seriously debilitated, his face had become puffy,

had tubes down his windpipe to provide air, down his nose to provide nourishment, in his abdomen to drain accumulative fluids, in his digestive tract to relieve gastric pressure and in his left thigh to relieve the pressure of blood clots. The effort in itself is remarkable considering he has had three major heart attacks.

'He has undergone emergency surgery twice – once to patch a ruptured artery to save him from bleeding to death, the second time to remove most of an ulcerated and bleeding stomach for the same reason. He has taken some 15 litres (4 gallons) of blood transfusions. His lungs are congested . . . his kidneys are giving out and his liver is weak. Paralysis periodically affects his intestines . . . he suffers occasional rectal bleeding. Ascites causes an accumulation of fluid in his abdominal cavity. Blood clots have formed and spread in his left thigh. He has lost 9.9kg (22lbs) from his pre-crisis 49kg (110lbs).' (Roy Porter, *The Greatest Benefit to Mankind: A Medical History of Humanity*, pb ed. (New York: W. W. Norton, 1999), p. 700.)

* Uraemia is a build-up of urea in the blood. It is a clinical state resulting from renal failure. The symptoms are often the result of acidosis affecting the blood, the result of an impairment of renal functions. It can be due to a disease of the kidneys or it can come from a stricture or blockage of the renal artery. It can also result from a build-up of back pressure or an obstruction to the ureter. Headaches can be a presenting symptom and drowsiness in daytime. It can lead to loss of consciousness and convulsions and it is a very dangerous condition, usually treated by dialysis.

† Lupus erythematosus is an auto-immune disease which affects the arteries supplying the skin or internal organs; it can affect the whole body, in which case it is known as systemic lupus erythematosus. It is a serious and potentially fatal condition, predominantly in women. The

almost certainly as a result of treatment with steroids, and he started to have intermittent renal dialysis. By 1980 his kidneys were failing. He had an unsuccessful kidney transplant and from then on had regular dialysis. Soon he was being kept alive by his kidney machine but it was not until December 1984 that it was officially admitted that he was suffering from a serious illness. He had to flee the country after losing the election in 1986 and died in Honolulu in 1989.

Mental illness

Mental illness tends to make politicians very secretive and this is because public opinion still, today, regards psychiatric illnesses as more frightening than physical ones. This leads some doctors to argue that releasing psychiatric information to the public deserves exceptional handling and that some parts can legitimately be withheld. But selective disclosure is not acceptable and politicians must educate public opinion and trust their judgement. Politicians have long been afraid that the revelation or announcement of any mental illness will damage their candidature. They remember the experience of Senator Thomas Eagleton, who was forced to resign as George McGovern's vice-presidential candidate before the 1972 presidential race when it was leaked that he had had three depressive episodes.* At the start of the twenty-

body's natural immune system turns inwards, attacks connective tissue and causes severe inflammation. Recent research suggests that the affected person is short of an enzyme called D Nase 1, which degrades DNA (deoxyribonucleic acid). Treatment in these cases can be with D Nase 1. Alternatively cases are treated with non-steroidal anti-inflammatory drugs which help to reduce joint pains. Anti-malarial drugs can reduce the skin rash. Corticosteroids help with pleurisy and neurological symptoms. Symptoms are arthritis, pleurisy, nephritis or infection of the kidneys, leading to kidney failure and sometimes dialysis. Neurological or psychiatric symptoms feature. The illness is found worldwide but more commonly amongst the Chinese and Afro-Caribbeans.

* Senator Eagleton was nominated by George McGovern as his running mate in the 1972 presidential election. He had been a highly successful politician in Missouri: in 1960, at the age of thirty-one, he became the state's attorney general and in 1964 its lieutenant governor. Then in 1967 he went to Washington as a senator. Shortly after his nomination by McGovern, amidst a mass of rumours, he held a press conference and announced he had been in hospital three times for 'nervous exhaustion and fatigue': firstly in 1960, after his state senatorial campaign, when he had electroconvulsive therapy (ECT); secondly in December 1964, after having been elected lieutenant governor, when he did not have ECT but just rest and treatment for a stomach pain; thirdly in 1966, when he was in the Mayo Clinic from September to October receiving ECT again for depression. Senator Mike Mansfield, the Democratic leader in the

first century public attitudes to mental illness contain less prejudice. But any presidential candidate would hesitate to take on still-existing prejudice against mental illness in general and electroconvulsive therapy in particular when choosing someone for a post which was once memorably described by a potential incumbent as 'not worth a bucketful of warm spit'.

Only two heads of government in the last hundred years have been formally certified as insane. The French President Paul Deschanel, referred to in Chapter 1, resigned voluntarily with what modern neurologists believe was frontotemporal dementia in 1920,[6] and in 1952 King Talal of Jordan was forced to step down because of schizophrenia.

A more enlightened attitude amongst the public towards mental illness depends on heads of government dealing honestly with all their own health issues. Heads of government have a duty to be open about their health, and the media have a duty to expose them when they evade the truth. It is unlikely that cover-ups of presidential illness of the magnitude perpetrated by Woodrow Wilson could happen in the United States now. Nor would the American press be as complicit now as it was in covering up Kennedy's illness. But the story told in Chapter 6 of how François Mitterrand was able to cover up his advanced prostate cancer for more than eleven years should be seen as a warning. The cover-up, admittedly assisted by French privacy laws, went on despite the lessons that appeared to have been learnt after the death of President Pompidou in office in 1974, whose illness had also been hidden from the French people. I used to think that the openness with which President Bush Sr dealt with his thyrotoxicosis presenting as atrial fibrillation in 1991 meant that we could expect truthfulness in the twenty-first century, but this has not proven to be the case, with Blair, Bush, Chirac and Sharon all covering up their illnesses.

Senate, said that he would routinely have been advised by the physician serving the Senate if any senator had any serious medical problem, but that to the best of his knowledge Eagleton had been in 'excellent physical and mental health' during his four years in the Senate. Many others defended Eagleton's fine political record. After defying calls for Eagleton's resignation, and in a polarised atmosphere about his own candidature, McGovern felt Eagleton should come off the ticket for the sake of party unity. Had Senator Eagleton been open throughout with McGovern's top aide, Frank Monkiewicz, and had McGovern made his choice of Vice President after allowing some public debate based on full disclosure of Eagleton's health, the outcome might have been different. But the public's fear of mental illness then was strong. A year later McGovern said he had been mistaken in removing Eagleton.

The role of personal doctors

How, then, are democratic societies to ensure that they have the information they need about the health of their political leaders? In the past the public has often had to rely solely on the statements made by the personal physicians of heads of government. But the primary responsibility of a personal physician to their patient means that they cannot be expected to balance the best interests of their patient against the best interests of the country. Personal physicians should not be expected to attempt to combine the two roles. When they do, it usually backfires. Take the example of Lord Moran, Churchill's personal physician, an eminent doctor and a president of the Royal College of Physicians. His attempt to combine the two roles ended in failure. He has rightly been criticised for his misleading public statements about Winston Churchill's health, particularly in 1953 (see Chapter 1). President Mitterrand's physician, Dr Claude Gubler, is another whose experience of trying to combine the two roles of personal physician and independent assessor failed. At a medical ethics enquiry in June 1996 Gubler admitted that his public disclosure of Mitterrand's illness so soon after his death had violated medical confidentiality but he claimed that he had been caught between two codes of honour and he wanted to acknowledge that he had signed medical bulletins revealing less than the truth. Requiring a personal physician to combine the two roles may not even be in the patient's best interests, never mind democracy's. Often a combination of secrecy and the political limits set on personal doctors results in the treatment for heads of government falling below the best standards. The best clinical practice, though readily available to a head of government, is simply not utilised because of their fear that the press and public will then discover the truth about their health. John F. Kennedy's initial period in office gives a good example of this.

Purists argue that any public statements by doctors about their patients are a breach of the Hippocratic oath.[*] Their view is that doctors should go to their graves with the secrets of their patients and not even leave behind any paper records for posterity. But there is another view and it is the one that I take –

---

[*] There are two versions of the oath, the classical version, 'What I may see or hear in the course of the treatment or even outside of the treatment in regard to the life of men, which on no account one must spread abroad, I will keep to myself, holding such things shameful to be spoken about', and the modern version, 'I will respect the privacy of my patients for their problems are not disclosed to me that the world may know'.

that history can sometimes gain from a personal physician's insight and that publication devoid of personal detail but dealing openly with the medical facts can be very valuable after a period of time, perhaps delayed until after close family members have given permission or died. The Shah's three closest doctors, Dr Abbas Safavian, Professor Jean Bernard and Dr Georges Flandrin, did reveal some information but did not cross this line of discretion and taste and they retained the confidence of the Shah's family. By contrast, Moran did cross the line and was rightly criticised by the family for publishing a book in 1966, so soon after Churchill's death, quoting from what he claimed was a diary of his time as personal doctor to Churchill,[7] though it was not a conventional daily diary. The model for the right way to release information by a personal doctor is that followed by the distinguished neurologist Lord Brain, whose son released his father's account, with the approval of the Churchill family, in 2000.[8] But in many ways, Gubler, unlike Moran, was right to want to disclose the Mitterrand cover-up soon after the event. By doing so he helped to ensure that a public debate took place; his disclosure was serving the national French interest and will hopefully lead to more openness in France and elsewhere. It can be argued too in Gubler's defence that he needed to demonstrate in a graphic way what an impossible position he had been in and had allowed to develop, given the demands made on him by Mitterrand.[9] Probably Gubler's mistake was not to publish initially in a medical journal and to go into too much personal detail about Mitterrand's personal reaction to his illness. By contrast, Moran's disclosures on Churchill had little immediate relevance for public policy though in the medium term they were helpful for historians.

Britain has a rule whereby some ministerial records are not made public for a period of thirty years, although it has been largely circumvented for government policies by freedom of information legislation. A reduction to twenty years would have the merit of not leaving so long a period of time to elapse that the record of history can be permanently distorted. After such a statutory waiting period and following the death of the patient, disclosure of all health details is, in my judgement, compatible with the Hippocratic oath. The personal physician of a head of government, if they disclose, should err on the side of discretion for non-medical information and should choose their words with care. It is also preferable to publish in a medical journal, where standards of objectivity with peer review are followed and there is no question of the doctor profiting from the revelation.

As for what we should expect from the personal physicians of heads of government when their patients are still alive, a guiding principle should be that personal doctors should not lie or consciously mislead if they do make public statements about their patient's health. To do so undermines public trust in the integrity and independence of the medical profession. A personal doctor has no mandate to disclose that which their patient refuses to sanction, but the power they do have – one that many doctors have used in the past– is the right to keep silent when their patient wants them to mislead. It would be wise for professional guidance to recognise this and recommend personal doctors not to sign any public medical bulletins on the health of their patients. Let that be done by the patient or their personal office, or by bringing in another doctor.

Independent medical assessment – before taking office

If the public cannot rely on personal physicians to keep them informed about the health of their head of government, how should they be informed? One way to find guidance on this question is to look to how practice has evolved in commercial boardrooms. Public companies worldwide have a duty to protect their shareholders from illness affecting their chief executive officers (CEOs). They rely on boards having some independent directors and on adopting rules of good governance. Such scrutiny month by month of company leaders is becoming far more detailed and effective than that which political cabinets exercise over their head of government. It is also becoming commonplace for the board of directors of a public company to insist on having a medical report prepared on their potential CEO prior to their appointment and many insist on regular yearly updates. Some boards insist on mentors to help executives with personal problems in their leadership style. Some companies in the United States are now insisting that new CEOs meet health status disclosure requirements and have surmounted legislative impediments hitherto cited as reasons for inaction.* In most such cases, however, the board does not receive the results as of right. A few boards insist that at least one board member be involved in the choice of the doctor to

---

* There are legal and ethical issues that have inhibited greater formal disclosure by CEOs in US business. These include the Health Insurance Portability and Accountability Act of 1996 (HIPAA) and the Americans with Disabilities Act (ADA). HIPAA generally does not allow an insurer or an employer group health plan to disclose information to the employer or other third parties without the individual's consent or authorisation. Moreover, individual claim information acquired in connection with routine employer health plan management may not be used for any other employment purposes. The ADA generally prohibits employment

make any assessment of the CEO; some are starting to require that the doctor must be independent, believing that independence cannot be guaranteed if the doctor chosen is already in a professional relationship with the CEO. The most demanding and the most effective arrangement is where the CEO agrees in advance that information relevant to their capacity to carry out the job can be passed to the senior board director or company chairman, if they are not also the CEO, by the independent doctor without specifically requesting permission of the CEO, just notifying them. In a very few companies, this has become in effect a tripartite agreement drawn up between the CEO, the board and the independent doctor. The chairman or the lead director of the board will be fully informed by the doctor of the CEO's health status and can determine how much of the medical information should be shared with colleagues. If this is becoming best practice for CEOs, why should something similar not apply to heads of government?

In 1960, the state of California voted to establish the Judicial Qualifications Commission to deal with judges who might be unfit to continue in office. Of the first ten cases that resulted in retirement, three were because of severe mental impairment, instability, erratic and perverse behaviour, failing memory, inability to concentrate or understand what was being said.[10] Judges were ruling on fellow judges and this has become the pattern, with the professions themselves trying to establish mechanisms for checking those whose decision-making can affect the public. In January 2007 the release of the FBI files of the late Supreme Court judge William Rehnquist showed that by December 1981 he had become addicted to the painkilling drug Placidyl, which was discovered when it was withdrawn during hospitalisation for back pain. He was weaned off the drug and this episode was not judged by physicians interviewed by the FBI as disqualifying him from being elevated, in 1986, to the position of Chief Justice. What this episode shows is that addiction can take hold of someone with few warning signs but also that it can be reversed. Regular independent medical assessment provides no guarantee that diagnostic signs will always be picked up, but they are the best

discrimination against a covered individual with a disability. The ADA also imposes restrictions on an employer's ability to mandate a post-offer physical exam unless such exams are mandatory for all employees. State law protections may also be implicated in such cases. The key ethical issue is whether the CEO has a responsibility to provide any necessary information as the company's leader, since his or her health can be a very sensitive issue in terms of the company's stability. Even if a CEO agrees, it has been argued that any contract to disclose health information can be deemed illegal based on the ADA.

safeguard that exists, along with greater openness from the head of government who is ill.

An important question – and it is not a straightforward one – is whether in democracies the electorate is entitled to know the results of an independent medical assessment of all the candidates before they stand for election directly or indirectly for the position of head of government. My answer is 'yes'. I believe this is necessary. It is not sufficient to rely on a probing press. Good governance, let alone public scrutiny and accountability, requires an independent public medical assessment of all candidates before party primaries, or prior to any election for the leadership of a political party. This is starting to happen, but left to their own devices, most politicians aspiring to be the head of government will not accept such disciplines. They will want to choose the doctor charged with making a medical assessment, and they will want to retain control over what is said to political colleagues and the press. In fact, many senior politicians – more than admit to it publicly – actually favour tougher legislation to limit the invasion of their privacy. There is still too great a reliance on the candidates' personal physicians, who usually carry out the public assessment ensuring selective and biased disclosure especially of potentially damaging information. So the public needs to be vigilant on this issue.

It would help if the medical profession, nationally and internationally, established a code of conduct over the issuing of public medical bulletins for prominent people. One guideline could be that a personal doctor's advice should remain simply that – personal; public statements on health matters should not be made by a personal doctor. Another guideline would be that an independent doctor is best used whenever a medical assessment is needed. Public statements could still be made by the patient or their staff on their behalf.

Democracies should be encouraged to enact legislation that makes public independent medical assessment mandatory on all candidates for the post of head of government, before they submit themselves to direct election nationwide or indirect election through their political party. It should be agreed in that legislation that the medical assessment would be published in a form that guarantees that the doctors' views are not censored. In this way voters would be in possession of the essential facts about the medical health of any candidate for head of government before entering the polling booth. The legal requirement for such an independent assessment might discourage some politicians from standing at all. Other politicians might wish pre-emptively to make public any medical history they had not hitherto released prior to its being revealed by an independent assessment. Nothing can stop politicians giving their medical history their own spin. Most would calculate that it is better to give their explanation well in advance so that there are no surprises left to affect their potential voters.

An independent medical examination is probably best overseen by a general physician or neurologist, but they must have the authority to call in any other specialised doctors and surgeons, particularly those skilled in psychological medicine, to undertake any special tests, including cognitive function tests, which have been considerably developed over the last few decades with further developments to come.[11]

In Britain, the Electoral Commission could, on advice from the Royal College of Physicians, agree a panel of independent doctors from which prime ministerial candidates could choose. Also they could agree the form the medical assessments would take and which other specialists might undertake and evaluate any specific tests. The independent doctor or doctors would then be guided by the Electoral Commission on how to release the information to the public. In other countries an analogous independent body could be vested with this responsibility. It is important that any medical examination of the politician, whether a candidate or an existing head of government, should be done without publicity so if faced with an adverse independent medical assessment that was about to be published they would be given an opportunity to stand down voluntarily with no medical findings being divulged.

What would have been the effect of such mandatory public independent medical assessments on heads of government in the past? We can only speculate but it is illuminating to do so. Had independent medical assessments been the rule in Winston Churchill's day he would no doubt have laughed off any adverse public assessment in 1945, joking about his health, while pictured puffing on his cigar with a glass of brandy in his hand. He might have been able to persuade public opinion to ignore assessments in 1951. By 1955, however, that would not have been possible. A public assessment then would have revealed the very serious heart attack he had had two years before, and how it had turned the old, self-confident Churchill into a sad figure who was staying beyond his time.

Another great leader whose career might have been affected by public disclosure of his medical condition is Franklin Roosevelt. After his new running mate, Harry Truman, had met Roosevelt in the White House on 18 August 1944, he said to the press that Roosevelt 'is keen as a briar'. In private, however, Truman told his assistant:

> I am concerned about the President's health. I had no idea he was in such a feeble condition . . . His hands are shaking and he talks with considerable difficulty . . . It doesn't seem to be any mental lapse of any kind but physically he is just going to pieces. I'm very much concerned about him.[12]

Would the American people have stood by Roosevelt in November 1944, when he was standing for his fourth term as President, if they had been able to read an independent medical assessment detailing his severe heart condition? Roosevelt was determined to run and he, like Churchill, might have scoffed at any independent assessment. He might have reminded everyone of the doctors' predictions when he had polio, claiming that they had told him he would never stand, let alone walk a few steps. It is possible, however, that knowing he would have to face such an assessment could have predisposed him to step down. In the 1944 campaign Roosevelt was able to draw on hidden reserves and just before the vote he appeared to recover his old strength, campaigning by open motorcade, spending hours in the rain in New York City, with much of his old verve. So even if an independent medical assessment had been given to the American people about Roosevelt's health in the summer of 1944, it is probable that voters would have elected him again that November. He was, deservedly, a national hero.

That 1944 presidential election raises a question mark over whether an independent medical assessment of Roosevelt, published in the midst of a war, would have meant that a democratic nation was divulging too much information about the health of its Commander in Chief. The same question would have applied to Churchill fighting an election in 1945 before VJ Day. Such realities show that it is very hard to prescribe rigid rules for a serving head of government. Some will argue, therefore, that there would have to be an exception made about the nature of any medical disclosures in times of war. I am against such a dispensation and, despite all the difficulties, believe that rules of disclosure about health prior to electing a head of government are an essential democratic safeguard in war even more than in peacetime.

How might an independent medical assessment have impacted on the careers of other big, but slightly lesser, figures? If Anthony Eden had been subjected to a public independent medical assessment before the 1955 general election he would probably have been given a relatively clean bill of health. He fought the election just having become Prime Minister and the voters would have been unlikely to hold disclosures about his failed operation and consequent intermittent cholangitis and other ailments against him.

If John F. Kennedy had known he faced a public independent medical assessment before the presidential election in 1960, he would have decided to reveal far more about his health much earlier, probably soon after Adlai Stevenson had fought the 1956 election, thereby giving the American public time to absorb the facts. He would almost certainly have dated his Addison's disease from his war service. Once that had been done I am not convinced his Addison's disease would have prevented him winning four years later. It might also have altered his own attitude and helped him recognise that as a public figure liable to periodic independent medical assessment, he would have to stop the indiscriminate use of drugs that brought accompanying mood changes. He might also have come round much earlier to accepting the need for a more disciplined approach to his medical treatment for Addison's disease, as well as for his back pain.

If Lyndon Johnson had faced an independent medical assessment in the 1964 presidential election, when his popularity was immense, he would have been able to ride out revelations about his heart condition. Also, given his nature, he probably would have managed not to reveal any details of his depressions and paranoia, ensuring any medical notes were not available and that his own doctors divulged very little. Much the same would have applied to Richard Nixon, who was very popular when running for re-election in 1972.

In Britain, after Harold Wilson was defeated in 1970, he was determined to come back and oust Edward Heath from 10 Downing Street, even though he had private anxieties about his own health. Yet before the 1974 general election he would probably have been found healthy enough in any independent public medical assessment to lead his party to victory. So the past record of a system of independent assessment does not show dramatic results. Where independent medical assessments are likely to have the greatest impact is in persuading those who are ill not to put their medical cover up to the test of having it revealed and exposed by independent examination.

Tony Blair, if he had had a public independent medical assessment before the three general elections which he won, would have had to give all the details of his arrhythmia of the heart. Again, it is likely that if he knew it was a statutory obligation to have an assessment he would have given medical details well before the leadership elections. More openness about his health would have done him no harm and would have meant that subsequent incidents would then have had little political impact.

Independent medical assessment – after taking office

What about serving heads of government, if they become ill while in office? This is more difficult and needs a different and more private system. Democracies should be encouraged to enact legislation for a mandatory annual independent medical assessment of their head of government, to be held in private. By keeping the assessment private an independent doctor could monitor the health of a serving head of government without creating public concern or igniting political controversy. Preferably, to keep a measure of medical continuity, the same doctor would be chosen as had done any previous public independent assessment on the head of government before being elected. The independent doctor would be required, by legislation, to report any concerns over his findings to a designated senior political figure. Realistically, mental capacity is likely to be the most sensitive and difficult aspect to assess and if there was any concern the independent doctor would be empowered to call in experts in psychological assessment and this would also be done without publicity. If the head of government's health gave no grounds for concern, there would be no reporting and there would be no publicity surrounding the annual assessment. Only if those findings called into question the head of government's capacity to discharge the powers and duties of his office would action then need to be taken, and then only by politicians.

A head of government becoming ill in office raises some very sensitive and sometimes profound questions. In a democracy any system allowing for involuntary removal from office could not automatically follow from independent medical assessment, however authoritative; nor should it follow from the recommendation of a grouping of doctors, however eminent. Independent medical advice must be considered in the first instance in private by the politician and their family, but then, if they decide to ignore the assessment, by a senior political leader who could be trusted to handle the findings confidentially and to take all relevant factors into consideration. The practical and unavoidable reality is that in most cases such a senior political leader would, initially, be from the same political party as the head of government and would, therefore, in part be conflicted. Such a senior politician might feel the need to consult leaders of the medical profession informally and weigh their confidential advice amongst all the many other factors. Then they would have to decide if the situation necessitated bringing the issue before colleagues in the Cabinet.

If there were a majority of the Cabinet who felt their head of government could no longer discharge their powers and duties, the senior political leader would then report, in the United States, to Congress; in France, the Assembly and Senate; in Britain, both Houses of Parliament; and in Germany, the Bundestag and Bundesrat. If those bodies, by an agreed majority, then decided that the head of government was unable to discharge the powers and duties of the office, their own relevant constitutional provisions should apply for choosing a successor. Authority could also be given to the senior politician to insist that a special private independent medical assessment be made between annual assessments if they became concerned about the head of government's health. As in the case of candidates to be head of government, the fact that such a procedure for independent medical assessment existed would be enough in most cases for an incumbent head of government, when ill, to decide voluntarily to step down.

The United States, through the Twenty-Fifth Amendment, has a more developed structure for dealing with illness in its head of government than most other countries.* There is a strong case for believing that this

---

* Section 4 of the amendment reads: 'Whenever the Vice President and a majority of either the principal officers of the executive departments or of such other body as Congress may by law provide, transmit to the President pro tempore of the Senate and the Speaker of the House of Representatives their written declaration that the President is unable to discharge the powers and duties of his office, the Vice President shall immediately assume the powers and duties of the office as Acting President.

'Thereafter, when the President transmits to the President pro tempore of the Senate and the Speaker of the House of Representatives his written declaration that no inability exists, he shall resume the powers and duties of his office unless the Vice President and a majority of either the principal officers of the executive department or of such other body as Congress may by law provide, transmit within four days to the President pro tempore of the Senate and the Speaker of the House of Representatives their written declaration that the President is unable to discharge the powers and duties of his office. Thereupon Congress shall decide the issue, assembling within forty-eight hours for that purpose if not in session. If the Congress, within twenty-one days after receipt of the latter written declaration, or, if Congress is not in session, within twenty-one days after Congress is required to assemble, determines by two-thirds vote of both Houses that the President is unable to discharge the powers and duties of his office, the Vice President shall continue to discharge the same as Acting President; otherwise, the President shall resume the powers and duties of his office.'

An inevitable weakness is that the Vice President, who is appointed by the President, plays such a crucial role and they may refuse to act. Vice President Thomas Marshall would not move against his friend Woodrow Wilson in 1919 and there is no reason to suppose he would have done so if this amendment had then been in force. Conversely, the Vice President may be antagonistic to the President or overly ambitious to succeed them. It is, nevertheless, understandable why in the American system it was felt that, for example, the Speaker of the

constitutional provision should have been invoked to force President Nixon to step down earlier. Robert Dallek believes:

> Because Nixon was so clearly impaired by Watergate in managing the Middle East crisis in 1973 and the peace negotiations in 1974, Kissinger would have done well to at least consult with other cabinet members about suspending the president's authority under the Constitution's Twenty-Fifth Amendment. While any such discussion would probably have produced no action, and might have undermined Kissinger's relationship with Nixon, at least it would have signaled Kissinger's greater concern with the national well-being than with Nixon's survival.[13]

A clear illustration of how Nixon was performing is the occasion on the evening of 11 October 1973, when Henry Kissinger, Secretary of State and head of the National Security Council (NSC), was informed that Edward Heath, the British Prime Minister, wished to talk to Nixon within the next half-hour about his concerns over the Middle East. Kissinger said to Brent Scowcroft, his deputy on the NSC: 'When I talked to the President he was loaded.' It was agreed to postpone the call from Heath to the next day. But what was striking about Nixon's condition was the way Kissinger and Scowcroft talked 'as if Nixon's drinking to excess had become part of the routine with which they had to live'. Days later, on 24 October, Nixon was almost certainly drunk again when Leonid Brezhnev warned on the hotline that if the United States would not agree to a joint military intervention, Moscow might act alone. This is discussed in Chapter 2. Kissinger helped promote the fiction that Nixon had personally managed this situation. This was no way for the most powerful and sophisticated democracy to conduct the nation's business at a time of crisis.

Nevertheless, sometimes in the past democracy has been well served by letting the leader's medical condition be considered as only one part of a spectrum of political considerations as to whether they should remain in office.

House of Representatives, who could come from another political party, should not be chosen to conduct this role. For much the same reasons, in Britain it should be the Deputy Prime Minister, in the French system the Prime Minister, in the German system the Deputy Chancellor, who is given the initiating role. They would be asked to make a political judgement about bringing their anxieties about the head of government's medical condition to the Cabinet after considering the independent medical report. Then, if the head of government refused to step down, the Cabinet's judgement would have to be endorsed by the respective legislative chambers before a final decision to remove them.

That is why having procedures for fixed medical examinations for all candidates before a head of government is elected is such an important preventative measure. That is why, too, procedures for an existing head of government must be sensitive to the complexities and dynamics of good government in a particular situation. It requires a balanced judgement to weigh up all the factors, not least the uncertain relationship between disease and the capacity to make decisions.

Ageing

Illness may not be the only reason why a head of government no longer seems capable of governing. Ageing on its own may have this effect. Age is a risk factor for depression and many other illnesses. It needs to be remembered, too, that older leaders, especially when ill, are more inclined to accept the status quo, become more indecisive, are often less open minded and more readily allow the political situation to drift. These characteristics were all too apparent in many of the elderly leaders of Europe between the two World Wars, particularly President Hindenburg. President de Gaulle apparently became worried by the precedents of Pétain and Churchill and did not want to cling on to office in a pathetic state of physical and mental decline. Marshal Pétain, who had become head of the renamed 'État Français' in 1940 at the age of eighty-four, was sometimes disorientated, even incoherent, and occasionally unable to recognise people. He also developed mild late onset of Parkinson's disease. Several of those close to de Gaulle heard him express the wish – although he did it very discreetly – that there should be someone who could warn him when the moment came that he was no longer in possession of all his faculties.

Yet when, at the age of seventy-eight, the time did come for de Gaulle to consider stepping down, he was still ready to justify holding on to power at the Élysée. His aide-de-camp, Jean d'Escrienne, described how, near the end of the day, he went into de Gaulle's office, where he was sitting at his desk, holding in front of him a sheet of writing paper. D'Escrienne saluted the President and de Gaulle showed him the piece of paper, which he then read from:

'Did you know that Sophocles wrote *Oedipus at Colonus* when he was ninety? At over eighty, Michelangelo was still doing admirable work in the Sistine Chapel and on the building of the dome of St Peter's. Titian was painting *The Battle of Lepanto* at ninety-five and the *Descent from the Cross* at ninety-seven.

Goethe was finishing Part II of his *Faust*, which is quite the equal of his earlier works, at eighty-three. At eighty-two, Victor Hugo wrote *Torquemada* and, at eighty-three, the second *Légende des Siècles*! Then there was Voltaire and today we have Mauriac![14]

De Gaulle was starting to delude himself. There is a huge difference between the decisions being made by an elderly head of government that affect millions of citizens and the creative capacity of this list of elderly artists and writers. The delusion of de Gaulle and many other elderly heads of government is that each believes himself uniquely capable of ignoring the passing of the years under the adage 'I am as old as I feel'. Heads of government often linger too long and conveniently forget that many of their own governments ensure that their key decision makers are compulsorily retired at ages well below that at which they still expect to continue to hold power. It is a dangerous vanity that allows heads of government to cling to office way beyond when most people retire. Why do many governments still expect to retain limits on retiring some key decision makers early? In the UK, admirals, generals and air marshals are often retired in their late fifties or early sixties. Chiefs of police retire early, consultant surgeons and physicians often have to retire at sixty-five. General medical practitioners in the UK, who work as independent contractors, have to retire by a certain age, as do magistrates and some judges. It is very rare in private or public business for a chief executive to be appointed over the age of sixty or to continue much after sixty-five. Yet legislators in many countries continue to ensure that they are exempt from any such practice or rules and stay on sometimes well into their eighties, as do some heads of government.

Nevertheless, governments are starting, rightly, to legislate for more flexible retirement ages. The fixed age is tending to go as the cost of funding pensions rises and better overall health means people want to go on working. But the corollary of lengthening the working life must be a greater readiness to retire when illness catches up – which it can do – without much warning. That means a greater readiness to accept medical advice and, in the case of key decision makers, regular independent assessment.

One of the simplest and best safeguards against hubris syndrome developing while in office would be if more democracies would enact legislation to ensure that no head of government could remain in office for longer than a set number of years. After Franklin Roosevelt was elected for a fourth term it was widely felt in the United States that there should be legislation to limit a

President's tenure in office. Accordingly, a law was passed limiting any President to two elected terms, meaning a maximum of eight years. No US President since has stayed in office for more than eight years in total and it is a provision that has served America well. Neither Truman nor Johnson, who, as Vice Presidents, first entered the White House to complete their predecessors' terms of office, sought, as they could have done, to stay over eight years by fighting a second presidential election of their own. Eisenhower, Reagan and Clinton all served eight years, with electorates appearing happy for them to stay longer. As popular Presidents at the end of their eight years, they might well have been able, had it been allowed, to fight and win a third term. Yet had they had a third term all three would have had serious illnesses early into such a term. Quite apart from the greater likelihood of illness, a limit of two terms greatly reduces the chances of leaders succumbing to the intoxication of power – the longer the head of government serves the more prone they are to developing hubris.

In Britain, there is no legislative limit on how long a Prime Minister can serve. There is also no fixed term for a parliament, although no parliament can remain for longer than five years without a general election unless an extension is authorised by both the House of Commons and the House of Lords. Britain should legislate to limit the number of years anyone can hold the office of Prime Minister to eight years of service, continuous or broken. Harold Wilson gave eight years' broken service. Margaret Thatcher, had she stepped down after eight years in May 1987, would have gone with her reputation very high and far better placed to be judged by history than after being removed by Conservative MPs in 1990. An eight-year limit would mean that Tony Blair would have had to step down no later than May 2005. He, in fact, won a third general election at that time but with a greatly reduced majority and he seemed surprised that it brought no new surge of authority. Sixteen months later he was told by Labour MPs he had to be out within the year.

In France there is no limit on the number of terms a President may serve but the actual length of the term of service between elections was cut by Jacques Chirac from seven years to five. So a two-term, ten-year limitation in France, had it been enacted at that time, would have had President Chirac stepping down in May 2005 rather than 2007. The Russian Federation from the start under Boris Yeltsin had a two-term, effectively eight-year, limitation. In Africa many of the colonial countries coming to independence initially had constitutions with a two-term limitation, mostly amounting to eight years. Tragically, as their personal power grew too many incumbent Presidents changed their country's constitution to extend their term in office, sometimes staying virtually for life, with damaging consequences. This trend is hopefully starting to be reversed.

Isolation

The environment of power that surrounds most heads of government has considerable impact on even the most stable personality. They are sustained by an executive civil service, have large numbers of political advisers, chauffeur-driven cars with police outriders and personal aircraft. They tend to travel from one VIP suite in one airport to another, live in grand houses owned by the state in the capital city and usually also in a rural part of the country. All this gives a standard of living that only a few very rich people in the world can match. But even more importantly it creates an isolation of the head of government, which is now buttressed by far greater personal security apparatus. The assassination of Olof Palme in 1986 while walking home from the cinema with his wife changed procedures even in Sweden. Most countries have greatly increased in size and scope the personal protection for their head of government with the terrorist threat.

When I first became a member of Parliament in 1966 I could walk along Downing Street without showing any pass, nod to the policeman on the door and enter No. 10 to be met inside by an attendant. At that time, only three Cabinet ministers had personal protection: the Prime Minister, the Foreign Secretary and the Home Secretary usually had only one, but sometimes two, security officers at any public occasion. Now many more politicians have personal protection and the number of police involved has expanded greatly. Today Downing Street is closed to the public, and barriers are raised and lowered in the road to admit cars. To watch the arrival of a US President at No. 10 is to witness a military operation. Also the comings and goings of the Prime Minister involve a major display of police, arms and vehicles. We have, sadly but for the most part necessarily, come a long way in Britain since 1945, when Violet Attlee drove her husband in their own car to Buckingham Palace to receive the seal of office as Prime Minister from George VI.

There is a yet more insidious isolation and that is the hierarchical structure, the deference within government which bolsters its leader so that they can easily come to believe that they are not as other men and women. There is, therefore, a much greater need for vigorous checks and balances on every head of government, to check their perks and the extent of the cocoon that surrounds them. The necessity for periodic endorsement by the electorate with the risk of defeat used to be one of democracy's most salutary experiences. Sadly, the beneficial effect of campaigning, with its levelling down, bringing the leader nearer to the life of the normal citizen, has not lasted. The trappings of power, particularly personal security, now stay with a head of government during an election, and this has meant they are shielded from normal electioneering. Ticket-only meetings stacked with party activists mean that old-style husting meetings have gone. John Major, as Prime Minister, mounting his 'soap box' to campaign in the 1992 general election already seems a distant memory.

Over forty years I have personally watched the metamorphosis of many politicians into heads of government in different countries. Heads of government have our lives in their hands. Too often those hands and the minds that control them become incapable of effectively making the best decisions. We have procedures for trying to ensure that key decision makers in commerce and business, and the armed services, are functioning at the peak of their capacity. It is time that all democratic nations took action to safeguard the capacity of their head of government.

Despots and regime change

It is one thing to lay down guidelines as to how democratic societies should deal with heads of government who have become too ill, too old or too hubristic to carry out their duties; it is quite another to prescribe for despots whose rule has become a danger to their people.

Many despots engage in behaviour which often makes them look, to the outside, as though they are suffering from a recognised mental illness. Yet this is seldom the case. As already argued, neither Hitler nor Stalin were 'mad' in any sense the medical profession recognises, whereas Mussolini was so, because of his depression, in his latter years. During my own political life, several despots, some of whom I had to deal with, seemed to popular opinion 'mad'. If those heads of government had ever come before an international criminal tribunal, I doubt if they, any more than Slobodan Milošević or Saddam Hussein, would have pleaded mental illness in their defence. If we are to deal with leaders who are such threats to their own people and sometimes to the wider world, the issue is not whether they are mentally ill but whether the world is ready to intervene. Just as democratic societies need to implement new procedures for dealing with illness in their own heads of government, so the United Nations needs to be readier to intervene to remove a leader or to bring about regime change where it can be shown that there exists a threat to the peace.

Three despotic leaders in particular over the last forty years, besides Saddam Hussein, illustrate this need: Pol Pot, Idi Amin and Robert Mugabe. When I became Foreign Secretary in 1977, Pol Pot had been leader of the Khmer Rouge in Cambodia for two years. He had been born Saloth Sar and adopted his *nom de guerre* in 1970. He had been a radical Marxist student in Paris and a member of the underground Communist Party, becoming its secretary general in 1962. He was attracted to the Russian anarchist Petr Kropotkin. His quiet demeanour went with a ruthlessness that mirrored that of Stalin and particularly Mao. He too attacked intellectuals, and people could be killed just because they wore glasses or spoke a foreign language. He believed in permanent revolution. On his taking power, 'money, law courts, newspapers, the postal system and foreign telecommunications – even the concept of the city – were all simply abolished'. With no regard for the two million people living there, he simply emptied the capital city of Phnom Penh in April 1975, driving people out into the surrounding countryside. 'Individual rights were not curtailed in favour of the collective, but extinguished altogether. Individual creativity, initiative, originality were condemned per se. Individual consciousness was systematically demolished.'[15] In more than three years one and a half million Cambodians, out of seven million, lost their lives.

There are no obvious categories of illness that can explain his fanaticism. The key to Pol Pot's personality seems to be that as a young child in a Buddhist school he learnt to suppress his individuality and he combined the nihilism of Theravada Buddhism with transcendentalism and Khmer superstitions. As Philip Short wrote in his biography, 'There were many causes of the egregious tragedy. The overconfidence of the country's new leaders, above all its principal leader, the man who would become Pol Pot, was but one element . . . Hubris is the besetting sin of despotism everywhere.'[16]

But our Western conscience cannot be allowed to forget how little we did. Only when Vietnam sent 100,000 men across the border into Cambodia, on 25 December 1978, was the killing ended. A misguided form of realpolitik drove the reaction of the United States and other countries, including the UK, which was in effect to ignore the crimes of Pol Pot because he opposed the Communists controlling Vietnam. But the genocide in Cambodia provided a dreadful legacy of US involvement in south-east Asia, on top of the Vietnam War.

In Africa, the President of Uganda, Idi Amin, was often characterised as a mad buffoon, but in fact he was a vicious sadist. The world is now more aware of this through the 2006 film *The Last King of Scotland*. In January 1971, at the age of forty-five, Amin had come to power as a result of a coup which ousted Milton Obote. Initially, he confined his killing mainly to soldiers whom he considered disloyal, but he soon became totally out of control, authorising hundreds of thousands of killings and committing crimes against humanity of a grotesque nature. His behaviour was bizarre and unpredictable. Some physicians hazarded the opinion he might be suffering the late stages of syphilis,* known as general paralysis of the insane. That diagnosis, however, was never substantiated and was later shown to be wrong since the disease is terminal and Amin eventually died from natural causes in 2003 in Saudi Arabia, where he was given refuge.

I am not ashamed to admit that when I was Foreign Secretary and totally frustrated by the inability to stop Amin's massacres, I contemplated his assassination and discussed it with a senior diplomat liaising with MI6. But in the years following the Second World War the culture against such action had become deeply rooted within the security services in Britain, and for very good reasons too. When assassination of genocidal leaders is considered as an option during peacetime, the downsides of taking such action will almost always outweigh the upsides. Eventually, in 1979, Amin was toppled by armed intervention by the Tanzanian government, outraged by attacks across their border and constant provocation. At the request of the then Tanzanian President, Julius Nyerere, I authorised UK financial assistance in a roundabout way to help pay for the ammunition the Tanzanian forces needed. 'Amin's rule had left Uganda ravaged, lawless and bankrupt, with a death toll put at 250,000 people.' But in this case it is hard to claim that outside military intervention in 1979 brought peace and stability. At Britain's insistence Obote was not reinstated as President and another, acceptable, Ugandan was installed.

---

* Syphilis is a sexually transmitted disease. Rarely is it a congenital disease. It is caused by *Treponema pallidum*, a spirochaete bacterium which can be seen in a blood smear under a microscope. Syphilis is treated with penicillin. It is divided up into three clinical stages, primary, secondary and tertiary. The tertiary phase usually manifests itself some years later, though the delay can be a matter of months, and then can present with a nerve defect, tabes dorsalis or general paralysis of the insane, sometimes characterised by grandiosity. Amin lived too long to have suffered from general paralysis of the insane.

However, Obote soon came back as President and until he was overthrown in 1985 his 'repression was as bad as Amin's had been', with some 300,000 civilian deaths.[17] Uganda under its hubristic President, General Yoweri Museveni, is still not stable, and Ugandan instability spread into Rwanda with the appalling genocide of 1994, which also went into Zaire (now the Democratic Republic of the Congo). The UN Security Council, led by the United States under President Clinton, refused to intervene in Rwanda with the enlarged rapid reaction force that had been called for by the UN's Canadian commander on the spot. There is little doubt that if Amin had been toppled by strong UN sanctions supported by Uganda's neighbours in 1975–6 it would have been a preferable scenario to the Tanzanian military invasion and the history of that whole region would have been much improved.

Robert Mugabe's ruthlessness became clear to me when I was negotiating with him over Rhodesian independence between 1977 and 1979.[18] But in none of my dealings with him did he tell obvious lies, nor did I see any sign of mental instability. He was, however, an ideological zealot, implacable and obdurate. He claimed to be a Maoist political leader, although MI6 discovered at my request that at the same time he was secretly attending mass in Maputo, the capital of Mozambique, having been educated in a Jesuit-run school in Rhodesia. On the basis of 'better a little crookedness than a lot of fanaticism', I judged in 1978 that Joshua Nkomo, rather than Mugabe, would make a better first leader of a democratic Zimbabwe. For a while I helped pursue secret negotiations with Nkomo to bring this about, eventually concluding in a meeting between Nkomo and Ian Smith, held in total secrecy in Lusaka, with Nigeria's Foreign Minister, Joe Garba present under General Olusegun Obasanjo's guidance, and with Zambia's President, Kenneth Kaunda, acting as host. The meeting should have ended with Nkomo flying straight back to Rhodesia to be saluted as Prime Minister at the foot of the aircraft's steps by General Peter Walls, the head of the Rhodesian army, bringing illegal independence to an end. A UK-backed and UN/Commonwealth-manned military and observer mission would have supervised a fair and free election within a year. It was not to be: another meeting was planned to be held in Lusaka but before then the initiative became public and the meeting never reconvened. Nyerere and Mugabe were totally against the whole concept.

I was somewhat embarrassed in the early 1980s that I had done this secret diplomacy, because against my predictions, Mugabe as the new Prime Minister appeared to preside over a remarkable period of reconciliation. Given what he and other black leaders had had to endure after Smith's illegal declaration of independence, Mugabe's reconciliation with the white rebels inside Zimbabwe appeared both generous and enlightened. But, sadly, Mugabe's conciliatory phase was fleeting and in October 1980, only six months after independence, Mugabe secretly signed an agreement with North Korea to train a new 5 Brigade, composed almost entirely of Shona-speaking former guerrillas, to deal with internal dissidents. Compared with the Zimbabwean army, 5 Brigade had different uniforms, better equipment and weaponry and a different chain of command. Mugabe then authorised 5 Brigade to use indiscriminate force, with beatings, arson and mass murder in January 1983 against the Matabele people. Also much to my surprise, Mugabe – who had railed so strongly to me against the corruption he saw as being associated with capitalism – slowly started to become ever more personally corrupt. He progressively destroyed parliamentary democracy, refusing all blandishments from other African leaders to step down from power.

By the start of the twenty-first century Zimbabwe was in the grip of an ageing fanatic. Mugabe had managed to decimate the country's once-flourishing agricultural production, gravely damage its economic stability and undermine the democratic basis of the 1980 constitution. By 2005 more than a third of Zimbabwe's population of twelve million needed donated food to avoid malnutrition. Two years later the country was in a downward spiral with hyper-inflation estimated at a staggering 11,000 per cent and Mugabe announced, at the age of eighty-three, that he was seeking a further six years in office. The world faced the moral dilemma that aid workers have wrestled with elsewhere: by helping to provide food one boosts the survival in office of those who have brought about the very humanitarian disaster one is trying to alleviate.

Mugabe had for some years been labelled 'mad' by the British and US press, an all too glib diagnosis to pin on him. Over thirty years I had resisted calling him that, believing that what Mugabe was doing was mirroring the brutality and destructive nature of Mao's form of communism, which he so admired. Then, in 2006, I saw a remarkable play, *Breakfast with Mugabe.** It gave a special African insight into what may be the root of Mugabe's troubles, in some way analogous to the role of superstition in Pol Pot's character. Historically accurate, the play is in part an exploration of W. H. Auden's famous

---

* Written by Fraser Grace, *Breakfast with Mugabe*, first performed in 2003 by the Royal Shakespeare Company at Stratford upon Avon, is set in State House, Harare, in 2001 with only four actors: Robert Mugabe, his second wife Grace, a white psychiatrist called in by Grace to see her husband, and a bodyguard who is also a secret policeman.

observation 'those to whom evil is done do evil in return'. What is emphasised and was known to many in the region is the implacable hatred Mugabe felt for Ian Smith for being refused compassionate release to see his three-year-old son before he died of malarial encephalitis in Accra in 1966. However, the play then goes on to depict the bitter departed spirit, a *ngozi*, having died violently, coming back in the shape of Comrade Josiah Tongogara* to haunt and bring terror to Mugabe, according to Shona tradition. Mugabe talks to a white psychiatrist and the play leaves one wondering about the deeper traditional forces that may be driving Mugabe.

That the new post-apartheid South Africa did not combine with the UN Security Council to ensure Mugabe's removal from power in Zimbabwe from the early 1990s may leave a lasting scar on both countries and the region as a whole. It may even, if some pessimists are correct, undermine South Africa's own democracy. How ironic that in 1965 a Labour government with a small majority, and with a Conservative opposition against the use of force, had felt unable to take military action to restore legality in Rhodesia – because a racist minority white South African government was supporting Smith and was refusing to help topple him through military intervention. Yet from 1997 a Labour government, with a large parliamentary majority and a Conservative opposition who wanted tougher action on Mugabe, still felt unable to intervene militarily, because this time a democratic South African government was refusing to help topple Mugabe.

The UN right to intervene

These brief examples – Pol Pot, Amin and Mugabe – show that humanitarian interventionism has limits, often set by realpolitik. This is not new: military interventions have always been restricted by calculations of military might,

---

* Tongogara was the charismatic guerrilla leader who headed ZANLA, the military wing of Mugabe's party, ZANU. He took part in the Anglo-American sponsored negotiations in Malta in 1978 and in the Lancaster House meetings in 1979. Many hoped he would become a key figure in an independent Zimbabwe. Tragically, before independence, Tongogara was killed in a motor accident. Some people believe Mugabe was responsible for Tongogara's death. But in the play Mugabe believes his death was an attempt by London to destabilise the country on the brink of freedom. Mugabe says: 'As a party we should have done more to avenge Tongogara's death. Perhaps the message of ngozi is we have left our debt of honour unpaid.' Later, in a crucial dialogue, the psychiatrist says to Mugabe: 'It's not always about power, Robert.' Mugabe replies: 'Ah. But it is.' Once again, a playwright may have shown more perception than politicians, diplomats and doctors about the true state of mind of a political leader.

political will and ideological commitment. This is best illustrated by NATO's refusal to intervene against the Soviet invasion of Hungary in 1956 and Czechoslovakia in 1968. Realpolitik lay behind the UN Security Council's indifference to the genocide in Rwanda and is visible yet again in Sudan. Kofi Annan as UN secretary general championed the principle of a 'responsibility to protect', to legitimise humanitarian interventions. This was accepted by the General Assembly in 2005.*

Annan's tenure as UN secretary general was marked by his determination to champion the doctrine of 'conditional sovereignty' and challenge the view that a nation's conduct of its internal affairs was inviolable. He told the General Assembly in September 1999, in the light of the UN having been bypassed over Kosovo: 'The state is now widely understood to be the servant of its people, and not vice versa.' Annan went on to declare that the UN member states must embrace a 'more broadly defined, more widely conceived definition of national interest'. No longer could the systematic extermination of the citizens of a strategically insignificant state be viewed as a matter of little or no concern to the Security Council. He was aware that after Kosovo, 'if the collective conscience of humanity . . . cannot find in the United Nations its greatest tribune, there is a grave danger it will look elsewhere for peace and justice'.

---

* The UN summit of heads of government in 2005 agreed the principle of a 'responsibility to protect'. Since they did not also advocate amendment of the UN Charter it was implicit that it could be done within the existing charter. It is reasonable, therefore, to assume that they were endorsing the responsibility to protect as overriding the charter's respect for national sovereignty. The Security Council in its interpretation of the charter cannot be overruled or 'judicially reviewed' by the International Court of Justice. This gives member states some flexibility in their interpretation of the charter. A UN Security Council resolution passed by the requisite majority of nine, with no vetos, that demands that a head of government step down, with the threat of military action under Chapter VII of the charter if they do not, is therefore legitimate. Similarly, so is a threat to invoke such a provision if the head of government does not start protecting their civilian population and living up to the requirements of the charter and the Universal Declaration on Human Rights. A threat to the peace, which is a political, not a legal, judgement, can override the charter's injunction not to interfere in another state's internal sovereignty.

How the Security Council interprets 'the responsibility to protect' in dealing with the genocide in Darfur in 2008 will start to define the UN for the twenty-first century. The permanent five on the Security Council face an immensely difficult challenge because the African Union is still too weak and is divided over Darfur. The leaders of the Sudanese government have shown a brutality and defiance of the UN that bodes ill for the whole country. However, in this case there is little evidence to allow one to ascribe all the problems within Sudan to a single, despotic leader. Kofi Annan served ten years, leaving at the end of 2006. Under the stress of allegations about his son's conduct he became depressed in the Easter period of 2003 and again in the spring and summer of 2004.

But a regime can be the target of sanctions as well as a head of government; if they personify its horrors and defects, then their regime has to be replaced. To enforce the stepping down of a head of government or regime, I have become more and more convinced that the UN must be readier to openly endorse a wider definition of a 'threat to the peace' within a broader interpretation of the UN Charter. This would mean that regime change could be demanded either by a short, sharp spell of economic and political sanctions or by the credible threat of military intervention. It means interpreting the UN Charter as giving the Security Council the right to insist on the removal of a particular head of government when it decides that their continuing in office creates a threat to the peace. In the autumn of 1977, in the wake of public horror at the circumstances surrounding the death of the anti-apartheid activist Steve Biko, when I was Foreign Secretary the UK supported President Jimmy Carter's administration with regard to the Security Council declaring for the first time that apartheid in South Africa was a 'threat to the peace' and that a mandatory arms embargo should be applied.

Military intervention should not be the first resort, but it needs to be available and not just after years of waiting. It is very important that the Iraqi debacle does not exclude future military interventions. The use of incentives, the 'carrot and stick' approach, is also important. It appears to have worked in dealing with Colonel Muammar Gaddafi of Libya. For many decades Gaddafi had been one of the heads of government frequently labelled 'mad'. This was despite him never having been identified as suffering from any known medical illness. He was well described by the late Stephen Egerton, then a young British diplomat, soon after the Libyan Revolution in the early 1970s:

> Gaddafi has his strict principles and once one grants this, there is a sort of crazy logic in what he says and does. But his logic is not of course ours, nor at this post do we believe it is the logic of most Arabs or of their leaders . . . I think he genuinely believes he is being 'called'. It is extraordinarily difficult for mere mortals to predict how the call will take him.

Indeed it was very difficult. Gaddafi over the years gained powerful supporters, not least Nelson Mandela, who was grateful for his support for the ANC over many years. It was Gaddafi's involvement in terrorism which troubled many countries. In the UK it was his regime's supply of Semtex to the IRA in the early 1980s. Its involvement in the 1986 bombing of La Belle, a Berlin discotheque used by US soldiers, killing three people and injuring 229 others, and the blowing up of the Pan Am plane over Lockerbie in 1988 led to Libya being sanctioned for sponsoring terrorism. President Reagan's 1986 retaliatory bombing of Libya and specifically of Gaddafi's own house, killing a close family member, was no doubt a factor in making him start to change his policies. Reagan was using the language of retaliation – unacceptable under the UN Charter – but made the long reach of the US Air Force clear to Gaddafi.*

Many pressures seem to have brought about Gadaffi's changed attitude to terrorism and readiness to halt Libya's nuclear weapons programme. Undoubtedly, Reagan's military decision was a factor in producing that result; the United States demonstrated that where support for terrorist activity was concerned, it would not feel inhibited in dealing with a government giving such support by a particular legal interpretation of the words in the UN Charter. What was missing, however, in addition, were positive inducements or incentives for Gaddafi to change.

President Clinton and then President George W. Bush, acting with Prime Minister Tony Blair, decided to add incentives to their armoury. While it was never admitted, they gave assurances to Gaddafi, as a personal incentive, that if he changed he would not later be toppled from power by military intervention from outside the country. Additionally, if Libya abandoned all support for terrorism and gave up trying to build a nuclear weapon then they would have all sanctions removed. Realpolitik triumphed. Libya agreed in 2004 to pay $35 million in compensation for victims of the Lockerbie air disaster and the United States in July 2006 dropped Libya from their list of terrorist countries. Yet for all the diplomacy of incentives, despotic leaders, who are not under normal democratic pressures from their own citizens, will not usually respond, unless there is also a credible threat.

---

* When Reagan bombed Libya, on 15 April 1986, Margaret Thatcher, as UK Prime Minister, deliberately never used or endorsed Reagan's word 'retaliation'. She justified giving permission for the US F-111 aircraft to use British airfields by referring to Reagan's actions as being of self-defence, thereby staying within the UN Charter's language, although she knew full well that Reagan was retaliating for Libyan involvement in the Berlin bomb incident. Reagan cited 'irrefutable' evidence that Gaddafi was behind the bombing and launched air strikes on Libya ten days later. A Berlin court ruled in 2001 that the bombing was organised by the Libyan secret service and aided by the Libyan embassy in the then-communist East Germany. It convicted four people of carrying out the bombing, and a federal court upheld their sentences in 2004. The La Belle case only took shape after Germany reunited in 1990 and East German secret police files were opened. The Stasi files led prosecutors to a Libyan who in 1996 agreed to cooperate with them. Among the evidence was an intercepted radio transmission from Tripoli to the Libyan embassy in East Berlin calling for an attack 'with as many victims as possible'.

In recent years a new threat, international legal action, has been developed. The trials of prominent heads of government are too recent to make any final assessment of their preventative effect. The legal approach has promise, but there cannot be absolute justice; there has to be a readiness to balance justice with reconciliation.* The advocates of absolute justice are loud in their condemnation of any actions to avoid holding a trial and often they are correct. Slobodan Milošević's trial was salutary, albeit a tragedy that a sentence was never passed, because of his death in prison. The long delays in that case in The Hague occurred in part because there was such a long charge sheet. A narrowly based initial charge, as in Saddam Hussein's trial, would have been wiser.

This conflict between reconciliation and justice is well illustrated by the case of the late President Augusto Pinochet, responsible for the widespread use of torture and the 'disappearance' of many Chilean citizens. Realpolitik played its part, after he was arrested in London, because of the crucial help that Pinochet and his government gave to the British armed forces during the Falklands War.† The British government appeared to 'call in the doctors' to provide a way of avoiding Pinochet's extradition to Spain for trial in 1998. However, this interpretation has been strongly denied by the then British Home Secretary, Jack Straw, who claims he made the decision on good medical evidence that Pinochet was not fit to be tried. Pinochet was sent back to Chile for his own government and people to decide whether to bring him

---

* There is frequently a conflict between reconciliation and justice and its resolution poses real dilemmas. It is very important that heads of government are now being prosecuted for crimes against humanity. Sometimes, however, it may still be necessary to grant some heads of government safe haven. Saudi Arabia did this quietly for Amin. France has done it for some of its African colonial leaders. It was argued that Mugabe's refusal to stand down from office had been made harder to achieve by what happened to Frederick Chiluba, former President of Zambia, who was charged with corruption, and by the transfer of Charles Taylor to the International Criminal Court in The Hague in 2006, after he had been promised refuge as part of a settlement of the Liberian crisis. (Tony Hawkins and Alec Russell, 'Zimbabwe's defiant dictator', *Financial Times*, 23 February 2007.)

† For years it was a closely guarded secret that within a week of the invasion of the Falkland Islands by the Argentinians in 1982, Chile, under Pinochet, agreed that Britain could have the unofficial use of its airfields and army bases nearest to the Falklands. Britain provided Chile with Canberra high-altitude spy planes equipped with high-specification photo reconnaissance equipment. These planes were flown to Belize, repainted in Chilean air force colours and then, after refuelling in Santiago, flown down to airfields in the Puntas Arena. The RAF crews stayed with the planes, providing invaluable information to the British task force commanders until the end of the war. (Andy Beckett, *Pinochet in Piccadilly: Britain and Chile's Hidden History* (London: Faber & Faber, 2002), p. 208.)

to trial rather than being arraigned before an international court, the effect of which was that the Chileans had to decide how much of their past compromise settlement should be upheld. Much of the UK's medical evidence about Pinochet did not appear to stand up to serious scrutiny – somewhat embarrassingly, Pinochet's health seemed to improve on his return to Chile for a few years prior to his death. Yet the British government could claim that the UK legal system had scrupulously followed the very important new legal provisions under international law. A sovereign head of state was for the first time no longer immune to charges of torture and was judged under the new system of international justice.

The Security Council should for the future operate on the basis that gross abuse of human rights that might, strictly speaking, fall short of genocide – which should automatically initiate action   could under the charter invoke a 'threat to the peace'. It would happen according to the doctrine of conditional sovereignty. This would add another 'arrow to the quiver' of the Security Council, enabling it to authorise mandatory economic and political sanctions and, if there were no response, military intervention.

In years past the Soviet Union and China would have automatically vetoed such interventions even if there were the necessary nine votes in the Security Council. In the twenty-first century that may change; a majority may be easier to assemble in the Security Council in some cases where humanitarian considerations are cited to force a head of government or regime out of office. But for this to happen we must all learn from the mistakes made in Iraq. The testing ground is likely to be Iran. The Security Council following any such intervention will not be bound to insist that any replacement government must always be democratic from the outset. But as the alternative of doing nothing is not acceptable to a swathe of world opinion and is incompatible with world order, from time to time the democratic countries may have to be prepared to compromise and accept replacement governments that are not initially democratic, provided they are at least representative. For similar pragmatic reasons the UN Charter never made it a requirement for member states to be democratic.

The international laws and conventions that we have at the start of the twenty-first century are the product of an emerging, but not perfect, civilised world. A world that has tried, through the UN, since 1945, to become ever more coherent. A world that has chosen to root itself in the moralities and the cultures of many civilisations which embrace almost all races, religions and creeds. A world that, for all its failings, has tried to forge respect for the UN

Charter. That world has 'Made in USA' stamped all over it with the associated presidential names of Franklin Roosevelt, Harry Truman, Dwight Eisenhower, John F. Kennedy, Jimmy Carter and George Bush Sr. Ever since 1945 opinion polls have shown that the American people believe it is not in the national interest for its government to ride roughshod over the UN, sensing that it is largely the United States' own creation. A reformed UN is urgently needed, and such reform needs to reignite all US governments' full commitment to the UN. This is what has been missing since 1991. The test for the UN is likely to be Sudan and in particular Darfur.

9

Conclusion

The sicknesses which heads of government have either brought to office or developed while occupying high office, and the consequences of being ill for the business of government, have been covered in some detail in this book. But there is also the interesting and far from uncommon phenomenon, as already discussed, whereby the very experience of holding office seems to infect heads of government with something that I have labelled 'hubris syndrome'.

The medical profession rightly eschews expressions such as 'madness' and 'lunacy' when talking about mental health. But it has been observed for centuries that something happens to some people's mental stability when in power, and the causal link between holding power and aberrant behaviour that has the whiff of mental instability about it was captured by Bertrand Russell's phrase 'the intoxication of power', mentioned in the Introduction (p. xix). Power is a heady drug which not every political leader has the necessary rooted character to counteract: a combination of common sense, humour, decency, scepticism and even cynicism that treats power for what it is, a privileged opportunity to serve and to influence – and sometimes determine – the turn of events.

Hubris is almost an occupational hazard for heads of government, as it is for leaders in other fields, such as the military and business, for it feeds on the isolation that often builds up around such people. Interestingly, the hubristic concept was picked up in a study of General Motors, when describing business leaders who deceive themselves and distance themselves from reality. The study argued that a point often comes when such individuals are no longer living in the same world as the organisation they lead, and it ended by describing the horror that arises from the claims of powerful mortals to be more than mortal. 'The Greeks called this hubris and they knew that the gods, whom we might refer to as reality, do not stand for it. They demand humility.'[1]

The havoc which hubristic heads of government can wreak is usually suffered by the people in whose name they govern. The virtues of a representative democracy lie in the scope it gives elected leaders to exercise real leadership and to show the decisiveness most voters prefer to hesitation, doubt and vacillation. But the exercise of that leadership needs to carry the trust of the electorate, which is usually lost when the leader crosses the borderline between competent decision-making and hubristic incompetence.

Medicine's approach to mental ill health often has to be conducted in the absence of any physical symptoms or disease markers: what alerts the practitioner to a problem is not a physical symptom but aberrant behaviour of some sort. Very often the medical profession may be unable to discover any cause of this behaviour but will nonetheless regard it as constituting mental ill health. Certain patterns of behaviour are categorised as symptomatic of specific syndromes. An identifiable syndrome once identified becomes easier to predict, prevent and perhaps even treat.

In adopting this approach, of categorising specific patterns of behaviour as symptomatic of defined syndromes, the medical profession is not so much *discovering* disease, as it might be said to have done in a straightforward sense when it discovered, say, tuberculosis, as *deciding* that certain patterns of behaviour should constitute a mental illness. This is a very important distinction because it highlights two quite distinct but equally valid practices for establishing what should and should not be recognised as illness. In agreeing to the existence of a particular syndrome, or clinical picture, the medical profession is not bowing to the unrefuted, objective evidence derived from experiment, as when some diseases are discovered, but is taking a collective, pragmatic decision that it is sensible to deem a certain pattern of behavioural symptoms. more often found together than separately, as amounting to an illness. A good example of this, though it took some time to acknowledge, is post-traumatic stress disorder. Here the condition cannot occur unless there has been a traumatic event. It is characterised by a set of signs and symptoms, such as flashbacks, hypervigilance and nightmares around the event, and now after much debate and controversy it is recognised as a medical syndrome.

I would like the medical profession to explore the hypothesis that there is a pattern of hubristic behaviour manifest in some leaders, particularly political leaders, which could legitimately be deemed to constitute a medically recognised syndrome, which I have called hubris syndrome. Some psychiatrists believe that hubristic behaviour is systemic, a product of the environment in which the head of government operates. On the other hand hubris appears to build up over time; it does not manifest itself quickly unless there has been a specific event such as 9/11. It gives the impression that it has become self-generating, that the individual is gripped by something which is no longer driven by outside factors but comes from within themselves. It is this element which comprises hubris syndrome.

Against past and present indications of the damage that hubris syndrome may be doing to a leader's rational decision-making, it seems wise not just for classical philosophers, playwrights and historians to study hubris, but for scientists, particularly medical doctors, to do so as well. There is a case for working on the supposition that there is an underlying syndrome in which a combination of signs and features are more likely to appear together than independently; it is for the medical profession to judge whether it forms a pathological category. I developed this argument in an article for the *Journal of the Royal Society of Medicine*,[2] and I hope a debate will now ensue.

The last fifty years have seen an explosion of sciences relating to people's mental make-up. Genetics, neuroscience, psychology and epidemiology are all forging ahead and finding new ways of augmenting one another. The enhancement of cognition by new drugs which improve intellectual performance is now a reality. The modest therapeutic success of acetyl-cholinesterase inhibitors has stimulated a search for better cognition enhancers, and drugs to beat dementia may start to be used by people whose cognitive function is in the normal range. We may well see psychoactive substances used not just to curb overactivity, as in ADHD, but to optimise performance, relieve distress, help people relax or aid sociability. While amphetamines used to be taken by political leaders, for example Eden and Kennedy, these newer drugs will as likely as not be used by their 21st-century counterparts. And the oldest drug of all, alcohol, is a prominent psychoactive substance.

There is good evidence for the involvement of several neurotransmitters in addiction, including dopamine, glutamate and gamma-aminobutyric acid.[3] As neuroscience evolves it seems perfectly feasible that it may be found that highly stressful jobs experienced over a period of time carry with them the possibility that there will be detectable changes in some of the substances of the brain (such as serotonin and dopamine, but there are many others). Such changes could affect mood and may provide an explanation for the sort of behavioural changes which can be identified as hubris syndrome. It is claimed by some that dopamine is a reward-related substance, with more released into the brain after a perceived success, and that there is a risk/reward mechanism; as people talked in the past of the thrill of an adventure, so today some talk loosely of a dopamine rush. All of this is far from proven but the linkages that are being established make neuroscience a field in which knowledge is growing fast.

No scientific explanation for hubris syndrome has yet been found and no such explanation may ever be found. However, watching the changes in the new sciences of the mind in my lifetime, as a former neurologist and politician, I believe they may ultimately provide an explanation of why some leaders succumb to hubris syndrome while others do not. It may be that hubris syndrome never has a medical cure or even a proven medical causation, but it is becoming ever clearer that, as much as or even more than conventional illness, it is a great menace to the quality of leadership and the proper government of our world. Yet it is difficult to identify when, as in the case of Bush and Blair, their public presentation is of being affable regular guys who can be trusted.

Curbing political leaders' hubristic behaviour has to rely on strengthening national democratic checks and balances. These have been built up over the years in both the US and the UK. The most important is vigilance and scrutiny by the Cabinet, for it comprises the people who see the most of their heads of government's true conduct in office. The readiness of Cabinet ministers to resign on principle is very important. Elliot Richardson resigned as US Attorney General rather than sack Archibald Cox, the special prosecutor, as ordered by President Nixon. Secretary of State Cyrus Vance resigned when President Carter against his advice ordered helicopters into Iran in a botched attempt to extract American hostages. As leader of the House of Commons Robin Cook resigned in 2003 over the invasion of Iraq. Had Colin Powell or Jack Straw resigned before the Iraq War the effect might have been considerable. Yet weighed against that is the chance offered to the general public to sack Bush and Blair respectively in 2004 and 2005, but both men won re-election. Even so, in mid-term elections in 2006 and 2007 there was considerable dissatisfaction recorded with each leader.

Press criticism was muted in both countries before the war in Iraq and for a while afterwards, either because the newspapers agreed with the decision to go to war or because they were embarrassed, having predicted a much more difficult military operation for the invasion than proved to be the case. Also it was very difficult to predict the insurgency without knowing more about the paucity of aftermath planning. There should have been more investigative journalism on both sides of the Atlantic and greater scrutiny by Congress and Parliament of aftermath planning.

In a democracy nothing can replace knowing more about the true nature and character of the people we vote in to become head of our government. The press have a key role to play in this. The importance of character is made clear in the work of the Jungian analyst James Hillman. In his book *The Force of Character*, he writes: 'The limiting effect of one's innate image prevents that inflation, that trespassing or hubris that the classical world considered the worst of human errors. In this way character acts as a guiding force.'[4] We need more clues, or alerting information, as to why some leaders may develop hubris when in office. The good sense of the people in a democracy is then more likely to ensure that those chosen have qualities in their character which are less likely to succumb to the intoxication of power.

The decisive leaders who are most likely to avoid hubris syndrome are usually those who are careful to retain a personal modesty as they stay in power, to keep as far as possible their previous lifestyle, to listen to those close to them – spouses, family and friends – and to eschew the trappings of power. These leaders try to consult carefully even if that process may not alter their opinions. They make errors of judgement but they are not often errors born of ignorance or stemming from contempt for the views of others. Above all, in a democracy, they accept that the inbuilt institutional checks and balances should be scrupulously respected and they make little or no attempt to circumvent them, whether in Cabinet or Parliament.

One of the best modern historians, David Reynolds, describes the hubris of leaders for whom their own personality is the key to their whole approach, with a surprising conclusion:

> A well-intentioned leader convinced of his rightness, whose confidence in his powers of persuasion bordered on hubris. Who squeezed out critical professional advice, controlling policy and information from an inner circle, and who played his best hands too early at the conference table. A leader whose rhetoric became increasingly extravagant and deceptive, yet whose apparent naivety may have been the outward face of a man who knew he had gone too far to turn back. Who does all this remind us of? For all their differences, Tony Blair's approach to summitry had a good deal in common with that of Neville Chamberlain.[5]

Other democratic heads of government who suffered from hubris syndrome in the last century, apart from Chamberlain and Blair, are David Lloyd George, Margaret Thatcher and George W. Bush. Theodore Roosevelt and Lyndon Johnson were hubristic but have been diagnosed as having had bipolar disorder.[6] Woodrow Wilson was hubristic but he suffered from arteriosclerosis, repeated strokes and dementia. Franklin Roosevelt looked as if he might be taken over by hubris when, in 1937, he fought and lost a battle with Congress over the Judicial Branch Reorganization Plan, affecting the nomination of justices to the Supreme Court. But, fortunately, he had a sense of humour and a certain cynicism, which meant he never lost his moorings in the democratic system. Raymond Moley, who knew Roosevelt well from 1928 until 1936, analysed the problem of 'mental intoxication' that comes with power when exercised in isolation over long periods:

> Until the very end of my association with Roosevelt I hoped that his quality of pragmatism would keep some of the windows of his mind open. I finally found . . . that he himself was slamming shut windows. He developed a very special method of reassuring himself of his own preconceptions . . . Ultimately, of course, a man closed off by one means or another from free opinion and advice suffers a kind of mental intoxication. He lives in a world of ideas generated only by himself, a world of make-believe.[7]

Against that assessment, one has to recognise the respect in which Roosevelt was held by many others who worked closely with him. His personal determination, ruthlessness, guile and optimism enabled the United States – in the midst of the Great Depression – to overcome its economic troubles; as he said, 'The only thing we have to fear is fear itself.' From 1941 to 1945 those qualities, in part the product of his illnesses, gave him the political authority to mobilise his country for war and to win that war in the interests of the whole world. I do not believe Roosevelt developed hubris syndrome. Nor did Winston Churchill.

Among dictators, Adolf Hitler developed hubris syndrome. Benito Mussolini was depressive and may have had bipolar disorder, and so may Mao Zedong. Both were essentially hubristic. Nikita Khrushchev had hypomania, as did a number of other dictators.

The last century could be seen as both the worst and the best in the political history of the world. Genocides and mass killing of civilians through wars waged worldwide provide the case for its being the worst. But the spread of democracy is a key measure of progress, and the hundred years between 1906 and 2006 the best for democracy. According to Freedom House, the New York-based organisation that systematically looks at democracy, there were no fully fledged democracies in 1900, a mere twenty-two in 1950. But by 2000 there were 120.

In the middle of the twentieth century the twenty-two democracies accounted for 31 per cent of the world population. Yet by the close of the century the 120 democracies (out of 192 nations) constituted 62.5 per cent of the world's population. In the twenty-first century we need to focus on deepening those democracies. This explosion of democracy in the latter half of the twentieth century represents the extension of universal suffrage, the fragmentation of the Soviet Union and the growth in multi-party competitive elections. More controversially, but I believe it to be the right course of action, we need to actively extend democracy. This is a particular challenge in relation to democracy for Arab and Muslim states, most of which have no history of any form of democratic government. Therefore it will take time; Afghanistan, Pakistan, Iraq, Iran, Syria, Jordan and Egypt are destined to be the proving ground for any such democratic reform strategy. If democratisation is to succeed then all the skills of diplomacy will be needed, which include patience, persistence and understanding, skills which have been so far in short supply in this region. After Iraq it will be easy to turn away from democratisation, blame the 'neocons' in the United States and try and find refuge in the scepticism and cynicism of those who acquiesced in Iraq's tyranny over the last thirty years. To do that would be a tragic misreading of events. The challenge is rather to learn from our many mistakes in Iraq and develop new skills on how to patiently advance the cause of democracy.

In this book I have tried to show, through case studies, the problems associated for the world when there is illness in heads of government, and also how illness may need to be redefined to include a hubris syndrome. I have suggested procedures for reducing the chances that a head of government will become ill in office or stay once ill. Such procedures were given world attention during the 2008 US presidential election since the Republican candidate, Senator John McCain, had undergone surgery for a melanoma on the left side of his face in August 2000. In 1999, when challenging George W. Bush for the Republican nomination, McCain gave the public an amazing amount of information about his health, 1,500 pages of medical and psychiatric records that had been part of a US Navy project on former prisoners of war. McCain, a war hero from Vietnam, promised to reveal all the information on his melanoma, which was classified on removal as being Stage IIa, before the American people voted on whether he should be their next head of government. I have also suggested procedures for promoting good government and respect for human rights, not just in democracies but throughout the world. The UN Security Council, including the undemocratic states that will continue to be members, needs to address the question of what action it, as part of the international community, is ready to take to deal with despots – despots who, whether medically ill or not, create massive suffering and, frequently, internal strife affecting their people and often neighbouring countries. This means intervention: political, economic and perhaps military. Intervention aimed at protecting the people from a head of government or regime, followed by intervention to help rebuild. Such intervention remains a noble mission for the UN and other international bodies in the twenty-first century.

Notes

Introduction

1. David Owen, *Time to Declare* (London: Michael Joseph, 1991), pp. 5–18.
2. David Owen, *In Sickness and in Health: The Politics of Medicine* (London: Quartet, 1976).
3. David Owen, *The Politics of Defence* (London: Jonathan Cape, 1972).
4. Written on 5 April 1887 to Mandell Creighton, the author of *A History of the Papacy during the Period of the Reformation.*
5. Barbara W. Tuchman, *The March of Folly: From Troy to Vietnam* (New York: Ballantine, 1985), pp. 32, 33.
6. Ibid., pp. 7, 33.
7. Bertrand Russell, *History of Western Philosophy*, 2nd ed. (London: George Allen and Unwin, 1961), p. 782.
8. Doris Kearns Goodwin, *Team of Rivals: The Political Genius of Abraham Lincoln* (New York: Simon & Schuster, 2005), p. xvii.
9. Joshua Wolf Shenk, *Lincoln's Melancholy: How Depression Challenged a President and Fuelled his Greatness* (Boston: Houghton Mifflin, 2005).
10. Source: MedicineNet website.
11. Jonathan R. T. Davidson, Kathryn M. Connor and Marvin Swartz, 'Mental Illness in US Presidents between 1776 and 1974: A Review of Biographical Sources', *Journal of Nervous and Mental Disease* (2006), vol. 194, pp. 47–51.
12. Owen, *Time to Declare*, p. 732.
13. Plato, *Phaedrus*, 238a, in Euthyphro/Apology/Crito/Phaedo/Phaedrus, tr. H. N. Fowler, Loeb Classical Library (Cambridge, MA: Harvard University Press, 1914); the Ancient Greek original has been added in italics by the author of this book.
14. Aristotle, *Art of Rhetoric*, tr. J. H. Freese, Loeb Classical Library (Cambridge, MA: Harvard University Press, 1926), 1378b.
15. David E. Cooper, *The Measure of Things: Humanism, Humility, and Mystery* (Oxford: Clarendon Press, 2002), p. 163.
16. Margaret Canovan, 'Hannah Arendt as a Conservative Thinker', in Larry May and Jerome Kohn (eds), *Hannah Arendt: Twenty Years On* (Cambridge, MA: MIT Press, 1996), p. 29.
17. Ian Kershaw, *Hitler 1889–1936: Hubris* (London: Allen Lane, 1998); Ian Kershaw, *Hitler 1936–1945: Nemesis* (London: Allen Lane, 2000).
18. David Owen, *The Hubris Syndrome: Bush, Blair and the Intoxication of Power* (London: Politico's, 2007).

Chapter 1: 1901–1953

1.   Margaret MacMillan, *Paris 1919: Six Months That Changed the World* (New York: Random House, 2002), p. 494.
2.   John R. Bumgarner, *The Health of the Presidents: The 41 United States Presidents to 1993 from a Physician's Point of View* (Jefferson, NC: McFarland, 1994).
3.   J. J. Brooks, H. T. Enterline and G. E. Aponte, 'The Final Diagnosis of President Cleveland's Lesion', in *Transactions and Studies of the College of Physicians of Philadelphia* (1980), vol. 2, pp. 1–25.
4.   Edmund Morris, *Theodore Rex* (New York: Random House, 2001), pp. 425–6.
5.   Jonathan R. T. Davidson, Kathryn M. Connor and Marvin Swartz, 'Mental Illness in US Presidents between 1776 and 1974: A Review of Biographical Sources', *Journal of Nervous and Mental Disease* (2006), vol. 194, pp. 47–51.
6.   David McCullough devotes a whole chapter to Roosevelt's asthma in his book *Mornings on Horseback: The Story of an Extraordinary Family, a Vanished Way of Life, and the Unique Child Who Became Theodore Roosevelt* (New York: Simon & Schuster, 2001).
7.   Candice Millard, *The River of Doubt: Into the Unknown Amazon* (London: Little, Brown, 2005), p. 17.
8.   Ibid.
9.   Edmund Morris, *The Rise of Theodore Roosevelt*, rev. ed. (New York: Modern Library, 2001), p. 297.
10.   Ibid., p. 736.
11.   Morris, *Theodore Rex*, p. 16.
12.   McCullough, *Mornings on Horseback*, p. 367.
13.   Ronald R. Fieve, *Moodswing: Dr Fieve on Depression*, rev. ed. (New York: William Morrow, 1989), pp. 132–3.
14.   'Mr Pulitzer's reply', *New York Times*, 16 December 1908.
15.   Millard, *River of Doubt*, p. 13.
16.   Ibid., p. 14.
17.   Ibid., pp. 335–6.
18.   Lucille D'Oyen Iremonger, *The Fiery Chariot: A Study of British Prime Ministers and the Search for Love* (London: Secker & Warburg, 1970), p. 228.
19.   Dick Leonard, *A Century of Premiers: Salisbury to Blair* (Basingstoke: Palgrave Macmillan, 2005).
20.   'The Impact of Wilson's Neurologic Disease During the Paris Peace Conference', in Arthur S. Link (ed.), *The Papers of Woodrow Wilson, vol. 58: April 23–May 9, 1919* (Princeton, NJ: Princeton University Press, 1988), pp. 612–13.
21.   Ibid., pp. 629–63.
22.   Edwin A Weinstein, 'Woodrow Wilson's Neuropsychological Impairment and the Paris Peace Conference', in Link, *Papers of Woodrow Wilson, vol. 58*, pp. 630–1.
23.   George Walden, *God Won't Save America: Psychosis of a Nation* (London: Gibson Square, 2007), p. 226.

24.   Bert E. Park, *The Impact of Illness on World Leaders* (Philadelphia: University of Pennsylvania Press, 1986), pp. 3–73.

25.   Colin Clifford, *The Asquiths* (London: John Murray, 2002), pp. 192, 193.

26.   Roy Jenkins, *Portraits and Miniatures* (London: Macmillan, 1993), pp. 126–7.

27.   Hugh Purcell, *Lloyd George* (London: Haus, 2006), p. 142.

28.   John Grigg, *Lloyd George: War Leader 1916–1918* (London: Allen Lane, 2002), pp. 11–13.

29.   Lord Beaverbrook, *The Decline and Fall of Lloyd George: And Great Was the Fall Thereof* (London: Collins, 1963), p. 141.

30.   Ibid., pp. 10–11.

31.   Kenneth O. Morgan, *Consensus and Disunity: The Lloyd George Coalition Government 1918–1922* (Oxford: Clarendon Press, 1979), p. 375.

32.   Ibid., p. 147.

33.   Ibid., pp. 259–60.

34.   MacMillan, *Paris 1919*, p. 188.

35.   Robert Lloyd George, *David and Winston* (London: John Murray, 2005), p. 164.

36.   C. P. Snow, *Variety of Men* (London: Macmillan, 1967), pp. 97–8.

37.   Purcell, *Lloyd George*, pp. 94, 93.

38.   Beaverbrook, *Decline and Fall of Lloyd George*, p. 233.

39.   Jacques Delamare (ed.), *Garnier Delamare: Dictionnaire des termes de médecine*, 26th ed. (Paris: Maloine, 2000), p. 259.

40.   François Boller, Annie Ganansia-Ganem, Florence Lebert and Florence Pasquier, 'Neuropsychiatric Afflictions of Modern French Presidents: Maréchal Henri-Philippe Pétain and Paul Deschanel', *European Journal of Neurology* (1999), vol. 6, pp. 133–6.

41.   Robert H. Ferrell, *The Presidency of Calvin Coolidge* (Lawrence: University Press of Kansas, 1998), p. 193.

42.   Stephen Graubard, *The Presidents: The Transformation of the American Presidency from Theodore Roosevelt to George W. Bush* (London: Allen Lane, 2004), p. 453, note 5.

43.   Davidson et al., 'Mental Illness in US Presidents between 1776 and 1974'.

44.   Graubard, *Presidents*, pp. 214–27.

45.   Donald R. McCoy, *Calvin Coolidge: The Quiet President* (Lawrence: University Press of Kansas, 1988), pp. 8, 30–31, 145, 159–63, 290, 389–91.

46.   Hugh L'Etang, *Ailing Leaders in Power 1914–1994* (London: Royal Society of Medicine Press, 1995).

47.   David Marquand, *Ramsay MacDonald* (London: Jonathan Cape, 1977), p. 640.

48.   Robert Self, *Neville Chamberlain: A Biography* (Aldershot: Ashgate, 2006), p. 256.

49.   David Reynolds, *Summits: Six Meetings That Shaped the Twentieth Century* (London: Allen Lane, 2007), p. 91.

50.   Ibid.

51.   William Manchester, *The Caged Lion: Winston Spencer Churchill 1932–1940* (London: Michael Joseph, 1988), p. 421.

52.   Alan Bullock, *Hitler: A Study in Tyranny* (London: Odhams Press, 1952), p. 143.

53. Ian Kershaw, *Fateful Choices: Ten Decisions That Changed the World 1940–1941* (London: Allen Lane, 2007), p. 65.
54. Ibid., p. 85.
55. Ibid., p. 409.
56. Ibid., pp. 409–10.
57. Rodric Braithwaite, *Moscow 1941: A City and Its People at War* (London: Profile, 2006), pp. 304–20.
58. Diary of Walther Hewel, 8 December 1941, Institut für Zeitgeschichte, Munich, ED 100.
59. Braithwaite, *Moscow 1941*, p. 307.
60. Kershaw, *Fateful Choices*, p. 423.
61. Dr Henry A. Murray, *Analysis of the Personality of Adolph Hitler* (1943), available from the Cornell University Law Library website (http://library.lawschool.cornell.edu).
62. Walter C. Langer, *The Mind of Adolf Hitler: The Secret Wartime Report* (New York: Basic, 1972).
63. Ibid., p. 126.
64. *New York Times*, 31 May 2005.
65. Langer, *Mind of Adolf Hitler*, p. 168.
66. Erich Fromm, *The Anatomy of Human Destructiveness* (New York: Owl, 1992), p. 546.
67. Ian Kershaw, *Hitler 1936–1945: Nemesis* (London: Allen Lane, 2000), pp. 726–8.
68. Laurence Rees, *Auschwitz: The Nazis and the Final Solution* (London: BBC, 2005), p. 21.
69. Kershaw, *Hitler 1889–1936: Hubris* (London: Allen Lane, 1998), p. 607.
70. Ibid., pp. 590–1.
71. Ibid., p. 841.
72. John Lukacs, *Five Days in London* (New Haven, CT: Yale University Press, 1999).
73. Kershaw, *Fateful Choices*, pp. 153, 155.
74. David Reynolds, *In Command of History: Churchill Fighting and Writing the Second World War* (London: Penguin, 2005), pp. 169–74.
75. Winston S. Churchill, *The Second World War, vol. 2: Their Finest Hour* (London: Reprint Society, 1951), p. 156.
76. David Bercuson and Holger H. Herwig, *One Christmas in Washington: The Secret Meeting between Roosevelt and Churchill That Changed the World*, pb ed. (Woodstock, NY: Overlook Press, 2006), p. 129.
77. Lord Moran, *Winston Churchill: The Struggle for Survival 1940–1965* (London: Constable, 1966), pp. 16–17, 644.
78. Field Marshal Lord Alanbrooke, *War Diaries 1939–1945* (London: Weidenfeld & Nicolson, 2001).
79. Anthony Storr, *Churchill's Black Dog, Kafka's Mice, and Other Phenomena of the Human Mind* (New York: Grove Press, 1965), p. 15.
80. Mary Soames, *Clementine Churchill by Her Daughter* (London: Cassell, 1979), p. 253.

81. John Colville, *Fringes of Power: Downing Street Diaries 1939–1955*, rev. ed. (London: Weidenfeld & Nicolson, 2004), p. 454.

82. Oliver Harvey, *The War Diaries of Oliver Harvey* (London: Collins, 1978).

83. John Connell, *Auchinleck* (London, Cassell, 1959).

84. Roy Jenkins, *Churchill: A Biography* (New York: Farrar, Straus & Giroux, 2001), p. 737.

85. Robert H. Ferrell, *The Dying President: Franklin D. Roosevelt 1944–1945* (Columbia: University of Missouri Press, 1998), pp. 35–42.

86. John C. Culver and John Hyde, *American Dreamer: The Life and Times of Henry A. Wallace* (New York: W. W. Norton, 2000), pp. 346–9.

87. Alanbrooke, *War Diaries 1939–1945*, p. 679.

88. John and Anna Boettiger, November 1943–February 1945 papers, Presidential Archive, Hyde Park, New York.

89. Moran, *Winston Churchill*, p. 226.

90. Alen J. Salerian and Gregory H. Salerian, 'A Review of FDR's Mental Capacity During His Fourth Term and Its Impact on History', *Forensic Examiner*, Spring 2005, pp. 31–38.

91. Charles E. Bohlen, *The Transformation of American Foreign Policy* (New York: W. W. Norton, 1969), p. 44.

92. Arthur M. Schlesinger Jr, Foreword, in Susan Butler (ed.), *My Dear Mr Stalin: The Complete Correspondence between Franklin D. Roosevelt and Joseph V. Stalin* (New Haven, CT: Yale University Press, 2005).

93. Ibid., p. xi.

94. Jeremy Isaacs and Taylor Downing, *Cold War: For 45 Years the World Held Its Breath* (London: Bantam Press, 1998), p. 12.

95. Butler, *My Dear Mr Stalin*, pp. xv, 29.

96. Roy Jenkins, *Franklin Delano Roosevelt* (London: Pan, 2005), pp. 165–6.

97. Geoffrey C. Ward (ed.), *Closest Companion: The Unknown Story of the Intimate Friendship between Franklin Roosevelt and Margaret Suckley* (Boston: Houghton Mifflin, 1995).

98. Doris Kearns Goodwin, *No Ordinary Time: Franklin and Eleanor Roosevelt – The Home Front in World War II* (New York: Touchstone, 1995), pp. 115–21.

99 Alan Bullock, *Hitler and Stalin: Parallel Lives*, rev. ed. (London: Fontana, 1993), p. 446.

100. Simon Sebag Montefiore, *Stalin: The Court of the Red Tsar* (London: Weidenfeld & Nicolson, 2003), p. 139.

101. Ibid., pp. 541–3, 550, 552.

102 Robert S. Robins and Jerrold M. Post, *Political Paranoia: The Psychopolitics of Hatred* (New Haven, CT: Yale University Press, 1997), pp. 5, 291.

103 Simon Sebag Montefiore, *Young Stalin* (London: Weidenfeld & Nicolson, 2007), p. 4.

104. Kershaw, *Fateful Choices*, p. 173.

105. Romano Mussolini, *My Father, Il Duce: A Memoir by Mussolini's Son* (Carlsbad, CA: Kales Press, 2006), p. 8.

106. Bullock, *Hitler and Stalin*, p. 996.
107. Sir John Colville, speaking on *Case History: Anthony Eden*, BBC Radio 4, 1998.
108. Jenkins, *Churchill*, p. 863.
109. As revealed in the BBC2 documentary *The Downing Street Patient*, 29 February 2004.
110. Lord Moran, *Churchill: The Struggle for Survival 1945–60*, rev. ed. (London: Robinson, 2006), pp. 366–7.
111. Soames, *Clementine Churchill by Her Daughter*, p. 508.
112. Colville, *Fringes of Power*, p. 662.

Chapter 2: 1953–2007

1. Robert P. Watson and Dale Berger, *Reconsidering Ike's Health and Legacy: A Surprising Lesson in Duty at the Little White House Residential Retreat* (Gettysburg, PA: Eisenhower Institute, 2006). www.eisenhowerinstitute.org/commentary/WatsonHealthIkeArticle.htm.
2. Clarence G. Lasby, *Eisenhower's Heart Attack: How Ike Beat Heart Disease and Held On to the Presidency* (Lawrence: University Press of Kansas, 1996), pp. 97–102.
3. Jerrold M. Post and Robert S. Robins, *When Illness Strikes the Leader: The Dilemma of the Captive King* (New Haven, CT: Yale University Press, 1993), p. 15.
4. Franz H. Messerli, Adrian W. Messerli and Thomas F. Lüscher, 'Eisenhower's Billion-Dollar Heart Attack – 50 Years Later', *New England Journal of Medicine* (2005), vol. 353, pp. 1205–7.
5. Geoffrey Perret, 'Lifesaver', in *Eisenhower* (New York: Random House, 1999).
6. Post and Robins, *When Illness Strikes the Leader*, p. 17.
7. Herbert L. Abrams, *The President Has Been Shot: Confusion, Disability, and the 25th Amendment in the Aftermath of the Attempted Assassination of Ronald Reagan* (New York: W. W. Norton, 1992), p. 173.
8. Robert A. Caro, *The Path to Power* (New York: Alfred A. Knopf, 1982), pp. 743–53.
9. Robert A. Caro, *The Years of Lyndon Johnson, vol. 3: Master of the Senate:* (London: Vintage, 2003), pp. 620–36.
10. Clark Clifford and Richard Holbrooke, *Counsel to the President: A Memoir* (New York: Random House, 1991), pp. 385–6.
11. Jeff Shesol, *Mutual Contempt: Lyndon Johnson, Robert Kennedy, and the Feud that Defined a Decade* (New York: W. W. Norton, 1997), p. 35.
12. Ibid., p. 361.
13. Robert Dallek, *Lone Star Rising: Lyndon Johnson and His Times 1908–1960* (Oxford: Oxford University Press, 1991), p. 556.
14. Liz Carpenter, *Ruffles and Flourishes: The Warm and Tender Story of a Simple Girl Who Found Adventure in the White House* (New York: Pocket,1971), p. 261.
15. Richard N. Goodwin, *Remembering America: A Voice from the Sixties* (Boston: Little, Brown, 1988), p. 398.

16. Ibid., p. 403.
17. Ibid., p. 390.
18. Robert Dallek, *Lyndon B. Johnson: Portrait of a President* (London: Penguin, 2005), pp. 376–7.
19. Vaughn Davis Bornet, *The Presidency of Lyndon B. Johnson* (Lawrence: University Press of Kansas, 1984), p. 294.
20. Barbara W. Tuchman, *March of Folly: From Troy to Vietnam* (New York: Ballantine, 1985), pp. 374–6.
21. Charles Williams, *The Last Great Frenchman: A Life of Charles de Gaulle* (London: Little, Brown, 1993), pp. 133, 180–1.
22. Jean Lacouture, *De Gaulle: The Ruler 1945–1970* (London: Harvill Press, 1991), pp. 502–3. The constitution laid down that 'by virtue of a specific delegation of authority and for a specific agenda, the Prime Minister may chair the Council of Ministers in the place of the President of the Republic.'
23. Williams, *Last Great Frenchman*, p. 465.
24. Lacouture, *De Gaulle*, p. 553.
25. Georges Pompidou, *Pour rétablir une vérité* (Paris: Flammarion, 1982), p. 201.
26. Tony Judt, *Postwar: A History of Europe since 1945* (London: Heinemann, 2005), p. 541.
27. Willy Brandt, *My Life in Politics* (London: Hamish Hamilton, 1992), p. 200.
28. Peter Merseburger, *Willy Brandt 1913–1992: Visionär und Realist* (Munich: DVA, 2002).
29. Brandt, *My Life in Politics*, pp. 286–97.
30. John Gambill, 'Potential Problems of Detecting and Treating Psychosis in the White House', *International Journal of Social Psychiatry* (1980), vol. 26, pp. 255–62.
31. James Reston, 'Let the voters beware', *International Herald Tribune*, 8 May 1975, quoted in William Safire, *Before the Fall: An Inside View of the Pre-Watergate White House* (Garden City, NY: Doubleday, 1975).
32. Anthony Summers, *The Arrogance of Power: The Secret World of Richard Nixon* (London: Victor Gollancz, 2000), pp. 363–4.
33. Ibid., pp. 333, 372.
34. David G. Winter, 'Things I've Learned about Personality from Studying Political Leaders at a Distance', *Journal of Personality* (2005), vol. 73, pp. 557–84.
35. Peter Morgan, *Frost/Nixon* (London: Faber & Faber, 2006), p. 4.
36. Jonathan R. T. Davidson, Kathryn M. Connor and Marvin Swartz, 'Mental Illness in US Presidents between 1776 and 1974: A Review of Biographical Sources', *Journal of Nervous and Mental Disease* (2006), vol. 194, pp. 47–51.
37. Quoted in Robert Dallek, *Nixon and Kissinger: Partners in Power* (New York: HarperCollins, 2007), p. 546.
38. Ibid.
39. Summers, *Arrogance of Power*, p. 537.
40. Zbigniew Brzezinski, *The Grand Failure: The Birth and Death of Communism in the Twentieth Century* (New York: Collier, 1990), pp. 154–5.

41. Jung Chang and Jon Halliday, *Mao: The Unknown Story* (London: Jonathan Cape, 2005), p. 42.

42. Zhisui Li, *The Private Life of Chairman Mao: The Memoirs of Mao's Personal Physician*, tr. Tai Hung-chao (London: Chatto & Windus, 1994).

43. Philip Short, *Mao: A Life*, pb ed. (London: John Murray, 2004), p. 315.

44. Ibid., pp. 603, 615.

45. Margaret MacMillan, *Nixon and Mao: The Week That Changed the World* (New York: Random House, 2007), p. 65.

46. Philip Ziegler, *Wilson: The Authorised Life of Lord Wilson of Rievaulx* (London: Weidenfeld & Nicolson, 1993), p. 487.

47. Ibid., p. 511.

48. Lawrence K. Altman MD, 'Reagan and Alzheimer's: a doctor notes', *New York Times*, 17 June 2004.

49. Richard Reeves, *President Reagan: The Triumph of Imagination*, pb ed. (New York: Simon & Schuster, 2006), p. 381.

50. The diaries have now been edited and published in one volume (Ronald Reagan, *The Reagan Diaries*, ed. Douglas Brinkley (New York: HarperCollins, 2007)).

51. Edmund Morris, *Dutch: A Memoir of Ronald Reagan* (New York: Random House, 1999), p. 622.

52. Hugh L'Etang, *Ailing Leaders in Power 1914–1994* (London: Royal Society of Medicine Press, 1995), pp. 55–6.

53. Altman, 'Reagan and Alzheimer's'.

54. Morris, *Dutch*, pp. 656, 664.

55. Lawrence K. Altman MD, 'Reagan's twilight', *New York Times*, 5 October 1997.

56. Reeves, *President Reagan*, p. 490.

57. Jorma Palo, 'The cover up of President Urho Kekkonen's dementia and its impact on the political life of Finland', *European Journal of Neurology* (1999), vol. 6, pp, 137–40.

58. Abrams, *The President Has Been Shot*, p. 179.

59. Ibid., pp. 181–2.

60. Ibid., pp. 162–3.

61. Ibid., p. 257.

62. Lawrence K. Altman MD, 'Reagan and Alzheimer's: Following path his mother traveled', *New York Times*, 8 November 1994.

63. George Bush and Brent Scowcroft, *A World Transformed* (New York: Alfred A. Knopf, 1998), p. 249.

64. Quoted in Philip Stephens, 'Blairism will outlive the departure of a battered Blair', *Financial Times*, 9 February 2007.

65. Hugo Young, *This Blessed Plot: Britain and Europe from Churchill to Blair* (London: Macmillan, 1998), p. 368.

66. David Owen, *Time to Declare* (London: Michael Joseph, 1991), p. 777.

67. General Sir John Hackett et al., *The Third World War: A Future History* (London: Sidgwick & Jackson, 1978).

68. Christopher Andrew and Vasili Mitrokhin, *The Mitrokhin Archive, vol. 2:
     The KGB and the World* (London: Allen Lane, 2005), p. 269.
69. John Lewis Gaddis, *The Cold War* (London: Allen Lane, 2006), pp. 243–6.
70. Strobe Talbott, *The Russia Hand: A Memoir of Presidential Diplomacy* (New York:
     Random House, 2002), p. 206.
71. Leon Aron, *Yeltsin: A Revolutionary Life* (New York: St Martin's Press, 2000),
     p. 590.
72. Aluf Benn, *Haaretz*, 5 January 2007.

Chapter 3: Prime Minister Eden's illness and Suez

1.   Quoted in Anthony Montague Browne, *Long Sunset: Memoirs of Winston
     Churchill's Last Private Secretary* (London: Cassell, 1995), p. 213.
2.   Lord Owen, Lord Henry Cohen History of Medicine Lecture, February 2005,
     subsequently published as 'The Effect of Prime Minister Anthony Eden's Illness
     on His Decision-Making during the Suez Crisis', *QJM* (2005), vol. 98,
     pp. 387–402.
3.   Gabriel Kune, 'Anthony Eden's Bile Duct: Portrait of an Ailing Leader', *ANZ
     Journal of Surgery* (2003), vol. 73, pp. 341–5.
4.   D. R. Thorpe, *Eden: The Life and Times of Anthony Eden, First Earl of Avon
     1897–1977* (London: Chatto & Windus, 2003), pp. 384–6.
5.   Robert Rhodes James, *Anthony Eden* (London: Weidenfeld & Nicolson, 1986),
     pp. 362–4.
6.   Sir Christopher Booth, speaking on *Case History: Anthony Eden*, BBC Radio 4,
     1998.
7.   Thorpe, *Eden*, p. 385.
8.   W. Russell Brain, 'Encounters with Winston Churchill', *Medical History* (2000),
     vol. 44, pp. 12–13.
9.   Clarissa Eden, *Clarissa Eden: A Memoir – From Churchill to Eden*, ed. Cate Haste
     (London: Weidenfeld & Nicolson, 2007), p. 183.
10. Ibid., p. 225.
11. James, *Anthony Eden*, p. 432.
12. Eden, *Clarissa Eden*, p. 228.
13. Anthony Nutting, *No End of a Lesson: The Story of Suez* (London: Constable,
     1967), pp. 34–5.
14. Eden, *Clarissa Eden*, pp. 186.
15. Thorpe, *Eden*, pp. 475–81.
16. Memorandum from Sir W. Churchill, 6 August 1956. Avon Papers, PM
     Personal Correspondence, ref. AP20/33/24, Special Collections, University of
     Birmingham. Also quoted in Martin Gilbert, *Winston S. Churchill, vol. 8: 'Never
     Despair' 1945–1965* (Oxford: Heinemann, 1988), pp. 1203–4.
17. Eden, *Clarissa Eden*, p. 237.
18. Guy Millard, 'Memorandum on Relations between the United Kingdom, the
     United States and France in the Months Following Egyptian Nationalisation of

the Suez Canal Company in 1956.' (Paper written in August 1957 and published by the Cabinet Office for UK Eyes Only on 21 October 1957). National Archives CAB 21/3314. This document does not spell out the detail of the collusion between France, Israel and the UK but is not exactly as originally written by Millard; that original version has disappeared.

19.   David Dutton, *Anthony Eden: A Life and Reputation*, pb ed. (London: Arnold, 1997), p. 423.

20.   Lord Deedes speaking on *The Downing Street Patient*, BBC2, 29 February 2004.

21.   Hugh Thomas, *The Suez Affair*, rev. ed. (London: Weidenfeld & Nicolson, 1986), pp. 43–4.

22.   Countess of Avon speaking on *Case History: Anthony Eden*, BBC Radio 4, 1998.

23.   Avon Papers, ref. AP39/4/2.

24.   Interview with Professor Malcolm Lader, *The Sunday Programme*, GMTV, 5 November 2006.

25.   Eden, *Clarissa Eden*, p. 260.

26.   Hugh L'Etang, *Ailing Leaders in Power 1914–1994* (London: Royal Society of Medicine Press, 1995), p. 10.

27.   James, *Anthony Eden*, p. 597.

28.   Ibid., p. 366.

29.   Nutting, *No End of a Lesson*.

30.   William Roger Louis, *Ends of British Imperialism: The Scramble for Empire, Suez and Decolonisation* (London: I. B. Tauris, 2006), pp. 653–6.

31.   Geoffrey Marston, 'Armed Intervention in the 1956 Suez Canal Crisis: The Legal Advice Tendered to the British Government', *International and Comparative Law Quarterly* (1988), vol. 37, pp. 773–817.

32.   Selwyn Lloyd personal papers, National Archives, ref. FO800/728, 52–3.

33.   Ibid., 58.

34.   Eden, *Clarissa Eden*, p. 248.

35.   *A Canal Too Far*, BBC Radio 3, 31 January 1987.

36.   Transcript of interview with Sir Richard Powell, papers of the Suez Oral History Project 1989–91, Liddell Hart Centre for Military Archives, King's College, London, ref. SUEZOHP 16.

37.   John Colville, *Fringes of Power: Downing Street Diaries 1939–1955*, rev. ed. (London: Weidenfeld & Nicolson, 2004), pp. 671–2.

38.   Eden, *Clarissa Eden*, p. 250.

39.   Thorpe, *Eden*, p. 519.

40.   Diary of Sir Evelyn Shuckburgh, Shuckburgh papers, ref. MS 191, Special Collections, University of Birmingham. Also published in edited form as Evelyn Shuckburgh, *Descent to Suez: Diaries 1951–56*, ed. John Charmley (London: Weidenfeld & Nicolson,1986).

41.   Professor David Dutton speaking on *Case History: Anthony Eden*, BBC Radio 4, 1998.

42.   Peter Hennessy, *The Prime Minister: The Office and Its Holders since 1945* (London: Allen Lane, 2000), p. 235.

43. Eden, *Clarissa Eden*, p. 250.

44. Thorpe, *Eden*, pp. 520–1.

45. Alistair Horne, *Macmillan 1894–1956: Volume I of the Official Biography* (London: Macmillan, 1998), pp. 420–3.

46. Dutton, *Anthony Eden*, p. 442.

47. Horne, *Macmillan 1894–1956*, p. 447.

48. James, *Anthony Eden*, p. 331.

49. Thorpe, *Eden*, pp. 515–19.

50. Louis, *Ends of British Imperialism*, p. 658.

51. Coulson to Lloyd, 30 October 1956, FO 800/741.

52. Lord Sherfield, speaking on *A Canal Too Far*, BBC Radio 3, 31 January 1987.

53. Lord Home, speaking on *A Canal Too Far*.

54. James, *Anthony Eden*, p. 617.

55. Hansard, HC Deb, 20 December 1956, vol. col. 1518.

56. Eden, *Clarissa Eden*, p. 261.

57. Avon Papers, ref. AP20/33/12A.

58. James, *Anthony Eden*, p. 532.

59. Bob Pierson Dixon's report of discussion with Sir Anthony Eden at Government House, Ottawa, 25–26 May 1957, Collection of Steve Forbes, New York.

60. Percy Cradock, *Know Your Enemy: How the Joint Intelligence Committee Saw the World* (London: John Murray, 2002).

61. Dutton, *Anthony Eden*, p. 424.

62. John W. Braasch, 'Anthony Eden's (Lord Avon) Biliary Tract Saga', *Annals of Surgery* (2003), vol. 238, pp. 772–5; Professor Gabriel Kune, speaking on GMTV, 5 November 2006.

63. Lord Butler, *The Art of the Possible: The Memoirs of Lord Butler, KG, CH* (London: Hamish Hamilton, 1971), p. 194.

64. Victor Sebestyen, *Twelve Days: Revolution 1956 – How the Hungarians Tried to Topple Their Soviet Masters* (London: Weidenfeld & Nicolson, 2006), p. 251.

65. Guy Millard, *A Canal Too Far*, BBC Radio 3, 31 January 1987.

Chapter 4: President Kennedy's health

1. Gretchen Rubin, *Forty Ways to Look at JFK* (New York: Ballantine, 2005), p. 125.

2. Robert McNamara, 'Apocalypse Soon', *Foreign Policy*, May/June 2005.

3. Aleksandr Fursenko and Timothy Naftali, *'One Hell of a Gamble': The Secret History of the Cuban Missile Crisis* (London: John Murray, 1997), pp. 240–3.

4. Trumbull Higgins, *The Perfect Failure: Kennedy, Eisenhower, and the CIA at the Bay of Pigs* (New York: W. W. Norton, 1987), pp. 58–60.

5. Robert Dallek, *An Unfinished Life: John F. Kennedy 1917–1963* (Boston: Little, Brown / London: Allen Lane, 2003), p. 362.

6. Arthur M. Schlesinger Jr, *A Thousand Days: John F. Kennedy in the White House* (Boston: Houghton Mifflin, 1965), p. 253.

7. Ibid.
8. Michael R. Beschloss, *Kennedy v. Khrushchev: The Crisis Years 1960–1963* (London: Faber & Faber, 1991), p. 114.
9. Arthur M. Schlesinger Jr, *Robert Kennedy and His Times* (London: Andre Deutsch, 1978), p. 454.
10. Schlesinger, *A Thousand Days*, pp. 246–7.
11. Richard Reeves, *President Kennedy: Profile of Power* (New York: Simon & Schuster, 1993), p. 77.
12. Richard N Goodwin, *Remembering America: A Voice from the Sixties* (Boston: Little, Brown, 1988), p. 173.
13. *Operation Zapata: The 'Ultrasensitive' Report and Testimony of the Board of Inquiry on the Bay of Pigs* (Washington, DC: Aletheia, 1981), p. 202.
14. Ibid., p. 39.
15. Irving L. Janis, *Victims of Groupthink: A Psychological Study of Foreign-Policy Decisions and Fiascoes* (Boston: Houghton Mifflin, 1972), p. 48.
16. Hugh Sidey, *John F. Kennedy, President*, new ed. (New York: Athenaeum, 1964), p. 126.
17. Dallek, *Unfinished Life*, pp. 369–70.
18. Janis, *Victims of Groupthink*, p. 165.
19. Medical records, John F. Kennedy Library, boxes 45, 48.
20. Robert Dallek, 'The Medical Ordeals of JFK', *Atlantic Monthly*, December 2002.
21. Dallek, *Unfinished Life*, Preface & p. 105.
22. James A. Nichols MD et al., 'Management of Adrenocortical Insufficiency During Surgery', *Archives of Surgery* (1955), vol. 71, pp. 737–40.
23. John F. Kennedy, *Profiles in Courage* (New York: Harper, 1956).
24. Janet Travell, *Office Hours: Day and Night – The Autobiography of Janet Travell, M.D.* (New York: World, 1968), p. 330.
25. Extract from oral interview of Pierre Salinger by Theodore White, John F. Kennedy Library, boxes 70–3.
26. William Alwyn Lishman, *Organic Psychiatry: The Psychological Consequences of Cerebral Disorder*, 3rd ed. (Oxford: Blackwell Science, 1998), p. 519.
27. Ernest Barcella, 'Health Profile of Our New President', *Today's Health*, February 1961. Also featured in the *New York Times*, 17 January 1961.
28. Dallek, *Unfinished Life*, p. 398.
29. Seymour M. Hersh, *The Dark Side of Camelot* (Boston: Little, Brown, 1997), pp. 231–2.
30. Beschloss, *Kennedy v. Khrushchev*, pp. 23–4.
31. *Foreign Relations of the United States 1961–1963, vol. 10: Cuba 1961–1962* (Washington, DC: Department of State, 1997), p. 305.
32. McGeorge Bundy, memo to Kennedy, 16 May 1961, National Security Files, John F. Kennedy Library, boxes 287–90.
33. Report of the Committee on Discipline, Regents of the University of the State of New York, 25 February 1975.

34. *New York Times*, Monday 4 December 1972, based on reporting by Boyce Reusberger and the paper's medical correspondent, Lawrence K. Altman, amongst others.
35. Dallek, *Unfinished Life*, p. 398.
36. Hersh, *Dark Side of Camelot*, pp. 235–6.
37. Lishman, *Organic Psychiatry*.
38. Reports of the Committee on Discipline, Regents of the University of the State of New York, 22 March 1973–25 February 1975.
39. Hersh, *Dark Side of Camelot*, pp. 234–5.
40. Dallek, *Unfinished Life*, p. 582.
41. Reeves, *President Kennedy*, p. 147.
42. Dallek, *Unfinished Life*, pp. 369–70.
43. Michael Beschloss, *The Crisis Years: Kennedy and Khrushchev 1960–1963* (New York: Edward Burlingame, 1991), pp. 189–91.
44. H. P. Rang, M. M. Dale and R. M. Ritter, *Pharmacology*, 3rd ed. (Edinburgh: Churchill Livingstone, 1995), p. 639.
45. Reeves, *President Kennedy*, p. 147.
46. Ibid., pp. 149, 154.
47. William Taubman, *Khrushchev: The Man and His Era*, pb ed. (London: Simon and Schuster, 2005), pp. xviii–xx.
48. Dr Bryant Wedge, 'Khrushchev at a Distance: A Study of Public Personality', *Trans-Action*, October 1968, pp. 24–8.
49. Nancy McWilliams, *Psychoanalytic Diagnosis: Understanding Personality Structure in the Clinical Process* (New York: Guilford Press, 1994), p. 248.
50. Taubman, *Khrushchev*, p. 577.
51. Ibid., p. xix.
52. Reeves, *President Kennedy*, p. 162.
53. Ibid., p. 166.
54. David Reynolds, *Summits: Six Meetings That Shaped the Twentieth Century* (London: Allen Lane, 2007), p. 204.
55. Reeves, *President Kennedy*, p. 172.
56. Reynolds, *Summits*, p. 202.
57. Alistair Horne, *Macmillan 1957–1986: Volume II of the Official Biography* (London: Macmillan, 1989), pp. 290, 303–4.
58. Reeves, *President Kennedy*, p. 181.
59. Dallek, *Unfinished Life*, p. 471.
60. Reeves, *President Kennedy*, pp. 242–3.
61. Dallek, *Unfinished Life*, p. 472.
62. Interview, 17 October 1967, Oral History, John F. Kennedy Library.
63. Susan E. B. Schwartz, *Into the Unknown: The Remarkable Life of Hans Kraus* (Lincoln, NE: iUniverse [*sic*], 2005), pp. 178–9.
64. Examination report by Hans Kraus MD written on 19 October 1961, in Dr George Burkley's medical notes for Patient X, John F. Kennedy Library.
65. Reeves, *President Kennedy*, p. 273.

66. Dallek, *Unfinished Life*, p. 473.
67. Laurence Learner, 'The Kennedy Men 1901–1963', *Boston Globe*, 11 November 2002.
68. Quoted in Dallek, *Unfinished Life*, p. 581.
69. Herbert S. Parmet, *JFK: The Presidency of John F. Kennedy* (New York: Penguin, 1983), p. 121.
70. Theodore C. Sorensen, *Kennedy*, pb ed. (London: Pan, 1966), p. 343.
71. Goodwin, *Remembering America*, p. 184.
72. David Owen, *The Politics of Defence* (London: Jonathan Cape, 1972).
73. Sorensen, *Kennedy*, p. 757.
74. John Lewis Gaddis, *The Cold War* (London: Allen Lane, 2006), pp. 75–8.
75. Robert McNamara, speech at the fortieth anniversary of the Cuban missile crisis, Havana, 11–12 October 2002.
76. Fursenko and Naftali, *'One Hell of a Gamble'*, pp. 281–3.
77. Beschloss, *Crisis Years*, p. 531.
78. Fursenko and Naftali, *'One Hell of a Gamble'*, p. 284.
79. Jeff Shesol, *Mutual Contempt: Lyndon Johnson, Robert Kennedy, and the Feud That Defined a Decade* (New York: W. W. Norton, 1997), p. 97.
80. Dallek, *Unfinished Life*, p. 576.
81. Anthony Summers and Robbyn Swann, *Sinatra: The Life* (New York: Alfred A. Knopf, 2005), p. 476.
82. Dallek, *Unfinished Life*, pp. 636–8.
83. Sidney Blumenthal, *The Clinton Wars* (New York: Farrar, Straus & Giroux, 2003), p. 786.
84. Dallek, *Unfinished Life*, p. 582.
85. Schwartz, *Into the Unknown*, p. 204.
86. 'The J.F.K. file', *New York Times*, 19 November 2002.
87. Dallek, *Unfinished Life*, p. 705.

Chapter 5: The Shah's secret illness

1. Robert Fisk, *The Great War for Civilisation: The Conquest of the Middle East* (London: Fourth Estate, 2005), p. 1281.
2. Alinaghi Alikhani, 'Introduction', in Assadollah Alam, *The Shah and I: The Confidential Diary of Iran's Royal Court 1969–1977* (London: I. B. Taurus, 1991), pp. 1–25.
3. Farah Pahlavi, *An Enduring Love: My Life with the Shah* (New York: Miramax, 2004), p. 261.
4. B. H. Kean, *M.D.: One Doctor's Adventures among the Famous and Infamous from the Jungles of Panama to a Park Avenue Practice* (New York: Ballantine, 1990), p. 230.
5. Quoted in Pahlavi, *Enduring Love*, pp. 266–7.
6. Ibid., p. 268.
7. Zbigniew Brzezinski, *Power and Principle: Memoirs of the National Security Adviser 1977–1981* (New York: Farrar, Straus & Giroux, 1983), p. 370.

8. Ibid., p. 396.
9. Mohammed Reza Pahlavi, *The Shah's Story* (London: Michael Joseph, 1980), p. 182.
10. William Shawcross, *The Shah's Last Ride: The Story of the Exile, Misadventures and Death of the Emperor* (London: Chatto and Windus, 1989).
11. Edward Mortimer, 'Iran: the greatest revolution since 1917', *Spectator*, 17 February 1979.
12. Pahlavi, *Shah's Story*, p. 215.
13. M. Bloom, 'The Pahlavi Problem: A Superficial Diagnosis Brought the Shah into the United States', *Science* (1980), vol. 207, pp. 282–4.
14. Cyrus Vance, *Hard Choices, Critical Years in America's Foreign Policy* (New York: Simon and Schuster, 1983), pp. 389–91.
15. Shawcross, *Shah's Last Ride*, p. 416.

Chapter 6: President Mitterrand's prostate cancer

1. Ronald Tiersky, *François Mitterrand: The Last French President* (New York: St Martin's Press, 2000), p. 321.
2. Claude Gubler, *Le Grand Secret*. Available in an English translation as *The Big Secret* at www.kantor.com. All subsequent references to Gubler refer to this text.
3. Jonathan Fenby, *On the Brink: The Trouble with France* (London: Little, Brown, 1998), p. 381.
4. Jacques Attali, *Verbatim, tome 1: Chronique des années 1981–1986* (Paris: Fayard, 1993).
5. Quoted in Richard J. Golsan, *Vichy's Afterlife: History and Counterhistory in Postwar France* (Lincoln: University of Nebraska Press, 2000), pp. 152–3.
6. Alistair Cole, *François Mitterrand: A Study in Political Leadership* (London: Routledge, 1994), pp. 11–12, 19–20.
7. David S. Bell, *François Mitterrand* (Cambridge: Polity Press, 2005), pp. 171–81.
8. Thierry Pfister, *Lettre ouverte aux gardiens du mensonge* (Paris: Albin Michel, 1999).
9. Tiersky, *François Mitterrand*, p. 133.
10. David Owen, *Balkan Odyssey* (London: Victor Gollancz, 1995), pp. 14–17.
11. Edouard Balladur, *Deux ans à Matignon* (Paris: Plon, 1995).
12. Quoted in Tiersky, *François Mitterrand*, pp. 228–43.
13. Hubert Védrine, *Les Mondes de François Mitterrand: À l'Élysée 1981–1995* (Paris: Fayard, 1996), pp. 56–7.
14. Owen, *Balkan Odyssey*, pp. 123–5.
15. Lieutenant-General Romeo A. Dallaire, 'Foreword', in Scott R. Feil, *Preventing Genocide: How the Early Use of Force Might Have Succeeded in Rwanda* (Carnegie Corporation of New York, 1998).
16. Adam Lebor, *'Complicity with Evil': The United Nations in the Age of Modern Genocide* (New Haven, CT: Yale University Press, 2006), p. 167.
17. Elaine Sciolino, 'Dead 10 years, Mitterrand, "the last King", lives on in French esteem', *International Herald Tribune*, 14/15 January 2006.

Chapter 7: Bush, Blair and the war in Iraq

1. Stephen Graubard, *The Presidents: The Transformation of the American Presidency from Theodore Roosevelt to George W. Bush* (London: Allen Lane, 2006), p. 39.
2. Lord Morgan, 'The Judgement of History', *Parliamentary Monitor* (2007), vol. 149, pp. 16–17.
3. Jonathan C. Randal, *Kurdistan: After Such Knowledge, What Forgiveness?* (London: Bloomsbury, 1988), p. 73.
4. John Kampfner, *Blair's Wars* (London: Free Press, 2003), p. 32.
5. Michael Gordon and Bernard Trainor, *Cobra II: The Inside Story of the Invasion and Occupation of Iraq* (New York: Pantheon / London: Atlantic, 2006), p. 13.
6. Charles Guthrie, 'The war of the generals', *Sunday Times*, 28 March 1999.
7. Bob Woodward, *State of Denial: Bush at War, Part III* (New York: Simon & Schuster, 2006), pp. 60–1.
8. Kampfner, *Blair's Wars*, p. 57.
9. Andrew Rawnsley, *Servants of the People: The Inside Story of New Labour* (London: Hamish Hamilton, 2000), p. 272.
10. Kampfner, *Blair's Wars*, p. 49.
11. S. Schachter and J. Singer, 'Cognitive, Social and Physiological Determinants of Emotional State', *Psychological Review* (1962), vol. 69, pp. 379–99.
12. Francis Beckett, 'Blair's Way', *Management Today*, 1 March 2005.
13. David Owen, 'Two-Man Government', *Prospect*, December 2003; David Owen, 'The Ever-Growing Dominance of No. 10 in British Foreign Policy since 5 April 1982', in Graham Ziegner (ed.), *British Diplomacy: Foreign Secretaries Reflect* (London: Politico's, 2007).
14. General Sir Rupert Smith, *The Utility of Force: The Art of War in the Modern World* (London: Allen Lane, 2005).
15. Louise Richardson, *What Terrorists Want: Understanding the Enemy, Containing the Threat* (New York: Random House, 2006), p. 96.
16. Christian Alfonsi, *Circle in the Sand: Why We Went Back to Iraq* (New York: Doubleday, 2006), p. 354.
17. Ibid., pp. 368–9.
18. George Tenet, *At the Center of the Storm: My Years at the CIA* (New York: HarperCollins, 2007), pp. 160, 255.
19. Bruce Riedel, 'Al-Qaeda Strikes Back', *Foreign Affairs*, May/June 2007.
20. Kampfner, *Blair's Wars*, p. 263.
21. Leaked memorandum of 29 April 2000 from Tony Blair to staff, reported in the *Times*, 18 July 2000.
22. David Marquand, 'A man without history', *New Statesman*, 7 May 2007.
23. Paul Scott, *Tony & Cherie: A Special Relationship* (London: Sidgwick & Jackson, 2005).
24. Quoted in Anthony Seldon, *Blair Unbound* (London: Simon & Schuster, 2007), p. 87.

25. Christopher Meyer, *DC Confidential: The Controversial Memoirs of Britain's Ambassador to the U.S. at the Time of 9/11 and the Iraq War* (London: Weidenfeld & Nicolson, 2006), p. 190.

26. Thomas E. Ricks, *Fiasco: The American Military Adventure in Iraq* (London: Allen Lane, 2006), p. 31, quoting the National Security Council summary of the conversation reported by the 9/11 Commission.

27. Jerrold M. Post (ed.), *The Psychological Assessment of Political Leaders: With Profiles of Saddam Hussein and Bill Clinton* (Ann Arbor: University of Michigan Press, 2003), p. 344.

28. Pierre Rentchnick, *Médecine et Hygiène*, 6 March 1991, p. 662.

29. Hugh L'Etang, *Ailing Leaders in Power 1914–1994* (London: Royal Society of Medicine, 1995), p. 66.

30. Robert Fisk, *The Great War for Civilisation: The Conquest of the Middle East* (London: Fourth Estate, 2005), p. 262.

31. Eliot A. Cohen, *Supreme Command: Soldiers, Statesmen, and Leadership in Wartime* (New York: Anchor, 2003), p. 208.

32. Tenet, *At the Center of the Storm*, p. 321.

33. H. D. S. Greenway, 'Fatal combination of hubris and incompetence', *Boston Globe*, 11 July 2003; J Freedland, 'The blind prophet', *Guardian*, 3 September 2003; Arthur Schlesinger Jr, 'Opportunity knocks', *American Prospect*, 21 November 2004; Charles A. Kupchan and Ray Takeyh, 'Middle East: reaping what Bush sowed', *International Herald Tribune*, 19 July 2006; Ricks, *Fiasco*.

34. Alfonsi, *Circle in the Sand*, p. 68.

35. Gordon and Trainor, *Cobra II*, pp. 500–1.

36. George Packer, *The Assassin's Gate: America in Iraq* (New York: Farrar, Straus & Giroux, 2005), p. 147.

37. Mark Danner, *The Secret Way to War: The Downing Street Memo and the Iraq War's Buried History* (New York: New York Review, 2006).

38. Ibid., p. 140.

39. David Owen, 'Next stop Iraq', *Wall Street Journal*, 15 November 2001.

40. 'Fall of a Vulcan', *Time*, 7 November 2005.

41. Danner, *Secret Way to War*, pp. 148–9.

42. Ibid., pp. 152–3 & 161.

43. Ibid., pp. 88–89.

44. Tenet, *At the Center of the Storm*, p. 310.

45. Danner, *Secret Way to War*, p. 91.

46. Charles Tripp, 'Militias, vigilantes, death squads', *London Review of Books*, 25 January 2007.

47. George Packer, *Assassins' Gate*, pp. 114–15.

48. David Fromkin, *A Peace to End All Peace: The Fall of the Ottoman Empire and the Creation of the Modern Middle East* (New York: Avon, 1990).

49. John Newhouse, *Imperial America: The Bush Assault on the World Order* (New York: Albert A. Knopf, 2003), p. 43.

50. Meyer, *DC Confidential*, pp. 8, 223–4.

51. Philippe Sands, *Lawless World: Making and Breaking Global Rules*, rev. ed. (London: Penguin, 2006), pp. 272–3.
52. Don Van Natta Jr, 'Bush was set on path to war, memo by British adviser', *New York Times*, 27 March 2006.
53. John Ware, 'Revealed: Blair was warned of looming disaster in Iraq', *Sunday Telegraph*, 28 October 2007.
54. Norman Dixon, *On the Psychology of Military Incompetence* (London: Jonathan Cape, 1976), pp. 399–400.
55. Michael Isikoff and David Corn, *Hubris: The Inside Story of Spin, Scandal, and the Selling of the Iraq War* (New York: Crown, 2006), pp. 417–19.
56. Meyer, *DC Confidential*, pp. 190, 224, 282.
57. Rajiv Chandrasekaran, *Imperial Life in the Emerald City: Inside Baghdad's Green Zone* (London: Bloomsbury, 2007), p. 33.
58. Robert D. Hormats, *The Price of Liberty: Paying for America's Wars* (New York: Times, 2007).
59. Bob Woodward, *Bush at War* (New York: Simon & Schuster, 2002), pp. 333 & 334.
60. Charles Cogan, *French Negotiating Behaviour: Dealing with La Grande Nation* (Washington, DC: United States Institute of Peace Press, 2003), pp. 205–9.
61. Sands, *Lawless World*, p. 273.
62. 'Blair's Mission Impossible: the doomed effort to win a second UN Resolution', *Financial Times*, 29 May 2003.
63. Van Natta, 'Bush was set on path to war'.
64. Bob Woodward, *Plan of Attack* (New York: Simon & Schuster, 2004), p. 285.
65. Ned Temko, 'Blair "ignored Chirac on Iraq"', *Observer*, 25 February 2007, reporting on Sir Stephen Wall's interview in a BBC2 three-part documentary on Tony Blair by Michael Cockerell.
66. Ibid.
67. John Vicour, 'A very different take on France's role in Iraq', *International Herald Tribune*, 20 March 2007.
68. Sands, *Lawless World*, Appendix X, pp. 328–42.
69. Matthew Parris, 'Are we witnessing the madness of Tony Blair?', *Times*, 29 March 2003.
70. Isikoff and Corn, *Hubris*.
71. David Hare, *Stuff Happens* (London: Faber & Faber, 2004).
72. Ron Suskind, *The Price of Loyalty: George W. Bush, The White House, and the Education of Paul O'Neill*, pb ed. (New York: Simon & Schuster, 2004), pp. 127, 149.
73. Peter W. Galbraith, *The End of Iraq: How American Incompetence Created a War without End* (New York: Simon & Schuster, 2006), p. 102.
74. Chandrasekaran, *Imperial Life in the Emerald City*, p. 77.
75. *Guardian*, 2 May 2007.
76. Chandrasekaran, *Imperial Life in the Emerald City*, p. 84.
77. Ricks, *Fiasco*, p. 158.

78. Tony Blair, *Today*, BBC Radio 4, 22 February 2007.

79. Seldon, *Blair Unbound*, p. 191.

80. Quoted in Joseph S. Nye Jr, 'Transformational Leadership and US Broad Strategy', *Foreign Affairs*, July/August 2006, p. 148.

81. Woodward, *State of Denial*, p. 241.

82. Ibid., p. 226.

83. Ibid., p. 82.

84. Ricks, *Fiasco*, p. 129.

85. On the Ground, Nicholas D. Kristof's *New York Times* blog.

86. Woodward, *Plan of Attack*, p. 249.

87. Tenet, *At the Center of the Storm*, p. 362.

88. Lawrence Wilkerson, *PM*, BBC Radio 4, 11 May 2007.

89. Woodward, *State of Denial*, p. 249.

90. Ricks, *Fiasco*, p. 407.

91. Ibid., p. 408.

92. John Yoo, *War by Other Means: An Insider's Account of the War on Terror* (New York: Atlantic Monthly Press, 2006), p. 39.

93. Ibid., p. 41.

94. Brian Urquhart, 'The outlaw world', *New York Review of Books*, 11 May 2006.

95. Gordon and Trainor, *Cobra II*, pp. 471–3. The same authors also describe how there were signs that an insurgency was already being planned in the reports coming from army field commanders in the early stages of the invasion (pp. 500–1).

96. Seldon, *Blair Unbound*, pp. 189–90.

97. David Gardner, 'Lost in Iraq: the illusion of an American strategy', *Financial Times*, 10 August 2007.

98. Ahmed Rashid, 'NATO's failure portends a wider war', *International Herald Tribune*, 1 December 2006.

99. Quoted in Andrew Pierce and Thomas Harding, 'Top aide's damning attack on Blair's Iraq war', *Daily Telegraph*, 22 February 2007.

100. Scott, *Tony & Cherie*, p. 227.

101. Review of Intelligence on Weapons of Mass Destruction, HC 898, 14 July 2004.

102. Kevin Woods, James Lacey and Williamson Murray, 'Saddam's Delusions: The View from Inside', *Foreign Affairs*, May/June 2006, pp. 6–8.

103. Tenet, *At the Center of the Storm*, pp. 375–83.

104. Tom Bower, 'Blair's defence over Iraq is crumbling', *Times*, 3 February 2007.

105. Christopher Ames, 'Revealed: the Iraq nuclear deceit', *New Statesman*, 7 May 2007.

106. Hansard, HL Deb, 22 February 2007, vol. 689, col. 1231.

107. Michael Barber, *Instruction to Deliver: Tony Blair, Public Services and the Challenge of Achieving Targets* (London: Politico's, 2007).

108. 'How not to run a country', interview with Lord Butler, *Spectator*, 9 December 2004.

109. General Sir Michael Rose, 'Enough of his excuses: Blair must be impeached over Iraq', *Guardian*, 10 January 2006.

110. Hansard, HL Deb, 29 June 2006, vol. 683, col. 1350.

111. Kampfner, *Blair's Wars*, pp. 302–3.

112. Philip Ziegler, *Wilson: The Authorised Life of Lord Wilson of Rievaulx* (London: Weidenfeld & Nicolson, 1993), pp. 222–3.

113. Mark Lawson, 'The truth about a special relationship: warmth can be riskier than distance', *Guardian*, 8 April 2006.

114. Peter Oborne, 'Now Blair silences the Tories with his Euroscepticism. What a genius!', *Spectator*, 25 June 2005.

115. Richard Horton, 'A monstrous war crime', *Guardian*, 28 March 2007.

116. Roger Cohen, 'Why Iraq's resistance differs from insurgency', *International Herald Tribune*, 14–15 January 2006.

117. Michael Scheuer, *Imperial Hubris: Why the West Is Losing the War on Terror* (Washington DC: Potomac, 2005), p. 203.

118. Daniel Bell, *The Cultural Contradictions of Capitalism*, 20th anniversary ed. (New York: Basic, 1996), pp. 48–9.

119. Al Gore, speech at the Commonwealth Club of California, San Francisco, 23 September 2002.

120. Geoffrey Wheatcroft, 'The tragedy of Tony Blair', *Atlantic Monthly*, June 2004.

121. Tony Blair speaking to Steve Richards, chief political commentator for the *Independent* and presenter of GMTV's *Sunday Programme*, October 2003.

122. Seldon, *Blair Unbound*, p. 102.

123. Hare, *Stuff Happens*, p. 10.

124. Norma Percy, 'An almighty splash', *Guardian*, 24 October 2005.

125. Geoffrey Perret, *Commander-in-Chief: How Truman, Johnson, and Bush Turned a Presidential Power into a Threat to America's Future* (New York: Farrar, Straus & Giroux, 2007), pp. 375, 392.

126. Kevin Phillips, *American Theocracy: The Perils and Politics of Radical Religion, Oil, and Borrowed Money in the 21st Century* (New York: Viking Penguin, 2006), p. 99.

127. James Saville and Dan Evans, 'Blair kept his heart problem a secret for 5 years', *Sunday Mirror*, 26 October 2003.

128. Paul Waugh, 'Clinton reveals Blair heart scare details', *Independent*, 26 February 2004.

129. Peter Oborne, *The Rise of Political Lying* (London: Free Press, 2005), p. 97.

130. Waugh, 'Clinton reveals Blair heart scare details'.

131. David Blunkett, *The Blunkett Tapes: My Life in the Bear Pit* (London: Bloomsbury, 2006), p. 550.

132. *Evening Standard*, 20 November 2003. See also 3.45 p.m. lobby briefing by Prime Minister's official spokesman on the same day.

133. Scott, *Tony & Cherie*, p. 219.

134. Oborne, *Rise of Political Lying*, pp. 276–7.

135. Stanton Peele, 'Personality and Alcoholism: Establishing the Link', in David A. Ward (ed.), *Alcoholism: Introduction to Theory and Treatment*, 3rd ed. (Dubuque, IA: Kendall/Hunt, 1990), pp. 147–56.

136. Kathleen T. Brady and Rajita Sinha, 'Co-Occuring Mental and Substance Use Disorders: The Neurobiological Effects of Chronic Stress', *American Journal of Psychiatry* (2005), vol. 162, pp. 1483–93.

137. John Heilemann, 'What's going on in George Bush's mind? A psychopolitical survey', *New York Magazine*, 5 February 2007.

138. Leo Abse, Tony Blair: The Man behind the Smile (London: Robson, 2001).

139. Justin A. Frank, *Bush on the Couch: Inside the Mind of the US President* (London: Politico's, 2006), p. 202.

Chapter 8: Safeguarding against illness in heads of government

1. Walter Lippmann, *The Public Philosophy: On the Decline and Revival of the Western Society* (London: Hamish Hamilton, 1955), p. 31.

2. Vanessa Raymont, William Bingley, Alec Buchanan, Anthony S. David, Peter Hayward, Simon Wessely and Matthew Hotopf, 'Prevalence of Mental Incapacity in Medical Inpatients and Associated Risk Factors: Cross-Sectional Study', *Lancet* (2004), vol. 364, pp. 1421–7.

3. Jonathan R. T. Davidson, Kathryn M. Connor and Marvin Swartz, 'Mental Illness in US Presidents between 1776 and 1974: A Review of Biographical Sources', *Journal of Nervous and Mental Disease* (2006), vol. 194, pp. 47–51.

4. Paul Preston, *Franco: A Biography* (London: HarperCollins, 1993), p. 778.

5. Jerrold M. Post and Robert S. Robins, *When Illness Strikes the Leader: The Dilemma of the Captive King* (New Haven, CT: Yale University Press, 1993), pp. 124–8.

6. François Boller, Annie Ganansia-Ganem, Florence Lebert and Florence Pasquier, 'Neuropsychiatric Afflictions of Modern French Presidents: Maréchal Henri-Philippe Pétain and Paul Deschanel', *European Journal of Neurology* (1999), vol. 6, pp. 133–6.

7. Lord Moran, *Winston Churchill: The Struggle for Survival 1940–1965* (London: Constable, 1966).

8. W. Russell Brain, 'Encounters with Winston Churchill', *Medical History* (2000), vol. 44, pp. 3–20.

9. Ronald Tiersky, *François Mitterrand: The Last French President* (New York: St Martin's Press, 2000), p. 337.

10. Ronald R. Fieve, *Moodswing: Dr Fieve on Depression*, rev. ed. (New York: William Morrow, 1989), p. 146.

11. Marshal F. Folstein, Susan E. Folstein and Paul R. McHugh, '"Mini-Mental State": A Practical Method for Grading the Cognitive State of Patients for the Clinician', *Journal of Psychiatric Research* (1975), vol. 12, pp. 189–98.

12. Quoted in interview with Harry H. Vaughan, Oral History, Presidential Archive, Harry S. Truman Library, Independence, MO.

13. Robert Dallek, *Nixon and Kissinger: Partners in Power* (New York: HarperCollins, 2007), pp. 524, 530–1, 622.

14.   Jean Lacouture, *De Gaulle: The Ruler 1945–1970* (London: Harvill, 1991), p. 573.

15.   Philip Short, *Pol Pot: Anatomy of a Nightmare* (New York: Henry Holt, 2005), p. 63.

16.   Ibid, p. 4.

17.   Martin Meredith, *The State of Africa: A History of Fifty Years of Independence*, pb ed. (London: Free Press, 2006), p. 238.

18.   David Owen, 'Africa', in *Time to Declare* (London: Michael Joseph, 1991), pp. 291–318.

Chapter 9: Conclusion

1.   Howard S. Schwartz, 'Narcissism Project and Corporate Decay: The Case of General Motors', *Business Ethics Quarterly* (1991), vol. 1, no. 3.

2.   David Owen, 'Hubris and Nemesis in Heads of Government', *Journal of the Royal Society of Medicine* (2006), vol. 99, pp. 548–51; Simon Wessely, 'Commentary: The Psychiatry of Hubris', *Journal of the Royal Society of Medicine* (2006), vol. 99, pp. 552–3.

3.   *Drug Futures 2025?: Horizon Scan* (Department of Trade and Industry, 2005), p. 20.

4.   James Hillman, *The Force of Character: And the Lasting Life* (Ballantine, 1999), p. 178.

5.   David Reynolds, *Summits: Six Meetings That Shaped the Twentieth Century* (London: Allen Lane, 2007), p. 393.

6.   Davidson et al., 'Mental Illness in US Presidents between 1776 and 1974'.

7.   Raymond Moley, quoted in Bert E. Park, *The Impact of Illness on World Leaders* (Philadelphia: University of Pennsylvania Press, 1986), pp. 280–1.

Index